# DIRECTIONS OF CHANGE
IN RURAL EGYPT

# DIRECTIONS OF CHANGE IN RURAL EGYPT

Edited by
NICHOLAS S. HOPKINS
KIRSTEN WESTERGAARD

The American University in Cairo Press

Copyright © 1998 by
The American University in Cairo Press
113 Sharia Kasr el Aini, Cairo 11511, Egypt
420 Fifth Avenue, New York, NY10018-2729
*http://www.aucpress.com*

This edition in paperback 2001

All rights reserved. No part of this publication
may be reproduced, stored in a retrieval system or
transmitted in any form or by any means,
electronic, mechanical, photocopying, recording,
or otherwise, without the prior written permission
of the publisher.

Dar el Kutub No. 4677/01
ISBN 977 424 663 2

Printed in Egypt

# Contents

| | |
|---|---|
| *Preface* | vii |
| *Weights and Measures* | ix |
| *Abbreviations* | x |
| Introduction: Directions of Change in Rural Egypt<br>Nicholas Hopkins and Kirsten Westergaard | 1 |

## I THE POLITICAL ECONOMY OF RURAL EGYPT

| | |
|---|---|
| 1. The Market's Place<br>Timothy Mitchell | 19 |
| 2. The Evolution of Agrarian Structures in Egypt: Regional Patterns of Change in Farm Size<br>François Ireton | 41 |
| 3. Beating Plowshares into Swords: The Relocation of Rural Egyptian Workers and their Discontent<br>James Toth | 66 |
| 4. Facing Structural Adjustment: Strategies of Peasants, the State, and the International Financial Institutions<br>Ray Bush | 88 |

## II CULTURAL REPRESENTATION: IDENTITY

| | |
|---|---|
| 5. Hegemony in the Periphery: Community and Exclusion in an Upper Egyptian Village<br>Reem Saad | 113 |
| 6. The Northwest Coast: A Part of *Rural* Egypt?<br>Soraya Altorki and Donald P. Cole | 130 |

## III CULTURAL REPRESENTATION: CONSUMPTION

| | |
|---|---|
| 7. Television and the Virtues of Education: Upper Egyptian Encounters with State Culture<br>Lila Abu-Lughod | 147 |
| 8. Conflict or Cooperation: Changing Gender Roles in Rural Egyptian Households<br>Kamran Asdar Ali | 166 |
| 9. The Vision of a Better Life: New Patterns of Consumption and Changed Social Relations<br>Kirsten Haugaard Bach | 184 |

vi   Contents

## IV  HEALTH

10. Being Sickly or Eating Well: The Conceptualization of Health and Ill-Health in an Upper Egyptian Village    203
    *Hania Sholkamy*

11. Health Units in Rural Egypt: At the Forefront of Health Improvement or Anachronisms?    219
    *Sohair Mehanna* and *Peter Winch*

## V  VILLAGE HISTORIES

12. Change and Continuity in the Village of Batra: Family Strategies    237
    *Malak S. Rouchdy*

13. Spaces of Poverty: The Geography of Social Change in Rural Egypt    256
    *Detlef Müller-Mahn*

## VI  DEVELOPMENT: THE ROLE OF THE MARKET AND DEVELOPMENT PROJECTS

14. Farmers and Cooperatives in the Era of Structural Adjustment    279
    *Mohamed H. Abdel Aal*

15. Rural Periodic Markets in Egypt    303
    *Mohamed M. Mohieddin*

16. Agro-Pastoralism and Development in Egypt's Northwest Coast    318
    *Donald P. Cole* and *Soraya Altorki*

17. Economic Changes in the Newly Reclaimed Lands: From State Farms to Small Holdings and Private Agricultural Enterprises    334
    *Günter Meyer*

## VII  DISPUTE SETTLEMENT: SOCIETY AND POLITICS

18. Men of Authority—Documents of Authority: Notes on Customary Law in Upper Egypt    357
    *Hans-Christian Korsholm Nielsen*

19. Culture and Mediation of Power in an Egyptian Village    371
    *Ahmed Zayed*

Contributors    389
Index    391

# Preface

In April 1997, a group of specialists on rural Egypt gathered in Aswan to consider the state of culture, society, and economy in contemporary Egypt. The group included anthropologists, sociologists, political scientists, and geographers, and participants were from Egypt and a variety of other countries. All had done recent field research in rural Egypt. The research sites ranged from Marsa Matruh in the Western Desert to Sharqiya governorate in the eastern Delta, and on to the reclaimed areas near Isma'iliya, and from Batra in the northern Delta, to Idfu in the southern governorate of Aswan.

The conference was a result of a research project covering the social organization of work and production in the two Upper Egyptian governorates of Qina and Aswan, conducted by the Social Research Center (SRC) of the American University in Cairo and funded by the Danish International Development Agency (DANIDA) in Cairo. The research project is part of a broader collaboration between the SRC and the Centre for Development Research (CDR) in Copenhagen, Denmark, funded by DANIDA through its ENRECA program, which also funded the conference. This book incorporates some of the results of the collaboration (papers by Abdel Aal, Bach, Nielsen, and Saad) along with work by many scholars who were not affiliated to the SRC/CDR research project. The editing of the book was also undertaken under the ENRECA program.

This book is the outcome of that gathering of lively, young scholars. It includes information on the changing economic situation in the countryside, particularly after the 'owners and tenants' law of 1992, which has now come into force, along with the effects of structural adjustment on agriculture, marketing, and rural life. A number of papers cover the changing and probably declining role of migration abroad in the strategies of rural Egyptians. Another set of papers treats the changes in consumption patterns, in house style, in dress fashion, and in the role of television. One of the basic measures of well-being is health, and that is covered directly in two papers. Other papers deal with social processes in rural areas, including dispute settlement and the response to development programs. Still further papers deal with the expansion of agriculture outside the traditional areas of the Nile Valley, and the increasing integration of the ecologically distinctive areas of the northwest coast of Egypt into the agrarian economy of the

Nile Valley. A final set of papers deals with representations of the rural population, the 'peasantry,' or *fallahin*, in the media, in statistics, and among themselves.

Overall, the papers show a rural Egypt that is full of life, constantly changing, and always teetering on the edge between progress and impoverishment. Though nothing is 'typical' of rural Egypt, these papers provide an up-to-date account of the stresses and strains, strivings and silences, progress and threat, that characterize the Egyptian countryside today. Geographically, the papers cover 'old lands,' 'new lands,' and the desert fringes. Topically, the range is from straightforward analyses of the social organization of production to cultural analyses of symbols and discourses. All of the papers focus on current directions of change and are sensitive in various ways to the influences that bear on Egyptian agriculture from the outside as well as the pressures internal to it.

The organizers and editors want to thank first of all the two host institutions, the Social Research Center of the American University in Cairo, and the Centre for Development Research in Copenhagen. Several figures in these two institutions were instrumental in encouraging this project in its early stages and throughout. We would like to extend particular thanks to Saad Nagi, the former director of the SRC, and Knud Erik Svendsen, the former director of the CDR. The current director of the SRC, Hoda Rashad, also gave her wholehearted support to the project, and joined in the Aswan discussions. This project would not have come into being without the support of the DANIDA office in Cairo, and in particular Ole Moesby, and later Kurt Mørck Jensen, Lis Jespersen, and Ali Kerdany. Throughout all the various phases of this project we benefited from our cooperation with the Governor of Aswan, His Excellency Salah Mosbah, who participated in both the opening and closing sessions of the conference.

During the conference itself, we profited from the help of two graduate students in sociology and anthropology from the American University in Cairo, Mona Abou Zeid and Dalia al-Naggar. Sami M. Kamel from the Aswan office of DANIDA was also unfailingly helpful. In the preparation for the conference, Neil Webster of CDR made a strong contribution; unfortunately a scheduling conflict prevented him from attending as we had hoped. Among others who helped at various times were John Davis of All Souls College, Oxford University, and Russell Stone of the American University in Washington. The Department of Sociology at the American University in Washington provided some technical support during the post-conference phase.

We are eternally grateful to all these institutions and individuals, and hope that they will regard this volume as at least partial recompense for their efforts.

# Weights and Measures

1 feddan = 1.038 acres or 0.42 hectares
1 feddan = 24 qirat
1 qirat = 175 square meters
1 ardeb = 198 liters = 5.62 US bushels
One US dollar was worth between 3.3 and 3.4 Egyptian pounds (LE) after 1991.

# Abbreviations

| | |
|---|---|
| AUC | American University in Cairo |
| CAPMAS | Center for Public Mobilization and Statistics |
| CARE | Cooperative for Assistance and Relief Everywhere |
| CDA | Community Development Association |
| DANIDA | Danish International Development Agency |
| ERSAP | Economic Reform and Structural Adjustment Program |
| GDP | Gross Domestic Product |
| GOE | Government of Egypt |
| GNP | Gross National Product |
| IBRD | International Bank for Reconstruction and Development |
| IFI | International financial institution |
| IMF | International Monetary Fund |
| NGO | Nongovernmental organization |
| PBDAC | Principal Bank for Development and Agricultural Credit |
| PHC | Primary health care |
| PL480 | Public Law 480 (of the U.S. Congress) |
| USAID | United States Agency for International Development |

# Introduction:
# Directions of Change in Rural Egypt

NICHOLAS S. HOPKINS and
KIRSTEN WESTERGAARD

This collection of studies deals with the directions of change in rural Egypt. At the end of the twentieth century, these changes appear as the culmination of a long process of transformation, and they announce probable trends for the beginning of the twenty-first century. We refer to direction*s* of change because change appears to be moving in more than one direction, and the papers in this book see some of these directions differently. There are changes in the life chances of rural people, and in their livelihood. Changes are implied in the transition from a centrally planned to a market economy. There are changes in the structure of society, and in the political expression of that structure. Yet other changes reflect the spread of education, and the power of television, as well as the cultural and economic impact of migration patterns of various sorts. People's lives are changing, partly through their own efforts, partly through force of circumstance. Some changes are in the domain of cultural construction, others in the domain of political economy. These changes are detailed and analyzed in the studies in this book. The authors in this collection see some of these changes as positive, others as negative, yet others as neutral. The implicit debate among the authors of this book is whether rural Egyptians are tending to be better off, or worse off.

A major interpretive issue is the question of whether a complex society such as rural Egypt is better approached in terms of its major structural features and the trends of change in these features, or in terms of the actors/agents and their culturally and economically motivated goal-seeking behavior. Some of the authors in this collection favor one of these broad approaches, some the other. The common position seems to be that while rural actors have considerable freedom to act, and to create their own worlds, they do this within a framework that is given by the global system, by the ruling classes in Egypt, and by the institutions inherited from their own past actions, such as the family. The picture of rural Egypt that can be gained from aggregate data is taken as one necessary backdrop to individual choice and action, together with the interpretation and evaluation of different outcomes that make action meaningful.

Some recent collections have focused on the economics of agriculture in Egypt (Faris and Khan 1993; Craig 1993; Fletcher 1996), as have some older studies (Abdel-Fadil 1975; Commander 1987). Taken as a whole, the focus of this collection is on the social and cultural dimensions. The collection offers a useful complement to other studies which focus on an economic and agricultural understanding and interpretation of rural Egypt. While all the cases in this collection are 'rural,' there is no implication that rural Egypt is a bounded unit. The studies are all grounded in particular cases which are more important than the label. In fact, many of the studies in this collection problematize the notion of rural Egypt.

## Rural Egypt

Does rural Egypt exist? At the risk of reifying the notion of rural Egypt, it is useful to give some figures as background to the studies in this book. The 1996 census showed that the percentage of the population of Egypt that is classified as rural actually rose from 56 percent in 1986 to 57 percent in 1996. Therefore, of a total Egyptian population of about 61.5 million, the total rural population was 35 million in 1996 compared to 28 million in 1986. Almost certainly this reflects an elusive definition of 'rural' and does not take into account the growth of the larger semi-urban or even urban communities in the rural sector. Part of the rise may be due to the faster rate of natural increase combined with a manageable rate of rural-to-urban migration.

Basically what is defined as rural in the census consists of everything outside the seats of governorates and district towns, that is, the urban is defined in terms of its administrative role, and the rural is residual. Rural Egypt specifically includes the agricultural areas of the Nile valley and the Delta, the 'new lands' (reclaimed lands), and the semiarid and arid zones of the northwest coast where pastoralism and rain-fed agriculture is carried out. The characteristic setting is of course the village, though this term covers a variety of situations from hamlets of a few hundred people to agro-towns of twenty thousand or more. On the valley fringes and in the desert people live in smaller clusters. Even in the valley there are people who live outside the village cluster, on their fields. Still, most people live in clustered communities ranging from several thousand up. The average 'village' size in Egypt is about seven thousand (in India, for example, it is about two thousand; in Turkey or Iran it is a few hundred).

One should certainly not confuse a rural person with a farmer, let alone a peasant, in spite of the fact that the term *'fallah,'* usually translated as 'peasant,' continues to have major currency. Although evocative, the term *'fallah'* has a wide range of meaning. Literally it means a tiller of the soil, a plowman (Wehr 1961:726), but is often used in the sense of a 'rustic' or a 'villager.' Large farmers sometimes describe themselves as *'fallah,'* which could be taken as disingenuous. Nowadays the term is sometimes used in contrast to the educated. 'Fellah' refers to a man who wears a *gallabiya* rather than trousers, a woman who dresses country rather than city. Some of the authors in this collection refer to peasants and others to farmers. Following Wolf (1969:xiv–xv), the editors understand a peasant to be a member of a community most of whose members earn their living from subsistence agriculture, while a farmer conducts agriculture within a market economy. In this sense, we feel that we are dealing in Egypt with farmers and not peasants.

Rural Egypt is historically food producing, and agriculture still predominates. An understanding of the social organization of agriculture is essential to a grasp of rural Egypt. Yet rural Egypt and agricultural Egypt are not coterminous. There are substantial numbers of people who earn their living outside agriculture, in government service, trade, transportation, and in the many factories that draw on rural people for their labor force.[1] This may take the form of off-farm employment for the head of household, or the head may continue to work in agriculture while other household members (often his children) work elsewhere. Relative to the past, for example, in 1952 at the time of the revolution and the first agrarian reform, rural society in Egypt is no longer so enclosed in an agrarian hierarchy. The rural and the urban interpenetrate each other far more than in the past. Writers in the 1960s referred to the ruralization of the city (J. Abu-Lughod 1961). Now the issue is the urbanization of the countryside—in terms of education, employment, architecture, and exposure to mass media such as television. People (men and some women) move easily back and forth between the cities and the countryside in search of profit, employment, entertainment, education, health care, and so on (Fanchette 1997).

Although less dominant than in the past, agriculture is still very significant. According to CAPMAS[2] and Ministry of Agriculture figures quoted by Fouad Ibrahim (1996:75), the proportion of the employed who work in agriculture declined from 53 percent in 1970–71 to 33 percent in 1991–92.[3] According to the same sources, agriculture's share in the national income dropped from 29 percent to 16.5 percent, and its share in exports by value dropped from 63 percent to 20 percent in the same period. It is also true that for nearly thirty years, Egypt has not been self-sufficient in food. "From being self-sufficient in food and a net exporter of agricultural commodities in the early 1970s, the country endured an annual net deficit in its agricultural trade balance in the 1980s" (Khedr et al 1996:55). It should be noted, however, that yields of most crops have risen, showing that agriculture is not stagnant.

Although rural Egypt is often treated as a whole, there is considerable variation, not only between the old and new (or reclaimed) lands, but also within the old lands themselves. This difference is often expressed as a distinction between the Delta, north of Cairo, and the Valley, to the south, but further distinctions are sometimes made. This contrast is illustrated by figures on poverty and on fertility. Rural Upper Egypt has both a higher poverty rate and a higher fertility rate than rural Lower Egypt. In Egypt for 1990–91, 34.1 percent of the rural population was estimated to fall below a poverty line based on consumption needs. The urban figure was slightly higher at 35.88 percent. The figure for the Valley is higher and for the Delta lower than this overall poverty figure of just over one-third of the population (Abdel-Latif and El-Laithy 1996:300; see also El-Laithy and Kheir al-Din 1992/93). The fertility rate also varies from urban to rural, and from Delta to Valley. The highest rate is in the rural Valley (5.19), compared to the urban Valley (3.80) and the rural Delta (3.45), with the lowest (2.66) in the urban Delta (Fargues 1997:129).

All these major regional distinctions are helpful, if oversimplified. Interregional variations particularly concern such ecological factors as the concentration of certain crops and animal raising practices (which in turn reflects differences in temperature, soil quality, and reliability of the water supply), as well as physical isolation. But there are other axes of difference: (1) Whether or not a region has a history of large estates, land reform cooperatives, or other special aspects in the history of land tenure; (2) Both off-farm employment and the marketing of agriculture produce reflect the proximity to major urban centers, new industrial sites (for example, Tenth of Ramadan City in the desert east of the Delta), tourist centers or simply axes of communication; (3) The existence of social structural features such as 'tribalism,' itself not a uniform phenomenon; (4) Variations in the division of labor by gender (women, for instance, are more likely to work in agriculture in the Delta than in Upper Egypt); (5) The presence of local crafts or other traditional industries. The studies in this collection provide ample material for an analysis of regional variation in Egypt.

## Structural Adjustment and the Market in Agriculture

Egyptian agriculture has long been highly intensive, both because there are on average two crops a year, and because of the high number of people who earn all or part of their livelihood from agriculture (as symbolized in the small holdings, averaging about 2.5 feddans (one hectare)). Egyptian agriculture depends almost entirely on irrigation from the Nile. Since 1952 this irrigation has allowed an expansion of agriculture into the 'new lands' reclaimed from the desert.

Agriculture has always had a relatively strong market orientation. For centuries there have been markets in at least some crops, and the scientists from the French expedition of 1798 reported a strong market orientation among Egyptian farmers. Even at the height of Egyptian socialism, in the 1960s, there was a market in land, although not a very active one, and there were active markets in labor, machine services, and in the sale of some crops. The government, through the cooperative system, was a monopoly provider of seeds, pesticides, and fertilizers, and the sole legal purchaser of many crops, but the farmer still had to ensure a profit which was his income. The Egyptian land reform was based on the notion of the independent small farmer (Marei 1957:243), even though that farmer was bound by regulations and institutions, such as crop delivery quotas and cooperatives. The family-based household continues to be the key unit for the analysis of the social organization of agricultural production.

Today, the agricultural sector leads in the reinforcement of a market economy in Egypt, both for historical reasons and because of the policy and support of the minister of agriculture, reinforced by major external donors.[4] Yet it is probably not the sector on which the overall success of economic liberalization will depend. Arguably the industrial sector, with the privatization of the public sector industries and the opening up of the country to imports which will compete with local consumer goods industries, is where the game will be played. Nevertheless, the sheer numbers of people involved in agriculture and the role of agricultural exports give that sector continuing importance.

The current debate about rural Egypt focuses on the issue of 'structural adjustment,' in other words, on the extension of the 'market' and its implications for how rural society is organized (M. Abou-Zeid 1997). It should be remembered that 'structural adjustment' is the current version of a much longer process. In practice, this means that the government is no longer a major supplier of inputs for agriculture nor a major purchaser of agricultural produce. When it does enter the market, it is one of many actors in the market rather than a non-market "state." One of the services that is being privatized is the provision of credit. Though the Principal Bank for Development and Agricultural Credit (PBDAC)[5] still provides 90 percent of the value of formal agricultural loans (Adams and Kamel 1996:256), it is increasingly acting as a private bank charging market-level interest rates, and it is under some pressure to adjust to the new free market economy by changing its corporate culture (Ibid.). There is even some discussion of privatizing the irrigation system through the establishment of user groups and the transfer of the costs of maintaining the system to the users, possibly spurred on by the threat of an overall water shortage in Egypt (Hopkins 1998). Moreover, with the withdrawal of the state from procurement, farmers must negotiate their prices with competing (and sometimes unpredictable) merchants.

A major change with far reaching implications is the amendment of the law governing owner–tenant relations,[6] subjecting them to supply and demand, rather than the previous system of administrative rent controls that gave tenants practical ownership of the land they were farming.[7] From 1992 to 1997, in a five-year interim period, tenants could continue to farm the land but had to pay a rent fixed at twenty-two times the land tax instead of seven times. After October 1997, all prior contracts were terminated, rents had to be negotiated periodically instead of being fixed by the state, and landlords were free to end any rental contract when it expired and to seek new tenants. Tenants who lost their lease were given priority in acquiring property rights in desert land, and no tenants could be expelled from their dwellings until the state provided a new house in the same locality.

This new 'owners and tenants' law was much discussed during the conference which forms the basis for this book, held in April 1997, about six months before the final implementation of the law. There are many skeptical references to it in the papers that follow. At the time of the conference, there was a concern that the actual transition would be quite violent. In the event, the physical violence was less than predicted (Essam El Din 1997), and seems to have occurred mostly in places such as Qina governorate, where social discrimination (such as that based on tribalism) combines with economic distress. The second level of concern in our conference was over the long-term affects of the law on equity. There were fears that this law would deepen the poverty of the poor, and accentuate the gap between the wealthy farmers and the landless and near-landless (see papers by Mitchell, Bush, and Toth). This concern runs through many of the papers in this collection, but it will take some years before the trend is visible.

What do these changes mean for the structure of agrarian society, and in particular for the well-being of rural people? Arguably,

Egyptian agriculture has always been more or less commercialized, and is now becoming more so. But many observers predict that these changes will bring about a greater polarization between the rich and the poor in rural areas as the rich use their political influence and social skills to dominate the situation, and especially to acquire additional rights over land at the expense of the small farmers. If they are successful in doing this, then logic suggests that many small farmers will be pushed down into the status of laborers or pushed out of agriculture and perhaps the rural areas altogether. Thus, in brief, is the argument that structural adjustment leads to impoverishment.

At the same time, there is much evidence that conditions of life in rural Egypt have been gradually improving, as measured by consumption as well as by the figures for life expectancy and literacy rates (Institute of National Planning 1996:140). This amelioration is due to a combination of income from labor migration (mostly abroad), from diversification of income sources at home, and from astute household strategies, as well as from government health and education policies. It is hard to say how widespread this relative prosperity is, or how much is due to better days for agriculture (as opposed, for instance, to migration income). So are we analyzing increasing prosperity—with the fear that it may be fragile—or gloom? Consumption levels are rising, and the rural population has adopted urban consumption patterns (housing and furnishings, clothing, television). It is revealing that three of the authors in this volume report being shown a modern bathroom in a village house. But with declining job opportunities abroad, and the freeze on government jobs, this increasing prosperity may be momentary if people do not find new ingenious solutions.

## Cultural Representations

The rural is incomprehensible without reference to the urban and the national. In this sense, Kroeber's old comment that "peasants are part-societies with part-cultures" (1948:284) retains its relevance, though now the lines of cleavage no longer run strictly between urban and rural, but represent different cultural positions even within the same family/household.

One of the major themes of this collection is that representations of rural life, and those held by rural people, are significant. They are significant because people act on the basis of them. These representations can be observed in various contexts—television programs, government programs, self-images, which are often 'urban' in origin. One enduring theme of course is precisely that of the contrast, and the significance of the contrast, between rural and urban. But other representations are important to people living in particular places, as they establish and maintain boundaries between culturally constructed social groups (gender, status groups or classes, lineages or villages), and define standards for health and welfare.

One set of cultural representations deals with people's skills for dealing with social processes and problems. Following Putnam[8] and others we can call this social capital—the known and tested strategies to achieve goals with regard to household and family continuity, to settle disputes or to start them, to cooperate, to deal with higher authorities, or to organize the division of labor by gender. These are the techniques that are part of the cultural tool kit of a particular set of people. There are several examples (Bach, Rouchdy, Nielsen, Zayed) in this volume of the ways in which rural Egyptians carry out these activities.

The repertory of social skills and knowledge has been extended in many ways by education. Education has spread enormously in rural Egypt in the last generation, and this change recurs in the papers in our volume though none attempts a broad overview of the shifts. At the least, education has meant that people now have access to skills outside the context of family, in a hierarchy that is bureaucratic rather than based on generation and seniority. Education is certainly important in its impact on social stratification, through the process that Bourdieu calls 'distinction.' But Abu-Lughod and Sholkamy also argue that through education and health the national elite is imposing its values on the rural populations.

The broad domain we call 'religion' is another area replete with cultural representations. It would certainly be fatuous to suggest that there is such a thing as 'rural religion.' Yet surely religion plays an important role in rural Egypt, as it does elsewhere in the country. Historically, the two main forms of the religious experience in Egypt, rural and urban, were the saint cult and the mystical brotherhoods. The saint cult was, in effect, a projection of the social pattern of patron–client relations into the supernatural sphere; the basic religious act was to seek the help or intercession of 'saints' (the 'beloved' of God) so that God would grant the wishes of the seeker, and the main ceremony, the 'moulid,' or annual saint's day celebration. The mystical brotherhoods taught and organized various means by which individuals could seek or demonstrate mystical union with God. These two forms of religious experience were analytically separate, but related in that the heads or founders of the brotherhoods often were considered to be religious intermediaries, and in that the brotherhoods often organized ceremonies at the festivals of the major saints (Biegman 1990). There appears to have been a kind of 'elective affinity' (Gellner 1981:61) between these two forms of religion and the social hierarchy of rural Egypt (Hopkins 1987:169–75).

Currently, a third religious style is common and is penetrating rural Egypt. This is what Geertz (1968:60) called the 'scripturalist' approach. The goal here is to determine what is God's will for us, on the basis of a study of texts, and to accept or obey that. In other words, it is a matter of "following a rule" (Weber 1978). This would appear to be more compatible with the urban and bureaucratic life style, or perhaps with the urbanizing and bureaucratic elements in rural Egypt (Gellner 1981). It is nonetheless spreading into rural Egypt through students, bureaucrats, and others, and is competing with, even hostile to, the other two styles. However, it is important to note that neither the spread nor the rivalry is recent. Berque (1957:36–37) reports a struggle between the Muslim Brothers and others in Sirs al-Layyan prior to the 1950s, while Ammar (1966:78) records a conflict in the Aswan village of Silwa in the 1940s, and Fahim (1973) and Kennedy (1977) report a similar struggle in the Nubian village of Kanuba (Aswan governorate) in the 1960s. Adams (1957) also analyzes diverse religious opinions in a Delta village. To the extent that the 'scripturalist' religious style is appealing to rural people, we need to understand why this form of religious expression appeals at the expense of more traditional forms. Is it, for example, an expression of the spread of urban values? We also need to understand the economic and social implications of accepting this world view, perhaps along the lines of Weber's analysis of Protestantism (Weber 1958). Only Toth's paper in this collection begins to address this question.

One feature that distinguishes rural and urban Egypt is the response to elections. Parliamentary elections in particular are taken very seriously in rural Egypt, and voting levels are fairly high. This is in contrast to the cities, where voting levels are low. This difference was observed by Janet Abu-Lughod (1972) a generation ago, and it is still true. This reflects the persistence of the political role of big families and wealthy men who mobilize their relatives, supporters, and dependents in political struggles with similar rivals (El-Karanshawy 1998). Comments in a number of papers in this collection show the importance of political conflict and elections at the local level (Altorki and Cole, Saad, Zayed, Rouchdy, Abdel Aal). However, what all their stories have in common is that the existing power structure is sustained—these are not stories of local political upheaval.

Violence as a possible political strategy is known and practiced in rural Egypt. It takes the form of vengeance feuds (Abu-Zayd 1965), or erupts during political struggles for local dominance, including elections, and is also part of the dialectic between people and government. Official violence against rural people is met with rural violence against the symbols of authority, and vice versa. Violence leads to deaths, but also includes many forms of threats and intimidation.[9] Violence is more a political strategy than an emotional outburst, and those responsible may be the paymasters more than the gunslingers. Recent political violence in Egypt has as often occurred in rural Egypt as in urban Egypt, but since the motives are often unreported, apart from general references to religion, it is hard to know what role agrarian tensions play in the genesis of this violence. Violence itself is as important by its representation as by its reality. As Mitchell notes (1991), what matters is not only the direct political outcome of violence but what is said, or not said, about it.

So far in this introduction we have tried to give an idea of the main themes of the book, and some general background for the papers in the collection. The two main themes are, on the one hand, the power and function of representations of different life styles, whether based on distinctions pertaining to urban versus rural, on educational attainment, or some other criterion, and on the other hand, the continuing importance of economic structures based on agriculture and other forms of employment. Now it is time to introduce the papers individually.

## The Studies in this Collection

We have grouped the nineteen papers in this collection into seven groups of unequal size, although any grouping is somewhat arbitrary and most papers could be classified in more than one group.

In the first group, the four papers by Mitchell, Ireton, Toth, and Bush raise issues relating to the general political economy of rural life in the context of Egyptian society. However, they also discuss particular cases and places. The common theme is to inquire whether policy relating to rural Egypt is taking the correct path; whether a policy that stresses the market makes any sense and is likely to benefit the majority of the population. Mitchell elaborates his case on the basis of field materials from Upper Egypt, while Bush focuses on the role of the international financial institutions and the state with regard to rural policy. Toth places the movement of rural people to the city in the context of a broader labor history of rural Egypt, and speculates that rural to urban migration lies at the roots of the growth of 'fundamentalism' (Islamism). Ireton takes a somewhat different approach, and provides a careful analysis of official Egyptian figures on landholding, showing that the trend towards deconcentration of holdings in the 'old lands' ceased in the 1990s, although with regional variations.

Introduction: Directions of Change in Rural Egypt 11

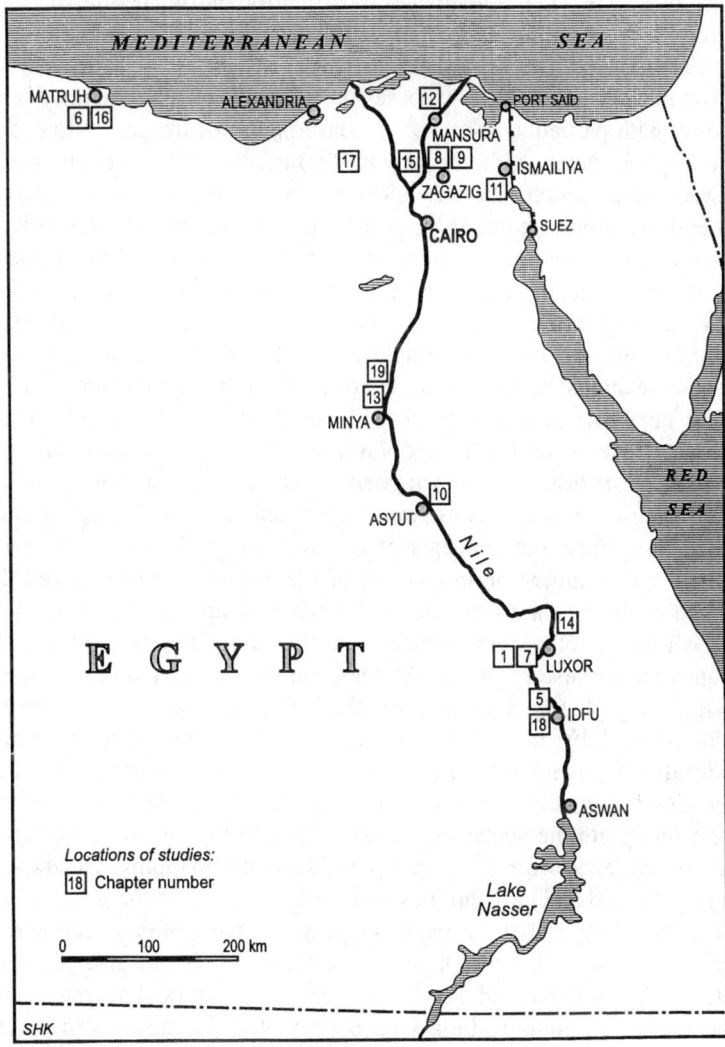

Figure 1 *Map of Egypt Showing Locations of Studies*

In the second group of papers we move from political economy to questions of identity. Saad disentangles various threads of identity in an Upper Egyptian village, stressing the way in which outside intervention in the name of development affects the sense of identity. On the other hand, Altorki and Cole raise the question of cultural boundaries within rural Egypt by focusing on the Bedouin of the northwest coast of Egypt. The self-image and identity of the people of this region is very strong and is maintained, in part, by establishing a contrast between themselves and the rest of Egypt.

The third group of papers focuses on questions of representation and culture, with particular reference to consumption of images and goods. Abu-Lughod deals with the cultural dimension of the relationship between rural people and the wider society, especially as articulated through television programs and the implicit content of educational materials and experiences. Asdar Ali raises the question of gender roles, and in particular, the meaning of changing forms of employment for rural men and women. Bach discusses the representation of a modern and urban life and shows the implications of this for changing patterns of social relations, notably the ability of people to work together.

The next pair of papers deals with health issues, and in particular various concepts of health and disease. Sholkamy focuses on two concepts in a village in Asyut: 'being sickly,' or persistent vulnerability to disease, and 'eating well,' as a health ideal. Mehanna and Winch also stress the concepts of disease that guide people in their actions in the context of an analysis of the role of government health units in the health care situation in a 'new lands' area near Isma'iliya.

The fifth set of papers includes two that use different methods to reconstruct the history of two villages, one in the Delta and the other in Upper Egypt. Rouchdy analyzes the history of a zone in the lower Delta marked by large landholdings and shows the succession of landlords and merchants through a focus on family history and the strategies followed by various actors throughout this history. Müller-Mahn interprets the social organization of a village in Minya on the basis of evidence from geography and especially mapping. He shows the place of old and new families and the marginality of the poor.

The penultimate set of papers returns to the political economy theme, but now with a thoroughly local focus. Abdel Aal uses survey material from Qina and Aswan governorates to demonstrate that cooperatives continue to be a valued alternative for farmers in these two governorates. Mohieddin compares markets in two governorates, Minufiya in the Delta and Minya in Upper Egypt, raising issues about the role of trade and commerce in contemporary rural Egypt. Cole and Altorki discuss the economic position of the sheepherding and farming populations of the northwest coast in the broader Egyptian economy, and illustrate this with comments on the role of development projects and government intervention. Meyer reviews the history of efforts to develop the 'new lands' west of the Delta and shows that small farmer settlement and medium-sized private farms are the most effective way to make use of these lands.

We conclude with a pair of papers dealing with dispute settlement and politics in Upper Egyptian villages. Nielsen concentrates on a rather formalized pattern of mediation and dispute settlement, currently marked by written documents, while Zayed analyzes the role of the elders in dispute settlement and in local politics generally, and shows how village-level political culture endures and maintains itself despite apparent modernization.

## Conclusion

Some tentative conclusions can be drawn from the studies in the volume, although a full analysis of the directions of change in rural Egyptian society would require filling in the gaps, notably with regard to the religious dimension. Our studies amply demonstrate the existence of stratification and sociocultural differentiation, but do not provide enough material to draw conclusions on the class structure of rural Egypt.

Recent decades have been ones of relative prosperity for rural Egypt, though many remain below the poverty line, and there is considerable apprehension among rural Egyptians as to whether this prosperity can continue given that some of the means (government jobs; migration to oil states; equity in access to land) have been cut off. Nationally, the gamble is that in a liberalized economy new energies will be released and efficiencies created that will result in greater prosperity, but it is far from clear that the small farmers and the laborers will benefit from these changes.

Rural Egypt has been culturally integrated into broader Egyptian society, although in a somewhat uncomfortable position. Its own culture, though clearly alive and dynamic as these studies show, is somewhat devalued and ignored at national levels in Egypt. Rural Egyptians remain adept at seeking their economic interests, at finding ways to cooperate when that suits them, at quarreling when that suits them, at making use of programs introduced by the authorities to advance local causes, and, in general, at constructing their own lives, both at the material and representational levels.

The future of rural Egypt will depend on decisions made by national leaders and by household members in the economic domain, and, of course, also on the position of Egypt in the world economy and emerging world society, in addition to the process of cultural globalization. The world capitalist economy and the globalized cultural system are changing so that Egypt is integrating into an evolving system. This brings both threats of impoverishment and opportunities for enrichment. The reality of changing rural life is surely a reflection of the rural policy of the urban elite and the government, but it is also created by the actions of its inhabitants, whose goal-seeking behavior fends off entropy.

## Notes

1 Richards (1991:70–80) notes that off-farm employment in the rural areas in the mid-1980s was around 40 percent. For a survey, see also Hopkins 1996.
2 CAPMAS, the Central Agency for Public Mobilization and Statistics, is the official statistics office for Egypt.
3 Although of course the population itself, and presumably the number of employed, rose so the total of those engaged in agriculture did not decline to such a great extent.
4 Minister of Agriculture Youssef Wally wrote in the forward to Fletcher's "Egypt's Agriculture in a Reform Era" (which was the result of a conference sponsored by USAID): "During the past decade the agricultural sector of Egypt has been gradually transformed by shifting away from central planning and government controls to increased reliance on market forces. This transformation preceded the more general structural adjustment that has been taking place throughout the economy since 1991" (Wally 1996:vii).
5 PBDAC is a semi-independent bank linked to the Ministry of Agriculture and is responsible for most loans to farmers.
6 This is Law 96 of 1992, amending the 1952 law on agrarian reform. The official publication is in *al-Jarida al-rasmiya*, issue 26bis(a), June 28, 1992, pp. 3–7. The most accessible source for the text is in *al-Ahram al-iqtisadi*, July 30, 1992, pp. 54–55, and an English translation was prepared by the Middle East Library for Economic Services, Cairo.
7 For a description of the system before the counter-reform, see Hopkins 1987:56–65.
8 Putnam writes (1995:67): "'Social capital' refers to features of social organization such as networks, norms, and social trust that facilitate coordination and cooperation for mutual benefit."
9 See the accounts of the Land Center for Human Rights in Cairo.

## References

Abdel-Fadil, Mahmoud. 1975. *Development, Income Distribution and Social Change in Rural Egypt, 1952–1970*. Cambridge: Cambridge University Press.

Abdel-Latif, Abla, and Heba El-Laithy. 1996. "Protecting Food Security For the Poor in a Liberalizing Economy." in Lehman B. Fletcher, ed. *Egypt's Agriculture in a Reform Era*. Ames, Iowa: Iowa State University Press. pp. 294–327.

Abu-Zayd, Ahmad. 1965. *al-Thar—dirasa anthropolojiya bi ahda qura al-Sa'id*. Cairo: Dar al-Ma'rif.

Abou-Zeid, Mona. 1997. "Structural Adjustment and the Egyptian Farmer: Towards Increasing Rural Differentiation?" unpublished masters thesis in Sociology–Anthropology, American University in Cairo.
Abu-Lughod, Janet. 1961. "Migrant Adjustment to City Life: The Egyptian Case." *American Journal of Sociology* 67:22–32.
Abu-Lughod, Janet. 1972. "Rural Migration and Politics in Egypt." in Richard Antoun and Iliya Harik, eds. *Rural Politics and Social Change in the Middle East*. Bloomington: Indiana University Press. pp. 315–34.
Adams, Dale W., and Ali Kamel. 1996. "Financial Reforms and Rural Credit: The PBDAC's Evolving Role." in Lehman B. Fletcher, ed. *Egypt's Agriculture in a Reform Era*. Ames, Iowa: Iowa State University Press. pp. 254–67.
Adams, John Boman. 1957. "Culture and Conflict in an Egyptian Village." *American Anthropologist* 59:225–35.
Ammar, Hamed. 1966 [1954]. *Growing Up in an Egyptian Village: Silwa, Province of Aswan*. New York: Octagon Books.
Berque, Jacques. 1957. *Histoire sociale d'un village égyptien au XXième siècle*. Paris, Mouton.
Biegman, Nicolaas H. 1990. *Egypt: Moulids, Saints, Sufis*. London: Gary Schwartz/SDU and Kegan Paul International.
Commander, Simon. 1987. *The State and Agricultural Development in Egypt since 1973*. London: Ithaca.
Craig, G. M., ed. 1993. *The Agriculture of Egypt*. Oxford and New York, Oxford University Press.
Essam El-Din, Gamal. 1997. "Peasant Rumblings, But No Revolt." *Al-Ahram Weekly*, Oct. 9, 1997, p. 3.
Fahim, Hussein. 1973. "Change in Religion in a Resettled Nubian Community in Upper Egypt." *International Journal of Middle East Studies* 4:163–77.
Fanchette, Sylvie. 1997. *Le Delta du Nil: densités de population et urbanisation des campagnes*. Tours, Centre d'Etudes et de Recherches sur l'Urbanisation du Monde Arabe (URBAMA), Fascicule de Recherche no. 32.
Fargues, Philippe. 1997. "State Policies and the Birth Rate in Egypt: From Socialism to Liberalism." *Population and Development Review* 23(1):115–38.
Faris Mohamed A., and Mahmood Hasan Khan, eds. 1993. *Sustainable Agriculture in Egypt*. Boulder and London: Lynne Rienner.
Fletcher, Lehman B., ed. 1996. *Egypt's Agriculture in a Reform Era*. Ames, Iowa: Iowa State University Press.
Geertz, Clifford. 1968. *Islam Observed*. New Haven, Yale University Press.
Gellner, Ernest. 1981. *Muslim Society*. Cambridge, Cambridge University Press.
Hopkins, Nicholas S. 1987. *Agrarian Transformation in Egypt*. Boulder CO: Westview.
Hopkins, Nicholas S. 1996. "The Egyptian Small Farmer and Off-Farm Employment." in Driss Ben Ali, Antonio di Giulio, Mustapha Lasram, and

Marc Lavergne, eds. *Urbanisation et agriculture en Méditerranée: conflits et complémentarités.* Paris: L'Harmattan. pp. 471–87, 575–77.
Hopkins, Nicholas S. 1998. "Irrigation in Contemporary Egypt." in Alan Bowman and Eugene Rogan, eds. *Agriculture in Egypt from Pharaonic to Modern Times.* Proceedings of the British Academy 96:367–385.
Ibrahim, Fouad N. 1996. *Aegypten: eine geographische Landeskunde.* Darmstadt, Wissenschaftliche Buchgesellschaft, 1996. (Wissenschaftliche Länderkunden, Bd. 42).
Institute of National Planning. 1996. *Egypt: Human Development Report 1996.* Cairo: Institute of National Planning.
El-Karanshawy, Samer. 1998. "Class, Family, and Power in an Egyptian Village." *Cairo Papers in Social Science* 20(1).
Kennedy, John (with Hussein Fahim). 1977. *Struggle for Change in a Nubian Community: An Individual in Society and History.* Palo Alto: Mayfield.
Khedr, Hassan, Rollo Ehrich, and Lehman B. Fletcher. 1996. "Nature, Rationale and Accomplishments of the Agricultural Policy Reforms, 1987–1994." in Lehman B. Fletcher, ed. *Egypt's Agriculture in a Reform Era.* Ames, Iowa: Iowa State University Press. pp. 51–83.
Kroeber, A. L. 1948. *Anthropology.* New York: Harcourt, Brace and Co.
El-Laithy, Heba, and Hanaa Kheir al-Din. 1992/93. "Evaluation de la pauvreté en Egypte en fonction des données sur les ménages." *Egypte Monde Arabe* nos. 12–13. pp. 109–44.
Marei, Sayed. 1957. *Agrarian Reform in Egypt.* Cairo: Imprimérie de l'Institut Français d'Archéologie Orientale.
Mitchell, Timothy. 1991. "The Representation of Rural Violence in Writings on Political Development in Nasserist Egypt." in Farhad Kazemi and John Waterbury, eds. *Peasants and Politics in the Modern Middle East.* Miami: Florida International University Press. pp. 222–51.
Putnam, Robert D. 1995. "Bowling Alone: America's Declining Social Capital." *Journal of Democracy* 6(1):65–78.
Richards, Alan. 1991. "Agricultural Employment, Wages and Government Policy During and After the Oil Boom." in Heba Handoussa and Gillian Potter, eds. *Employment and Structural Adjustment: Egypt in the 1990s.* Cairo: American University in Cairo Press. pp. 57–93.
Wally, Youssef. 1996. "Foreword." in Lehman B. Fletcher, ed. *Egypt's Agriculture in a Reform Era.* Ames, Iowa: Iowa State University Press, pp. vii–viii.
Weber, Max. 1978 [1907]. "The Concept of 'Following a Rule.'" in W. G. Runciman, ed. *Weber: Selections in Translation.* Cambridge, Cambridge University Press. pp. 99–110.
Weber, Max. 1958. *The Protestant Ethic and the Spirit of Capitalism.* New York: Scribner's.
Wehr, Hans. 1961. *A Dictionary of Modern Written Arabic,* ed. J. Milton Cowan. Ithaca: Cornell University Press.
Wolf, Eric R. 1969. *Peasant Wars of the Twentieth Century.* New York: Harper and Row.

# I
# THE POLITICAL ECONOMY OF RURAL EGYPT

# 1

# The Market's Place

TIMOTHY MITCHELL*

The dominant theme in the description of the rural Third World at the close of the twentieth century remains the story of its capitalist transformation. The theme is exemplified in rural Egypt, where the reform and removal of state controls through the program known as structural adjustment is intended to turn the land and its produce into market commodities and remake the countryside for the twenty-first century as a fully capitalist economy. There are several ways to critique this story of capitalism's advance. In the case of Egypt one can question how seriously some of the market reforms have been applied, ask about the ways they have been resisted or evaded, point to the increasing hardship and poverty they have caused, attack them for reversing the 1952 land reform and other political achievements, and criticize their appropriateness for the way most households survive and make a living. What remains remarkably difficult, however, is to account for what is happening in the countryside in a way that not only questions the extent or desirability of the advance of market capitalism, but avoids telling it as the story of capitalism.

Let me suggest why one might want to avoid telling capitalism's story. The power of the market economy reveals itself not only in the transforming of people's lives and livelihoods but in its influence over the way we think. It is one of those ideas that we seem able to grasp only in terms that the phenomenon itself dictates. There are many different ways to describe the nature of the market economy, yet every description carries a common assumption. It is variously said to be

---

* I have changed the names and certain descriptions of people in the village discussed in this essay. I am grateful to all of them, and especially those I have called Rajab, Zaynab, Mona, and Salim, for their help and hospitality. Special thanks to Butros Wadi', and also to Lila Abu-Lughod, Siona Jenkins, Reem Saad, David Sims, and the editors of and other contributors to this volume. A National Endowment for the Humanities Fellowship at the American Research Center in Egypt gave me the time to write this essay.

based upon principles of self interest, profit making, the proper organization of pricing and other forms of information, the accumulation and reinvestment of capital, the exploitation of labor, and a continuous historical process of expansion and transformation. Different accounts may highlight or ignore different features from this list. But every attempt to describe the capitalist economy inevitably attempts to capture what distinguishes the market from the non-market system. The distinction gives capitalism its identity.

Telling the narrative of capitalism requires that it have such an identity. As Gibson-Graham argues, there must be some characteristic that is the essence of capitalism, so that as it develops and expands one can recognize its occurrence and put together its story.[1] As one tells the story, this essence supplies the theme that enables the narrative to move forward. It provides a logic that becomes the source of historical movement and the motor of social transformations. In contemporary rural Egypt, one can attribute the spread of free-market practices to the force of self-interest and individual economic freedom, once the restraints of state control and other non-capitalist arrangements are removed. Or, following a different conception of capitalism's essence, one can ascribe the changes to the power of Egyptian and international capital, driven by the need to accumulate and reproduce. Whichever way one tells the story, what is happening in rural Egypt, or anywhere else in the rural Third World, receives its logic and meaning from the movement of the principle of market capitalism.

This logic does not mean that there are no other factors at work. The narrative gives a place to all kinds of non-capitalist features. The countryside may contain what one thinks of as traditional practices or precapitalist social arrangements, which resist the spread of the market or even interact with it in some kind of transitional articulation. It may contain political forces that present obstacles to the spread of capitalism or distort its operation. People may have social values or cultural norms that differ from those of the market. What characterizes all these additional features, however, is that when they are placed within the larger story of capitalism they are determined by its logic. The narrative marks them as non-market factors, meaning that it defines their identity and significance in terms of what they are not. Their role is that of negative elements. They stand outside the principle of the market, as external, non-dynamic, generally residual, mostly local factors. As the exterior of capitalism, moreover, although they may impede its progress or distort its path, they do not shape its essence. They play no part in defining its nature. The market economy is understood to be a universal form constituted only from its own internal logic. The local and residual features encountered in a place like rural Egypt do not affect its real nature.

Is there an alternative way to make sense of what is happening in the countryside? Can one find a way to take the evidence of local variation and complexity and make it challenge the narrative of the market? Can one do so without positing the existence of a precapitalist or non-capitalist sphere, a position that always invokes the universal nature of capitalism? To begin to do so, one would have to stop asking of rural Egypt, is it capitalist or not? One must avoid the assumption that capitalism has an 'is' and take more seriously the variations, disruptions, and dislocations that make each appearance of capitalism, despite the plans of the reformers, something different.

I propose to explore these questions by drawing on some recent experience of a rural community in southern Egypt. What I offer is not a systematic study but a selection of observations and incidents that can help address these issues. There are several aspects of the village's experience I will discuss, but to give a focus to the account I want to look in particular at the question of wheat.

Wheat offers an appropriate theme for a critique of economic discourse. It has often served as a symbol of popular resistance to the market. In Egypt, Jordan, and beyond the Arab world, efforts in recent years to end national protection against the world market have been marked by major riots protesting the increase in the price of bread. More than two decades later, no discussion of the economic reforms of the International Monetary Fund (IMF) in Egypt passes without reference to the bread riots of January 1977.[2]

Following the 1977 riots, as all the accounts of the reform process relate, the Egyptian government moved more slowly and surreptitiously towards the reintroduction of world market prices for wheat. Protection had begun in 1941 as a measure to counteract the food shortages and price inflation caused by war. In 1966 the government introduced ration cards to control distribution after the United States cut off its supply of subsidized wheat. When non-market US wheat returned in enormous amounts after 1973, the ration system changed from a form of quantity control into the almost unlimited supply of highly subsidized bread.[3] From the mid-1980s, as the US began to demand market prices for the wheat it had previously dumped (with the express aim of creating a future market), the Ministry of Supply started to increase the price and reduce the availability and quality of subsidized bread and flour. It also stopped issuing ration cards for children born after 1991. At the same time, the Ministry of Agriculture began to introduce policies demanded by the US to create an uncontrolled domestic market in wheat and most other crops. The Ministry claimed to have ended government control of all crop areas, quotas, and prices by 1987, except for rice, cotton, and sugarcane, and for all except sugarcane by 1992. The control of marketing and processing was also changed. In the case of wheat, the public sector's share was reduced to about 50 percent of production after 1992, when the private sector was allowed to begin importing wheat flour.[4]

What has been the experience of these changes in rural Egypt? The village from which I want to draw some observations is located in a sugarcane producing region of Qina governorate. It lies about six kilometers from the town of Luxor on the other side of the Nile and on the periphery of its tourist industry.[5] Bread is the village's staple food, but it has no bakeries and almost none of its more than two thousand households buys bread already baked. Instead they use wheat flour to make the large loaves known as *'aysh shamsi*, leavened in the sun and baked in earthen ovens at home. The dozen or so largest landowners use only wheat from their own fields, but the rest depend in part or whole on sacks of purchased flour. As the government-subsidized *baladi* (local) flour was made scarcer, more expensive, and of worse quality, all except the very poorest households came to depend increasingly on *fino* (highly refined, mostly imported) flour purchased from local merchants at unregulated prices.

Many households with small landholdings dealt with these changes by growing increasing amounts of their own wheat, which they process at one of the tiny, one-room village mills and use entirely for household bread-making. Zaynab, for example, who owns twenty qirats (five-sixths of a feddan) and used to produce little or no wheat, now grows wheat on more than half her land. With eight children but no grown men to feed, a strong yield will supply all her needs for the year. The Mahmud household farms four feddans and now uses more than half the land for wheat, although with three married sons and their wives and children the crop will not quite supply their needs. Rather than running out of home-grown wheat, which makes bread of superior texture and taste, the women add a little *fino* flour each time they bake. The village's largest landowner, Salim, who controls over three hundred of its 2,750 feddans, produces an enormous surplus of wheat, which he sells to grain merchants from Qina or other large towns. Unlike the small holders, however, he has not increased his wheat acreage since the deregulation of the market, preferring (for reasons to be explored) to keep most of his land in sugarcane.

The Ministry of Agriculture produces statistics that reflect the increased production of wheat, at least among small holders, and may exaggerate it. The official figures for the country as a whole report that levels of wheat production stagnated at just under two million metric tons a year from the start of the 1980s until 1986/87, then suddenly doubled to more than four million tons by 1990 and over 4.5 million by the mid-1990s. The biggest increase came in 1987/88, immediately following the removal of area restrictions, quotas, and fixed procurement prices, when production jumped by 40 percent in one year.[6] The Ministry, the IMF, and the US Agency for International Development (USAID) regularly cite these figures as the best proof of the success of their program of free-market reforms. While acknowledging that there has been a significant increase in wheat production, one can point to two problems with this use of the figures. First, the system of compulsory cropping and low procurement prices that preceded the 1987 reform, which particularly affected small farmers, gave them a strong incentive to disguise the size of wheat yields. Small holders who were required to grow a quota of sugarcane or other commercial crops and sell them to the government at low prices also had good reason to divert part of their land to crops they could eat themselves, including wheat. At the very least they would ensure that any particularly poor soil was allocated to government crops, not those consumed at home. ("There's my sesame," 'Amm Mahmud used to say, pointing to a barren patch of whitish soil that never produced anything). These sorts of practices may well have increased during the 1980s, as procurement prices dropped in real terms, subsidized flour became harder to obtain, and consumer prices for other foods increased sharply. The stagnant yields of the years before 1987, which according to the official view made necessary the shift to an unregulated market, may in fact reflect, in whole or in part, the small holders' unreported diversion of land and crops to better serve their own needs. To the extent that this is the case, which is something one has no way of measuring, the impact of the free-market reforms may have been greater on the statistics published by the state than on what farmers actually grow.

Second, it is curious that those telling the story of Egyptian agriculture at the end of the twentieth century as one of successful movement toward a free market should produce as the best evidence of its progress the fact that farmers are moving not toward the market but toward increased self-provisioning and protection from the market. The rationale for the deregulation of agriculture was that farmers would respond by growing more so-called high-value crops, especially export crops such as cotton and vegetables, drawing themselves more fully into the national and transnational market economy and thereby increasing their own and the nation's income. This did not happen. In the six years following the 1987 deregulation, the area planted with cotton, the two main vegetable crops (tomatoes and potatoes), and most other vegetables, declined.[7] The area planted with grain and fodder crops serving mostly household production, on the other hand, remained steady, and in the case of the two staple grains, wheat and rice, dramatically increased.[8]

In the village itself several smallholders reported experimenting with growing vegetables after the government controls were lifted, with mixed results. In 1988, Ahmad Hasan planted two qirats of eggplant and sold the crop for LE700—a good return. The following year he planted six qirats, half his landholding. There was a shortage of irrigation water for one month, the crop dried out, and his entire yield filled barely three baskets. He sold the crop for LE20. Others reported planting tomatoes and getting LE2 or 3 per kilo, selling directly to a man with a truck who shipped them to Rud al-Farag wholesale market in Cairo. Then came *'ayyam Saddam,'* the 1990–91 Gulf crisis, when tourism collapsed, and with it the price of vegetables. People were selling two or three kilos for just fifty piasters. Some told of other disaster stories, while many more were unable even to consider taking such risks.

Instead, one finds farmers adopting other strategies to increase their income, but these often take them in different directions than the market. To prepare one of her strips of land for planting the 1996/97 crop of wheat, Zaynab hired a distant cousin who uses a wooden plow, drawn by a cow and its calf. During the eight years since she started farming her own land she had always previously hired tractors. By the end of the 1980s, these had almost entirely replaced animal-drawn plows—a process encouraged by government subsidies and USAID programs to promote the import of agricultural machinery.[9] The ending of subsidies, however, had removed some of the cost advantage of the tractor (LE1.50 to LE2.00 to plow one qirat, compared to LE2.50 for the cow). Zaynab had also learned that animal-drawn plows produce a better yield, because they do not compact the soil as tractors do, especially when making tight turns at the ends of the narrow, elongated strips that small farmers own. Moreover, she talked the owners of neighboring plots into hiring the same plow and received a discount in return that made it cheaper than the tractor (it helped that the plow was owned by a relative). The owner is now in such demand that he has hired a partner to do the plowing, in return for one third of the income. Machines have a limited life and their cost includes the cost of their replacement. The cow trains its own calf as it plows, and in two or three years the calf will take its place. Fueled with home-grown fodder and producing its own replacement, the cow represents another part of people's engagement in a logic that moves away from or at cross-purposes to the logic of the market.

These alternative strategies do not create a separate sphere of practice that might be labeled traditional or non-market and contrasted to the market sphere. On a strip of land in a different part of the village, also prepared for wheat, Zaynab hired a tractor to plow. The tractor's owner, Abu Qumsan, farms an adjacent strip and Zaynab depends on his son, who drives the tractor, for other favors during the year. The father owns only three feddans, much less than any other tractor owner, so he is particularly dependent on renting out the tractor to work his neighbors' plots. Zaynab decided it would be prudent to maintain good relations with him by continuing to hire his tractor. Elsewhere in the village, to give a different example, farmers have begun to reintroduce the use of camels, particularly to carry the sugarcane crop. Like the animal plow, camels had been almost completely replaced by tractors over the previous decade. But then a number of young men from different hamlets in the village began to invest in camels. They use them to carry sugarcane in the mornings, then deck them with saddles and decorated cloths and take them to the ferry where tourists disembark from Luxor, to earn money offering rides through the village.

Sugarcane offers a more complex case of this embrication of what it is difficult to distinguish as market and non-market practices. The Mahmud household, with four feddans and three married sons, while increasing their wheat crop to more than two feddans, still keeps one feddan devoted to the year-round production of sugarcane. This is their only cash crop. The rest of the land grows maize and berseem for animal raising, and onions, *mulukhiya*, and other small crops to feed the household. The cane provides the income to purchase seeds, diesel for the irrigation pump, and the fertilizer they require for growing household crops. The feddan of cane will earn between LE4,500 and LE5,000 from its sale to the government sugar factory. The factory pays part of this amount in advance, providing a cash loan early in the year on which the household now depends. This is another reason why they keep the sugarcane—if they switched to another crop they could not survive the growing season without the loan. They are involved in production for the market, but its purpose is to support the much larger system of self-provisioning. This is true for the village as a whole, and probably for the entire country. The pattern is the reverse of that described in the old debates on the articulation of modes of production, and far more complex. Rather than a subsistence sector surviving in support of capitalism, market crops, protected and promoted by the state, survive in support of self-provisioning.

Small and medium-sized farmers like the Mahmud household have no interest in extending the production of a market crop such as sugarcane, beyond the needs of their household production, precisely because of the expense and loss involved in getting it to the market.[10] They cut and strip the cane themselves with the help of neighbors and relatives, but they must hire a tractor and trailer to carry it across the village to the light railway line running to the mill in Armant, fifteen kilometers to the south, and a pair of men to load the railway wagons. For a feddan of cane, the tractor costs LE500, the loaders LE300. As Rajab Mahmud says, "The tractor takes our profit." The mill workers take some too, he swears, for when they weigh the cane at the factory they always cheat and record a lower weight for each farmer's wagons. Household crops, on the other hand, which they also cut themselves, are carried to the house on a donkey or by hand, or in a pick-up truck rented for a few pounds if the field is further away. No one else takes their profit.

These same considerations produce a different logic for the handful of very large landowners, for whom sugarcane has comparatively low labor costs. Salim, for example, who grows more than a hundred feddans of cane, hires teams of day laborers at LE5 each per day (in 1996/97) for the planting, weeding, and harvesting of all his crops. His sons and nephews help to supervise the laborers working in different areas of the village and he employs a handful of permanent workers to drive the tractors he owns and operate his irrigation pumps and other machinery. Since all his crops carry the cost of hired labor, sugarcane is no more expensive to grow than wheat, maize, or broad beans. In fact its labor costs are much cheaper. The cane stays in the ground for three to five years, reducing the cost of planting, and needs fertilizing only three times a year. Salim's crop is so large that its harvesting takes five months, from late December until May. He employs wagon loaders continuously through this period, at a discount. He pays them only LE2 per ton of loaded cane, compared to the LE2.50 or LE3 that small holders pay to hire loaders by the day, making his labor costs as much as 50 percent lower. Most importantly, villagers do much of his harvesting for free. Those with little or no land use the leaves *(gilwah)* of the cane as fodder for household water buffalo. Mona, for example, who owns only a few qirats and rents several more to grow berseem, depends on the *gilwah* as an additional source of fodder. She helps harvest in the fields adjacent to her house and sends her sons to more distant plots. They do the difficult and physically dangerous work of cutting and stripping the cane without payment, or for a token amount, in exchange for taking the leaves, which have no market value. The interaction of paid and unpaid labor determines that the same crop which small farmers find the most costly to produce is for large landowners the cheapest. But the profits that lead large owners to grow sugarcane rather than wheat depend upon a large supply of villagers with little or no land, willing to do the most arduous work of all without payment.

I have been calling sugarcane a market crop, but this is misleading. The mill that buys the crop is owned by the government, which fixes the purchase price. Yet this is not the misleading part. If the government were to privatize the Egyptian Sugar and Refining Company, the farmers would still not be able to chose to whom to sell their crop or at what price. The crop takes eighteen months to grow when first planted and stays in the ground for at least two further nine-month cultivations, so farmers have no way to respond to the ups and downs of international sugar prices.

What is misleading is the very idea that there can be a free market in sugar. As a crop that requires the year-round sun of tropical or semi-tropical regions, and one whose harvesting cannot easily be mechanized, cane is the only staple food in the world whose cultivation and export is not dominated by the rich countries of the temperate zone. This anomaly was first overcome, three hundred years ago, by colonizing the Caribbean and enslaving Africans to grow cane there. When the US and Europe lost control of their Caribbean dependencies in the mid-twentieth century, they responded by promoting the cultivation of sugar beet, an inferior crop that requires extensive use of chemical herbicides and had to be protected with price supports and import quotas. Surplus beet sugar was then dumped on the world market, depressing and destabilizing the price of cane sugar and costing its Third World producers billions of dollars each year in lost revenues.[11] The price of sugar in the US includes the hundreds of thousands of dollars the sugar industry pays each year buying votes in Congress in order to keep the subsidy system in place.[12]

Just as sugarcane cannot easily be understood as a market crop, so too with the case of wheat. There is a similar difficulty in describing the movement of wheat outside the village as a market system. As with sugarcane, cotton, and other major crops, the agricultural policy reforms in Egypt were unable to deregulate the price of wheat. From 1992, private merchants were allowed to import wheat flour, ostensibly creating a free market in white *(fino)* flour. In practice, however, the reform replaced Egyptian government controls with a series of other restrictions and controls, running from the world market to the village merchant. At the global level, the marketing of wheat is controlled by half-a-dozen US grain-trading corporations, some of them privately owned. Production prices depend on an extensive system of US and European Union price supports, required to keep afloat their large and otherwise unprofitable commercial producers. The failure of large-scale commercial wheat production dates back more than a century, to the emergence of a global market in wheat between the 1870s and 1930s. As Harriet Friedman has shown, the emergence of the market did not follow a logic one could describe simply as capitalist. It coincided with a global shift from large-scale commercial farming to the increasing production of wheat by family farms. Relying on their own unpaid labor, household producers were more efficient, flexible, and resilient than large farms using wage labor. From the 1930s, as the crisis of large grain producers worsened, the US and other governments began to introduce a system of price supports, which Washington extended after World War II into a program of subsidized grain exports that aimed to convert first Europeans, and then parts of the Third World into consumers of meat-based diets, which require much higher levels of grain production. In the 1970s and 1980s, the largest recipient of subsidized US grain was Egypt, where cheap wheat imports helped depress farm incomes and diverted government spending to other sectors, especially the military.[13]

In the US and Western Europe, government subsidies kept wheat prices high to protect politically powerful producers. Total annual subsidies in US agriculture reached about $29,000 for each farmer (or forty times Egypt's per capita GNP).[14] A separate system of support, using food coupons and welfare payments, made bread affordable for the poor.[15] In Egypt, where producers had no political power and a far greater proportion of the population could not afford the inflated prices of the world grain market, the government used subsidies differently, to keep consumer prices low. As mentioned earlier, in the late 1980s, the US began to demand market prices for its wheat, forcing Egypt to embark on the program of agricultural policy reform. The Egyptian government eliminated subsidies from most other goods, cut the quantity and quality of subsidized flour, and began adding corn flour to the wheat. Despite strong IMF pressure to abolish bread subsidies, however, the government was unable to eliminate the program. The private sector wheat market had to coexist with the system of government supply.

Farmers in the village were now caught in the resulting confusion. The Ministry of Agriculture claimed to have ended the system of area restrictions, quotas, and fixed procurement prices. The Ministry of Supply and Trade, however, working with the governorate authorities, still attempted to procure about 12–15 percent of local wheat production, at a fixed price (LE100 per ardeb in 1996 and 1997). The land reform cooperatives, which supply seeds and fertilizer, demanded in return that the owners of each holding (the *nimra*, or original land-reform unit, which is usually now shared among several second or third-generation owners) sell to the government one ardeb (150 kilograms) of wheat. In the summer of 1996, a crisis erupted when the price of wheat on the commercial market rose much higher than the government's price, and the Ministry of Supply was unable to obtain its wheat. The Qina Governorate authorities responded by suspending development projects in any village that failed to supply its quota, forcing farmers to supply the missing wheat by purchasing on the market, where prices jumped even higher. The authorities also reduced the supply of subsidized flour to each distributor. In Aswan Governorate to the south, local authorities required that anyone seeking permits or other government assistance produce a document showing that they had supplied their quota of wheat. In at least one district this requirement was imposed on every village household, including those growing no wheat or even farming no land at all. To obtain the appropriate document, villagers had to pay the cooperative a sum covering the cost of purchasing wheat on the market to resell to the government. The authorities had banned the transport of wheat between governorates, so villages had to smuggle supplies through the desert to avoid the road blocks and inspection points that now operated as frontiers on the main roads.[16] The official accounts of Egypt's successful transition to a rural market economy have not discussed these unusual arrangements.

There are further reasons why the movement of wheat outside the village does not resemble the model of a free market. The international cartel of grain trading corporations that controls world supplies is now copied within Egypt. A small group of merchants controls the commercial importing of wheat flour and fixes the price.[17] Within the village itself, the commercial distribution of flour is also tending toward a local oligopoly. Three or four merchants in the village have official concessions to sell subsidized flour from the Ministry of Supply. Commercial sales of flour are now concentrated in the same hands. By far the biggest of these merchants is Hasan Qinawi, who, with his brother Ibrahim, inherited his father's village shop and transformed it in the mid-1990s into a wholesale operation that began to monopolize the supply of flour in the district.

One of the reasons why the supply of flour cannot operate freely as a market is that for most people in Egypt, bread is a staple. The government has reduced or eliminated almost all other food subsidies, but cannot end the supply of subsidized bread. In the village, bread forms a large part of almost everyone's diet. Compared to the flat loaves of *'aysh baladi* eaten in the towns, the thick *'aysh shamshi* loaf is extremely filling. For the poorest households, it is almost the only food, taken with a cup of black tea at breakfast and dipped in a bowl of *mulukhiyya* to give it moisture as the main meal.

The staple nourishment that bread can provide is the result of a major resource within the village, a resource that shapes the wheat market yet cannot itself be marketed—the labor of bread-making. The work women do in kneading and baking their bread and supplying fuel for the bread oven is one of the major means of creating household wealth. Most women bake every four or five days, often working jointly with a sister-in-law, neighbor, or daughter kept home from school, to share the huge labor of producing fifty or sixty loaves. The work is integrated with the other household labor of child rearing, laundry, cooking, and cleaning, and is closely connected with animal raising. Pats of buffalo dung, together with the remains of the maize or corn leaves used as animal fodder, mixed with dung from the donkey, provide the main source of fuel for the bread oven. (Households needing extra supplies can spread a little dung on leaves outside the house, provoking every passing donkey to provide some more). Cardboard boxes, used school notebooks, and other new forms of refuse in the village provide an additional source of fuel. Tourist groups from Luxor that visit the temple near Zaynab's house bring boxed lunches, whose packaging she has arranged to recycle in her oven. Dried scraps of bread from her table are never wasted, but carefully collected and fed to the poultry. Even the ashes from the bread oven are reused, as fertilizer in the fields.

This form of food production cannot be reproduced commercially, given the market costs of fuel and labor, so *'aysh shamshi* is not available for purchase. In the wealthiest landowning households, women who are spared some of the other chores of animal raising and collecting fodder still produce their own bread. Even the handful of younger, better-off women who live in the small apartment buildings near the ferry, from where their husbands commute to work as lawyers or pharmacists in Luxor, still usually return to their mothers' homes in the village every few days to bake bread.

The system of self-provisioning begins with the growing of wheat and the raising of domestic animals. No household is self-sufficient, for most lack enough land to support themselves entirely, and those with large landholdings purchase tea, sugar, and other goods they cannot grow. But self-provisioning involves far more than the resources represented by government figures for wheat production and numbers of farm animals. The village household produces its staple diet not only by raising crops and animals but by an intensive system of food manufacture. Neither the labor used to make bread nor the fuel is a market commodity. The same is true of the labor used in milking the buffalo and producing cheese, clarified butter, and other household milk products, or in preparing poultry to eat. This manufacturing system is probably the country's largest industry, at least in terms of the numbers it employs. Yet it has no official place in the government's program of agricultural reforms. Contemporary methods of estimating the country's gross domestic product include some guess at the value of crops directly consumed by those who grow them. But the reforms are concerned with removing obstacles to the operation of market laws and understand the nature of Egyptian agriculture according to the model of a market. This model has no place for the industry of domestic food manufacture and the crops and livestock that support it, except a residual and insignificant one.

The result of working with the model of the market has been to demonstrate its failure. Ending the compulsory government purchase of crops at low prices probably stimulated production. The yields of several major crops appear to have increased significantly. But some of this increase may have been due to more accurate reporting and much of the rest to the continuing introduction of high-yielding crop varieties, which have no necessary connection with market principles. (Egypt now holds the world record for yields of sugarcane, the one crop that the government still entirely controls). In general, the free-market reforms produced results opposite from those their proponents anticipated. Instead of moving towards high value export crops, such as cotton and vegetables, farmers increased their production of staples such as wheat, maize, and rice. Markets did not work, because of monopolization, hoarding, and speculation, and the exposure of farmers to international price swings that make free-market farming impossible all over the world. Acreage controls and floor prices had to be retained or reintroduced. Furthermore, even the reformers acknowledged that "the costs," as they put it, of their policies had "become much more apparent." These included "growing unemployment, falling real wages, higher prices for basic goods and services, and widespread loss of economic security."[18]

Reformers claimed that these hardships were the necessary price for removing the barriers to agricultural growth. Once the growth began, the hardships would be overcome. Since removing the barriers exposed farmers to global price instability and local price fixing, however, it did not stimulate real growth. The World Bank had claimed that the old system of price controls was penalizing farmers and reducing agricultural GDP by 20 percent.[19] Yet in the seven years following the removal of controls after 1986, despite the reported increase in yields, agricultural GDP stagnated or even declined.[20] The reformers subsequently admitted that they did not know whether the old price controls had depressed output or what effect government interventions had on overall agricultural performance.[21] Moreover, apparent success in the other major area of economic reform, currency stabilization, encouraged large flows of foreign capital into Egypt, which the IMF claimed were causing the real exchange rate to become overvalued, perhaps by as much as 30 percent.[22] If so, the decline of real agricultural income, as well as the obstacles to the further promotion of agricultural exports, were even greater.

Far from a temporary phenomenon, the costs of the reforms were to become a central part of the reformers' long term plans for rural Egypt. Following the creation of a commercial market in crops, the next goal was to be a free market in land. The 1952 agrarian reform gave agricultural tenants and their heirs security against eviction and fixed the maximum rent at seven times the land tax. The US government and international financial agencies argued that this arrangement was "creating disincentives to a more efficient use of land," although there was no logic or evidence to support them.[23] A law to abolish the 1952 reform was pushed through parliament in 1992. The maximum rent was raised from seven to twenty-two times the land tax for a five-year period, after which rents and tenancies were to be uncontrolled and all tenants could be freely evicted. Parliament enacted the law without any studies of its possible impact, nor even accurate figures about the number of tenants affected or the size of their landholdings.[24]

The eviction of small tenants is not the only part of the reformers' longer term plans. A conference in Cairo in March 1995 bringing together representatives of USAID, the Ministry of Agriculture, agribusiness consulting firms, and some of the US and Egyptian academics they employ, concluded that Egypt's agricultural future depended principally on increased use of technology to encourage 'falling labor use,' which in turn would release additional labor for industrial employment. This surplus labor, together with lower prices paid to farmers for producing food, would "help keep real urban wages low and industry more profitable."[25] The transitional costs of higher unemployment, falling real wages, and increased economic insecurity were now revealed as a long term goal of the reforms.

Perhaps to hasten this process of pauperization, the conference repeated the demand of the US government and the IMF for the early removal of the remaining subsidies on bread and flour, on the grounds that keeping staple food affordable resulted in "waste" and "excess consumption," proposing instead that a smaller amount of aid be given to the "ultrapoor 20 percent of the population."[26] This smaller figure would probably not even cover the proportion known to be suffering from serious malnutrition.[27] It might even increase that proportion, for there is no evidence that those who eat subsidized bread are guilty of over consumption. Even among the two-thirds of the population classified as non-poor, food accounts on average for almost 50 percent of household expenditure, a large part of it consisting of bread and other carbohydrates. Surveys indicated that the average calorie intake of this better-off two-thirds remained below the minimum recommended allowance, even before most of the price increases and wage cuts of the 1990s.[28] If the US government was concerned with waste and excess consumption, it perhaps needed to look elsewhere. Its own estimates suggest that five percent of Egypt's population are affluent by US standards and that the top two percent (over one million people) are "exceptionally and often ostentatiously wealthy."[29] There is no evidence that this class purchases a significant quantity of subsidized bread. The bread reached only 75 percent of the urban population in 1984, and it has since declined in quality and availability.[30]

Reading the proposals and reports of the proponents of free-market reforms for Egyptian agriculture, one is struck by the almost complete absence from their accounts of any of the detail or particularity of rural Egypt. One encounters no farmers or villages in their writing. Much more, too, is missing. Many of the most sweeping reform proposals are unsupported by adequate evidence. The demands to abolish price controls, crop quotas, food subsidies, and the protection of tenants, were made with no reliable knowledge about the effects of these programs or the likely consequences of their removal. The result of removing them was a dramatic decline in rates of agricultural growth, a massive shift away from high value crops such as cotton, a huge drop in Egypt's most valuable manufactured export, cotton textiles and clothes, and repeated crises of overproduction or underproduction of different crops. None of this, however, has prevented the reformers from announcing the success of their plans. We should see the significance of these endless reports and announcements less in marking progress along the path of capitalist development, but more in constantly reiterating the language of market capitalism, thereby reproducing the impression that we know what capitalism is and that its unfolding determines our history.

How instead should we understand rural Egypt and its relation to the market system? There appear at present to be two alternatives, neither of them without problems. One stresses the non-capitalist nature of small farming and sees it as an alternative system of self-provisioning and subsistence, surviving in some sort of articulation with the capitalist sector, in particular providing cheap labor to the large farmers. The problem with this view is that it fails to account for local complexity and the multiple forms of involvement with the market. What are portrayed as two opposed systems are in practice impossible to disentangle. The other approach sees household-based farmers as small capitalists. It stresses the variety of ways in which they deal with the market and the entrepreneurial skill with which they turn meager resources into a basis for survival.[31] This view makes better sense of the complexity of social relations and the central role of small farmers in what is called the market system. But in stressing the identity of household farmers as small capitalists, it presents no real alternative to the story of the market. This means that what happens in rural Egypt is ultimately based on the logic of capital. Other sorts of elements play only a secondary role and do not affect the development of capitalism itself.

The alternative, as Gibson-Graham has illustrated in the different context of the global finance industry, would be to start by questioning the assumption that there is some universal social form called capitalism, to which Egyptian farmers relate.[32] The variety of processes described as capitalist or market are not a self-contained system, to be imported intact into rural Egypt. One of the proponents of free-market reforms in Egyptian agriculture says their introduction "requires a seamless web" of simultaneous changes in the agricultural system.[33] But the system cannot be seamless, for it must be stitched together out of people and practices already involved in a multitude of agrarian and other social relations. The project of free-market capitalism not only encounters this range of existing practice, it depends upon it to proceed. In the village, as we saw, the major cash crop is sugarcane, whose profitability rests upon the use of unpaid, non-market labor for harvesting. The majority of cane growers, moreover, produce a cash crop not as market entrepreneurs but to support a larger system of self-provisioning. Self-provisioning itself is not incidental to the free-market project. The goal of capitalist expansion through lower wages requires farm workers who avoid the market cost of food by supplying part of their own consumption needs directly. Crops intended mostly for the farm household now account for more than two-thirds of the crop area.[34] Even production intended for the market is often based on forms of organization that cannot easily be described as capitalist, such as the coerced labor of the military production sector, the oligopolies that control commercial animal raising, or the forms of patronage and kinship ties through which local merchants like the Qinawis or large-scale farmers like Salim manage their operations.

The picture of rural Egypt that emerges cannot easily be described as a system of small capitalists incorporated into a larger capitalist economy. Nor, however, does there exist a separate non-capitalist sector in articulation with a market system. Rather, the so-called capitalist agriculture encouraged and developed by the free-market reforms includes and depends upon a far wider range of practices that do not fit with any common definition of the essential nature of capitalism.

These apparently non-capitalist elements are so numerous and so central that they have decisively shaped the outcome of the free-market reforms. The most obvious example of this is that relaxing crop quotas and acreage controls led to a boom not in market and export crops but in staples and self-provisioning. The removal of marketing controls led not to a free-market system but to cartels and price-fixing on one side and reintroduction of floor prices and acreage controls on the other. Advocates of the market attribute these setbacks to the incomplete nature of the reforms, or the improper sequence, or unanticipated side effects. In other words, they ascribe them to the failure to introduce the market system as a "seamless web." Instead, we should see them, not as a coordinated resistance to the market, but as the displacements and reformulations that occur because of the dependence of so-called capitalist arrangements on such a multitude of seemingly non-capitalist elements. Given this dependence, we cannot easily describe the latter as non-capitalist. But once we introduce them into the description of capitalism, any attempt to attribute an essence to capitalism has to be abandoned.

The forms of displacement and reformulation I have described are not in any sense merely a characteristic of transitional arrangements, where supposed market principles are introduced into a non-market system. As my discussions of the role of subsidies in US agriculture, of slavery in the origins of capitalism, or of the world sugar and grain markets indicate, these displacements are found everywhere. At the same time, the conclusion to be drawn is not that the situation in rural Egypt is therefore essentially no different from that of US farmers, or that the local reformulations might represent a coherent or organized challenge to the project known as global capitalism. The project remains one that has immense concentrations of power and resources on its side. The conclusion, rather, is that we need to become much more attentive to the failures, diversions, and changing directions of the project. The power of what we call capitalism rests increasingly on its ability to portray itself as a unique and universal form, on reproducing a view of history and of economics in which the market is the universal system, constituted and propelled forward by the power of its own interior logic. The displacements and reformulations of the capitalist project show its dependence on arrangements and relations that this logic needs to portray as non-capitalist. By revealing the absence of an interior logic, they force us to look elsewhere for its power.

## Notes

1 This discussion draws on the insightful argument of Gibson-Graham (1995). On the critique of essentialized notions of the economy see Mitchell (1995a). On contesting the discourse of capitalist modernity in accounts of the Third World see, among others, Mitchell (1991); Bhabha (1994); Prakash (1990a, 1990b); and Spivak (1988).
2 See for example, "Kabir khubara' al-iqtisadiyin bi-sanduq al-naqd al-dawli:....." *al-Ahram*, Jan. 25, 1997, p. 21; Douglas Jehl, "Egypt Adding Corn to Bread: An Explosive Mix?" *New York Times*, Nov. 27, 1996, p. A4.
3 See Alderman and Von Braun (1982).
4 Khedr, Ehrich, and Fletcher (1996, p. 63).
5 There is no space in this essay to give a full account of the political economy of the village, or to discuss the ways tourism affects its life; see Mitchell (1995b).
6 Khedr, Ehrich, and Fletcher (1996:66), using data from the Department of Agricultural Economics and Statistics, Ministry of Agriculture and Land Reclamation, Cairo; 1995/96; *al-Ahram*, Jan, 20, 1997, p. 13.
7 Khedr, Ehrich, and Fletcher, (1996: 63, 67); "al-Hukuma tahammalat 522 malyun ginayh li-l-mawsim al-qutn 96/97," *al-Ahram al-iqtisadi* Feb. 24, 1997, p. 40.
8 See Nassar, Sands, Omran, and Krenz (1996:92), citing data from the Department of Agricultural Economics and Statistics, Ministry of Agriculture and Land Reclamation, Cairo.
9 On the mechanization of Egyptian agriculture, see Hopkins (1987), and Hopkins, Mehanna, and Abdelmaksoud (1982).
10 A detailed survey of farmers and marketing carried out in 1989–91 found the costs of marketing—that is, the proportion of the final consumer price taken by transportation, merchants, and others, compared to the proportion left to the farmer, or what economists term 'marketing efficiency'— to be of important concern to the farmers (Mehanna, Hopkins, and Abdelmaksoud (1994:133).
11 The World Bank calculates that in 1983 the sugar protection policies of the industrialized countries caused Third World producers to lose $7.4 billion in revenue, cutting their real income by $2.1 billion and increasing price instability by 25 percent. See *World Development Report 1986*, Washington DC; The World Bank, and World Commission on Environment and Development, *Our Common Future*, Oxford and New York: Oxford University Press, 1987, p. 82.
12 The Center for Responsive Politics cites the sugar industry as one of the most glaring examples of how pressure groups use money to influence voting in Congress. In 1996, the industry paid an average of $13,000 to the sixty-one senators who voted to preserve sugar subsidies, compared to an average of $1,500 to those who voted against. *Cashing In: A Guide to Money, Votes, and Public Policy in the 104th Congress*. Washington DC: Center for Responsive Politics, Jan. 1997. "US politicians' votes 'tied to

*The Market's Place* 37

funding,'" *Financial Times*, Jan. 23, 1997, p. 1. The price of US sugar also includes the cost of the embargo on Cuban sugar, another part of the protection system.

13 See Mitchell (1995c).
14 The figure of $29,000 is from the Organization for Economic Cooperation and Development, cited by Kevin Watkins, "Fast Route to Poverty," *The Guardian Weekly*, Feb. 16, 1997, p. 29. Egypt's 1994 per capita GNP was estimated at $720 (World Bank, *World Development Report 1996*, p. 188).
15 In 1993, the US food stamp program served 27 million people and cost $27 billion (FY 1994). Another $8 billion was spent on other subsidized food programs, including the School Lunch and the Women, Infants, and Children programs (United States Department of Agriculture, *Agriculture Fact Book 1994*, pp. 76–79).
16 I am grateful to Reem Saad for the Aswan information, which describes events in the Idfu district.
17 In January 1997, the Minister of Supply acknowledged the existence of this cartel and promised government legislation against monopolies to give the cartel "a harsh rap on the knuckles." "Basic commodities abundant in Ramadan," *The Egyptian Gazette* Jan. 10, 1997, p. 10.
18 Fletcher (1996a:4).
19 Dethier (1989).
20 The index of the real value of agricultural output (1980=100) was calculated at 145 in 1986, 158 in 1987, 144 in 1992, and 154 in 1993. See Rady, Omran, and Sands (1996:153), based on unpublished data from the Department of Agricultural Economics and Statistics, Ministry of Agriculture and Land Reclamation, Cairo.
21 Khedr, Ehrich, and Fletcher (1996: 61).
22 "Tadaffuq ru'us amwal ajnabiya kathira li-Misr qad yamthul quwa daghita 'ala taghyir si'r al-sarf wa bi-l-tali yu'aqqid min al-wad' al-iqtisadi," *al-Ahram*, Jan. 25, 1997, p. 21, quoting the views of Dr Arvind Subramanian, Permanent Representative of the IMF in Egypt. See also Fletcher (1996a: 5).
23 Okonjo-Iweala and Fuleihan (1993:134). If tenants hold land in perpetuity and can pass it to their heirs, there is no reason to assume they behave toward it any differently than those who own the land. Nor is there any evidence that they do so. Arguably, removing this security is more likely to discourage tenants from improving the land or maintaining its quality. If so, it is not the 1952 law, but those demanding its repeal that are "creating disincentives."
24 Law 96 of 1992, amending law 178 of 1952, known as the First Agrarian Reform Law. For a fascinating account of the political debate surrounding this law, see Saad (1998).
25 Fletcher (1996b:333–34).
26 Khedr, Ehrich, and Fletcher (1996:75).
27 A 1991 survey found that stunting (low height for age) affects 23 percent of urban children and 34 percent of rural children under five years of age.

In rural Upper Egypt, the rate reaches almost 40 percent. Rady, Omran, and Sands (1996:159).

28 Based on the 1990/91 Income, Expenditure and Consumption Survey (Cairo: Central Agency for Public Mobilization and Statistics, 1993), Abdel-Latif and El-Laithy (1996:299–301) estimate that the non-poor (defined as those with household incomes above a poverty line of LE3,994 in urban areas and LE3,399 in rural areas, representing the annual cost of basic food and non-food needs) had an average daily per capita calorie intake of 2,488 in urban areas and 2,468 in rural areas. The Food and Agriculture Organization of the United Nations recommended a minimum level for that year of 2,540 calories (Rady, Omran, and Sands 1996:159).

29 US Embassy report quoted in Economist Intelligence Unit, *Egypt: Country Profile 1996/97*, p. 22.

30 Alderman and Von Braun (1984).

31 Mehanna, Hopkins, and Abdelmaksoud (1994); Hopkins (1987).

32 Gibson-Graham (1995).

33 Fletcher (1996a:3).

34 Nassar, Sands, Omran, and Krenz (1996:9). Berseem, maize, wheat, and rice, the four largest crops accounting for 70.2 percent of the crop area, are produced mostly for household use. A survey in 1989–91 of 665 farmers in three different parts of the country, found that about 70 percent of those growing wheat, almost 80 percent of those growing maize, and nearly half of those growing berseem used the crop entirely for their own consumption. Most of the rest sold only a part of the crop, and often to other households within the village, almost entirely so in the case of berseem (Mchanna, Hopkins, and Abdelmaksoud 1994:68–77).

## References

Abdel-Latif, Abla, and Heba El-Laithy. 1996. "Protecting Food Security for the Poor in a Liberalizing Economy" in Lehman B. Fletcher, ed. *Egypt's Agriculture in a Reform Era*. Ames, Iowa: Iowa State University Press. pp. 294–327.

Alderman, H., and S. Von Braun. 1982. *Egypt's Food Subsidy and Rationing System: A Description*. Washington DC: International Food Policy Research Institute.

Alderman, H., and S. Von Braun. 1984. *The Effects of the Egyptian Food Ration and Subsidy System on Income Distribution and Consumption*. Washington DC: International Food Policy Research Institute.

Bhabha, Homi K. 1994. *The Location of Culture*. London and New York: Routledge.

Center for Responsive Politics. 1997. *Cashing In: A Guide to Money, Votes, and Public Policy in the 104th Congress*. Washington DC: Center for Responsive Politics.

Dethier, J. 1989. *Trade, Exchange and Agricultural Pricing Policies in Egypt*. World Bank Comparative Studies. Washington DC: World Bank.

Economist Intelligence Unit. *Egypt: Country Profile 1996/97.*
Fletcher, Lehman B. 1996a. "Introduction and Overview." in Lehman B. Fletcher, ed. *Egypt's Agriculture in a Reform Era.* Ames, Iowa: Iowa State University Press. pp. 3–8.
Fletcher, Lehman B. 1996b. "Egypt's Agricultural Future" in Lehman B. Fletcher, ed. *Egypt's Agriculture in a Reform Era.* Ames, Iowa: Iowa State University Press. pp. 331–41.
Gibson-Graham, J.K. 1995. "Identity and Economic Plurality: Rethinking Capitalism and 'Capitalist Hegemony.'" *Environment and Planning D: Society and Space,* 13:275–82
Hopkins, Nicholas S. 1987. *Agrarian Transformation in Egypt.* Boulder: Westview.
Hopkins, Nicholas S., Sohair R. Mehanna, and Bahgat Abdelmaksoud. 1982. *The State of Agricultural Mechanization in Egypt: Results of a Survey.* Cairo: Ministry of Agriculture, Agricultural Mechanization Project.
Khedr, Hassan, Rollo Ehrich, and Lehman B. Fletcher. 1996. "Nature, Rationale and Accomplishments of the Agricultural Policy Reforms, 1987–1994" in Lehman B. Fletcher, ed. *Egypt's Agriculture in a Reform Era.* Ames, Iowa, Iowa State University Press. pp. 51–83.
Mehanna, Sohair, Nicholas S. Hopkins, and Bahgat Abdelmaksoud. 1994. "Farmers and Merchants: Background to Structural Adjustment in Egypt." *Cairo Papers in Social Science* 17:2.
Mitchell, Timothy. 1991. *Colonising Egypt* (2nd ed.). Berkeley: University of California Press.
Mitchell, Timothy. 1995a. "Origins and Limits of the Modern Idea of the Economy." *Working Paper Series,* no. 12, Nov. Ann Arbor MI: Advanced Study Center, University of Michigan.
Mitchell, Timothy. 1995b. "Worlds Apart: An Egyptian Village and the International Tourism Industry." *Middle East Report* 196. pp. 8–11, 23.
Mitchell, Timothy. 1995c. "The Object of Development: America's Egypt" in Jonathan Crush, ed. *Power of Development.* London and New York: Routledge. pp. 129–57.
Nassar, Saad, Fenton Sands, Mohamed A. Omran, and Ronald Krenz. 1996. "Crop Production Responses to the Agricultural Policy Reforms" in Lehman B. Fletcher, ed. *Egypt's Agriculture in a Reform Era.* Ames, Iowa, Iowa State University Press. pp. 84–111.
Okonjo-Iweala, Ngozi, and Youssef Fuleihan. 1993. "Structural Adjustment and Egyptian Agriculture: Some Preliminary Indications of the Impact of Economic Reforms" in Mohamed A. Faris and Mahmood Hasan Khan, eds. *Sustainable Agriculture in Egypt.* Boulder and London: Lynne Rienner. pp. 127–39.
Prakash, Gyan. 1990a. "Writing Post-Orientalist Histories of the Third World: Perspectives from Indian Historiography." *Comparative Studies in Society and History* 32(2):383–408.
Prakash, Gyan. 1990b. *Bonded Histories: Genealogies of Labor Servitude in Colonial India.* Cambridge, Cambridge University Press.
Rady, Abdel Moneim, Mohamed A. Omran, and Fenton B. Sands. 1996.

"Impacts of the Policy Reforms on Agricultural Income, Employment and Rural Poverty" in Lehman B. Fletcher, ed. *Egypt's Agriculture in a Reform Era*. Ames, Iowa: Iowa State University Press. pp. 149–64.

Saad, Reem. 1998 "State, Landlord, Parliament and Peasant: The Story of the 1992 Tenancy Law in Egypt" in Alan Bowman and Eugene Rogan, eds. *Agriculture in Egypt from Pharaonic to Modern Times*. Proceedings of the British Academy 96: 387–404.

Spivak, Gayatri Chakravorty. "Can the Subaltern Speak?" in C. Nelson and L. Grossberg, eds. *Marxism and the Interpretation of Culture*. Basingstoke: Macmillan Education, 1988. pp. 271–313.

United States Department of Agriculture. *Agriculture Fact Book 1994*

World Commission on Environment and Development. 1987. *Our Common Future*. Oxford and New York: Oxford University Press.

World Bank. *World Development Report 1986*. Washington DC.

World Bank. *World Development Report 1996*. Washington DC.

# 2

# The Evolution of Agrarian Structures in Egypt: Regional Patterns of Change in Farm Size

FRANÇOIS IRETON

Since the beginning of the 1960s, the share of the active agricultural population in the active rural population has noticeably declined. There has been, simultaneously, a diversification and a growth of non-agricultural activities in the countryside, and an increase in the number of working rural residents with jobs in town or abroad. While the active rural population increased, the number of males (six years of age and above) working in agriculture has been constant for the last thirty-five years. In 1960, 3.82 million, or 81 percent, of a total active male rural population of 4.72 million, were engaged in agriculture. In 1986, 3.97 million, or 65 percent, of 6.1 million male rural workers, were classed as engaged in agriculture.[1] Everything points to the persistence of this stagnation until now. The share of agricultural income in the total income of rural people has declined even faster, since the number of those working in agriculture who have second jobs has increased in this period. The number of heads of farm households with outside jobs was 118,000 in 1960, or 7.2 percent of the 1.64 million existing heads of farm households, while they were 700,000 in 1990, or 24.2 percent of the 2.9 million heads of farm households.[2] The income sources of households which are at least partly agricultural (and of rural people in general) have diversified. Not only are there heads of households with outside jobs, but also other members of these domestic groups now work outside the agricultural sector (in crafts, construction, industry, trade, and rural services, in both the formal and informal sectors, as well as in the public bureaucracy).

While there has been an overall stagnation of the number of males active in agriculture, there has also been, over thirty years, a major transformation of the internal structure of the work force. In 1960, the heads of farm households were only, at most, two-fifths of the roughly 4.2 million males active in the agricultural sector, while in 1990, not counting the female heads of farm households, they constituted exactly two-thirds. The numbers of family helpers and of salaried workers, both permanent and occasional, have thus declined by one million in thirty years (dropping from 2.4 million to 1.4 million), while the rise in the number of household heads was just able to compensate for this decline.

In examining this intricate relationship of the employment and income structures of members of households which were at least partly agricultural, it seems less useful than ever to distinguish the agricultural and non-agricultural spheres, or the rural or urban ones, and, instead, to consider the 'agrarian economy' as a separate reality. This is of particular importance at a time when we can observe, even in Egypt according to some, the 'end of the peasantry,' that is, of those who lived almost exclusively from working the soil. The transformation of agrarian structures is nonetheless a central aspect of the changes affecting rural Egypt, and we need tools to analyze both the spatial diversity of the components of a differentiated socioeconomic agrarian reality, and their recent evolution.

There is only one systematic source able, despite many inadequacies, even defects, to allow us to grasp at once, in all the seventeen rural governorates of Egypt and over a significant period (thirty years), the spatial diversity, the evolution, and the internal differentiation of agrarian structures. This is the general agricultural census which the Egyptian government has carried out six times, in 1929, 1939, 1950, 1961, 1982, and 1990. The last three form the basis of the analysis in this paper.

This is not the place to sketch a chronological, geographic, and socioeconomic picture of Egyptian agriculture. Among the many possible themes for analysis, this chapter focuses on the evolution of the regional and socioeconomic diversity of the conditions for access to farm land. Three different aspects of this question can be studied:

1. The overall 'demography' of access to land (the evolution of the number of domestic groups or households which have access to land and which live, in part at least, from working that land).

2. The quantitative dimension of unequal access to land: the distribution of land among households (the differential evolution of the number of farm units according to their size and the distribution of land which results from that, as well as the processes of concentration or deconcentration of landholdings).

3. The qualitative dimension of unequal access: the matrix of social relationships which form around agricultural land (the dynamics of

distribution of types of access to landownership, tenancy, or mixed—according to the status of the farmer: owner, tenant, or both, as well as the evolution of the relationship between the structure of land ownership and the agrarian structure).

For practical reasons, this paper is limited to the analysis of the first aspect, although the choice of the other two might have been even more revealing. The last two are directly linked to two questions frequently raised at present (by the peasants themselves, and by researchers, journalists, activists, and politicians) concerning the development of an Egyptian agriculture undergoing deregulation and almost total liberalization. First, with the end of subsidies to inputs and the full realization of a 'free' market for agricultural products, is there a process of 'natural' selection of farms and is there a tendency towards a concentration of landholding? Second, what contribution to this selection process will the removal of the cap on land rent make?

But before tackling these two points, we must first establish the dynamic of the growth of the numbers of farms. It is preferable not just to describe the state of affairs in 1990, but to place the 1990 situation in a diachronic perspective, while keeping as the geographic framework for the analysis the nine Delta governorates and the eight Nile Valley governorates which have substantial cultivated areas. At the end of the paper, we examine the regional evolution of the inequalities of the distribution of land among farms.

## 1. Trends in the Numbers and the Average Size of Egyptian Farms (1939–1990)

*National Data*

In 1939, the total area of farmed land in Egypt[3] was 6,036,000 feddans, with exactly one million farms (see Figures 1 and 2). The average size of these farms was thus six feddans (see Figure 3).

During the 1940s, and corresponding to a strong rural-to-urban migration, the total number of farms barely increased while the area of farm land increased by a hundred thousand feddans (or 1.5 percent of the usable agricultural land). Therefore, the average farm size rose slightly. In the 1950s, when the cultivated land expanded even more slowly than in the previous decade, the number of farms increased considerably to 1.64 million, and the average farm size dropped to 3.8 feddans. This increase resulted from three main factors: First, the application of the first phase of the agrarian reform; second, the increase in the national population growth rate—which rose from 1.2 percent per year for the period from 1927–37, to 1.8 percent per year

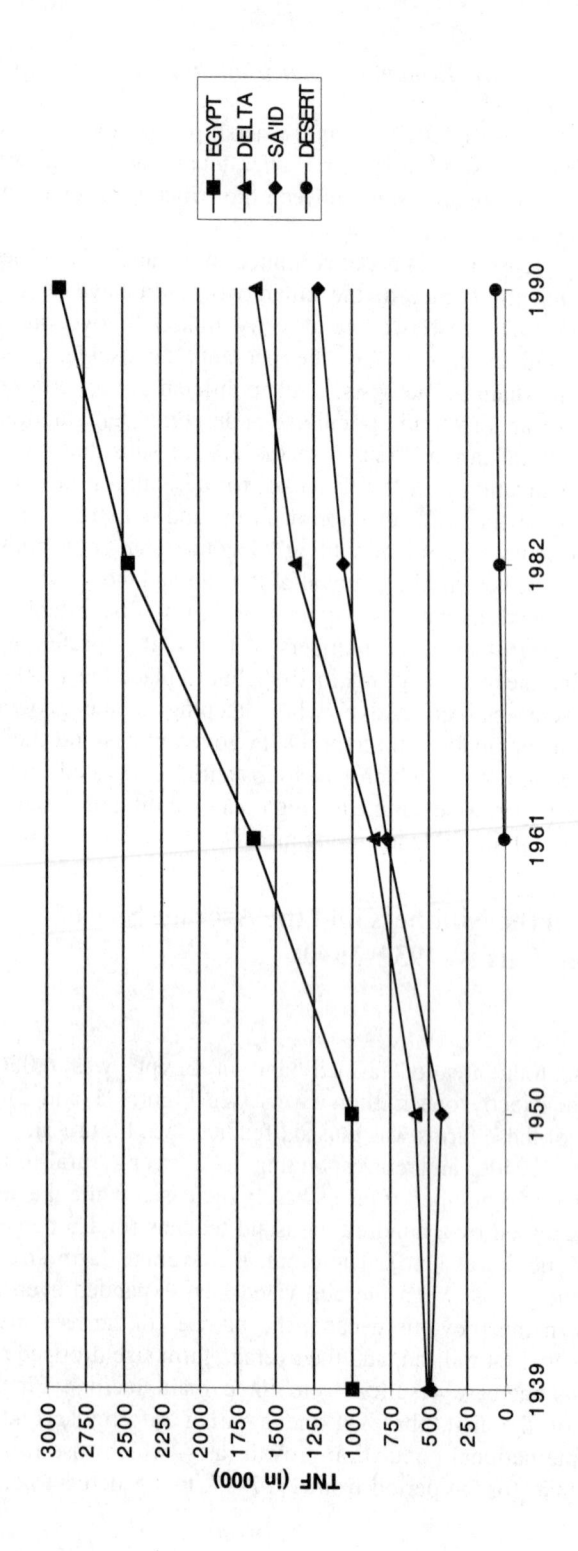

Figure 1 *Total Number of Farms in Egypt and the Three Main Regions (1939–1990)*

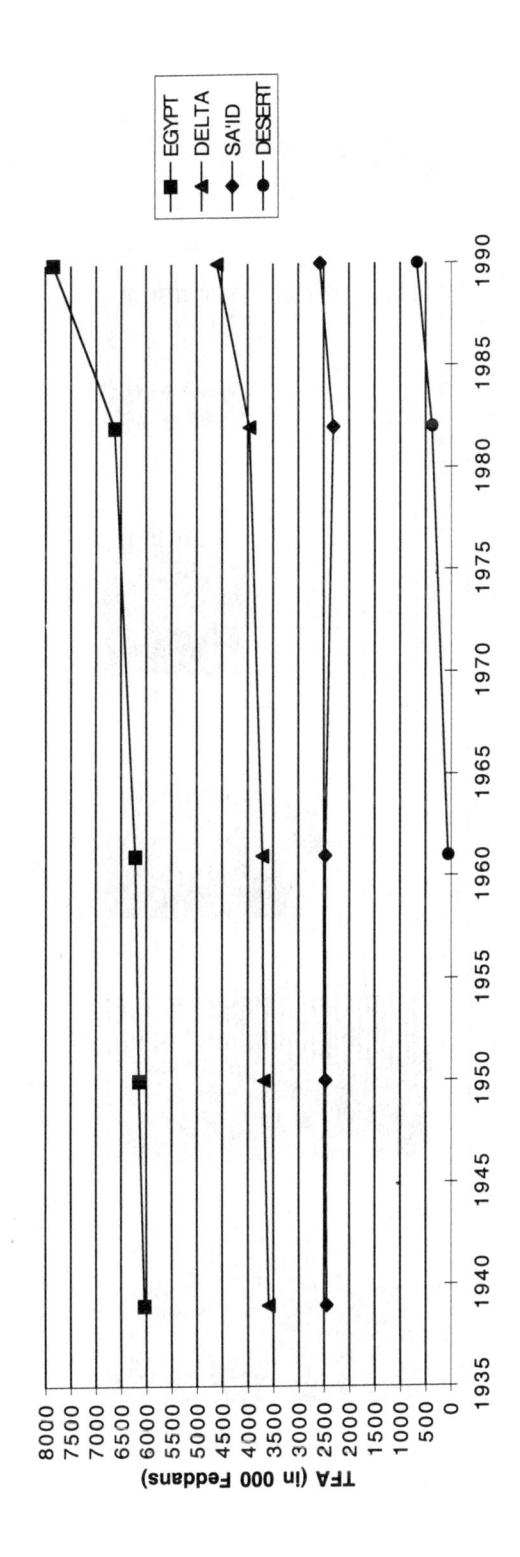

Figure 2  *Total Farm Area (TFA) in Egypt and the Three Main Regions (1939–1990)*

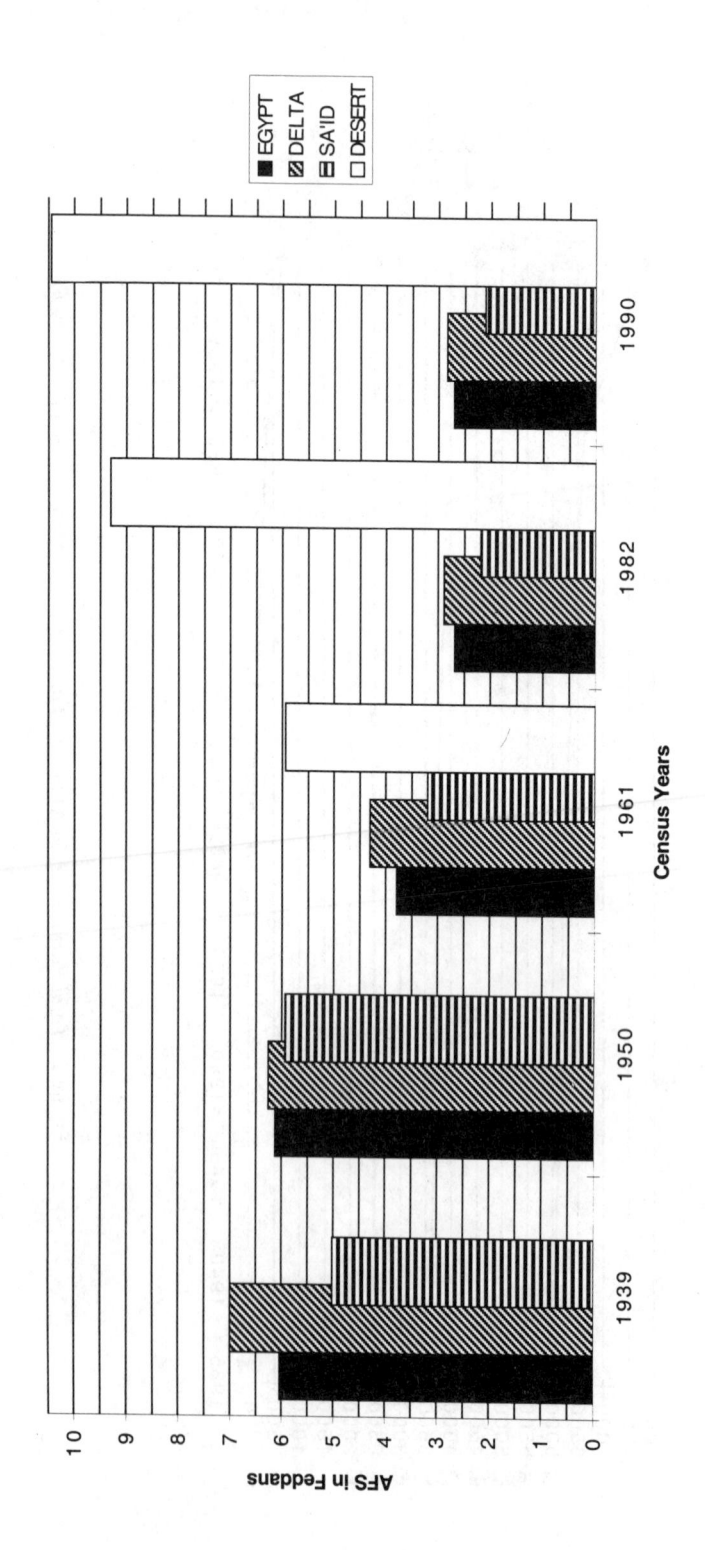

Figure 3 *Average Farm Size (AFS) in Egypt and the Three Main Regions (1939–1990)*

during the period 1937–47, and to 2.5 percent per year during the period 1947–60, resulting in the acceleration of the division of farms among farmers' sons, more of whom survived; and finally, a slight reduction, compared to the previous decade, in the rate of emigration from the countryside to the cities.

Over the next twenty years (1961–82), the rate of growth of the farmed area tripled compared to the rate of the 1950s. The farmed area increased from 6.22 to 6.63 million feddans, or 6.5 percent. Meanwhile, the number of farms increased to 2.47 million, an increase of 50 percent. This represented an average annual rate much less than that of the preceding decade (2 percent compared to 4.5 percent). The average farm size dropped by one-third in twenty years, falling to 2.7 feddans in 1982. The rate of farm creation diminished, in spite of the sharp weakening of urban migration after the end of the 1960s, due to a large proportion of farmers' sons changing occupations while remaining at home, through a major creation of non-farm jobs in the countryside. Emigration of young people from rural areas to oil-producing countries, which was significant after 1974, also helps explain this drop in the rate of creation of new farms through division of existing farms. Finally, in the 1980s, there was a major upswing in land reclamation, including the completion of reclamation works undertaken earlier. As a result, the total farmed area grew by one-fifth, reaching 7.85 million feddans. The number of farms amounted to 2.9 million in 1990, while the average annual growth rate was almost equal to the preceding period, and the average farm size remained about 2.7 feddans.

These aggregate data at the national level disguise the macro-, meso-, and micro-growth patterns. Here we will examine briefly the macro or regional level, and then discuss growth at the second level, that is, the governorate.

## The Delta, the Sa'id, and the Margins

Over the fifty-year period analyzed here, the average farm size in the Sa'id (the Nile Valley) remained less than that in the Delta by about a quarter (see Figure 3). In 1939, the average farm size in the Sa'id was five feddans, compared to seven in the Delta; in 1961, it was 3.2 feddans, compared to 4.3; and in 1990, 2.1 feddans, compared to 2.8. The farmed area remained about the same in the Sa'id between 1939 and 1961 (see Figure 2); then it declined by 150,000 feddans during the 1960s and 1970s due to the expansion of towns and villages, and the lack of new lands brought under cultivation through land reclamation; and, finally, it grew again in the 1980s, adding a quarter million feddans, so that the total in 1990 was 2.57 million feddans. In the Delta, on the other hand, the growth of the farmed area, at least in the peripheral areas, was always greater than the loss of cultivable land due to urban sprawl. These gains were modest from 1939 to 1961 (110,000 feddans), but were 2.5 times greater over the next twenty years, and six times greater during the 1980s. The farmed area of the Delta thus gained 1.1 million feddans in fifty years, an increase of more than a quarter compared to the 1939 area, while in the Valley, the increase was only 5 percent.

Under these conditions, if the rate of increase of the numbers of farms had been equal in the two regions, then there would have been an increase in the difference of the average farm size. However, as we have seen, this ratio remained steady. The lack of growth in the farmed area in the Sa'id was compensated for by a slower rate of growth in the number of farms (see Figure 1). The number of farms was almost the same in 1939 (0.51 million in the Delta and 0.49 million in the Valley), but the number of farms tripled in the Delta, while in the Sa'id the number rose by two and a half times. The total number of farms in the Delta rose to 1.63 million in 1990, a 317 percent increase, and in the Sa'id to 1.22 million, a 250 percent increase. While the growth of numbers of farms was steady in the Delta, it was more irregular in the Valley, where the number of farms first decreased in the 1940s, through the disappearance of farms of less than one feddan, grew during the 1950s at a rate higher than that of the Delta, and then continued to grow during the last thirty years, but at a rate lower than that of the Delta. Despite all this, the average farm size in the Sa'id has continued to decline, albeit slightly, in the 1980s, dropping from 2.2 to 2.1 feddans, while in the Delta the size has been stable.

The farmed areas of the desert governorates have grown considerably in the last thirty years thanks to land reclamation efforts. In 1961 only small areas (in the tens of thousands of feddans) in the oases of the Western Desert were farmed, while in 1990, farms created on the desert fringes, mostly around the New Valley oases, amounted to 64,000 and covered 0.67 million feddans, with an average farm size of 10.5 feddans, which is quite high for Egypt.[4]

Whether we are dealing with the total farmed area or with the number of farms, the macro-regional analytic framework does not provide a satisfactory result, since it groups together very distinct dynamics which the meso-regional framework allows us to see better. Using this level, and a shorter period (1961–90) we are able to follow the change in the *number* of farms, which has varied considerably by governorate, the change in the total *area* occupied by these farms, which also varies geographically, and finally the changes in the average farm *size*, which is an approximate index of meso-regional differences in agrarian structure resulting from changes in the first two.

## 2. Regional Dynamics in the Number and Average Size of Farms (1961–1990)

The average farm size (SIZE) of each governorate in 1990 ($SIZE_{90}$) reflects three factors: the average farm size of the governorate at the beginning of the period ($SIZE_{61}$), the change, during these thirty years, of the total farm area of the governorate (the index of which is indicated by $AREA_{61-90}$, base 100=1961), and the change in the number of farms in each governorate (the index of which is indicated by $NUMBER_{61-90}$, base 100=1961). The relationship is expressed by a simple formula:

$$SIZE_{90} = SIZE_{61} \times (AREA_{61-90}/NUMBER_{61-90})$$

Let us examine briefly the three variables comprising the right side of this equation.

*Average Farm Size by Region in 1960 (See Figure 4)*

$SIZE_{61}$ is taken as a given, resulting from earlier processes. In 1961, four governorates, located on the fringe of the Delta, stand out, since the average farm size ranged from 7.5 to 5.5 feddans. Of these four peripheral governorates, two were large (Bahayra and Kafr al-Shaykh) and two were small (Dumyat and Isma'iliya). Part of their agricultural land had been reclaimed from uncultivated areas at the edge of the Delta at the beginning of the twentieth century, and then more in the 1950s. The first three of these governorates can be identified under the label of northern and western Delta. The $SIZE_{61}$ of the other thirteen governorates ranged from 4.5 to 2.1 feddans. In descending order, one can note the adjoining eastern Delta governorates of Daqahliya and Sharqiya, together with Fayum and Aswan governorates, with a $SIZE_{61}$ of 4.4 feddans; then the three governorates of the middle valley (Bani Swayf, Minya, and Asyut) with a $SIZE_{61}$ between 3.9 and 3.4 feddans; finally, the governorates of the central and southern Delta, whose average farm size ranged from 3.3 feddans for Gharbiya to 2.4 feddans for Minufiya and Qalyubiya, to which one can add the adjacent governorate of Giza, with a $SIZE_{61}$ of 2.5 feddans. One can sum up the situation by identifying four homogeneous geographical regions, including twelve governorates, with respect to their 1961 average farm

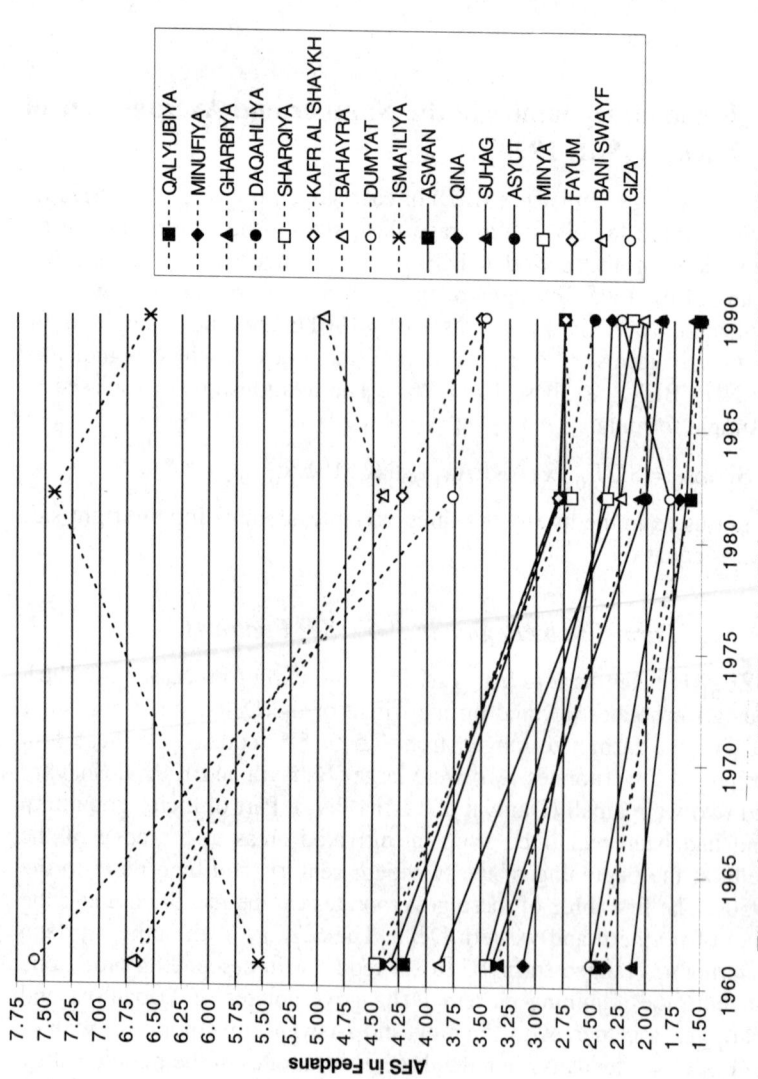

Figure 4 *Average Farm Size (AFS) by governorate (1961-1982-1990)*

size, to which can be added five spatially isolated governorates whose $SIZE_{61}$ differs from those of the adjacent governorates. In addition to the already mentioned Isma'iliya and Fayum, these five include the only large non-homogenous region, Upper Egypt (southern Sa'id), whose three governorates cover the spectrum from 4.4 feddans in Aswan, to 2.1 feddans in Suhag (the lowest in Egypt), and 3.1 in Qina.

### Thirty Years of Evolution in Farm Area, by Governorate

The known variations in the total farm area[5] (caught by the index $AREA_{61-90}$) result from the size of the sum of increases in the farm area (mostly from reclaiming desert areas) and losses (mostly due to expansion of built-up areas and public 'facilities', both urban and rural). Population growth, which varies among governorates, may be responsible for most of the extension of the built-up area onto farm land, but, although the losses due to this phenomenon are far from negligible, since the land that disappears in this way has high yields, they are made up by adding reclaimed land. Reclaimed land outweighs lost land in twelve of the seventeen governorates, and substantially so in five cases. Land reclamation determines the value by governorate of $AREA_{61-90}$. There are three types of governorate:

(a) Those where the values of $AREA_{61-90}$ range from ninety-two to ninety-seven, indicating a decline in the total farm area. This type includes three governorates, two of which, Minufiya and Gharbiya, are located in the interior of the Delta and have no area for expansion, while the third is Aswan, where narrow strips of cultivated land upstream from the High Dam were flooded at the beginning of the study period.

(b) Those where the values of $AREA_{61-90}$ are substantially greater than a hundred (with a range from 115 to 303). These governorates are on the periphery of the Delta and thus adjacent to reclaimable desert land (such as Sharqiya, with an $AREA_{61-90}$ of 128, Bahayra with 169, and Isma'iliya with 303) together with the somewhat similar Kafr al-Shaykh (115) and Giza (139).

(c) Those where the values are around a hundred (from ninety-eight to 104), which is the case of nine of the ten remaining governorates—Minya alone being slightly outside this range with a figure of 107.

### The Regional Demography of Farms: An Explanatory Model (See Figure 5)

While the first two 'independent' variables are exogenous and poorly correlated with each other,[6] the third, $NUMBER_{61-90}$, is largely

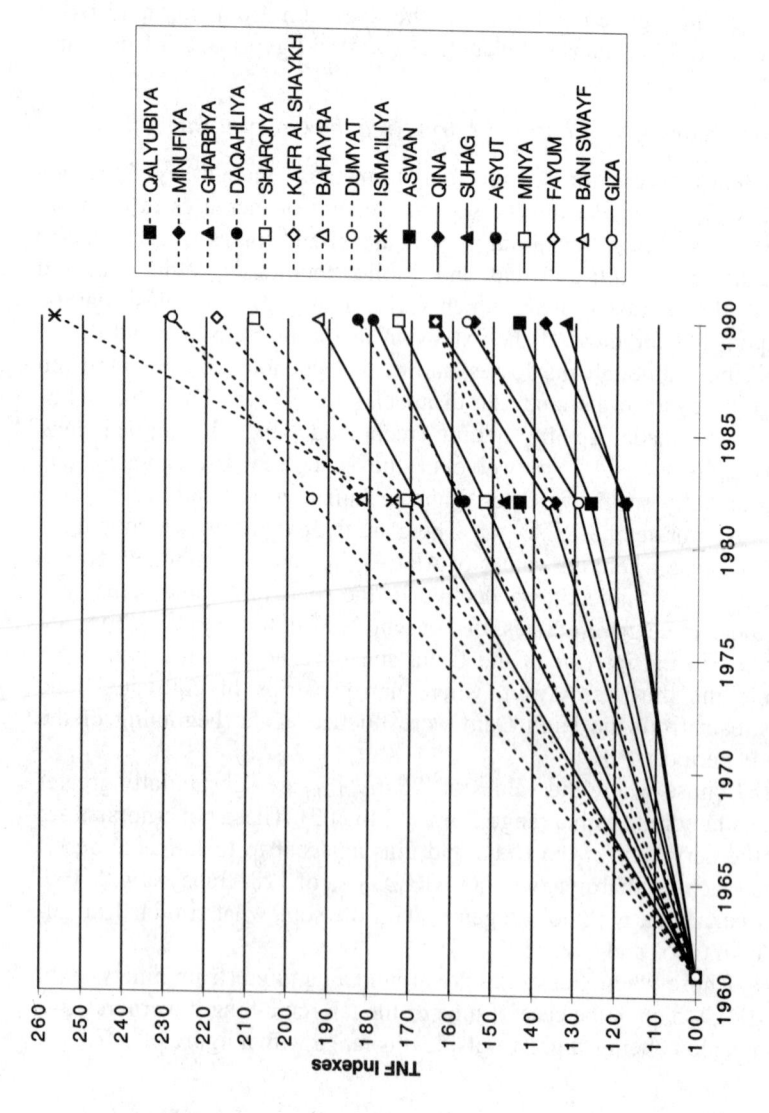

Figure 5 *Index of Number of Farms (TNF) by Governorate (1961–1982–1990) (1961=100)*

endogenous in the sense that it depends on the first two. One can hypothesize the existence of regulating mechanisms which limit the growth of the number of farms in governorates characterized by the weakest figures for $SIZE_{61}$, whereby, once the average *farm* size approaches a lower threshold, the subdivision and thus the multiplication of these farms is, for economic reasons, blocked. The expansion of the total area farmed acts to delay the moment when this threshold is reached. Thus the co-variability of $SIZE_{61}$ and $AREA_{61-90}$ by governorate explains 84 percent, a significant amount, of the variation of $NUMBER_{61-90}$ by governorate.[7] Of course, the principal actual mechanism by which the number of farms increases is their division through inheritance by male heirs, and this factor in turn is linked to the fecundity of farm families. To a lesser degree, other factors come into the picture, the creation of owned farms on new lands and the creation of rented farms in the old lands, and these processes are also in part determined by demography. Nevertheless, the introduction of an additional variable reflecting, very imperfectly, the spatial variation in fecundity, giving rise to a growing 'pressure' on the land during the study period, does not improve at all the ability of the model proposed above to account for the spatial variation of $NUMBER_{61-90}$. Such a model would assume that the agricultural land of the governorates was subjected, during the study period, to 'demographic pressure' with variable intensity in space, but which was regulated in a 'decompression chamber' for each governorate, on the one hand by the existing pressure (to which the $SIZE_{61}$ corresponds), and on the other by the continuing possibility of expansion of the volume of this decompression chamber (to which the $AREA_{61-90}$ corresponds), with the two regulating variables absorbing almost all the intergovernorate differentials in demographic pressure, and producing, with unequal strength, the growth rate of the number of farm units. (The weight of the $SIZE_{61}$ was much stronger, as we have seen, than that of $AREA_{61-90}$).

Given this mechanism, one might expect that a map of the levels of growth of the numbers of farms by governorate would be easily superposed on the $SIZE_{61}$ map, and this is indeed the case. Moreover, as a function of the $AREA_{61-90}$ that characterizes them, the three upper valley governorates (Aswan, Qina, and Suhag) form a homogeneous unit (which, as we have seen, was not the case with the $SIZE_{61}$). Thus there are five homogeneous regional groupings:

(a) In the northern and western Delta governorates (Bahayra, Kafr al-Shaykh, and Dumyat), and in Isma'iliya, where the $SIZE_{61}$ was highest and the expansion of farm land ranged from 15 percent to 200 percent, the number of farm units increased from 118 percent to 129 percent over thirty years for the first three, and by 157 percent for Isma'iliya.[8]

(b) The group with the next highest $NUMBER_{61-90}$ includes the two eastern Delta governorates. The eastern Delta is a somewhat less homogeneous entity than the preceding one. The rate of growth of the number of farm units in Sharqiya, for instance, was higher than in Daqahliya (109 percent, compared to 83 percent), but these numbers fall clearly between those of the northern and western Delta on the one hand and those of the central Delta/lower valley on the other.[9]

(c) The values for $NUMBER_{61-90}$ which hold for the four governorates which make up the central Delta/lower valley region (Minufiya, Gharbiya, Qalyubiya, and Giza) fall between 155 and 164 (in other words, the number of farm units has increased from 55 percent to 64 percent), making this region the penultimate in order of descending values of $NUMBER_{61-90}$, and the most homogeneous in this respect. This homogeneity derives from the interaction of two independent variables: the $SIZE_{61}$ and the $AREA_{61-90}$. The $SIZE_{61}$ of Gharbiya, which is clearly higher than those of the other governorates in this group (3.3 feddans, compared to 2.4 feddans) is traded off against the greatest agricultural land loss (its $AREA_{61-90}$ is 92).[10]

(d) To the south of this region there is a group of four governorates of which only two, Minya and Asyut, have had a homogeneous change process in the last thirty years. With a $SIZE_{61}$ of 3.4 feddans and with the number of farm units having grown by three-quarters, there is a residual factor of +9 percent for Asyut governorate, which preserves this homogeneity despite the considerable expansion of the agricultural land in Minya governorate and the slight drop in agricultural land in Asyut. The two governorates of Fayum and Bani Swayf have evolved in ways opposite to the predictions of the model. While their farmed area is almost constant, Fayum, with a $SIZE_{61}$ of 4.3 feddans has a $NUMBER_{61-90}$ of only 164, and Bani Swayf, with a $SIZE_{61}$ of 3.9 feddans, has a high $NUMBER_{61-90}$ of 193.[11] One should hesitate, in these conditions, to speak of a spatial entity called 'middle valley/Fayum,' but it is nonetheless clear that, although not very homogeneous, this region contrasts with the two geographic groupings that border it on the north and the south, because of the dynamics of growth of the number of its farm units.

(e) A homogenous 'upper valley' is characterized by the three lowest $NUMBER_{61-90}$ scores for all the seventeen governorates analyzed here. They range from 132 for Suhag to 144 for Aswan, with Qina in between. The number of farm units in this region has only increased by a third in thirty years, compared to an average growth of about 75 percent for the middle valley/Fayum. The homogeneity of the dynamics of the upper valley is only possible insofar as the three governorates escape partly from the model suggested here. (There are substantial negative residues, of -17 percent for Aswan, -14 percent for Qina, and -8 percent for Suhag.) It is not only that, given their SIZE$_{61}$ (4.2 and 3.1 feddans, for Aswan and Qina respectively), these two governorates not only 'should' have experienced a greater multiplication of the number of farm units, but also even Suhag governorate, which had the lowest SIZE$_{61}$ in Egypt and whose farmed area slightly declined, is characterized by a NUMBER$_{61-90}$ which is lower than that which the model predicts.

The dynamics of the process of multiplication of farm units produces three quite homogeneous geographic groupings: northern and western Delta, central Delta and lower valley, and upper valley (these three are respectively first, fourth, and last in descending order of their NUMBER$_{61-90}$ level), as well as two less homogeneous regions (eastern Delta and middle valley/Fayum, ranking second and third), which are quite distinct from the spatially adjacent groupings. Moreover, the notation of eight substantial residues (greater than 5 percent in either a positive or a negative direction), derived from the very simple model suggested here, shows that this model is better able to account for the dynamics of the numbers of farm units in the Delta (including Giza) than in the Valley. There are two significant positive residues for the ten governorates in the first group and four negative and two positive residues for the seven in the second group. Thus the relative absence of change in the upper valley (quite homogeneous according to the NUMBER$_{61-90}$ score), and the significant change in the middle valley/Fayum (not very homogeneous), are both only partly predicted by the model. One or several factors with limited spatial impact must be added to the two variables analyzed here.

We can examine one possible factor briefly. One of the regulating mechanisms limiting the multiplication of farm units consists in the professional mobility outside agriculture of the heads of farm households or of some of their heirs.[12] The rural zones of the three governorates of the upper valley (along with Minufiya in the Delta) are those where the emigration of the agricultural population (indicative of mobility outside agriculture of the heads of farm households and their potential heirs) has been the highest during the twentieth century. On the other hand, the middle valley governorates are characterized by much lower emigration rates from agricultural areas. This contrast in migration pattern would explain the large negative residues which we find in the upper valley, in Aswan and Qina governorates. Given their average size at the beginning of the study period, the farm units have been less divided than 'foreseen,' because of the great mobility away from agriculture. Likewise, this would explain the positive residues which characterize the middle valley (apart from Fayum). Given their original average size, the units have been more divided than the model would have 'predicted,' given the modest amount of mobility.

One can hypothesize that, among the causes of this differential mobility, the average cropping intensity of the farm units (relationship of the harvested area to the cultivated area) plays an important role. The small size of a farm is compensated for by its high cropping intensity (the coefficient can rise to three in the case of vegetables), which favors keeping the active population (especially heads of farm households and their heirs) in agriculture, thus perpetuating the division of farm units (and vice versa in cases where the cropping intensity is low). We know that cropping intensity in the upper valley remained lower, until the middle of the 1970s,[13] than that of the middle valley. In this region, the higher intensity would thus have favored the lesser mobility outside agriculture and the greater division of farms, the opposite of the case in the upper valley.

When we turn to the Delta, the peripheral governorates are also marked by a lower cropping intensity than that found in the central Delta (which should encourage mobility outside agriculture and produce $NUMBER_{61-90}$ scores lower than they actually are). However, on the one hand, this difference is smaller than the difference which, in the 1960s and 1970s, separated the upper and the middle valley and, on the other hand, two phenomena counter the possible effects of this lower level of intensity in the peripheral Delta. First of all, the $SIZE_{61}$ of the governorates in this region is very high, even on old lands, compared to the rest of the territory, and this allows a substantial subdivision of farm units (all the more so because their intensity has increased over a thirty-year period). Secondly, many of those who left their farms on the old lands, or did not take over those of their fathers, moved in terms of space, without advancing professionally, settling as farmers in the rapidly expanding new lands (this phenomenon is shown by the high $AREA_{61-90}$). Thus, they established new farm units, often in the same governorate. The fact that, in the model proposed here, the residues characterizing the Delta governorates are only weakly present is explained by the neutralization of the modest difference in cropping intensity between the center and the periphery of the Delta. This occurs under the influence of the *size* of the differentials (distinguishing these regions from one another) between $SIZE_{61}$ and $AREA_{61-90}$, working in the same direction and affecting $NUMBER_{61-90}$. The comparison of the processes at work in the upper valley and in the peripheral Delta shows particularly well the explanatory power of the $AREA_{61-90}$.[14] This explanatory power also expresses the near absence of variation from one governorate to another in the upper and middle valley and in the central Delta, which reveals in the model numerous residues for which only cropping intensity can account. This is because $SIZE_{61}$, the only element that varies between these regions, cannot by definition account for cropping intensity.

The need to take cropping intensity into account can be confirmed through one final example. Qalyubiya, in the central Delta, is one of the two governorates in lower Egypt for which the model proposed shows a substantial residue (+9 percent). Its $SIZE_{61}$ is low, its agricultural land has not increased in thirty years, and the $NUMBER_{61-90}$ is thus quite a bit higher than the model would predict. But in Qalyubiya, which is next to Cairo and into whose territory Greater Cairo is currently expanding, peri-urban gardening has developed in a substantial way, bringing with it a large increase in the cropping intensity. This has reduced the minimum farm size required to generate an income capable of sustaining a family. Only the important residues for the governorates of Fayum and Sharqiya cannot be easily absorbed by the introduction of the cropping intensity into the model.

The analysis of the residues left by the model leads us to observe that the principal independent variable, the average farm size, is not at all a simple variable. There are three reasons for this: (a) Rural Egypt is not a homogeneous territory, neither in terms of its ecology or agronomy, nor in terms of infrastructure (such as irrigation), nor in terms of socioeconomic patterns; (b) the distribution of farms according to size is not the same in each region, and there are regionally differentiated dynamics of inequality of access to land (see conclusion); and, (c) finally, farms of the same size, located in a homogeneous region, are themselves differentiated according to various criteria, such as cropping intensity, types of tenure, crop mix, productivity of the land and of labor, the level of mechanization, and the external resources linked to off-farm employment. These three types of factors contribute to the variations in the complex relationship between farm size and the revenues (or subsistence) which can be drawn from the farms, and thus to the plurality of growth dynamics of the numbers of farms of different sizes. Factors of different types can appear together: the regional cropping intensity scores, for instance, vary as a function of the modes of irrigation appropriate for the regions and the distribution of farms by size in these regions, since intensity is strongly but negatively correlated with farm size.

The regionally differentiated dynamics of growth of the numbers of farms has only been studied from its overall trend over the thirty-year period. However, it is useful to compare the most recent trends of this dynamic, that of the last inter-census period (1982–90), to that of the preceding period (1960–82). From this database, two types of profile are in contrast (see Figure 5).

(a) One profile shows an annual growth rate of the number of farms which is higher in the second period than in the first. Isma'iliya governorate shows the most extreme version of this profile, since the growth of the number of farms accelerated in the second period, although the farmed surface rose steadily from 1961 to 1990. Diametrically opposed to the spectrum of the $NUMBER_{61-90}$, this profile is also clearly that of the governorates of the upper valley, the region characterized by the lowest values of this index. The growth rate of the number of farms is quite low in the first period, and grows noticeably in the second period, sketching out the beginnings of a 'catch-up,' which might be explained by the fact that the cropping intensity has risen to the national level in this region since the introduction of perennial irrigation after the completion of the High Dam in the 1960s. With a smaller gap between the two growth rates, this same profile also characterizes the governorates of the central Delta/lower valley region, which is the penultimate region in terms of the level of its $NUMBER_{61-90}$. Although its $SIZE_{61}$ was already low, pressure on the land, in the 1980s, grew even more in this region of 'high population densities.'

(b) A profile consisting of an annual growth rate of the number of farms which is the same for both periods. This is the case in the governorates of the three other regions, including Bahayra, where the agricultural area expanded considerably in the 1980s.

It is noteworthy that, however low the average farm size was at the end of the first period, in no governorate did the rate of growth of the number of farms slow down during the second period.

## Trends in Farm Size (See Figure 4)

The data from which we started concerned the $SIZE_{61}$ by governorate and the processes (changes in agricultural area and in the growth of the number of farm units) which have affected these data during the period under study. This allows us to account for the evolution of the average farm size in the different governorates. There are four main points:

1. In general, the higher the $SIZE_{61}$ was, the faster the reduction of this measure between 1961 and 1990.
2. The size of the gaps between the maximum and minimum $SIZE_{61}$ and between the equivalent scores in 1990 were reduced

during the study period (especially between 1961 and 1982, for reasons that will be seen below). Apart from the governorate of Isma'iliya, this gap was 5.5 feddans at the beginning of the study period and only 3.5 feddans in 1990 (2.1 if one excludes Bahayra). If one omits the three governorates of the northern and western Delta, the gap drops from 2.5 to 1.5 feddans (see Table 4).

3. During the period from 1982 to 1990, in nine of the seventeen governorates, the rate of decline of the average farm size decelerated relative to the preceding period, while in three governorates (Aswan, Qina, Fayum) the average farm size remained essentially stable, and in three others (Giza, Bahayra, Sharqiya), the 1961–82 trend was reversed and the average farm size began to grow. This phenomenon is explained by the sizable growth in the agricultural area of these governorates during this period.

4. However, the original gaps between the $SIZE_{61}$ of the governorates were large enough that their rank order in 1990 did not change, except for Minya and Qina, which rose a couple of rungs between 1961 and 1990, and for Giza, for the reason mentioned in the previous point.

## Conclusions and Prospects: Spatial Inequalities and Socioeconomic Inequalities

The process of reduction in the average farm size affected all governorates, but not to the same extent. This process was linked to the differential dynamics of growth in the numbers of farms and to the variations (positive, nil, and negative) in the size of the agricultural area. One outcome is that the spatial inequalities measured by the gaps between average farm sizes in the different governorates have been reduced. But here we have underlined the fact that the average farm size for a particular area is an abstract indicator, as are all those based on an understanding of 'central values.' What about the dynamics of the distribution around these central values, by governorate? More concretely, was the reduction of spatial inequality matched by a reduction, inside each unit, of socioeconomic inequalities with reference to access to land? Has there been a number of regional processes of deconcentration of land as a resource for farms? At what speed? Has there been a reduction in the spatial variation of patterns of unequal access to land? The previous analyses only introduce these more basic questions, whose answer requires substantial development beyond the limits of this article. Nevertheless, we will attempt to respond to these questions in a succinct and descriptive manner by way of conclusion.

Through the use of the Gini coefficient[15] (G)(see Figure 6), we can

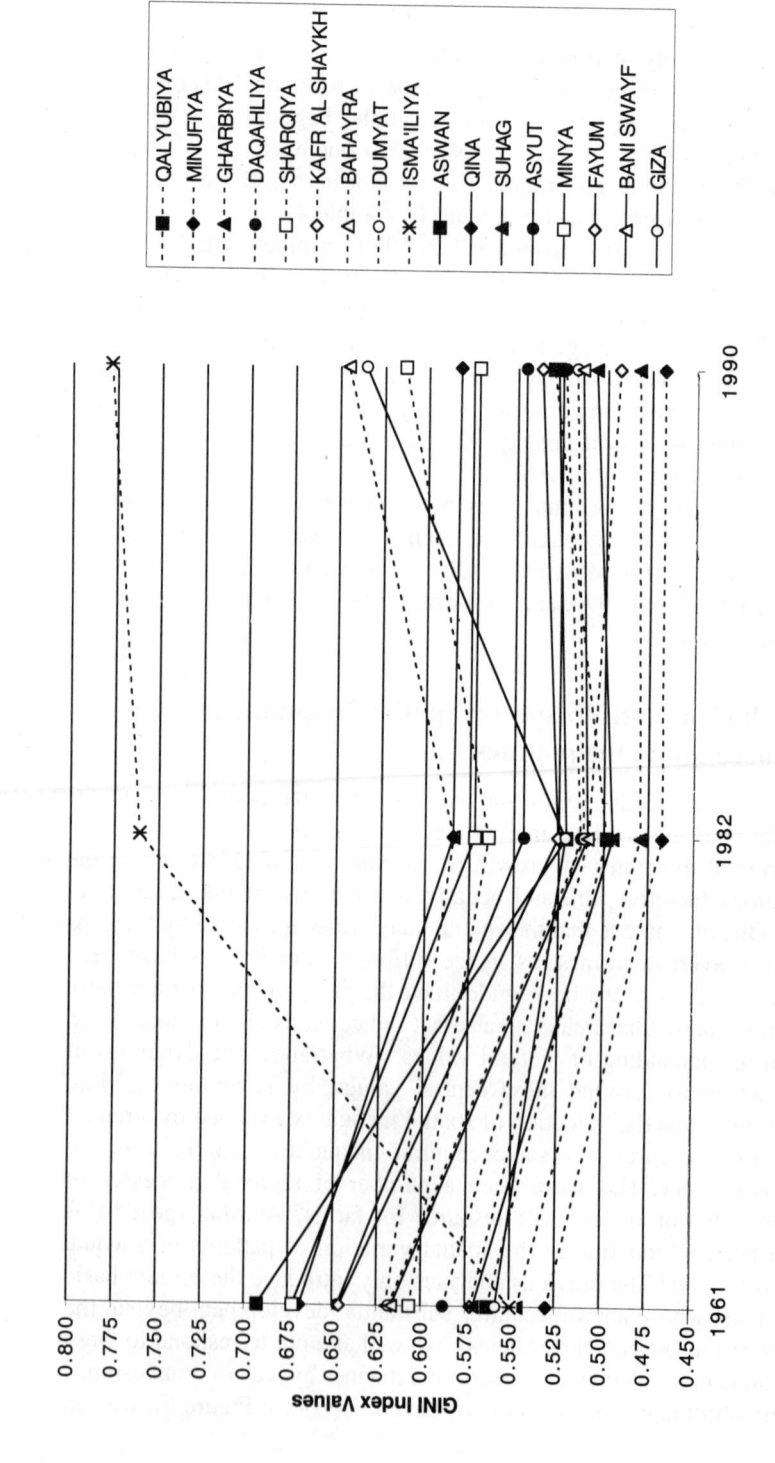

Figure 6 *GINI Index Values of Farm Distribution by Size, by Governorate (1961–1982–1990)*

trace an important and regular process of deconcentration of land resources from 1939 to 1982 for agricultural land in Egypt as a whole. G dropped from 0.78, indicting an extremely unequal distribution of land, to 0.57,[16] and then tended to reflect a reconcentration of land during the 1980s, so that G rose to 0.60 in 1990. This higher figure in 1990 was largely due to the establishment of large farms on new lands. In the old lands, we can only note the important conclusion that between 1982 and 1990 there was a stabilization in the distribution of land resources, which marks the end of a forty-year period of deconcentration. At the level of governorates, in 1960, when the national level of G was 0.63, the spectrum of G ranged from 0.69 (Aswan) to 0.53 (Minufiya), or a swing of a magnitude of 24 percent relative to the national level of G. All the governorates, except Isma'iliya, experienced a substantial process of deconcentration between 1960 and 1982, and Egypt recorded a slight reduction in the spatial inequality of land distribution by governorate. In 1982, except for Isma'iliya, the spectrum of governorate Gs ranged from 0.59 (Qina and Bahayra) to 0.47 (Minufiya), or a variation relative to the national level of G (0.57) of a magnitude of 20.5 percent, compared to 24 percent twenty years earlier.

In the 1980s, three governorates out of seventeen experienced a substantial reconcentration. These included the governorates of Bahayra and Sharqiya, whose G was among the four highest in 1982, at around 0.58, and the governorate of Giza (whose G of 0.53 was in the middle range). The Gini coefficient for these three governorates in 1990 ranged from 0.65 and 0.62. Giza governorate experienced the most intense reconcentration of land in Egypt during the 1980s. These three governorates, along with Isma'iliya, witnessed the largest increase in land surface, over this ten-year period, due to land reclamation. This intense process of reconcentration is thus directly linked to the very high average size of farms established in these reclaimed new lands. We cannot be sure that land reclamation is the only cause of reconcentration in Giza governorate, since Qalyubiya governorate, also adjacent to Cairo, experienced the same process of reconcentration, but to a lesser degree (low G of 0.50 in 1982, rising to 0.53 eight years later), even though the governorate includes no new land.

There are six other governorates, very homogeneous in the 1980s from the point of view of the concentration of access to land, which recorded a low degree of reconcentration. These were Aswan, Suhag, Fayum, and Bani Swayf in the Valley, and Daqahliya and Dumyat in the Delta. Of these, only Fayum, Daqahliya, and Dumyat acquired new desert land. Their G was situated between 0.50 and 0.53 in 1982 and between 0.51 and 0.54 in 1990.

In five governorates, making up two distinct groups from the point of view of the degree of concentration of farms, the distribution of farm holdings remained practically unchanged. These five included, on the one hand, Minufiya and Gharbiya, in the central Delta, which had already achieved in 1982 the highest degree of deconcentration (their G were respectively 0.47 and 0.48), and, on the other hand, Qina, Asyut, and Minya in the Valley, whose G in 1990 fell between the first and second groups. Among these five governorates, only Minya recorded a significant increase in its land area in the 1980s through land reclamation.

Finally, the process of deconcentration during the period 1961–82 continued in Kafr al-Shaykh during the 1980s. Kafr al-Shaykh became one of the three most 'egalitarian' governorates, together with Minufiya and Gharbiya—all three situated between the two branches of the Nile.

As for Isma'iliya, its agricultural area, which consists entirely of new land, tripled from 1961 to 1990, and the Gini coefficient rose from 0.55 at the beginning of the period to 0.76 in 1982. It was the only governorate where the Gini coefficient rose during this period. It then remained at this level during the 1980s.

The period 1961–82 was marked by two aspects of a single process. On the one hand, in all governorates, except Isma'iliya, there was a reduction in the degree of socioeconomic inequality with regard to the distribution of land among farms. On the other hand, there was a reduction in inequality between governorates with respect to the degree of internal socioeconomic inequality which characterized them. The 1980s, schematically, saw the deconcentration process stop in all governorates (except Kafr al-Shaykh), which was a major phenomenon. This halt characterized the old lands of the Nile Valley and the Delta. In the governorates which experienced a reconcentration, this was almost entirely linked to the expansion of agricultural land through reclamation.

Will the 1990s see the beginning of a process of reconcentration in the old lands? We have seen that there has been a small trend in this direction in three governorates (Aswan, Suhag, and Bani Swayf), which do not have any new land and where the agricultural area of the old lands grew smaller or stagnated. This reconcentration is certainly a goal of some liberals, who advocate a profound modification of Egypt's agrarian structures through the creation of 'modern' farms, ranging from ten to thirty feddans, mechanized, giving high yields, and producing surpluses for internal consumption and export. The new law deregulating land rent and the 'return' to determining rents 'by the laws of the market alone' may well have the effect of not only fully

*The Evolution of Agrarian Structures in Egypt* 63

liberalizing the agricultural sector, but also, whether intended or not, of encouraging a trend toward reconcentration, due to small tenants abandoning their plots since they cannot afford the new rent. It is still too early to judge, but the threat is there. Whatever may happen, the 1990s certainly marks the end of a trend toward a reduction in unequal access to land, which began in the 1930s, and which was accelerated by the agrarian reform of 1952.

## Notes

1 These data come from the population censuses of 1960 and 1986 and cover all those aged six years or above. We know in general that, when there is a population census, the permanent male labor force in agriculture (farmers, family helpers, and wage-earners) report this fairly reliably, as do the farmers with off-farm jobs but whose main income derives from agriculture. On the other hand, temporary agricultural workers (family helpers or wage-earners, seasonal or irregular workers) are only reported as active in agriculture if they are working at the time of the census. It is even more difficult to estimate the number of women who are active in agriculture.
2 The figures on multiple jobs come from the agricultural censuses of 1961 and 1990. In these censuses, heads of farm households were only taken into account if they had land.
3 This area includes farms of all statuses (for example, belonging to private individuals, to foreign or Egyptian companies, cooperatives, or the state). A small part of this land is not cultivated, for a variety of reasons. The notion of a 'farm unit' corresponds to that of *'hiyaza,'* that is, all the land managed as a single unit, whether that land is owned, rented, or otherwise.
4 With the partial exception of some fruits and vegetables, the average yields of these reclaimed lands have been lower than those on old lands.
5 This is simple area farmed, as distinct from the cropped area resulting from growing more than one crop a year.
6 The $R^2$ between these variables is only 0.12, and Student's $t$ test shows the low degree of significance of the connection (only about 0.2).
7 The regression is the following:
$NUMBER_{61-90} = 83.53 + 14.69\ SIZE_{61}{***} + 0.31\ AREA_{61-90}{***}$
$(t=5.81)(t=3.78)$
$R^2 = 0.84$; d.f. 14 *** : significant at the 1 percent level
Since the coefficient of partial correlation of $SIZE_{61}$ with $NUMBER_{61-90}$ is $r = 0.84$ (significant at the 1 percent level) and that of $AREA_{61-90}$ with $NUMBER_{61-90}$ is $r = 0.72$ (also significant at the 1 percent level), the first variable contributes more than the second to explaining the variations in $NUMBER_{61-90}$.
8 The linked variations of the two independent variables completely take into account the growth of the number of farms in these four governorates. Of seventeen governorates, nine are characterized by negligible residues (less than 5 percent of the adjusted $NUMBER_{61-90}$ score), four by positive

residues (ranging from +7 percent to +12 percent of the adjusted NUMBER$_{61-90}$ score), and four others by negative residues (ranging from -7 percent to -17 percent of this score).

9  The residue which characterizes the NUMBER$_{61-90}$ score for Daqahliya is almost null, while that of Sharqiya is +10 percent.

10  In the regression, Gharbiya is characterized by a near absence of residue, although the 'residual factors' contribute to the homogeneity of the NUMBER$_{61-90}$ of the central Delta/lower valley region, especially because the growth of the number of farms in Qalyubiya, characterized by a residue of +9 percent, is higher than the scores of the two independent variables would lead one to think.

11  In the first case, a residual factor works negatively (-8 percent of the adjusted value), and in the second, it works positively (+12 percent).

12  Another is to postpone the division of the farm unit through inheritance.

13  Basin irrigation, based on the annual flood of the Nile, was conducted on much of the land of the upper valley until the second half of the 1960s, just before the completion of the High Dam. Overall, flood irrigation allowed no more than a single harvest in the winter, in addition to the cultivation of some marginal crops on the un-flooded high lands. To this should be added the vast areas, mostly devoted to sugar, irrigated year round by high power pumps. The cropping intensity coefficient for the upper valley at the end of the 1950s was only 1.2, while it was 1.8 in the middle valley. After the upper valley went over completely to year round irrigation, it took about ten years before the two coefficients corresponded.

14  In the Delta periphery, although the expansion of the agricultural land permitted a geographical mobility that favored the creation of farms and thus kept the NUMBER$_{61-90}$ high, it limited professional mobility outside agriculture, linked to a low intensity, thereby slowing down the increase in farms. This explains why cropping intensity did not have visible effects, and why the model did not produce any residues. In the upper valley, on the other hand, the low intensity did encourage professional mobility out of agriculture, and thus slowed down the increase in the number of farms, because there was no new land on which to settle the excess farmers and heirs from these governorates.

15  The values of the Gini concentration index can range from 1 (total concentration: one farmer monopolizes all the land in the governorate) to 0 (total equality: all farms have the same size).

16  The Gini coefficient in 1939 corresponds to what one would now call a Latin American type of inequality, and the Gini coefficient in 1982 is still a little higher than the egalitarian south east Asian distribution (such as, in Japan and Taiwan). The 1952 and 1960 agrarian reforms are only partly responsible for this deconcentration process.

# References

Kingdom of Egypt, Ministry of Agriculture. 1946. *Agricultural Census of Egypt 1939.* Cairo. (in Arabic).

Kingdom of Egypt, Ministry of Agriculture. 1946. *Agricultural Census of Egypt 1939.* Cairo.

Republic of Egypt, Ministry of Agriculture. 1957. *Agricultural Census of Egypt 1950* Vol. 1. Cairo. (in Arabic).

United Arab Republic, Ministry of Agriculture. 1967. *Fourth Agricultural Census 1961* Vol. 1, Part 1. Cairo. (in Arabic).

Arab Republic of Egypt, Ministry of Agriculture and Land Reclamation. 1987. *Nata'ig al-ta'dad al-zira' 'an al-sana al-zira'iya 1981–1982.* Cairo: Ministry of Agriculture. (One volume for each governorate). (in Arabic).

Arab Republic of Egypt, Ministry of Agriculture and Land Reclamation. 1995. *Nata'ig al-ta'dad al-zira' 'an al-sana al-zira'iya 1989–1990.* Cairo: Ministry of Agriculture. (One volume for each governorate). (in Arabic).

# 3

# Beating Plowshares into Swords: The Relocation of Rural Egyptian Workers and their Discontent

JAMES TOTH

## Introduction

One of the most commonly examined sectors of the Egyptian economy is agriculture. And one of the most thoroughly discussed issues in the economic literature on rural Egypt is determining the exact percentage of surplus or redundant labor. Ever since Wendell Cleland first estimated (1936:35), during the height of the Great Depression, that as many as 80 percent of all workers in the Egyptian countryside were chronically unemployed or underemployed, and therefore constituted a large mass of expendable surplus labor, numerous neo-Malthusian economists have either raised or lowered this single percentage. But in applying a 'marginalist' model of economic efficiency, few, if any of these scholars seriously questioned the accepted axiom of excess, unnecessary labor.

After the Korean War, the development theories of the economist W. Arthur Lewis (1954) further fueled this discussion. Lewis argued that redundant farm workers could be harmlessly removed from the countryside, shifted to urban locations, and used to cheaply staff new factories financed by foreign investors. In turn, agricultural production would be rationalized and streamlined, farm plots consolidated, and relocated rural workers replaced by mechanized equipment. Yet this theory concealed more than it revealed. For, in addition to covering up the fact that capitalism in general favors unemployment so as to keep its labor costs low, it went on to misrepresent the nature of rural Egyptian society by not only describing it as overpopulated and overly procreative, but also by characterizing it as passive and static.

The Egyptian countryside exhibits a technical division of male labor that consists of two distinct branches—village farm work and distant migrant labor. The very existence of migrant wage labor ought to have been the first clue that in Egypt, seasonally unneeded farm workers were not then necessarily unemployed. Not only did rural laborers have other options besides the binary choices of 'farm work' or 'no work,' but in addition, other sectors of the Egyptian economy were already exploiting this seasonally available labor force. These economists and their theories never took into account such complexity, and thus missed the point that unemployed or underemployed agricultural workers were not therefore necessarily redundant and nonessential. Rural workers were not simply inert, expendable inputs who could be easily siphoned off without damaging agricultural production, and then relocated to the cities in such large numbers that urban life did not suffer either. Indeed, by their own actions and agency, rural workers significantly discredited the theory of surplus labor and showed that it occupied more the realm of ideology than the domain of scientific thinking.

It is this agency which I wish to chronicle in this essay in order to understand just how rural workers negated these calculations, percentages, simplifications, and scholarly discourses. For in Egypt, contrary to the Lewis model, the transfer of labor, crops, and capital from the countryside to the city did not take place smoothly, without resentment from the workers or without harm to the nation. Moreover, the depiction of rural Egyptians as passive and static agents is belied by the disruption they caused, first in the countryside as their departure from farm work left production shortfalls, trade deficits, and financial difficulties in their wake, and second in the city as their incomplete incorporation into the informal sector propelled them first into spontaneous riots and later into militant religious organizations.

The departure of farm laborers from the countryside was not merely an economic gesture, despite their avowed goal of obtaining better wages and a higher standard of living. For it meant abandoning the intimate ties of village life, with its familiar rhythms and fond attachments. Forsaking the village, then, was as much an act of political desperation for rural workers as were the more concerned disruptions they provoked once they relocated to the city. Migration, either temporary or permanent, was one rudimentary way of resolving their rural predicament. Once in the city, however, they met with equally difficult circumstances. These problems were no longer settled merely by moving. Instead, ex-rural workers took part first in clashes over city bread prices and then later in the Islamist opposition to urban inadequacies and injustices. And although these displaced laborers had come to reject their simple rural roots, the urban disturbances they initiated echoed in familiar ways the political habits they had learned in the village.

The narrative begins in 1960, for this year witnessed the convergence of five state policies—high dam construction, land reclamation, nationalization, introduction of cooperative organizations, and price controls—that together mark the beginning of intensive state domination of the countryside. The 1952 land reform had proved insufficient since it had only affected 3.6 percent of rural families and 5 percent of the cultivated area (Abdel Fadil 1975:9)—essentially, the estates of the palace and the Turkish elite. The more far-reaching economic reforms of 1961, however, coupled with the unsettling political investigations following the Khamshish affair five years later in 1966 (Ansari 1986), were much more disturbing, for they demonstrated the state's serious intent to control and dominate the agricultural sector.

## Where Have All the Workers Gone?

In 1961, Egypt experienced major failures in its vital export crops. Cotton production fell 40 percent despite a record sown area, and a drop in rice yields, together with an increase in domestic consumption, created a major decline in the amount of rice available for export as well (Hansen and Nashashibi 1975:50–51). Coming on the heels of Egypt's new Five-Year Plan and the nationalizations that launched 'Abd al-Nasir's Arab Socialism, this agricultural crisis had more than just rural consequences. Foreign exchange earnings plummeted 38 percent, from LE121 million in 1960–61 to LE75 million in 1961–62, and forced the government to curtail its ambitious plans for industrialization (Waterbury 1983:94). In order to obtain LE20 million in foreign currency needed for continuing its operations, the government desperately turned to the International Monetary Fund (IMF) for assistance.

In May 1962, Cairo reached an agreement with the IMF in exchange for its promise to curb imports, restrain government expenditures, and devalue its currency. Egypt lowered its pound 24 percent, from 35.2 piasters per US dollar to 43.5 piasters, in order to receive short-term credit. As a result, the prices for imports rose dramatically, while the inelastic status of Egypt's exports further deteriorated. Consumer prices increased on average while agricultural revenues and incomes fell, so that the ripple effect of the cotton crisis soon came to engulf most Egyptian consumers (Hansen and Nashashibi 1983:106).

*What was behind the 1961 agricultural crisis?*

In May 1961, at the height of a severe boll weevil infestation, the Agricultural Committee of Parliament issued a decree requesting the urgent allocation of LE1 million not only to purchase chemical pesticides but also to subvene the wage costs of a multitude of 'emergency' seasonal workers to fight the plague of cotton worms (Parliament Records 1961:715). Yet pest control is much more a labor intensive activity than it is a technical matter of chemical spraying. For the overall process, particularly in its earlier stages, requires countless numbers of hands deftly passing over the maturing cotton leaves looking for worms and intensely scouring the ground looking for their burrows (el-Togby 1976:74–83). Normally, such work employs women and children, but the high demand for their labor often exceeds their local supply. Men, however, should they otherwise be inactive, frequently pitch in and supplement their efforts.

Yet in 1961, if more workers had to be hired for these emergency operations, then the countryside's regular male labor force must have been experiencing some unusual shortages. In a country where the number of rural workers was thought to be well in excess of what was optimally needed for agriculture, such labor shortages appear quite astonishing.

*Where could these workers have gone?*

In January 1960, construction work had begun on building the spectacular High Dam at Aswan. In tandem, the government's land reclamation program in Tahrir province had received a financial transfusion so that its infrastructure would be completed at the same time as the High Dam. Building these projects were monumental undertakings. The amount of manual labor required was staggering. Wages for unskilled laborers at Aswan approached LE10 a month (Little 1965:117), equal to forty-two piasters a day for a six-day working week or thirty-six piasters a day for a seven-day week. Others earned less for working on subcontracted projects. The average farm wage for 1960 is not known, but in 1959 it was twelve piasters a day and in 1961 it rose to 12.6 piasters (Abdel-Fadil 1975:66). Thus wages at the High Dam were more than three times those in agriculture. In land reclamation, wages were lower. Laborers from the province of Bahayra , working through the government Employment Office, earned between eighteen and twenty-two piasters (Barada'i 1972:23), well below the thirty-six or forty-two piasters estimated for daily High Dam wages, but almost twice as high as those paid in village farm work. No wonder such migrant work seemed more appealing. Yet their departure left women and children overburdened and unable to adequately complete the necessary pest control operations to insure good cotton harvests.[1]

In 1960, a number of important Egyptian businesses, including the entire cotton sector, had already been expropriated. On July 23, in the middle of the 1961 cotton season, President 'Abd al-Nasir announced even more property expropriations and confiscations, the magnitude of which shocked employers and property owners throughout the country (Waterbury 1983:73-76). He also announced a second land reform law that cut ownership ceilings and land assessments to half those promulgated in the first reform of 1952. A month later, the government declared all agricultural bank loans interest free and gave state cooperatives a monopoly on distributing seeds and fertilizers (Abdel-Fadil 1975:Chapter 1).

These new institutional changes in property ownership, marketing, and credit proved extremely distressing. Few rural employers were willing to take any economic risk that might result in personal misfortune by paying workers higher wages despite the growing shortage of labor. Nor were they any more inclined to increase wages thereafter, for the government program to expand the network of agricultural cooperatives, as a means of strengthening its policy of agricultural price controls, was soon initiated as the state's response to the 1961 crisis.

The cooperatives provided the mechanism for the government to appropriate capital from agriculture in order to finance its plans for promoting industrialization first and then later subsidizing urban consumption. With large landlords marginalized by the two land reform laws of 1952 and 1961, price controls could then be imposed and capital transfers realized without much resistance. By controlling prices paid to farmers, the state left them little, if any, extra income (Cuddihy 1980:iv and 29). Such savings by farmers could have been invested in reversing the flow of workers by paying higher wages, in purchasing machinery to replace them, or else creating a viable domestic market. Instead it was appropriated by the state. Rural poverty thus became a condition explicitly engineered by government policies—farmers were kept poor— rather than being a case of bad luck, ignorance, unresponsiveness, or culture.

Egyptian agriculture essentially remained a labor-intensive business—increase labor, and production increased; remove labor, and production fell, unless workers were replaced by substitutes or machines. When men left, they were replaced by women and children, but not perfectly. Equipment proved expensive, and only became widespread later. Labor-intensive agriculture therefore continued to be the source of the country's exports and food. Exports earned hard currency, and domestic cultivation reduced food imports that depleted foreign currency reserves. Chronic shortfalls in both then reduced

Cairo's hard currency accounts which required IMF loans to make up the deficit. Such credit, however, did not come without strings attached. Such conditions subsequently weakened individual economies and undermined the national one, thereby reducing the credibility of both the government's Five-Year plan and 'Abd al-Nasir's Arab Socialism.

Before 1961 the state had been a rather silent 'night watchman,' operating more as a distant agent, merely maintaining polarized property relations and overall social stability than as one intimately involved in micro-managing economic relations. Yet afterward, the government inserted itself more centrally into the economic life of the country, a position, however, that was not accepted without opposition.[2]

## Organizing the Dispossessed

In 1962 and 1963, agricultural activity picked up, but only temporarily. By 1964, agriculture again became paralyzed. To make matters worse, sales of imported US wheat to Egypt, which previously were paid for in local soft currency under the PL480 program, began requiring hard currency transactions instead. Revoking financial credits for US PL480 wheat sales would have been inconsequential if sufficient quantities of wheat had been grown domestically. Production shortfalls in cotton decreased the accumulation of hard currency; deficits in cereal yields meant importing foreign wheat to pacify urban consumers. In order to pay for imported grain, Egypt had to dip into its foreign currency reserves, already low because export cotton production had declined.

This placed even greater production and financial burdens on Egypt's agricultural sector. The government continued to mis-schedule its projects. First, it initiated infrastructure construction at Aswan and on the desert fringes of the Nile Valley. Later, it formulated policies of confiscating property, expanding agricultural cooperatives, and imposing price controls. Then in 1964, in order to secure more workers for these national projects, the government organized a momentarily successful workers' union—the General Union for Agricultural and Migrant Workers or GUAMW. In all cases, government planners deluded themselves into thinking that the countryside contained unlimited numbers of surplus workers. In reality, such numbers were critically missing. Instead, men opted for migrant labor rather than remaining in farming. The women and children who replaced them became so thinly distributed that not enough workers were able to produce the food and export crops Egypt needed so desperately to advance the state of its economy.

Already, from 1961 to 1964, provincial efforts at organizing migrant labor had resulted in the elimination of brokerage commissions and corruption. Wage advances had become regularized and labor requirements had been reduced. The safety of long-distance transportation was improved and migrant workers were provided with free food and better shelter. Yet pressure to do more increased. In the spring of 1964, following a dramatic presidential speech, Parliament finally established the GUAMW. Between April and July, twenty-seven provincial branches and four thousand union committees were formed. Local elections promptly chose committee officers and representatives to the national union. National union elections were scheduled for July 12 (Toth 1991).

One of the serious flaws in establishing the national union was that it included white collar employees from government ministries and companies. The July voting elected more white collar employees into leadership positions than manual workers. And even the label 'manual worker' is suspect since many of these union leaders were educated enough to assume the duties of their new post. This suggests that they were in fact not working with their hands at all. Among union officers, seven out of ten were non-workers, and out of ten members on the board of directors, six were listed as non-workers (*al-Akhbar*, Jul. 12 & 13, 1964).

Was the GUAMW then, with its non-worker leadership, simply another example of the corporatist labor organization reportedly found elsewhere in Egypt (Bianchi 1989:Chapter 5)? Was this state-organized union merely what June Nash once labeled a "labor control mechanism" (1985:153)? In fact, the new union was not entirely a government artifact. Despite its white collar leadership, it still became a significant arena for struggle over the control of labor and income.

After these summer elections, the national union set about doing what most labor organizations do: mobilizing its members and holding mass meetings. The first two meetings proceeded in a calm, corporatist fashion, indicative of the new leadership style (*al-Jumhuriya*, Aug. 19, 1964; *al-Akhbar*, Nov. 17, 1964). Yet at the third meeting, held in Aja, Daqahliya, migrant workers and their middle-class allies aggressively confronted unsympathetic union officers over the issue of prohibiting corrupt labor brokers and transferring all their employment and welfare activities to the union (*al-Masa'*, Nov. 15, 1964). The unexpected outcome was an autonomous worker-led organization in Daqahliya that broke away from the national union, whose headquarters were in Cairo. Such militancy clearly demonstrated that the economic demands of rank-and-file rural laborers were not to be taken lightly, despite the wishes of the union's more staid leadership.

Later, following the Six Day-War, Egypt was no longer able to financially support the benefits the GUAMW had won. Yet in its first three years, the union gained an impressive number of important victories—raising wages, improving work-site conditions, and attracting national attention—which coaxed large numbers of agricultural workers to register with the GUAMW, to enlist with rival government agencies, or even to continue working through honest private brokers. The precise extent to which the initial provincial organizations, the summer elections, and the rousing fall meetings lured local agricultural workers into migrant labor is not easily measured, but Egypt continued to experience crippling labor shortages. As the GUAMW improved wages and conditions, even more workers left agriculture. No longer content simply to exchange reduced incomes earned in the village for abuses encountered in migrant labor, rural workers insisted on receiving their full entitlements. Such agitation, and the union's early achievements, had the unintended consequences of being too successful, and, once again, of leaving far too few male workers back on the farm.

Labor shortages persisted, and once again agricultural production problems in cotton, rice, and, in 1964, wheat, wreaked havoc on the national economy. Not only were foreign currency reserves depressed, but now the United States was demanding hard dollars for its grain. Cotton production declined 20 percent from 1964 to 1966. To compensate for the subsequent imbalance of trade, Egypt resorted to deficit financing, borrowing an average of LE60 million annually up to 1966. Egypt was forced to restrict wheat grain imports and to draw on its foreign exchange reserves to pay for what was already traded. This contributed to food shortages that raised retail food prices by 11.5 percent and added to the overall price inflation that gripped the country. The value of imported wheat and wheat flour in 1965–66 (LE55 million) exceeded the value of all Egyptian exports to Western markets (LE52 million). In meeting its import demands, Egypt fell into arrears in servicing its external commercial debt (Waterbury 1983:95–98).

During the period 1960–64, Egypt's GNP had expanded 5 percent per year. But in the two years preceding the war with Israel, its GNP grew at the rate of just 0.3 percent annually. By 1965 and 1966, a second crisis had appeared in Egyptian national financing, which again had its origins in agricultural production. Thus on the eve of the 1967 debacle, Egypt was in serious economic straits. Cairo had so depleted its foreign exchange reserves that it was no longer able to purchase parts and equipment from abroad (Goldschmidt 1988:125).

The June war demonstrated that the manufacture of essential

military armament and munitions, which had relied on imported machinery, had been starved of foreign currency. Parts for repairing damaged battle equipment were not in stock. The drain on its hard-currency reserves had reduced Egypt's ability to engage successfully in combat. The foreign currency earned by insufficient cotton exports was not even enough to pay for the imported wheat that compensated for shortfalls in domestic grain production, much less to pay for foreign components and spare parts. Thus a labor-induced agricultural crisis helped contribute to Egypt's humiliating military defeat by reducing the nation's foreign currency reserves. Such failure in agriculture was the outcome of attracting large numbers of rural workers to work first in Aswan and later in Tahrir, handicapping village employers by jeopardizing their incomes, and then further encouraging the exodus by establishing a momentarily effective union for migrant laborers.

## Opening the Door to Urban Unrest

After the June defeat, the government enacted severe austerity measures. Consumption costs climbed, incomes stagnated, and forced capital transfers expanded. Government budgets were cut, except for defense expenditures. The result was what Waterbury called a period of "seven lean years" of retrenchment, stretching from 1967 to 1974 (1983:112). Although rural workers had left agriculture for migrant labor when new jobs had opened up in Aswan and Tahrir, and when the GUAMW had won concessions on wages and working conditions, now such employment had become no more rewarding than farming.

Beginning in 1974, however, new global conditions began to expand the unskilled labor market. Rural workers once again disrupted agriculture, this time by leaving both migrant labor and agriculture for expanding urban opportunities indirectly resulting from a growing regional economy based on oil. Following the October 1973 war, when the state changed its regulations toward labor emigration and permitted large numbers of skilled urban workers to travel abroad for higher waged employment, new building jobs opened up domestically that attracted many rural workers. Urban construction wages rose to three to five times the level of those in agriculture (Hansen and Radwan 1982:74–75).

The vast number of small, flexible informal sector contractors and sub-contractors made it easy to absorb new arrivals from the countryside, and the skills rural workers had learned in the village fields and migrant labor camps easily prepared them for these new construction jobs (The General Organization for Housing 1981 vol. 2:120, and vol.

3:G.4–6, 34). Yet ex-rural laborers who became momentarily unemployed still waited in anticipation for further construction work instead of returning to agriculture. For despite the inflated size of the work force, both the intermittent nature of construction work and the paternalistic ties to employers made this expectation reasonable. And even after 1985, when Egypt's construction sector began to slow down, many deactivated workers found jobs in the informal sector or in services, averse to ever going back to alternating between farming and migrant labor.

Eventually, more city dwellers meant creating more jobs. This required greater investment, which in turn depended on the government attracting foreign capital through its Open Door policy and, to a lesser extent, on expatriate workers remitting their income to finance informal sector activities. However, in the late 1970s, the government's investment strategy failed to expand productive activities, and after 1985, when regional oil revenues fell, labor remittances declined significantly (Waterbury and Richards 1990:67). Neither was able to keep pace with the growth in demand for more employment, income, and consumption. Instead, insufficient investment generated corruption, social polarization, and urban unrest, aggravating Egypt's economic difficulties that eventually required more IMF intervention.

The accomplishments of the Open Door policy were limited. Most new investment was in banking, tourism, and luxury housing. Few invested in productive enterprises (Waterbury 1978:206–23). As a result of the influx of foreign capital, inflation, which had been holding steady at a relatively moderate 8 percent, grew to 25 percent. Job generation remained sluggish when public sector enterprises stagnated, and new private and joint sector activities employed capital intensive technology instead of labor. The construction, informal, and service sectors supplied numerous jobs but even more were demanded. Consumer prices escalated without an attendant rise in income or income sources. Additional dependents soon overwhelmed family budgets since they were unable to find new jobs (Waterbury 1983:171–81; Hirst and Beeson 1981:207–10).

The Open Door economy also aggravated Egypt's chronic deficits in its balance of payments. The government import bill, especially for food, increased enormously, reflecting in part the precipitous rise in world energy prices, in part the steady growth in Egypt's population, but in large part the widespread stagnation that still afflicted domestic agriculture. For the problems of shortfalls in agricultural exports and food crops, and balance of trade deficits, which rural labor had caused in 1961 and 1964, had never really disappeared, even when male workers returned to their villages after the Six-Day War. Throughout the 1970s and into the 1980s, labor shortages resumed, price controls tightened, food imports increased, cotton exports stagnated, industrial output slumped, balance of payments difficulties deepened, and the national debt grew.

In order to resolve these financial problems, the IMF drafted a stabilization plan in the spring of 1975. Legislative approval for the plan was postponed until after the parliamentary elections of October 1976. But once the elections were over, the government announced on January 18, 1977, that in accordance with the IMF, it was reducing a number of essential subsidies and raising prices on basic consumer goods. Egyptians in Cairo and other major cities reacted violently when they heard the news.

The January riots revealed the degree of discontent and dissatisfaction in Egypt's working classes that altogether alarmed state officials. The demonstrations were first organized by skilled laborers from the formal sector and state-owned industries. Only later did workers from the informal sector join in. Once confronted by the police, this clutter of protesters turned to riot. Nathan Brown once argued (1990:112–13) that although underlying complaints among peasants may be longstanding, such spontaneous outbursts of violence take place only when they are directly confronted with an immediate threat to their livelihoods. Once the proximate threat disappears, so too does the violence. Thus the singular demand of the Cairo rioters was to rescind the price increases and subsidy reductions despite the various other grievances of those employed in public-sector factories and informal sector businesses. Once the radio announced their restoration, the immediate crisis vanished, and so the rioting subsided. But the fundamental dissatisfaction that gave rise to it continued to simmer.

Ex-rural workers who had moved to cities soon discovered that despite their higher wages, the cost of urban living was even greater. The government services they had come to expect as part of their entitlement—education, health, housing, training, transportation—were also not forthcoming, for government budgets either had not been restored since the 'lean years' of the early 1970s or else had been cut under pressure from the IMF. Debt repayments consumed much of what little was left for social services. Thus nonexistent services, unemployment and underemployment, inflation, and stagnant incomes made city life terribly precarious.

Any hope of improving economic conditions and changing state policy through legitimate channels, such as labor unions or political parties, had declined after the administration reorganized the political system. In April 1974, strengthened by his success in the October war just seven months earlier, President al-Sadat had proposed major modifications in Egypt's single political party, the Arab Socialist Union (ASU). These reforms essentially meant the exclusion of recalcitrant factions—workers, peasants, students, academics, and their advocates—who opposed his Open Door policy.[3] Since they were too large to censure outright, these troublesome factions, instead, were muzzled by affiliating them with new political parties too weak to influence government policies and operations. As a result, many members of the underclass who had previously spoken out through various ASU departments were no longer able to attract attention to their critical conditions.

Thus, demonstrations, riots, and attacks against the state became the sole avenues of dissent. In the end, the government both resumed its consumer subsidies and received its international credit. Workers, however, both rural and ex-rural, remained upset over the ever-escalating cost of living, the stagnation of incomes, and the uneven pace of job generation and economic development generated by state policies.

Urban flight had once been a practical, though unsophisticated, political response for the rural poor. Now, however, there were no more places they could move to at their skill level, even more so when emigration abroad declined after 1985. Stuck in an increasingly inhospitable city, labor's political tactics shifted. Indeed, the urban mob action of January 1977 soon began to coalesce into more organized forms of opposition.

In 1979, Egypt's president was coaxed into signing the Camp David treaty, in large part by US promises of extended food aid to compensate for grain shortages (Richards and Waterbury 1990:145). In 1982, Egypt transacted one sixth of all international wheat flour sales (*The Wall Street Journal*, Jan. 19, 1983:32). By 1987 Egypt had become the fourth largest importer of wheat (Sadowski 1991:15). In November 1991, imported foodstuffs, including wheat, accounted for 70 percent of Egypt's total food consumption (*al-Wafd*, Nov. 29, 1991). Rural workers who once had played a vital role in providing cheap foodstuffs were no longer cooperating. Their growing exodus, however, was generating more problems than just labor shortages. It generated still larger trade deficits, foreign debt, and inflation. Egypt's entire economy and political autonomy were seriously limited by its difficulties in agricultural production.

## The Islamist Solution

After 1985, crop production stabilized and then grew as price controls were gradually lifted. This encouraged mechanization and permitted wage and income increases for those still active in agriculture. Nevertheless, Egyptian agriculture had become, as Simon Commander concluded, a sector of part-timers and moonlighters who temporarily returned to farming at night or on weekends (1987:168). All segments of the rural community were diversifying their occupations. The propertied strata of the village had taken advantage of 'Abd al-Nasir's free education and sent their sons and daughters to public schools, and later on to urban universities so as to obtain better non-farm employment. Those in the middle had mastered new skills in the army or trade schools; now they commuted between countryside and city, tending their village plots whenever they could. Those at the bottom who had once toiled as poor migrant workers had left the countryside altogether for seemingly better opportunities in towns and cities.

Yet as more and more of these urban transplants began experiencing income and job limitations, they sought to change the state policies and policy makers that had given rise to them. Unplanned riots had intimidated officials, but only momentarily, and thus proved ineffectual in securing permanent policy changes. Increasingly, ex-rural laborers upset over their poverty began linking up with equally discontented ex-rural university graduates, both unable to find appropriate employment, earn higher incomes, and achieve a better lifestyle in a stalled economy. Joined together through strong bonds of paternalism, these two segments donned the garments of religious radicalism that sought to purify the government and purge it of the duplicity and fraud of what they saw as a parasitic and autocratic elite. In short they joined an Islamist movement that constituted the politics of rural-to-urban migration.

Over the past three years, I have been discreetly conducting field work among friends and acquaintances in one of the major towns of Egypt's southern Sa'id which had become a notorious 'hot-bed' of Islamic radicalism and militancy. Here I have capitalized on an informal network of old friends acquired while managing an international program of community development in the mid-1980s. Because of tight security, the research has remained somewhat restricted; nevertheless I have been able to delineate the contours of this religious movement and the government's response to it.

At first, this new brand of Islamist radicalism remained limited mostly to rural middle-class students and ex-students whose religious zeal led them to establish charitable service associations in the name of Islam. It was not until after the petroleum-induced recession hit Egypt in 1985 that it began to include members of Egypt's disaffected urban working classes that contained large numbers of ex-rural laborers. Then, the state closed down the Islamic investment companies whose *zakat* donations were funding Islamic development initiatives, took over private mosques and reallocated their charitable funds, and arrested and imprisoned dedicated Muslims who had been providing alternative welfare resources. As a result, social services deteriorated drastically. Members of the working classes were particularly hard hit. Rural ex-laborers and ex-rural professionals who had both joined these associations then united together to transform these unsatisfactory conditions fundamentally. Denied access to legitimate political participation and subjected to increased government persecution, some Islamist groups turned to violence. Religious radicals who previously had just preached their opposition turned into Islamist militants who began translating their words into holy combat. It seemed to my informants at the time that Egypt stood at the brink of a religious civil war.

These radical organizations are reminiscent of the social protest movements Eric Hobsbawm documented (1959:Chapter 2) for southern Italy before this region was incorporated into a unified modern nation. There, secret societies also brought together a disgruntled rural middle class and a discontented class of poor, both displaced by the encroachment of nineteenth century capitalism. Before the Italian mafias turned criminal after 1860, their early actions may well have included acts of rebellion described by the state instead as illegal crimes (cf. Brown 1990:6–7). Egypt's Islamic associations may have been similarly characterized as 'terrorist' organizations because they dared to challenge the legitimacy of the prevailing order.

The two class segments that subscribed to Islamic radicalism had both experienced the dislocation of rural-to-urban migration. Ex-rural, middle-class university students had first come from diversified farm families and had since graduated into an uncertain job market. These included well-educated but nonetheless alienated white-collar professionals—doctors, engineers, lawyers, teachers, accountants, civil servants —who were strongly supported by disgruntled members of the underclass who found it increasingly difficult to stretch their limited incomes to cover rising consumption costs. Ex-rural workers had migrated to the city and found employment in the construction, service, and informal sectors but still remained destitute and impoverished. These two segments were strongly linked together through a paternalism that treated each other as both equals and unequal at the very same time.

The rural middle class had benefited extensively from the new free education policies of the 'Abd al-Nasir administration. They were highly motivated and accomplished, and many participated in campus Islamic associations of the 1970s. Upon graduation, however, these students discovered that despite their costly education—dearly paid for not only in money but also in the personal sacrifice of their families—the road to gaining better professional employment and achieving higher status that leads inevitably to the capital city was essentially blocked by the ascriptive wall of Cairene elite society. Frustrated when wealthy family connections took precedence over merit, many instead migrated to Libya, Iraq, and the Gulf to acquire the better incomes unavailable at home.

However, after 1985, many professionals returned to stay. Many reactivated the piety and spirituality learned during their college days and reinforced while working abroad. They chose to emulate the life of the Prophet Muhammad, to grow beards and dress in white robes, and to perform charitable acts and good deeds that would bring them closer to their religion. But many remained thwarted in their quest for upward mobility. They therefore channeled their frustration into mobilizing an equally discontented ex-rural working class. The tone was one of moral outrage. The adversary became those corrupted by opportunism and contact with Western authorities (Ibrahim 1996:9; Ansari 1986:Chapters 9 & 10).

In the 1970s, the exodus of rural workers from the countryside had increased rapidly after the seven years of economic stagnation that followed the June 1967 war and after the three-fold increase in petroleum prices that followed the Egyptian–Israeli war of October, 1973. Ex-village workers migrated to the cities in large numbers[4] and replaced emigrant workers in the construction sector, where the wages and organization attracted those who had previously been overworked and underpaid in the countryside. These laborers became attached to specific building contractors and small workshop owners through strong ties of paternalism that they had once employed in their villages and which were again effective in the cities in order to guarantee employment opportunities and to preserve a readily available work force, even in periods of temporary inactivity.

After 1985, fewer skilled urban workers traveled abroad, and those who did came home sooner. Back home, they mixed with their unskilled colleagues in the provincial cities and towns who had never emigrated and together sought work in a construction sector whose investments were already declining. Patron–client relations allowed lesser skilled laborers to stay tied to construction bosses and workshop proprietors despite growing unemployment so as not to return to their villages where conditions were even more hopeless. Many of these unemployed or underemployed workers, constrained by high prices, low wages, and unemployed kin, came to rely heavily on the charitable acts and good deeds of pious professionals to get them through tight times. Such desperate circumstances firmly attached needy laborers to charitable professionals in ways that extended far beyond the specific welfare activities.

Both professionals and workers subscribed to the values of an imagined rural community. Middle-class village students attending urban universities as the first in the history of their families to do so were unfamiliar with the impersonality of large campuses, crowded classrooms, and indifferent professors. Rural workers moving into the city and finding employment in construction crews, workshops, and services were unaccustomed to the cold bureaucracy of government offices, large companies, and rapid commercial transactions. Nostalgia and uncertainty drove both groups into the more familiar, intimate surroundings of the Islamic associations.

Yet ironically, the creed of these religious associations was not the same as that which these villagers had left behind. Village Islam had been textured by the passive quietism of Sufism, saint shrines, and miracles. Urban Islamist associations rejected such 'superstition' and instead exhibited the political activism of *salifiyism*, legalism, and righteousness (Gilsenan 1992:Chapter 10). The rural to urban shift had been paralleled by a transformation from 'traditional' to 'modern.' However, it was not a secular modernity, but rather a religious one inherited from the doctrines of Muhammad Abduh and Hasan al-Banna.

These associations thus attracted ex-villagers by providing an intimacy reminiscent of the old rural community, but in the process transposed their beliefs from tolerant submission to indignant radicalism. They united those who wished to practice a more devout and pious Islam with those who were in dire straits, forming a core of religious activists and loyal supporters potentially useful for partisan action. Although very few of these associations ever reached the violent intensity practiced by *al-Jihad* or *al-Jama'a al-Islamiya*, many members, I was told, did switch to these more combative associations once government persecution increased. Nevertheless, most enthusiasts embraced a non-militant religiosity which advocated performing good deeds and pious acts on the one hand, and bestowing devout blessings and grateful loyalty on the other.

Since the start of skilled labor emigration abroad after 1973, university-trained professionals who remitted their ample salaries home allocated a significant portion toward performing Islamic good deeds, pious acts, and funding community development and charity projects. In the early 1980s, such financing increased even further with the profit-sharing and monetary transactions routed through Islamic investment companies. Moreover, the supervision over the *zakat* funds of local privately-operated mosques by like-minded colleagues guaranteed that the bulk of these donations would reach the surrounding communities and those in need.

Subsumed under the name of good deeds and pious acts, these activities delivered a wide range of important social benefits, such as providing hospital beds for the poor, low-cost health clinics, affordable housing, after-school tutoring, complimentary textbooks, clothing exchanges, veterinarian services, small-scale business assistance and low-cost credit, and guidance through the labyrinthine state bureaucracy for permits, licenses, and taxes. All of these constituted critical services that the government simply could not or would not provide. Cairo had written off the Sa'id and neglected to provide essential welfare benefits. Instead, the gap was filled by the myriad of small community initiatives funded by labor remittances, *zakat* funds, and Islamic investment companies, and intended to provide a strong Islamic presence.

These religious benefactors gained, in turn, from the allegiance they won from undertaking their good deeds and pious acts, whether they participated legally in community politics or else unlawfully in militant Islamic associations. When Islamist technocrats entered political contests in the countless number of governorate, city, town, and district level election campaigns and partisan appointments, they received overwhelming support and loyalty from those they had once assisted. When pious but alienated professionals exhorted their followers to berate and attack the government for its fiscal corruption that had eliminated social services, working-class clients dutifully joined them and actively promoted their agenda. Thus, poor laborers and ex-rural workers approved and followed those who had once helped them with difficult problems, and who were now seeking their support in strengthening their religious message and in establishing a virtuous and honest administration. Paternalism sealed the bonds connecting the activist with the masses.

After 1985, the funding available for the vital services that compensated workers for their lack of sufficient income fell precipitously because of permanent labor repatriation and the decline in overseas remittances, together with the government's crackdown on Islamic investment companies, its takeover of private mosques, and its repression of Islamic activists.

The good deeds, charitable acts, and material welfare provided to those at the bottom of the social hierarchy seemed to be far removed from those engaged in senseless demagoguery or wanton terrorism. Indeed, the spiritual attitude and religious demeanor of the devout professionals I met appeared beyond reproach. Yet the cumulative effects of constant government arrest, torture, and humiliation pushed many over the thin line that, until then, had separated them from those committed to violence. While some still remained hopeful that the political and electoral process would eventually establish a legitimate avenue for social change, a growing number moved beyond the limits of peaceful transformation as they began to realize that militancy offered the only practical way to change state and society fundamentally.

In many provincial towns and cities, men wearing full beards and white robes and women dressed in the dark *naqab*, the complete Islamic covering, said they were routinely arrested, questioned, sometimes tortured, humiliated, jailed, or released. Homes of suspected militants were bombed and burned. Many militants never came to trial, but instead were fatally shot in police crossfire when security forces came to arrest them. Their families were heartbroken and terrified by this persecution. Neighborhoods became divided, both sympathizing with those whose piety had earned them great admiration and frightened that their sympathy might make them suspect as well. Anger swelled, and, in response, many acts of police misconduct were repaid by outraged relatives—not through organized retribution, but by individual acts of revenge. That most religious violence erupted in the Sa'id may be more a testimony to this region's 'tribal' practice of seeking revenge for the dishonor of family members—*al-tha'r*—than to an exceptional concentration of state repression. Police brutality also occurred in Cairo, Alexandria, and the northern Delta, but without this remnant of tribal tradition, such acts went unavenged. Nevertheless, arrests and mistreatment silenced many who participated in Islamic development associations.

When the government took over local private mosques and appointed its own clerics, it deposited most of the *zakat* donations into government banks and decided where the little that remained was to be distributed. This resulted in less funding for local social services and a further loss of important welfare and charity activities. As successful programs and services closed for lack of funds and authorization, the government did not compensate by providing alternative services of its own. This made life even more difficult and precarious for Egypt's working classes. In addition to this, the political system prevented them from voicing their concerns or further pressuring officials for better treatment. Consequently, they felt even more powerless and more angry. Throughout the late 1980s and 1990s, the growing political gap between elite secular parties on the one hand, and both frustrated provincial professionals and the unorganized urban working classes on the other was filled by local Islamic populist associations that came to pose a serious challenge to the state.

IMF adjustments and economic constriction continued to generate poverty and anger at the bottom, and corruption and opportunism at the top, that together were eroding the state's ability to sustain solid economic growth, and wearing down the government's legitimacy in creating a national consensus. Increasingly, only the state's security forces were able to buoy the government's sagging authority. The Islamic opposition, unable to share power and alter the current configuration of economic policies and policy makers, turned instead to more militant means to achieve its political goals. In the end, the state continued operating much as before, yet ever fearful that once again, changes in the nation's top leadership would take place only after another funeral.

Rural workers had once moved into the cities in order to improve their lives and livelihood. But their ambitions soon proved equally unfulfilled, for the same state that had made the village unbearable was now making the city just as intolerable. Still culturally attached to the countryside, they joined those organizations that embodied the social practices and transposed values of rural life. In response to government repression, this discontented working class joined forces with a disenchanted professional class to demand the funding, services, and justice to which they felt entitled. The government in Cairo was slow to respond, and when it did, restrictions from the IMF prevented a satisfactory response. Egypt's weak financial and political position did not permit a better response.

## Conclusion

This essay has shown that fitting Egyptian agriculture into the mold of the Lewis model and its 'marginalist' economics ultimately resulted in breaking the cast. Simple calculations of presumed surplus labor ignored a more complicated rural division of labor than neo-Malthusian economists had imagined. The lived experience of rural workers was more down to earth, more intricate than these unsophisticated 'marginalist' models depicted. The Lewis model of expendable rural labor effortlessly transferred to unaffected urban employment sites was shown to be invalid by the workers' very own agency. It resulted in an agricultural economy that suffered from crop failures and production shortages, which in turn contributed to foreign exchange problems, trade deficits, balance of payment difficulties, debt crises, and eventually to limitations on Egypt's national autonomy.

Nor was the application of the Lewis model painless for rural and ex-rural workers, whose first form of refusal and resistance appeared in overcoming the inertia of social ties and commitment to village life and in leaving their home communities. Rural-to-urban migration generated considerable hostility, the attraction of bright lights notwithstanding. This anger occurred not in the countryside so much as in the city when, upon arrival, the bright lights dimmed. Opposition to the government first erupted in riots in January 1977, and later, after 1985, fueled the rise of Islamist radicalism and militancy. Had the state and its international patrons allowed incomes to rise when it increased prices, workers could have afforded the more expensive consumption and accumulated the savings that would have generated a domestic market for purchasing the machinery and goods that the industrial sector manufactured. Instead, the lack of legitimate channels for protest and dissent compelled workers to use other means to present their demands and demonstrate their opposition.

Both spontaneous riots and militant organizations recall the rural politics that ex-villagers left behind—first in the outburst of 'communal action' that reacted to immediate outside threats, then later in the establishment of 'secret societies' that defended the nation against dangers to a traditional way of life. The indignation and anger generated by growing unemployment, economic difficulties, and inadequate services in the city transformed these village practices into powerful urban weapons against the state. As the resentment and opposition from ex-rural workers and others steadily increased and multiplied, these weapons obstructed the nation's future economic development.

## Notes

1 Transplanting rice shoots from nursery to field also takes place in the summer, a task that competes with cotton pest control activities. In 1961, inadequate supplies of male and non-male labor generated low harvests here, too.
2 This timing coincides with the increase in governmental activity Donald Cole and Soraya Altorki observed for Egypt's Western Desert. See their chapters (6 and 16) in this volume.
3 For a list of those speaking out against the dismemberment of the ASU, see Waterbury's description [1978:253–54] of the parliamentary hearings that were held in September 1974.
4 Although the annual rate of rural-to-urban migration in Egypt actually declined from 2.1 percent in the 1960s to 1.9 percent in the 1970s, these represent percentages of the total national population which was in fact growing much faster than the amount of those moving from countryside to city. Indeed, the absolute number of rural migrants in Cairo alone practically doubled, from an annual rate of 702,000 from 1960 to 1970, to an

annual rate of 1,100,000 from 1970 to 1980. The percentage for the 1980s was even lower—1.7 percent—even while the absolute rate was still higher: 1,430,000 migrants yearly [Ibrahim 1996:100]. One should note that this migration is for Cairo alone and does not include provincial towns and cities like those in southern Egypt. Egyptian statistics measure migration as *inter*-governorate movements, mostly to Cairo, Alexandria, and the Canal cities. Yet I consider intra-governorate movements just as important, if not more so, where rural workers move within their governorate to its district towns and capital city. Even were workers to remain residing in the village, their absence from agricultural and migrant employment and their permanent engagement in construction result in the same problem of farm labor shortages, agricultural deficits, and national economic problems.

# References

Abdel-Fadil, Mahmoud. 1975. *Development, Income Distribution and Social Change in Rural Egypt, 1952–1970*. Cambridge: Cambridge University Press.

Ansari, Hamied. 1986. *Egypt: The Stalled Society*. Albany: State University of New York Press.

Barada'i, Husayn. 1972. "'Ummal al-Tarahil fi Misr." *Majalat al-'aml. Kitab al-'aml*, no. 103.

Bianchi, Robert. 1989. *Unruly Corporatism: Associational Life in Twentieth Century Egypt*. New York: Oxford University Press.

Brown, Nathan. 1990. *Peasant Politics in Modern Egypt*. New Haven: Yale University Press.

Cleland, Wendell. 1936. *The Population Problem in Egypt*. New York: Columbia University Press.

Commander, Simon. 1987. *The State and Agricultural Development in Egypt since 1973*. London: Ithaca Press.

Cuddihy, William. 1980. *Agricultural Price Management in Egypt* (Staff Working Paper no. 388). Washington DC: The World Bank.

The General Organization for Housing, Building, and Planning Research, the Steering Committee of the Ministry of Housing, and the World Bank. 1981. *Construction/Contracting Industry Study: Final Report* (3 volumes.). Cairo: Arab Republic of Egypt, Ministry of Housing.

Gilsenan, Michael. 1992. *Recognizing Islam: Religion and Society in the Modern Middle East*. New York: I. B. Tauris.

Goldschmidt, Arthur. 1988. *Modern Egypt: The Formation of a Nation-State*. Boulder: Westview.

Government of Egypt. 1961. *Parliament Records*. First Legislative Portion. Third Regular Meeting. Eleventh Session. May 8, 1961.

Hansen, Bent, and Karim Nashashibi. 1975. *Egypt: Foreign Trade Regimes and Economic Development*. New York: National Bureau of Economic Research.

Hansen, Bent, and Samir Radwan. 1982. *Employment Opportunities and*

*Equity in Egypt.* Geneva: ILO.
Hirst, David, and Irene Beeson. 1981. *Sadat.* London: Faber & Faber.
Hobsbawm, Eric. 1959. *Primitive Rebels: Studies in Archaic Forms of Social Movements in the Nineteenth and Twentieth Centuries.* New York: W. W. Norton.
Ibrahim, Saad Eddin. 1996. *Egypt, Islam, and Democracy: Twelve Critical Essays.* Cairo: American University in Cairo Press.
Lewis, W. Arthur. 1954. "Economic Development with Unlimited Supplies of Labour." *Manchester School of Economic and Social Studies* 22(2):139–91.
Little, Tom. 1965. *High Dam at Aswan: The Subjugation of the Nile.* New York: The John Day Company.
Nash, June. 1985. "Deindustrialization and the Impact on Labor Control Systems in Competitive and Monopoly Capitalist Enterprises." *Urban Anthropology and Studies of Cultural Systems and World Economic Development* 14(1–3):151–82.
Richards, Alan, and John Waterbury. 1990. *A Political Economy of the Middle East: State, Class, and Economic Development.* Boulder: Westview.
Sadowski, Yahya. 1991. *Political Vegetables: Businessman and Bureaucrat in the Development of Egyptian Agriculture.* Washington DC: Brookings Institution.
El-Togby, Hassan Ali. 1976. *Contemporary Egyptian Agriculture.* New York: The Ford Foundation.
Toth, James. 1991. "Organizing Migrant Workers: The Egyptian Experience." in Nicholas S. Hopkins, ed. *The Informal Sector in Egypt. Cairo Papers in Social Science* 14(4):66–77.
Waterbury, John. 1978. *Egypt: Burdens of the Past, Options for the Future.* Bloomington: Indiana University Press.
Waterbury, John. 1983. *The Egypt of Nasser and Sadat: The Political Economy of Two Regimes.* Princeton: Princeton University Press.

*Newspapers*

*al-Akhbar*
*al-Jumhuriya*
*al-Masa'*
*al-Wafd*
*The Wall Street Journal*

# 4

# Facing Structural Adjustment: Strategies of Peasants, the State, and the International Financial Institutions

RAY BUSH*

## Introduction

The Egyptian peasantry has been treated as passive and malleable by state officials throughout the twentieth century. The Government of Egypt (GOE) and officials of the international financial institutions (IFIs) have operated with very limited views of what constitutes agricultural modernization. Yet the state has failed to sustain economic and political development premised on the extraction of rural surplus. The reasons for that failure derive both from the inefficiency of state intervention and from the vibrancy and coping mechanisms of farmers (Brown 1990; Kazemi and Waterbury 1991).

Egyptian agriculture and farmers are now nevertheless at a turning point which has been provoked by economic adjustment in agriculture beginning in the mid-1980s, prior to the formal agreement with the IFIs in 1991. Policies of economic adjustment, liberalization, and privatization have accelerated the pace of rural change. Decades of resource scarcity, rural impoverishment, and GOE inefficiency have created conditions for an accelerated process of social differentiation and class formation. The most seriously affected are the poorest 90 percent of Egypt's rural population—those with access to less than five feddans of land—and the rural landless, for whom changes in the

---

* Research for this chapter was funded by the Economic and Social Research Council (UK) grant number L320253119 as part of a larger project "Coping With Poverty and the Environment: Social Transformation in Egypt." I gratefully acknowledge that support and research assistance from the late Mohamed Abou Mandour, Hassanine Kishk, Mohamed Hakim, Ibtissam el Gafaarawi and Lamia Raai.

Agrarian Reform Law, accelerating price increases on farming inputs (not matched by increases in farm gate prices), declining quality of land and water, and increases in the cost of education, health, energy and transportation, are all now challenging local strategies for coping with crisis.

Economists talk often about the benefits of reform, improvements in farm gate prices, new incentive structures, and the value of a new market structure (Fletcher 1996; Handoussa 1994; Handoussa and Potter 1991; Handoussa and El-Din 1995), yet the beneficiaries of these reforms are only the minority with access to wealth and power, able to shape and accumulate capital from the emerging markets.

Here I explore why the reform program is exacerbating rural inequality and failing to sustain early reported rises in productivity (Fletcher 1996). I also highlight that it is mistaken to place sole blame for Egypt's agricultural crisis upon the Egyptian state. In so doing, reformers have failed to break from recurrent false characterizations of Egyptian agriculture this century. I argue that the program of reform, built around ignorance of the Egyptian countryside, fails to recognize the complex way in which rural politics and the gender division of labor affect agricultural modernization. The IFI strategy is premised upon accelerating rural social differentiation. Inequality provides the social drive for betterment (and impoverishment) and in generating winners and losers in the adjustment game, landowners can shape production systems for export crops and reap the benefits of comparative advantage. Rural poor and landless, those dispossessed and marginalized by market deregulation, can either work in the countryside or migrate to towns in search of employment. This rationale is premised on economic growth and a local bourgeoisie which is prepared to invest rather than strip the countryside of its assets. Yet the linking of agricultural development and income generation to the vagaries of the external market has failed to deliver projected rates of growth. For example, the value of agricultural exports between 1989 and 1991 fell from $407 million in 1989/90 to $355 million in 1991/92 (Abou Mandour 1996). It remains easier for the IFIs and the state to promote a uniform and undifferentiated strategy for agricultural modernization than one premised upon detailed analysis of what rural production systems actually look like, what makes them work, and who is involved in the labor process.

The issues of local politics and political power, and the role of women in the countryside, are sidestepped by the IFIs and GOE, not only because this is the solution of facility but also because the Egyptian state, at different times, continues to be in a contradictory position vis-à-vis the adjustment process. President Mubarak has often noted publicly that it is the GOE, in his view, which controls the Structural Adjustment Program (SAP). Government 'ownership' of adjustment programs ensures that the IFIs can distance themselves from criticism for failure yet still enable them to claim approval for success. The GOE must accept responsibility for the slowness of the pace of reform, the continuing inability to deliver public-sector companies for privatization, and the debacle following the failures of private fertilizer companies and a revamped PBDAC[1] to ensure that the agricultural sector receives sufficient levels of inputs, infrastructure provision, and provide efficient market structures.

The state bureaucracy resists the scaling-back of its activities since this will curtail its power, and of course there are still many who see the efficacy of state intervention in economic and social life. Meanwhile, the ruling political party, and others in mainstream politics, are set to gain from aspects of economic liberalization. For example, some of these actors have significant interests in land ownership and will benefit from the liberalization of markets in land. Others own companies whose activities are linked to input provision, marketing and export of crops, as well as irrigation and water management systems.

It is only by recognizing the character of this contradictory relationship which the state has to economic reforms, and setting it alongside the actual relations of production and social reproduction in the countryside, that we can get a better idea of the struggles linked to SAP and the outcome of adjustment. This also informs our view of the way in which the uneven incorporation of peasants into Egyptian politics is shaped with considerable continuity from previous historical periods. Moreover, it raises the question why, despite criticism, it has thus far been impossible to build a coalition against liberalization in agriculture (in Egypt and elsewhere); and why the building of such a coalition will require a concerted attempt to unravel the nature of GOE tactics and strategy in relation to Egypt's peasantry. Discussions like this also raise questions as to the impact, or not, of political liberalization linked to market deregulation. For example, will the emergence of civil society be possible in Egypt's countryside? If political space can be created for this kind of liberalization, will it promote greater democratization-arenas for peasants to express themselves and their interests and to set their own political agendas independent of existing party provision?

The debates about SAP in agriculture are informed by previous discussions concerning the Egyptian countryside. In the next section, I suggest that the challenge of economic reform is now threatening the ability of small landholders to continue their conditions of rural existence, and that unless this is recognized there will be impoverishment and political mobilization to an extent not previously experienced in rural Egypt.

## Structural Adjustment and Agricultural Reform

The IFIs argue that distortions in the Egyptian economy are promoted by the dominance of an unproductive, rent-seeking state. The solution is for the state to retreat from economic activity. The IFIs argue that liberalization and privatization will allow Egypt to discover its true comparative advantage on international markets. They also argue that the increased inequality associated with the reforms will be offset by rising overall levels of welfare, and that the retreat of the state will allow a productive private market sector to emerge (IBRD 1992; USAID 1992a, 1992b, 1995). The IFIs also assert that reform will promote a more open and transparent policy framework.

It is possible to trace a continuous thread in the shared strategy between the agencies since the early World Bank report on economic management in Egypt during a period of transition, written in 1978 (Ikram 1980; IBRD 1992a; USAID 1990, 1992a, 1992b). The IFIs argue that there are essentially four main obstacles to agricultural growth in Egypt: (1) The legacy of inappropriate pricing policies; (2) an anti-competitive statist institutional framework; (3) the need for technological innovation; and (4) inefficient and ineffective management of land and water resources. Population growth is an additional worry for the agencies. The vehicle advocated by the agencies for reforming Egypt's ailing agricultural sector is the application of a neo-liberal market policy to 'roll back' the state from interfering in the allocation of resources.

The World Bank, globally, is in another phase of its declared strategy to promote the erosion of poverty. Yet there is little evidence of this in Egypt. That begs the question whether it is an intentional absence, or whether news of shifts in policy at the newly labeled 'listening bank' have simply not filtered down to Cairo. The influential IBRD report of 1992 did nevertheless argue that their strategy to revitalize agriculture needed to recognize "various characteristics of the rural economy" (IBRD 1992a:7). These included the importance of non-farming activities, the prominence of women in agricultural development, and the role of farm size in agricultural growth.

While the World Bank recognizes these three important dimensions to Egyptian agriculture, there is little evidence that they are included in policy formation. The IFIs, moreover, seem to focus solely upon farming in the Nile Delta, ignoring any regional variation in farming systems, relations of production, or gender division of labor.

The strategy which has followed from this characterization of Egypt's agricultural crisis by the IFIs is raising productivity and rural incomes by divesting the state of previous duties, supporting the introduction of new land tenure legislation, and promoting more efficient resource use by instigating methods of cost recovery. There seems to have been no recognition of the contradictory impact which the growth of landlessness resulting from rent increases may generate, not least as possible impetus to join the disaffected Islamist opposition. Nor does there appear to have been serious discussion of the impact that landlessness may have on the type of landlord system which could arise from the new legislation. We can only speculate whether the landlords emerging from the changes in land tenure will be 'efficient' capitalist farmers or unproductive 'rentiers,' many of them senior members of the ruling political party and other government officials. This latter outcome would of course also undermine any IFI expectation that 'rent-seeking' will automatically cease with the retrenchment of the state. Instead, it is likely that market liberalization will merely legitimate previously criticized practices of spoils politics or corruption *(al-fasad)* (cf. Gibbon, Havnevik, and Hermele 1993). There is already discussion in the Egyptian press of cases of corruption relating to the embezzlement of public funds, the use of public office for private gain, and of collusion between the public and private sector, effectively contradicting reformers' views extolling the virtue of even-handed market liberalization.

The problem of rent-seeking and market failure was graphically illustrated by the humiliating outcome for the GOE and the IFIs of the deregulation of the fertilizer sector. Contrary to the goals of the reform program, liberalization of fertilizer production failed to improve the efficiency of supply within the domestic market. Instead, deregulation led to the emergence of three oligopolistic producers who, first, dramatically increased the price of fertilizer from LE21 to LE90 a packet between 1994 and 1996, and who, second, preferred to export their production, benefiting from an export price of LE800 per ton, compared with the local delivery price of LE450 per ton. That rush to export led to serious supply problems in 1994 and 1995, which had a disastrous impact on agricultural production. Finally, at a time of increased IFI pressure on the GOE to deregulate the public sector more quickly, the inefficiency of deregulation in fact led the PBDAC to reactivate public-sector fertilizer provision. The price of chemical fertilizers rose by between 350 percent and 667 percent in the period 1987–93.

Table 1: *Fertilizer Price Increases, 1987–93 (LE per ton)*

| Type | 1987 | 1993 |
|---|---|---|
| Urea | 149 | 505 |
| Ammonia | 58 | 301 |
| Gypsum | 48 | 250 |
| Potassium | 57 | 380 |
| Superphosphate | 75 | 400 |

Source: Abou Mandour (1996)

The final thrust of the IFI prescription for reducing Egypt's rural crisis is the call for export-led agricultural growth (Baroudi, 1993). This provides the theoretical gloss of comparative advantage to the policies advocated by the agencies. The spokes of price incentives, technological innovation, especially green revolution technology, and private capitalist investment are intended to provide the strength and support for the hub of liberalization and the opening of the Egyptian economy to the international market. IFI discussion of export-led growth also provides an insight into what they understand by 'food security.'

According to the USAID, the shift towards the production of high-value, low-nutrition foodstuffs, especially for the European market, such as strawberries, fine green beans, peppers, and tomatoes, as well as grapes, peaches, and other citrus crops, could yield as much as $100–150 million a year up to 1996. (USAID 1992:2–3; interviews with USAID, January and April 1994). For the World Bank, "[i]n the new liberalized environment, farmers are expected to follow market signals that would lead them toward production of those crops in which Egypt has a comparative advantage" (IBRD, 1992a:39). (This argument is echoed elsewhere in this volume.)

The IFI strategy for agricultural transformation is for modernization by a process of commoditization. That process requires specialization and standardization to "reduce the variations, obstacles and *unpredictability* of natural environments" (Bernstein, 1990:6–7). This strategy is pursued without recognition of the specific way in which rural production is organized. There is continuity from previous periods when peasant concerns, such as poverty, access to the means of production, and environmental assets like land and water, were marginalized. The difference between the late 1990s and the policies of the preceding thirty years is that decades of rural underdevelopment have lead to a potential turning point in the contemporary period. A refashioning of the countryside has taken place in the 1990s which has undermined the viability of small holders and landless peasants and worker-peasants (those with jobs both in the countryside and in the town).

The modernization of Egyptian agriculture is now shaped to meet conditions of economies of scale and technical efficiency. These have led policy makers to promote standardization of farm units by reducing the viability of small holdings and changing tenancy rights. The standardization of rural units of production leads to increased social differentiation, which meets two needs of policy makers, one of which is unspoken. The undeclared aim is the need to sustain a rural social order which does not effectively challenge the status quo. While the reforms to tenant–landlord relations challenge the well-being of poorer peasants in a more serious way than ever before, they are offset by the rhetoric which maintains that price reforms compensate for increased costs of inputs and land, and that where they do not, they are the necessary, but unintentional, outcome of market deregulation which inevitably creates winners and losers.

The second aim of policy makers is to ensure that reforms which affect the size of peasant landholdings also facilitate their integration into the broader agricultural sector and the economy as a whole. Underpinning the new agenda for agricultural reform is the characterization of the way in which production is organized. The main focus of the reformers is the misconceived view of the farm unit as a single economic actor which performs the role of allocating its resources for goal maximization.

## Continuity and Change: The Politics of Agricultural Modernization?

The neo-liberal problematic for reformers dates back to 1991, but the role it assigns to Egypt's farmers is a familiar one. There is continuity in the way in which agriculture and the *fallahin* have been perceived by the state for more than a hundred years. The agricultural sector is valued for what it can deliver in terms of surplus. That surplus has been accumulated by state actors and large landowners, and it has also been used, albeit unevenly, for investment in non-agricultural activity. Indeed, the political leadership since Nasir has had the declared view that agriculture can provide both the capital necessary for industrialization and cheap food for a burgeoning urban proletariat.

With these declarations, it is perhaps all the more surprising that policy makers have shown only a limited interest in the welfare of the people who grow crops and produce agricultural surplus. Their concern instead has been with sustaining access to land and other assets for landed interests, rather than with the quality of life of the agricultural producers and rural communities (Brown 1991:218). There has also been a failure to examine relations of production in agriculture and in the social reproduction of rural Egypt. In this way, the state has neglected the real and self-perceived interests of rural producers and has focused instead on the nature of environmental assets (land and water quality) and also on the issue of agricultural production. When discussion of people has entered the policy making equation it has invariably been to criticize the rate of population growth, that is, to depict people as a hindrance rather than as an essential component of the rural productive process (inter alia, Lillian Craig Harris 1988; Fletcher 1996).

This dominant characterization of Egypt's peasantry is supported historically by the way in which farmers have been viewed and treated by state actors—as pawns that can be manipulated by public policy. That was certainly a feature of the early nineteenth century and the strategy of Mohammed Ali. His granting of land-use rights to clients and office holders culminated in a rural power structure which inhibited growth because of its bipolar rural class structure, with, on the one hand, a powerful minority landowning and merchant class, and, on the other, the vast mass of poor peasants.

Although the rhetoric of the Nasir reforms was to promote equity and social justice, the vehicle for this was a series of incomplete land reforms. Nasir remained rooted in the view that rural surplus was the main source of capital for industrial growth (El-Ghonemy 1992; Saunders and Mehanna 1986). Moreover, while trying to break the political power of the pashas, Nasir depoliticized the peasantry and frustrated rural radicalism (see Toth, this volume).

There has been a continuous thread in the way in which Egypt's peasants have been perceived by the state. This view is typified in the remarks of one seasoned commentator: "Conservatism and insularity are manifested in the social practices of villagers, in their attachment to old agricultural methods, in their patience in adversity that derives from religious belief" (Vatikiotis 1991:9). This view led the same commentator to note that, "Conservatism, isolation and a long established traditional social structure comprise what one might call Egypt's permanent 'Egyptianity'" (1991:9). This view of Egypt's farmers has done much to justify persistent state intervention in Egyptian agriculture. Yet while it is clear that the state has been formally central to the way in which agricultural production and distribution have been organized, it would be quite wrong to assume that the IFI rhetoric of 'the state' representing 'bad,' and 'private' and 'the market' representing 'good,' is anything other than ideological posturing. This convenient and oversimplistic characterization of the role of the Egyptian state in agriculture has very little explanatory power of the precise impact which the state may or may not have at any given time. It masks the importance of indigenous strategies of coping with state policies which has often reduced their effectiveness. It also underplays the significance of the ways in which peasants have preserved and transformed their local environments. The reification of 'the state' as political actor in agricultural production masks the social dynamics of production, the perceptions and nature of rural conditions of existence, and the dynamism of those relationships. These include patterns of coping with environmental change, cropping and employment patterns, gender division of labor, and the shifting of boundaries of social class and inequality.

The failure to understand these issues means that reformers are unable to understand the mechanisms for social change in the countryside. There is no excuse for that. There is a rich literature on the problems of agricultural modernization in Egypt, and the failure of the IFIs and the GOE to engage with the 'agrarian question' is sloppy and reflects, at best, intellectual laziness (Abdel-Fadil 1975; Radwan and Lee 1986; Adams 1986; Glavanis and Glavanis 1983; Seddon 1986; Hopkins 1988, 1993). The literature on the agrarian question has focused on the reasons for a perceived stalling of class polarization and rural proletarianization. Reasons for a delay in agricultural modernization, and for proletarianization, have included the idea that the rural bourgeoisie restricted the transfer of rural surplus to the industrial sector and that state intervention blocked class polarization. Additionally, Hopkins argues that a block to the universal spread of capitalist relations of production is a result of the persistence of peasant household producers. Hopkins argues that the household remains an economic unit despite the emergence of capitalist farmers, the increased use of technology, and the large rural population of free wage labor. He argues that while these processes may have undermined the viability of many peasant producers, the village has also retained and transformed many of its productive practices to accommodate outside forces like the state and the market (cf. Weyland 1993; Glavanis 1989).

The continued, yet transformed role of the household in agricultural production undermines IFI strategies for agricultural modernization. For while the categories of household and family production may be merely ideal types of family economic and social organization, they provide a way to examine the more complex and interrelated relationships between and within households and families and the specific way in which divisions of labor and social relations of reproduction operate. Such variations of the ways in which households may produce and reproduce themselves are not conducive to a uniform reform policy. If households are complex organizations, shaped by culture, social values, and concerns which are not determined merely by economic decisions, then reform strategies should be similarly nuanced and not structured solely around the view that individuals make decisions based on rational economic choice (Hopkins 1993:186; Elson 1996). Households follow various and complex strategies for production and reproduction and during periods of stress cope with economic and environmental forms of crisis. Patterns of coping and survival are shaped by different social relations of production, people's differential access to resources within households, and the village class structure: Patterns of survival also relate to shifts in the character of national economic crises, which in turn are linked with international capitalist restructuring—in the contemporary period, with SAP.

## The Limits of State Power

Government intervention has been a continuous theme in the fortunes and crises of Egypt's peasantry. Blaming governments for poor economic performance is also the central plank in the IFIs ideological assault on the state in developing countries. Yet it is insufficient to simply assert that rolling back the state will necessarily improve efficiency and productive allocation of resources. For this view of the state assumes more than it demonstrates—and it also now seems contrary to the revised Washington World Bank view that 'development without an effective state is impossible' (IBRD 1997).

The IFI criticism of state intervention in Egypt has assumed that the state is strong, efficient, well-maintained and staffed, and able to do what states in capitalist societies do well, namely sustain the economic interests of the dominant capitalist class within the shell of liberal social democracy (Hoare and Smith [Gramsci] 1971; Miliband 1969; el-Sayyid 1996). The IFIs also assume that there is a strong and vibrant bourgeoisie available and *willing* to fulfill functions vacated by the state. The IFIs make assumptions about the Egyptian state which are eurocentric and ill-founded. In short, the role of the Arab state has been 'over-stated' (Ayubi 1995). While it may be true to say that the Arab state is a 'fierce state' (some are clearly more fierce than others), it is not a 'strong state' (Hansen 1991). Its infrastructure power is weak. It is difficult for it to collect revenue like income tax, and it has failed to establish government by ruling through a bloc of social classes which govern with *legitimacy* and where elections may lead to regime replacement without the use of violence (Ayubi 1995; Beetham

1994). Indeed, contrary to the declared view of the IFIs that economic liberalization will be accompanied by political democratization, there seems instead, since 1991, to have been a tightening of political control by the ruling party which has reduced openness, transparency, and participation. The 1995 election, for example, was dogged by accusations and counter-accusations of political violence and vote-rigging, and since the early 1990s, tens of thousands of Egyptians have had even rudimentary human rights violated by the state in its strategy to crush Islamists.

There are two further issues which need to be considered with specific reference to the role of the state in managing agricultural development. The first is the extent to which the state is effective in implementing its policy changes in the countryside. The second issue is to question the extent to which the market is an effective mechanism promoting agricultural growth.

It is now established that while the "presence of the state in rural communities is palpable" it is also "unpredictable" (Berry 1993:46). In other words, it does not always follow that if a government promotes a particular policy it will achieve its desired outcome. Peasants, for example, are able to escape government control; they may, as they have done in Egypt, refuse to grow cotton in cotton-designated areas, and instead grow more financially rewarding crops. Such peasant defiance has a long history (Schulze 1991:179).

The mistaken view that state policy will always achieve its desired end does not account for the different interests of class actors or the structure of political institutions. In many ways, as Berry has commented in another context, the IFI prescriptions for agricultural reform "ignore the interplay between individual action and institutional structure, and ... imply that rural development programs have definitive consequences which can be clearly labeled successes or failures" (Berry 1993:45). The outcome of government rural development policy cannot be read from stated policy. It is more appropriate to try and explain the outcome of policy initiatives and their rural impact within the context of the nature of the particular economic and political struggles involved.

The IFIs and the GOE however, operate naively and with conceit. They assume that their policy initiative will automatically generate the declared aim. The IFIs go one step further. They are little concerned with the effect of the removal of government from economic activity as long as market deregulation is in place. The IFIs have shown very little interest in the actual consequences of market-driven formulas for rural people's well-being nor, more generally, in the type of agricultural growth and the winners and losers that market-driven formulas create.

Its rhetorical consideration for the poor and short-term losers from structural adjustment has become convenient camouflage for its ideological persistence with market-driven formulas and reinvigorating failed policies of comparative advantage. It has now become clear that the interests often served by the IFIs are those of the sanctity of free trade and the defense of US interests overseas. An example of this is the conflict described by Wade (1996) between Japan and the IBRD over the assertion by the Japanese state of the importance of government intervention for economic growth in East and South-East Asia.

Instead of arguing that Egypt's agricultural problems are the result of too much government intervention, it is more accurate to say that it is precisely government *neglect* of agriculture that has aggravated food security. Agricultural budgets have declined, and rural investment in effective rural infrastructure, including health and education, has not kept pace with urban demands on the state.

The second issue to explore further is whether the market will act as an efficient and effective conduit to facilitate agricultural growth. This is an issue which Tim Mitchell also examines in this volume. I have already commented on the market failure in Egypt's fertilizer sector since its deregulation, and yet despite that debacle the IFIs and the GOE pursue liberalization as the panacea for Egypt's economy. Nothing is said about what market forces represent, why they should ipso facto raise productivity—apart from a notion of increasing incentives. Nothing is said either about which social class will substitute, and with what effect, for the state or parastatal authorities in providing the necessary agricultural inputs and marketing after the state has relinquished its position.

## The Agricultural Reform Law

A major aspect of the IFI strategy for reform is the issue of the privatization of land tenure. Indeed, it is arguably now at the heart of the Egyptian reform process and will remain so as the outcome of increased rents for tenants newly deprived of legal rights of inheritance are felt across the country at the end of 1997. The new land tenancy act of 1992, Law 96, affects about two million tenants who support about 14 million family members. The law allows rents to be set by market forces after 1997, and allows landlords to set the length of tenancy agreements and to evict tenants who for decades have been legally secure on their farmland.

Changes in land tenancy at a time of economic retrenchment will create newly dispossessed farmers who will be unable to find employment as landless laborers or migrants: the macro-economy is simply unable to create employment for those pushed out of the countryside. That will especially be the case now. A Shura Council[2] report has detailed the disastrous impact that economic reform has had on reducing "average rates of growth of GDP per capita to less than 1 percent [1992–95] ... and that a third of the population now live under the poverty line" (cit. in *Al-Ahram Weekly* Dec. 19, 1996).

There is another major consequence of the new land act. There is little recognition in Egypt that it has promoted a new politics of opposition. Increased rural violence, attacks on landlords, rural demonstrations, and unrest have accompanied the new land act and yet they have been characterized by the GOE as either aspects of personalized anger against neighbors or the result of outside agents (*Al-Ahram Weekly* Aug. 28, 1997). As a commentator for *al-Sha'b* newspaper noted in early 1997, "The GOE had thrown a time bomb in the form of the new law in front of tenants. It had then retreated with fingers in its ears and with eyes closed in the hope that it would not witness an explosion." Yet the level of rural opposition, localized protest, and, in May 1997, a protest meeting near Tahrir Square in central Cairo by peasant activists is unprecedented in recent time (Land Center, 1997; *Al-Ahram Weekly* Jul. 10, 1997; *Le Monde* May 28–Jun. 3, 1997; *Afaq 'Arabiya* Jan. 16, 1997). The economic reforms have reinforced the class status of the large landholders, enhanced obvious and real sources of economic power, and polarized village and household access to resources.

The continuity in the way the Egyptian countryside is viewed by policy makers is therefore largely expressed in the way the state is viewed as an effective tool in the management of agricultural resources. Whether efficient or not and whether active or not, the state has been viewed as a major actor capable of intervention and shaping the lives of the *fallahin*. The actual efficacy of that intervention historically can be questioned, and in the process, it is necessary to discuss what type of intervention is necessary in the contemporary period, what social forces will replace the state if it eventually capitulates to IFI interests, and whether IFI interests are more desirable, or simply different, than the interests of state actors since Nasir.

One of the consequences of viewing the state as a major actor in agricultural development has been a preoccupation among policy makers in government and the IFIs that remedies for agricultural decline should focus on supply side issues. The IFIs, for instance, focus attention on issues of environmental accounting, pricing of environmental assets, reforming landlord–tenant relations, and promoting the liberalization of markets. These concerns largely ignore issues which underpin the *demand* for agricultural assets and which ensure viable and sustainable production. This preoccupation is not accompanied by an understanding of people's choices and expectations. The concerns of poor households for collective or communal action are ignored or undermined by market-oriented formula. That is because many poor people's incorporation into the market is marginal or uneven and is either not recognized by policy makers, or is not viewed as being equally as important as that of more powerful and economically stronger market participants.

## Egyptian Agriculture at a Turning Point

Egyptian agriculture is now at a turning point leading to accelerated rural social differentiation. This is the result of government policies of market liberalization which have undermined rural conditions of existence. Market liberalization is further monetarizing the rural economy in ways which will make dependence upon access to the cash economy the single most important vehicle for safeguarding standards of living. Moreover, it is increasing the pressure on women's time and labor power in a way still unrecognized by policy makers. The market economy, moreover, especially at a time of economic contraction, penalizes those with limited financial resources or access to cash.

Market-driven solutions to Egypt's problems neglect the existing ways in which rural people address their uneven access to resources. There is little attention paid to the way in which people cope with crisis and the impact of market failure. The GOE and IFIs have, among other things, used a simple and crude linking of poverty with environmental degradation. They have focused on notions of peasant ignorance, poor technological know-how, and the anachronistic view that common resource management undermines sustainability. Policy makers have failed to consider deeper issues of land reform and sociopolitical reform which might empower larger numbers of poorer households and enable them to shape and promote their own agenda for reform and draw on local expertise of agricultural production. Current strategy merely emboldens the larger landholders and absentee landowners with significant off-farm income-earning possibilities. This signifies the loss of the great opportunity offered by the current period of transformation, while, simultaneously, it poses political questions which the GOE is unwilling to engage.

Evidence from four villages in Lower Egypt confirms that the peasantry has considerable insight and awareness of what is being promoted by the reform process and that it is crucial for the reformers to listen to local farmers. Respondents were very much aware that the implications of market deregulation was threatening their abilities to withstand economic crisis. Data were assembled in 1992 to establish socioeconomic profiles of sixty households in two villages in Giza and Daqahliya. In 1994–95, further material from 120 households was gathered in Dumyat and Qalyubiya (for a detailed discussion see Bush 1995; and Bush et al 1996).

The villages were in contrasting locations geographically, and they varied in size, access to infrastructure, and in the type of agricultural activity. Common to the respondents' concerns were threats to improvements in health, education, and rural infrastructure. These threats resulted from the economic reforms and changes in tenure legislation. Respondents viewed the impact of economic reforms as the reason for the decline in village service provision. It was especially felt to be the cause of lengthening queues at health centers and a reduction in the actual delivery of services. However, respondents who either had access to more than two feddans of land or who had access to higher yielding land were more sympathetic to the economic reforms. Landowners, as opposed to tenants, recognized benefits and increased income-earning opportunities from market liberalization.

It is perhaps surprising, however, that following the initial enthusiasm for market liberalization, and the erosion of the influence of cooperatives and state provision, respondents stressed the importance of the need for a new set of structures to be erected to ameliorate the impact of recurrent market failure. (Similar responses were given to Abdel Aal, also in this volume, for Upper Egypt.) Tenants stressed the need for collective strategies to offset the impact of the most recent agrarian reform law and the need for a revitalized cooperative which did not simply allocate its resources to influential community members.

Since the increase in the price of agricultural inputs, peasant access to labor migration as a source to supplement farm income has become increasingly important in all villages. Access to off-farm income was crucial to sustaining coping strategies during economic adjustment. Yet the opportunities for work were declining as competition for employment locally and regionally intensified. Sources of access to cash as an indicator of rural inequality have assumed more significance in the last five years. While commentators of peasant differentiation have usually stressed access to land, its fertility and size, as well as the breed, sex, and number of livestock in accounting for levels of rural inequality, it is the increased incursion of the market into peasants' lives which has shaped the importance of their access to sources of off-farm income in their calculations for survival.

Table 2: *Summary of Survival and Livelihood Strategies*

| Strategies for increasing resources | Strategies for increasing the efficiency of current resources |
| --- | --- |
| Intensification of the labor process | Change in diets which may involve changes in food preparation |
| Greater participation of women in labor process | Reduced number of visits to health centers and fewer children in school |
| Increased petty-commodity production | Change in overall consumption patterns |
| Decline in cultural association | |
| Migration: local and international | Increased pressure on women's labor time |
| Asset sales | |
| Theft | |

At a village-wide level, villagers indicated the need for a strategy of economic growth and an ability to sustain the character of their livelihoods, which combined self-initiative with continued, but recast, government regulation. For example, in the Qalyubiya village, which suffered, like most in the Delta, from poor drainage, salinization, and rising water levels, villagers were frustrated by the lack of rapport with government. On their own initiative, villagers had sought the development of a new drainage station which required relatively small-scale financial assistance, but which the government refused to provide.

Villagers looked for a relationship with government which they hoped would draw on village mobilization around issues of environmental management and poor infrastructure provision. This would require the government to slow the pace of price increases for farm inputs and land reform and moderate the influence of powerful merchants who benefited significantly from market liberalization. In neglecting initiatives from villages, the GOE was clearly losing an opportunity to establish a legitimacy which in future it may need. The GOE was either making the choice that it preferred to continue the tradition of neglecting the majority of rural voices for greater sympathy with larger landholders, or it was making a non-decision. That non-decision supported the status quo of rural differentiation and furthered the goals of the IFIs in promoting agricultural modernization with empowered merchant entrepreneurs.

A major problem with the policies of the GOE and IFIs, especially at a time of considerable debate regarding environmental degradation, is their failure to recognize the importance of the varied and more sustainable farming systems, cropping patterns, and reliance upon the interrelationship between farming and wage labor employment used by resource-poor farmers. Among the resource-poor farmers and those neglected by the GOE and IFIs are women. Women are especially affected by policies of liberalization and the changes in the tenant–landlord relationship.

Women in all of our villages had become increasingly involved in the market economy in the last five years. Their labor time within and beyond the household increased as they were the main providers of caring and nurturing responsibilities with regard to health and education provision. As social services came under pressure resulting from government cutbacks and the implementation of user charges, women sought to find alternatives to state provision. As food prices increased, women spent more time in the market place searching for cheaper substitutes, especially for meat. As a result, household diets changed in response to increased prices. Women were increasingly drawn into the agricultural labor process, working longer hours on family farms and for wages on neighboring farms. Women also sought to extend income-earning opportunities through involvement in petty commodity production.

Debates about the marginalization of rural women have mostly gone beyond measuring the importance that privatization of tenure may or may not bring them: a priori privatization is unlikely to improve their conditions of existence. Instead, what is required are effective rights to land *utilization* for the women who cultivate the land. While many commentators repeatedly express the view that there is no discrimination against women when it comes to their ability and legal rights to hold land, it is clearly the case that the ability of women to retain access to the financial output of the land, as well as adequately to have a say in the agricultural labor process, is shaped by household patterns of power and more generally the balance of forces characterizing the specific local gender division of labor.

While the World Bank has made considerable progress by including women in debates about rural development, it continues to make a fundamental error. It locates the problem for rural women as the non-recognition of their work. Yet the issue now is surely not the need to focus on the important contribution which women make to a myriad of different and often interrelated activities, and how men have benefited more than women from this (Boserup 1970), although this bears repeating. Rather, the issue is *how* women are incorporated into those activities, with what consequences and opportunities, and how they impact on decision-making structures.

Reformers in Egypt fail to recognize that there is the need to understand the persistent exclusion of women from some economic activities as well as to offer a proper understanding of what women's inclusion in the labor process actually means in terms of their conditions of existence. Elson (1994), among others, has noted that particularly with SAPs, policy makers are only concerned with monetary aggregates of the productive economy and not with human resources, issues of the reproductive economy, or indicators of health, nutrition, education, and skill development. This male bias of policy makers disregards women's work because it is not seen to be part of the economic matrix which constitutes national accounting figures. Women's work is not accounted for because much of it takes place on family farms and constitutes income-earning within the household. Moreover, women are assumed to be able to withstand the rigors of adjustment to agricultural 'modernization' because women's time is seen to be infinitely flexible—a persistent view in the representation of women in Egyptian rural life. There is, moreover, the overall assumption that economic policies of the IFIs are gender-neutral, yet they fail to recognize the differential way in which women enter into economic market relationships. IFI policies assume all economic relationships are relationships which are solely structured around tradable activities, and they therefore fail to recognize the range of activities which women do and the way in which they are incorporated into market activities (see also Dasgupta 1993:305–42).

## Conclusions

Farmers and peasant society in Egypt have been viewed for more than a hundred years as mere supports for more privileged sections of the Egyptian social formation—rural landowners, government officials, and an urban elite. This unequal treatment is not unique to Egypt, of course. Nevertheless, the Egyptian case of rural underdevelopment now offers an acute illustration of a turning point promoted by structural adjustment. While the agreements between the IFIs and the GOE for reforming Egypt's political economy are not without tension, in agriculture they have been driven with a particular pace and endeavor not repeated in other sectors. This pace of reform now threatens to promote a disjuncture from the past which may prove difficult to heal. A consequence for the aggressive modernization of Egyptian agriculture, which has been structured by a particularly crude and simplistic model reminiscent of 1950s US modernization theory (Mitchell 1995), will be to generate a hitherto unheard of pattern of vulnerability and rural dispossession.

This characterization will no doubt be criticized for being dramatic and alarmist. It may even be challenged by some of my assertions and evidence regarding the ability of peasants to cope and transform their own environments. It is nevertheless the case that even the most resourceful economies suffer transformations which radically alter previous methods of coping and promote impoverishment from which it is impossible to recover. Recently, Dasgupta (1993) has given a substantial defense for preventing the catalysts of destitution by policy makers who have little understanding about rural decision-making. Commenting on how policy makers reify private property rights as the vehicle for sustainable rural development he noted that:

> It is not difficult to see why common-property resources matter greatly to the poorest of the rural poor in a society, or therefore, to understand the mechanisms through which such people may well get disfranchised from the economy even while in the aggregate the society is enjoying economic growth (Dasgupta 1993:291).

These mechanisms of dispossession include shifts in population size and density and also predatory governments and 'thieving aristocracies.' Dasgupta is led to the view that:

> Resource allocation mechanisms which do not take advantage of dispersed information, which are insensitive to hidden (and often not-so-hidden) economic and ecological interactions ... which do not take the long view, and which do not give a sufficiently large weight to the claims of the poorest within rural populations (particularly the women and children in these populations) are going to prove environmentally disastrous (1993:294).

There is always the hope that even the IFIs will recognize that their policies lead to impoverishment resulting from accelerated social differentiation, and that while they view this as a desirable outcome for the acceleration of agricultural transformation because of the incentive structures that it creates, the strategy may only yield such benefits in the short term. Increased levels of productivity, as witnessed in Egypt since 1992, have not been sustained and have not met the desired IFI targets. Is it still too much to ask now that even the IFIs and the Ministry of Agriculture will start listening to peasant voices about strategies which are sustainable and which promote greater rural empowerment, thereby ensuring peasant commitment to a successful agricultural strategy for the next millennium?

## Notes

1 The Principal Bank for Development and Agricultural Credit, the main agricultural bank in Egypt.
2 The Shura Council is the upper house of the Egyptian parliament.

## References

Abdel-Fadil, Mahmoud. 1975. *Development, Income Distribution and Social Change in Rural Egypt (1952–1970): A Study in the Political Economy of Agrarian Transition*. Cambridge: Cambridge University Press.
Abou Mandour, Mohamed. 1996. "Economic Reforms in Egyptian Agriculture." in R. Bush, S. Bromley, M. Abou Mandour, eds. *Al-Iqtisad al-siyasi li-l-islah fi Misr: al-Bank al-Dawli wa-al-zira'a w-al-fallahin*. Cairo: Al Mahrusa Publishing House.
Adams, R. 1986. *Development and Social Change in Rural Egypt*. Syracuse NY: Syracuse University Press.
Ayubi, N. N. 1991. *The State and Public Policies in Egypt since Sadat*. Reading: Ithaca Press [Political Studies of the Middle East, 29].
———. 1995. *Over-stating the Arab State*. London: I. B. Tauris.
Baroudi, Sami. 1993. "Egyptian Agricultural Exports since 1973." *The Middle East Journal* 47(1):63–76.
Beetham, D. 1994. "Conditions for Democratic Consolidation." *Review of African Political Economy* 21(60): 157–172.
Bernstein, H. 1990. "Agricultural 'Modernisation' and the Era of Structural Adjustment: Observations on Sub-Saharan Africa." *Journal of Peasant Studies* 18(1)1:3–35.
Berry, S. 1993. *No Condition is Permanent: The Social Dynamics of Agrarian Change in Sub-Saharan Africa*. Madison: University of Wisconsin Press.
Boserup, E. 1970. *Women's Role in Economic Development*. New York: St. Martins Press.
Bush, R., S. Bromley, and M. Abou Mandour, eds. 1996. *al Iqtisad al Siyasi li-l-islah fi Misr: al-Bank al-Dawli w-al-zira'a w-al-fallahin*. Cairo: Al Mahrusa Publishing House.
Bush, R. 1995. "Coping with Adjustment and Economic Crisis in Egypt's Countryside." *Review of African Political Economy* 22(66):499–516.
Brown, N. 1990. *Peasant Politics in Modern Egypt: the Struggle against the State*. New Haven and London: Yale University Press.
———. 1991. "The Ignorance and Inscrutability of the Egyptian Peasantry." in F. Kazemi and J. Waterbury, eds. *Peasants and Politics in the Modern Middle East*. Miami: Florida International University Press. pp. 203–21.
Dasgupta, P. 1993. *An Inquiry into Well-Being and Destitution*. Oxford: Clarendon Press.
El-Ghonemy, M. R. 1992. "The Egyptian State and Agricultural Land Market 1810–1986." *Journal of Agricultural Economics* 43(2): 175–190.
El-Sayyid, M. K. 1996. "Bureaucracy and Political Change in Egypt." in Dan Tschirgi, ed. *Development in the Age of Liberalization: Egypt and Mexico*. Cairo: The American University in Cairo Press. pp. 109–17.

Elson, D. 1994. "Micro, Meso, Macro: Gender and Economic Analysis in the Context of Policy Reform." in I. Bakker, ed. *The Strategic Silence, Gender and Economic Policy*. London: Zed Books in association with the North-South Institute. pp. 33–45.

Fletcher, L., ed. 1996. *Egypt's Agriculture in a Reform Era*. Iowa: Iowa State University Press.

Gibbon, P., K. Havnevik, and K. Hermele. 1993. *A Blighted Harvest, The World Bank and African Agriculture in the 1980s*. London: James Currey.

Glavanis, K. 1989. "Commoditization and the Small Peasant Household in Egypt." in K. Glavanis and P. Glavanis, eds. *The Rural Middle East: Peasant Lives and Modes of Production*. London: Zed Books. pp. 142–62.

Glavanis, K. R. G. and P. ·M. Glavanis. 1983. "The Sociology of Agrarian Relations in the Middle East: The Persistence of Household Production." *Current Sociology* 31(2):1–109.

Handoussa, H. 1994. "The Role of the State: The Case of Egypt." *Working Papers Series* 9404. Cairo: Economic Research Forum.

Handoussa, H. and G. Potter, eds. 1991. *Employment and Structural Adjustment: Egypt in the 1990s*. Cairo: American University in Cairo Press.

Handoussa, H. and H. K. El-Din. 1995. "A Vision for Egypt in the Year 2012." Paper presented to workshop on *Strategic Visions for the Middle East and North Africa*. Gammarth, Tunisia, 9–11 June.

Hansen, B. 1991. *The Political Economy of Poverty, Equity, and Growth*. Oxford: Oxford University Press

Harris, L.C. 1988. *Egypt: Internal Challenges and Regional Stability*. London: Routledge and Kegan Paul. Chatham House Papers, 39.

Hoare, Q. and G. N. Smith, eds. 1971. *A. Gramsci, Selections from the Prison Notebooks*. London: Lawrence and Wishart.

Hopkins, N. S. 1988. *Agrarian Transformation in Egypt*. Boulder: Westview, and Cairo: American University in Cairo Press.

———. 1993. "Small Farmer Households and Agricultural Sustainability." in M. A. Faris and M. H. Khan, eds. *Sustainable Agriculture in Egypt*. Boulder and London: Lynne Rienner. pp. 185–95.

Ikram, K. 1980. *Egypt: Economic Management in a Period of Transition*. Baltimore and London: Johns Hopkins University Press.

International Bank for Reconstruction and Development. 1992a. *Arab Republic of Egypt: An Agricultural Strategy for the 1990s*. Report number, 11083-EGT. Washington and Cairo.

———. 1992b. *World Development Report*. Oxford: Oxford University Press.

———. 1997. *World Development Report: The State in a Changing World*. Oxford: Oxford University Press.

Kazemi, F. and J. Waterbury, eds. 1991. *Peasants and Politics in the Modern Middle East*. Miami: Florida International University Press.

Land Center. 1997. *Activity Report*. Cairo: Markaz al-Ard. (translated from Arabic).

Miliband, R. 1969. *The State in Capitalist Society*. London: Weidenfeld and Nicolson.

Mitchell, T. 1995. "The Object of Development." in Jonathan Crush, ed. *Power of Development*. London: Routledge. pp. 129–57.

———. 1991. "The Representation of Rural Violence in Writings on Political Development in Nasserist Egypt." in F. Kazemi and J. Waterbury, eds. *Peasants and Politics in the Modern Middle East*. Miami: Florida International University Press. pp. 222–51.

Radwan, S. and E. Lee. 1986. *Agrarian Change in Egypt: An Anatomy of Rural Poverty*. London: Croom Helm.

Saunders, L. W. and S. Mehanna. 1986. "Village Entrepreneurs: An Egyptian Case." *Ethnology* 25(1):75–88.

Schulze, R. C. 1991. "Colonization and Resistance: The Egyptian Peasant Rebellion, 1919." in F. Kazemi and J. Waterbury, eds. *Peasants and Politics in the Modern Middle East*. Miami: Florida International University Press. pp. 171–202.

Seddon, D. 1986. "Commentary on Agrarian Relations in the Middle East." *Current Sociology* 34(2):151–72.

Toth, J. 1991. "Pride, Purdah, or Paychecks: What Maintains the Gender Division of Labor in Rural Egypt?" *International Journal of Middle East Studies* 23:213–36.

USAID/Egypt. 1990. "Agriculture Briefing Paper." Cairo.

———. 1992a. "Country Program Strategy FY 1992–1996: Agriculture." Cairo

———. 1992b. "Country Program Strategy FY 1992–1996: Environment." Cairo.

———. 1995. "The Egyptian Agricultural Policy Reforms: An Overview. Agricultural Policy Conference." Cairo, 26–28 March.

Vatikiotis, P. J. 1991. *The History of Modern Egypt from Muhammad Ali to Mubarak*. London: Weidenfeld.

Wade, R. 1996. "Japan, the World Bank, and the Art of Paradigm Maintenance: The East Asian Miracle in Political Perspective." *New Left Review*, no. 217:3–36.

Weyland, P. 1993. *Inside the Third World Village*. London: Routledge.

## Interviews

Officials at the Ministry of Agriculture and Land Reclamation, April 2, 1994.
Officials at the PBDAC, April 6, 1994.
Officials at USAID, Cairo, January 18, 1994; April 7, 1994.
Officials at US Embassy, April 3, 1994.

## Newspapers

*Al-Ahram Weekly* Dec. 19, 1996
———. Aug. 28, 1997
———. Jul. 10, 1997
*Le Monde* May 28–Jun. 3, 1997
*Afaq 'Arabiya* Jan. 16, 1997

# II

# CULTURAL REPRESENTATION: IDENTITY

# 5

# Hegemony in the Periphery: Community and Exclusion in an Upper Egyptian Village

REEM SAAD*

## Introduction

This paper attempts to describe and characterize aspects of social organization that affect and inform different modes of communal and collective action in an Upper Egyptian village. In particular, I wish to stress the fact that the idea of 'community,' which is so central to both anthropological and development discourse, has no local equivalent. Rather than 'community,' we find various forms of collective identity which, in turn, correspond to different forms of collective action. The place that 'the village' and 'the community' (and of course the village community) have occupied in both anthropological and development literature has tended to obscure this multiplicity of levels of belonging and identity, the various bases of stratification and differentiation, and the many ways in which villagers associate for purposes of collective action. While it is true that there is nothing specific about the Egyptian village when it comes to this issue, and that, in general, sociological categories never quite fit the social reality they seek to describe, the situation requires special attention when such categories provide the basis for outsiders' actions and intervention. With the present pattern of development characterized

---

\* This chapter is a result of field work carried out over the period of one year (Jan. 1996–Feb. 1997) in a village in the Governorate of Aswan. This work was done as part of a project entitled, "Organization of Work and Production and the Role of Participation in Qina and Aswan," sponsored by DANIDA, Cairo. I am also grateful for the help I received from everyone at the Idfu Primary Health Care Project (DANIDA): the project sociologists, Ms Wafaa Bahr and Mr Shukri Sayed, who generously shared with me their findings on Manara, and especially the project advisor, Ms Anette Cramer, who provided me with a candid interview and who graciously received my critical approach.

by a growing role for NGOs and development agencies carrying out interventions at the village level, the idea of 'the community' gains special importance and acquires a concreteness it does not always possess in reality. From 'community,' which is usually taken to correspond to the visible, physical boundaries of various human settlements, development practitioners tend to deduce homogeneity and a unified collective interest. This paper would like to address the possible consequences of such assumptions.

This paper uses ethnographic evidence from the Upper Egyptian village of Manara[1] in order to illustrate the multiple forms of collective identity and corresponding forms of collective action. The second part of the paper highlights one aspect of the interaction between village and outside in the context of the politics of community development. The specific focus is one activity undertaken as part of the Primary Health Care Project initiated in the village by DANIDA.

## Bases of Collective Action in Manara

Manara, which is located in the Governorate of Aswan, is an administrative center ("mother village") hosting the Village Local Popular Council which serves not only Manara, but also another small village and a number of satellite hamlets existing mainly at the edge of the desert which borders the village from the west. A census carried out by the DANIDA Primary Health Care Project estimates the number of inhabitants in the core area at around 6,500.[2] However, the population estimate according to the Manara Village Local Popular Council is 12,000. This discrepancy is due to the inclusion of the other village and the satellite hamlets.

Manara is a place which shares a number of characteristics with the rest of the Egyptian countryside, but also has a number of local specificities generally found in Upper Egypt. Among the general characteristics it shares with the rest of rural Egypt is the decreasing importance of agriculture as a primary occupation and the corresponding increase in the number of government employees. This is a village of small landowners and government employees. Although the majority of the inhabitants are landowners, this is not their primary occupation. According to both DANIDA[3] and the Village Local Popular Council statistics, the number of people who state their main occupation as government employee exceeds that of those who list agriculture. There is no history of large landowning in the village, and at present the largest holding is ten feddans. In general, holdings are evenly distributed, with the average holding being between one and two feddans. Sugarcane, a lucrative cash crop, predominates.

One feature which Manara shares with the Qina/Aswan region, is the key role that 'tribalism' plays in the social organization of the village. Tribalism here has several meanings and it is important to examine the different ways in which this notion is employed, not only because of its significance in understanding the dynamics of collective action and identity in this particular village but also to stress the great variations that exist in the practice of tribalism in Upper Egypt. The tribal violence which marked the 1995 parliamentary elections, particularly in one village in the northern part of Qina governorate, has reinforced the wide-spread idea that tribalism is synonymous with a premodern form of social organization that is rigid and fanatic.

In Manara, the term *'gabila'* (tribe), has an obvious presence and is indeed considered the major way in which the village is organized. Yet, what we see is mainly a large number of families with no obvious genealogical or ancestral link. The village is divided into five geographical/residential parts that are simply called the 'fifths' *(akhmas)*. These have tribal names which are supposedly linked genealogically to the smaller units which comprise them. Each fifth is in turn divided into a number of *durub* (singular, *darb*), which could mean streets, but here are really quarters or clusters. The *durub* are subdivided into *buyut* (houses/households/families). It is interesting that it is these smallest units (which are in practice extended families) which people refer to as 'tribes.' However, people describe the general way in which the village is organized as following 'the tribal system.'

Although people claim that the five clusters which form the village are five major tribes of which they are all descendants, I have not met anyone who can confirm the actual link between his/her extended family and the encompassing structure. This is certainly different from other cases, where tracing and proving genealogical links is constantly practiced, and where tribal elders normally keep detailed written records tracing ancestry and descent.

The *darb*, which normally comprises three or four *buyut*, functions as an intermediate structure between the family and the village. It was once described to me as the 'middle branch' *(al-far' al-wasat)*. It is primarily the place where events pertaining to the individual take on a public or communal significance. Each *darb* has a guest house *(madyafa, khayma,* or *diwan*—all used interchangeably) which is built and used collectively by the male residents of the *darb*. Each *darb* has a treasurer who is responsible for collecting the *firda* (literally, levy). The *firda* is levied on each married man, who pays LE1 every month for the purpose of the routine maintenance of the *khayma*.

The guest house is opened on occasions such as receiving condolences in cases of death and congratulations in cases of marriage or pilgrimage. Residents of the *darb* have obligations toward one another on such occasions. For example, in the case of the death of any member, the rest of the families are responsible for providing meals for the family of the deceased at the guest house for the duration of the condolences period (usually one week). In cases of return from pilgrimage, members of the *darb* share in buying a calf to be slaughtered and offered at the guest house for those coming to congratulate the returning pilgrim. In the latter case, the money collected monthly is usually supplemented by extra donations from the married male members of the *darb*. In all these occasions, in addition to the two Muslim feasts, male elders of the different families of the *darb* are expected to be present at the guest house to receive visits from the rest of the village. Visits are especially expected from men of other *durub* of the same fifth.

The *darb* is thus more than a neighborhood. Despite the fact that the residents are not necessarily connected by kinship ties, the *darb* is a significant unit of communal solidarity which provides a framework both for regulating reciprocity within the unit and structuring links with the rest of the village. Although the types of collective action that take place within the *darb* cannot be considered 'participation' as normally understood by development practitioners, the form and structure of regulating responsibility at this level provide the model for mobilization at a larger scale intended for organizing and implementing different types of actions motivated by a shared interest, rather than individual and social everyday events.

*Participation in the Periphery*

'Participation' in Manara centers mainly around the organization and implementation of 'self-help' projects at the village level. In this respect, Manara is an exemplary village. Over the last decade, the village raised money and implemented a number of projects. The most important of these are the building of an impressive three story Azharite school (primary, preparatory, and secondary), the establishment of a preparatory school, and the provision of the building for the telephone exchange and post office.[4]

Implementation of these projects naturally requires a high degree of coordination and mobilization. The way in which these projects are decided upon and implemented follows the 'tribal' and residential pattern in this village. In relation to these projects, it is not the *darb* but the 'fifth' which is the operative unit for collective action. Each 'fifth' has two or three leaders, who are generally elders with prominent positions in society. The leaders of the five 'fifths,' together form

## Hegemony in the Periphery 117

the informal leadership of the village. They meet in one of the public places, either the mosque or the school, and the village residents are expected to abide by their decisions. After a decision is made to go ahead with a certain project, the cost is estimated and it is the duty of the treasurer to collect the money (also called *firda*) from each married man in his 'fifth.'

The projects are conducted in coordination with the relevant government departments through the mediation of representative institutions of the village, either the Village Local Popular Council or the community development association (CDA). It is usually the case that the informal leadership of the 'fifths' includes members of these institutions. This leadership is usually referred to as *'al-kubar bitu' al-balad,'* meaning the big men of the village, which, especially to outsiders, usually connotes their knowledge, wisdom, and command of respect.

Although the people of Manara are generally proud of their ability to coordinate such activities and regard their village as a model one in terms of 'self-help,' this issue is at the same time a source of a pervasive feeling of bitterness. People fear that the fact that they can 'look after themselves' will induce more neglect from the government; that they will be abandoned rather than rewarded for their activities. In these circumstances, it is indeed reasonable and legitimate that residents of Manara often asked why they had to pay for the same thing that other villages get for free. This sense of injustice was heightened after the construction of two schools started in a neighboring village with a smaller population using allocated local government funds. The only explanation (and it is a plausible one) that Manara villagers could give for this discrimination is that a resident of that village was a member of the Shura Council.[5]

In response to this neglect, Hagg Ahmad 'Ali told me, "We are like orphans. We have no one to care for us." This statement is significant in two ways. Although told at the occasion of the news of the building of the two schools, it expresses a profound sentiment that goes much beyond that particular incident. In Manara (as in most other parts of rural Egypt), people have a deep sense of 'peripheralization.' They constantly complain, and rightly so, of the fact that resources and services tend to be concentrated in Cairo, and that they are neglected and forgotten. An example which may seem trivial but one which presents a constant reminder of this situation has to do with TV channels. In Manara, only channels one and two can be received, while in Cairo, viewers can choose from among nine channels, including the regional channel of Aswan which Manara villagers do not receive.

The second significant aspect of Hagg Ahmad's statement concerns his position. He is the President of the Board of Directors of the Agricultural Cooperative, and is, by Manara's modest standards, a large landowner. He is also one of the leaders of the Isma'iniya 'fifth' and is a respected village elder. In short, he is by all measures a representative of 'the village elite.' What is worth noting here is that the condition of being on a periphery, and the deep bitterness engendered as a result of this is something that people experience and express as 'a village' rather than a particular class or identity group. Elite and non-elite are largely in the same boat.

This situation should clarify why the notion of 'urban bias,' most commonly associated with the work of Michael Lipton,[6] is still useful, despite the many criticisms leveled against it. Lipton's main argument is that the major struggle in developing countries is between the rural classes and the urban classes, and that development policies have been extremely biased in favor of the urban classes, resulting in both inequity and inefficiency. In a critique of Lipton's approach, Keith Griffin criticizes the use of this notion as the core of one's analysis. He argues that "urban bias is essentially a geographical or residential notion. It views conflicts over policy as arising primarily from where people live (rural versus urban areas) rather than, say, from the economic sectors in which they derive a livelihood (industry versus agriculture), or from their position in the class hierarchy."[7] But even from a sheer residential viewpoint, living in rural areas entails a number of material consequences and disadvantages that are shared among rural inhabitants regardless of their class position. Rural areas have much fewer facilities and worse amenities, and a feeling of neglect and peripheralization is shared among rural dwellers. This feeling contributes both to a unified rural world view and to a sharpening of an 'us–them' distinction based on this very residential category rather than any explicit class-based distinction.

## *Differentiation in Manara*

It is with this in mind that I now proceed to discuss the elements of differentiation and heterogeneity that exist in Manara. Contrary to the situation in other parts of rural Egypt, landownership does not play a significant role in a horizontal stratification in Manara. Instead, what seems to be the crucial determinant of elite power is a high bureaucratic position and/or access to powerful outsiders. A high-ranking government position is not only a source of financial security, but is also a source of power. It is a main source for important contacts, especially outside the village, and a much needed asset necessary for solving a variety of problems that villagers face in their everyday life.

These could range from interceding with representatives of the police or the Village Local Popular Council, to turning a blind eye while a new house is being erected on agricultural land, to the biggest favor of all which is helping someone to get a government position.

Nevertheless, while high-ranking government employees are potentially powerful patrons, not all of them actually are. Bureaucratic power is normally consolidated with access to one or more of the local political positions which are fiercely fought over. Seats on the Village Local Popular Council and the Board of Directors of the Community Development Association are supposedly elected positions. They are normally filled by high-level bureaucrats, and provide their holders with considerable clout. Given the local election system, which is primarily based on party lists, and given that the ruling National Democratic Party is the only one that is active in the village, access to the Village Local Popular Council depends mainly on having the right contacts with the party leadership at the district level. There is, however, an informal process of primary selection which takes place at the village level and attempts to ensure that 'candidates' represent the different parts of the village.

Membership of the CDA board, while a less glamorous position than that of the Village Local Popular Council, has recently become a source of considerable power, mainly because of the decentralization of foreign aid projects and donor preference to deal with NGOs rather than governments.[8] CDAs which are supposedly grassroot voluntary organizations formed in almost all villages are closely supervised by the Ministry of Social Affairs. In Manara, as in most other places, CDAs are now the link between donors and local communities. Despite the low membership fee, the general assembly in Manara has few members. Annual elections do not take place regularly, and the present board, formed exclusively of high-ranking government employees, has been serving for a number of years without change.

Apart from the bureaucratic elite, a further element of heterogeneity in Manara concerns the existence of a number of what could be termed 'marginal groups.' These are: the Copts, members of the Bani Hilal tribe, the family of potters *(al-fakharaniya)*, and al-Hiwan, who are predominantly fishermen. Apart from the Copts, who are original inhabitants of Manara and consider themselves (and are considered to be) among the 'people of the village' *(ahl-al-balad)*, the rest of these groups consider themselves and are considered as outsiders.

Despite the fact that the ethnic diversity found elsewhere in the Aswan region is not evident in Manara in its typical form, and that these groups cannot be considered as 'ethnic groups' in the obvious sense, their place and position in the social structure of the village stresses their difference vis-à-vis a homogeneous and dominant majority. Members of each of these groups live together in different parts of the village, which are referred to by the names of the respective groups. They are predominantly landless, and each group has a distinct professional specialization. The most obvious sign of their different position vis-à-vis the majority is that there is no intermarriage between any of these groups and the rest of the village. They are partially integrated in the village mainly through sharing in *darb* and other collective obligations. However, contrary to the rest of the village residents, all four groups primarily identify with larger structures that exist outside the village. The following is a brief description of each of these groups:

### Bani Hilal

In Manara, there are only four families of the Bani Hilal tribe, which is dispersed over the three southernmost governorates of Egypt: Suhag, Qina and Aswan.[9] They identify with other members of the tribe, whose central organ is the Association of the Sons of Bani Hilal located in Aswan city. They traditionally specialized in carrying and selling water and in livestock breeding, a profession they still practice today. Alternatively known by the derogatory name *'jamas,'* members of this group are practically outcasts. They are regarded and treated with the greatest contempt and are regularly referred to as "lowly and of lowly origins" *(watyin wa asluhum wati)*. It is only with the greatest difficulty that I found someone who would introduce me to them, and when that person finally agreed, he left me at the door of one of them, rudely refusing the owner's polite invitation to enter and have a glass of tea.

### The Hiwan

There are a number of Hiwan families who now work mainly as fishermen and traders. Their name derives from a profession that they no longer practice, which is treating snake and scorpion bites. They are considered as outsiders to the village.

### *'Fakhraniya'* (potters)

The potters are one extended family of twenty-five members. They do not identify themselves as a tribe but are related to and identify with other *fakhraniya* in various parts of Qina and Aswan, having especially strong links with those of the Idfu region. Their links with others were expressed to me by one of the women as follows: "We are dispersed all over the place, but at important moments we are one people *(sha'b wahid)*." This mainly refers to events of deaths or marriages where the other members of the group are informed of such events by letters or telegrams.

## Copts

There are around thirty Coptic families in the village, which has one church attended also by Copts of neighboring villages. Copts in Manara all share in one *khayma* (guest house). They consider themselves, and are considered as, *ahl al-balad*, and they talk of themselves as *'Basali,'* a label distinguishing the original inhabitants from those whose origins lie elsewhere. However, Copts in this village identify themselves primarily as Copts, and share with other Egyptian Copts a wide-spread minority sentiment of being second-class citizens. Apart from mixing with the Muslim majority at places of work and in schools, there is very little dealing between Copts and Muslims. Social obligations (especially paying condolences) are observed, and relations are generally cordial but superficial. They are part of the Isma'iniya 'fifth' and pay *firda* for collective projects. To an outside observer, this balance of segregation and integration seems to work as a guarantor of peaceful coexistence. However, I was reminded of how volatile this situation is upon discovering a few months after my first visit that there were two major incidents of violence against Copts, both following rumors that Copts were expanding their public space. The first incident was when the church was completely demolished by a crowd of Muslims leaving the Friday prayers in the mid-1960s, and the second involves sabotaging and blocking the construction of the Coptic guest house, accompanied by physical attacks on Copts by masked youth in the late 1980s. But it is equally important to mention that this second incident was recounted to me by some Muslim friends. They told me how the whole village was distressed, and how everybody cooperated in order to track down the attackers. These were finally discovered and were severely punished by their elders.

### Collective Interests and Elements of Exclusion

The condition of the periphery influences the role of the elite of this village. On the one hand, they take the initiative and take on the tasks and responsibilities associated with carrying out collective projects in the village. On the other hand, while much of their action answers to collective interests, they also control resources and resource distribution to a great extent.

The building of the Azharite school (or simply Al-Azhar, as it is referred to in the village) provides an example for this dynamic. The impressive three-story building is the pride of the village and is very often cited by its residents as a testimony to their ability to accomplish great things. However, this is not just a place for providing education for the village children but an opportunity for providing much sought after government employment for the village youth, whether as teachers or as workers and janitors, according to their level of education. The village leaders who carried out the organization and implementation of the project were also responsible for negotiating with and contacting Al-Azhar authorities. As a result, they had control (or at least a strong influence) over the distribution of new jobs. In fact, there is a wide-spread story in the village that jobs were reserved for the sons and relatives of the village leaders involved in the project. Apologists of the village leadership express the view that it is a 'right' they acquired in return for volunteering to organize the work. Most of the villagers, however, see things differently, resenting the village leaders' monopoly over such valuable resources.

For members of marginal groups, the case was even worse. The exclusion of the marginals is not an issue to which the dominant majority would give any thought. Apart from the Copts, who were by definition excluded from getting jobs at an Islamic institution, it was unthinkable that a member of the Bani Hilal or the Hiwan would receive such a coveted post. The fact that jobs were not given to the marginals may not in itself constitute strong evidence for the exclusion of marginals, since their numbers are small and the vacancies are in fact limited. However, the significant aspect for members of these groups was that the Azhar jobs were symbolic of the fact that they were excluded. It is here that the term *'kubar al-balad'* takes on the meaning of powerful versus powerless, and expresses a sense of remoteness from decision-making circles, as opposed to the meaning associated with respect, wisdom, and knowledge in which it is usually used to describe village-level decision-making processes.

Before ending this discussion, it is important to present another usage of the concept of 'tribalism' which came up in a very significant context. Manara is one of fourteen villages *(nag')* which make up the region of Busayliya, and they consider themselves to be 'one people,' and identify themselves as *Basali* vis-à-vis other groups within the governorate of Aswan. There are several versions of, what could be considered as, a 'myth of origin,' which considers the fourteen villages as branches of one genealogical tree. It is interesting to note that the Copts of Manara also consider themselves as descendants of the same tree.

This regional identification informs 'participation' and mobilization at a higher political level. Most importantly, it determines the voting behavior in parliamentary and Shura Council elections. Although the Busayli identity is sometimes referred to as 'tribal,' the more common term used is that of Busayli nationalism *(al-qawmiya al-Busayliya)*, and it is often used in jest.

From the above, we can get a sense of the variety of forms of collective action that take place in the village. It is part of a continuous social process that is at once a result and an instrument of reproduction of various sentiments of collective identity. These actions span a range extending from the extended family to the mini-region of the supposed tribal origin. Although the village as administratively defined provides a significant marker of communal borders, it is by no means the only one. The village displays a social organization which accommodates marginality, but only according to the terms set by the dominant strata of the dominant group.

## The Development Project

The presence of both national and foreign development agencies involved in different types of projects is now a fact of life in most Egyptian villages, and Manara is no exception. In 1996, Manara was chosen as one of fourteen villages targeted by the DANIDA Primary Health Care Project (PHC) operating in the district of Idfu. The project is mainly concerned with training local health trainers and with upgrading water and sanitation facilities in target villages. According to the project advisor, the criterion for choosing the villages in which to work was CARE's recommendation that project villages should have active CDAs. The Project Document which guides the activities of the implementation unit states that all activities have to be carried out through the village CDA, on the assumption that it is a grassroot organization representing the interests of the community. The project stressed the role of the community in defining its needs, rather than imposing a ready-made package on the village. With 'participatory development' becoming the standard approach adopted by international NGOs and development agencies,[10] "it is the community itself that decides ...," as the currently much-used saying goes.

Development projects that involve potential financial gains for selected beneficiaries, particularly those involving loan schemes, have been severely criticized for accentuating divisions within society, and creating a fertile ground for nepotism and corruption.[11] To the credit of the DANIDA project, it does not involve such inevitably disruptive high stakes. It is, however, interesting for this very reason. Even for a project which has not resulted (and is not bound to result) in a major restructuring of power relations, we find that the very process of linking with the target 'community,' and especially the need to establish mediating agents, not only fulfills the agency's need to enter the community but also provides these 'mediating agents' with the service of establishing them as the 'legitimate representatives' of the 'community,' and enhances their power vis-à-vis the village through their actual or perceived access to the resources of these powerful outsiders.[12]

My purpose here is not to evaluate the viability or effectiveness of the DANIDA PHC Project. Rather, I am going to use one activity initiated by this project as an example of the influence outside agencies could have on the communities they work with, and to present some of the unintended consequences of interventions based on certain assumptions about 'community' and 'participation.'

### Integration and Segregation: The Street Naming Project

The activity I would like to focus on is that of putting up signs with street names in the village. This activity was chosen as a way of letting the village know of the project and with the purpose of mobilizing the villagers and ensuring their participation.[13] I was surprised when I arrived in Manara after a week's absence to find all the houses with numbers on them, and the streets with blue street signs characteristic of major cities. The street names where those of Islamic figures. When I asked one of my acquaintances in the village about the new signs, he laughed, and said sarcastically, "We've now become exactly like Alexandria, overnight!"

When I asked at the PHC Office who had chosen the street names, I was told by the project sociologists, "We did not decide on the names. It was the community itself which chose them,"—community here meaning members of the CDA.

The street naming activity, in my view, was not a very fortunate way of acquainting the villagers with the project, nor did it bring about the intended mobilization and participation. To start with, it introduced a confusing message as to what the project was about. It is an activity whose results were much more visible and concrete than those of the main activities of the project pertaining to health would be. The overnight appearance of house numbers and street signs indeed made people aware of DANIDA's presence, but it also led many villagers to start calling DANIDA 'the numbering company.'

At another level, and as mentioned before, the acute sense of peripheralization that pervades the village heightens the value of contact with outsiders. As mentioned earlier, this project was not about the disbursement of money nor does it entail any substantial material benefit for particular individuals. Members of the CDA were asked to choose a number of the village youth to hang the signs in return for LE1 per sign. This was soon to be a cause of wide-spread discontent in the village. People started saying that the CDA members gave the 'jobs' to their children, and a feeling of exclusion set in.

Perhaps the most significant aspect of the consequences of the street naming activity was its symbolic component, that is, the names themselves that were chosen for the streets.[14] Even before we examine the names, it has to be said that the idea of 'streets' was itself imposed. The pattern in which the village is laid out and organized, with its various divisions and subdivisions was known to all its residents. The five 'fifths' have names, and so do the *durub,* and the smallest units, the *buyut.* All of these are both social and geographical entities. They are clusters or quarters rather than 'streets' in the linear sense, associated with urban order and making the anonymous city space usable. One learned, high-ranking bureaucrat, thinking that this would please me, expressed his enthusiasm for this move as it would "bestow a civilized look on the village."

As mentioned above, with very few exceptions, the streets were named after Islamic figures. This was regarded by DANIDA sociologists as a good thing as it would evade the issue of tribalism and fights between families as to whose name would be used on the sign. It was regarded as a supra-tribal and non-controversial solution. Nevertheless, it is a reflection of the dominance of the Islamic discourse in today's Egypt, and of the belief of the rural middle class (in this case represented by the CDA members) of what is a respectable, official, and sober thing to do. As a further sign of being sophisticated and learned, the CDA members chose the names of some obscure figures that are not familiar to the majority, and a couple of them difficult to pronounce. A perplexed farmer, who found difficulty in pronouncing the name of his own street, asked me plaintively, "Are we supposed to know all these names by heart?"

Furthermore, the Islamic names did not prevent all rivalry among families. One interesting objection to the street names came from one of the prominent men of the village, Hagg Sa'd, who is a member of the Village Local Popular Council and has a long-standing rivalry with the CDA board. The street in which he lives was named after one of the Prophet's followers. He was outraged and had a public row with two members of the CDA board for not naming the street after his family. His argument for that rested on the fact that all the land which comprised the so-called street belonged to him and his family. "There should be respect for private property," he said.

A more significant consequence of the new names was that

marginal groups felt further marginalized. Contrary to my initial assumption, Copts were not antagonized by the fact that the streets had predominantly Islamic names. For them, segregation by religion was the natural order of things. Rather than differentiating between groups on the basis of tribes and families, such as other villagers did, the Copts regarded the rest of the village as simply 'Muslim.' They had another reason for being resentful, though. The street in which they lived was called "al-Khur" (simply meaning the low land), and it was not changed. Copts I talked to did not object to the Islamic street naming, but to the fact that their street was not changed into "the Copts' street." Not obtaining the sign that they wanted was a reminder of their lack of voice and power, reinforcing their feeling of marginality and minority.

What applied to the Copts applied also to the other marginal groups, especially the Bani Hilal and the Hiwan tribes. The Bani Hilal lived on one side of the street where the Village Bank is located. The street is now called "Bank Street." Given the perceived low status of the Bani Hilal by the rest of the village, there was no suggestion that the street where they lived should be named after them. In this case, there was no need to place an Islamic name that would overrule the tribal claim. What is important, however, is that members of the Bani Hilal used to call the street the Bani Hilal. Similarly, the Hiwan called the areas in which they lived by the names of families from within the tribe, while others in the village referred to these areas by the name of the *darb*.

I am quite sure that multiple place names will continue to be used and that the new names nailed to the village walls will not easily become the primary way in which villagers identify various parts of their village. However, before the signs were fixed, there could have been more room for accommodating diversity and for the marginals to influence the integration–segregation balance. The development project, and specifically the street naming, tended to impose an outside order which also accentuated in various ways the hierarchies in the village.

## Conclusion

I have tried here to provide a close and critical look at the politics of 'development' and 'participation' in one village. I showed the link between elements of the social structure and organization on the one hand, and the different types of collective action based on these on the other. In Manara, the mobilization pattern that operates for the reproduction of family, neighborhood, and communal ties provided the model for collective action at the village level, resulting in the successful accomplishment of a number of self-help projects. Residents of Manara are indeed to be congratulated for their initiative and good organization. But why should they have to engage in self-help initiatives? What does the idea of self-help really mask? And why do tax-paying citizens have to pay for such basic services and infrastructure as school buildings and telephone and post-office buildings, whereas their counterparts in upper-class Cairene quarters never have to 'participate' in this manner? The wide-spread feelings of peripheralization and neglect possessed by Manara villagers are largely justified. It is perhaps this shared experience of deprivation which contributes to a sense of a 'village community,' and is also crucial for an understanding of the nature of rural elites. The building of the Azharite school is a good example of how collective interests are served and differentiation reproduced, simultaneously. Community is, as Robertson says, an 'uneasy truce' rather than an embodiment of altruism.[15]

With regard to communities, Robertson also argues that "... divisions of interest and identity may be latent but may erupt into open conflict when some new activity, such as a development project, presents itself."[16] The street naming project reinforced and brought to the surface latent trends of polarization. Members of the bureaucratic elite were confirmed as the legitimate representatives of 'the community,' while the voiceless and marginal were further pushed to the sides. This situation was a direct result of DANIDA's need for local mediators (elite members) linking them to their target community. These do not only represent the community vis-à-vis development agencies, but simultaneously act as representatives of the agencies vis-à-vis their communities, a position which boosted their power and was instrumental in reinforcing inequalities.

The intention of this chapter was neither to malign this particular project, nor to do away with the idea of 'community' altogether. I was trying to unpack some of the terms taken for granted, such as 'tribalism' and 'participation,' and refer them to concrete instances. Moreover, this chapter drew attention to the various strands that constitute the dynamics of power in present-day rural Egypt.

## Notes

1 This is a pseudonym.
2 The Idfu PHCP Community Unit.
3 The Idfu PHCP Community Unit, p. 11.
4 It has to be said that those social groups who will obviously not benefit from a particular project are exempt. For example, the Christians did not

participate in the building of Al-Azhar school, and the landless are not expected to participate in a proposed project for building a fertilizer warehouse. The Azharite school system is a parallel educational system at all levels under the supervision of al-Azhar University and the Ministry of Religious Endowments *(awqaf)*.

5 The Shura Council is the partly elected, partly appointed upper house of the Egyptian parliament.
6 Lipton 1977.
7 Griffin 1977, p. 108.
8 See Abdel-Rahman 1993.
9 For further information on Bani Hilal and their position in the social structure of Upper Egypt, see Abnoudi 1988, pp. 7–43.
10 The ambiguity and lack of agreement as to what 'participatory development' actually means has been noted by many (see Watson 1996, p.1; and Hinton 1996, p.28). Helen Watson also notes how "... the concept has suffered the typical fate of all things which undergo the transformation from periphery to center, the change of status from something progressive, new and exciting to that of the accepted, familiar and established." (Watson 1996, p. 2).
11 See, for example, Sholkamy 1988.
12 Alternatively, this situation could be compromising, as described by Rachel Hinton (1996, p. 31) for a Nepalese refugee community in which refugee representatives were held accountable by their community for actions undertaken by relief agencies and on which the representatives had no real control, and sometimes not even information.
13 According to the project advisor, street naming was not the decision of the Idfu Implementation Unit but was set out for them in the Project Document following recommendations of a planning mission.
14 For an interesting analysis of street naming as a tool of political manipulation, see Faraco and Murphy 1997.
15 Robertson, p. 146.
16 Ibid., pp. 146-47.

## References

Abdel Motaal, Doaa. 1995. "Reconstructing Development: Women at the Moqattam Settlement of the Zabbaleen." unpublished MA thesis, American University in Cairo.

Abdel-Rahman, Maha Mahfouz. 1993. "Local Self-Help—Local Self Defeat: A Study of the Potentials and Drawbacks of Community Development Associations in Upper Egypt." unpublished MA thesis, American University in Cairo.

Abnoudi, Abdel-Rahman. 1988. *al-Sira al-Hilaliya*. vol. 1. Cairo: Akhbar al-Yawm.

The Idfu Primary Health Care Community Unit. 1996. *Participatory Village Assessment: Final Report*. Idfu: DANIDA.

Faraco, J. Carlos Gonzalez and Michael Dean Murphy. 1997. "Street Names and Political Regimes in an Andalusian Town." *Ethnology* 36(2):123–48.

Griffin, Keith. 1977. "Review of Michael Lipton, 'Why Poor People Stay Poor: Urban Bias in World Development.'" *Journal of Development Studies* 14(1):108–10.

Hinton, Rachel. 1996. "NGOs as Agents of Change? The Case of the Bhutanese Refugee Programme." *Cambridge Anthropology* 19(1):24–56.

Lipton, Michael. 1977. *Why Poor People Stay Poor: Urban Bias in World Development*. London: Temple Smith.

Robertson, A. F. 1984. *People and the State: An Anthropology of Planned Development*. Cambridge: Cambridge University Press.

Sholkamy, Hania. 1988. "'They are the Government:' Bureaucracy and Development in an Egyptian Village." unpublished MA thesis, American University in Cairo.

Volpi, Elena. 1995. "Development and Community Organization: Informal Garbage Collectors in Cairo." unpublished MA thesis, American University in Cairo.

Watson, Helen. 1996. "Introduction." *Cambridge Anthropology* 19(1):1–4.

# 6

# The Northwest Coast: A Part of *Rural* Egypt?

SORAYA ALTORKI and DONALD P. COLE*

## Introduction

During the course of joint field work in 1986 on change and development in Saudi Arabia (Altorki and Cole 1989), a university-educated man in his late twenties questioned one of us as to whether we considered his community, 'Unayzah, to be a village or a city. Neither of us had any doubt about 'Unayzah's status as an urban community. It had an estimated population of seventy thousand, was the capital of a local emirate, and had a large *suq* that served the community and a wide hinterland, as well as numerous government offices and schools, banks, clinics, hospitals, and so on. 'Unayzah was definitely not a village but a city and, indeed, had been a city for at least a couple of centuries. The young 'Unayzah man readily agreed that his community had been a great city in the past. "But I think 'Unayzah is now a village," he insisted.

What was the message behind this apparent contradiction? On one level he was simply stating the obvious—that Riyadh, Jeddah, Dammam, and other Arabian cities have grown much more rapidly than 'Unayzah. They have left it behind as a calm, quiet community that is still relatively homogeneous. However, from city to village implies what we understood to mean a downgrading of 'Unayzah's relative importance within the context of the wider and changing Arabian culture, society, and economy. Thus, his question and his answer provided what we considered to be an oblique but, given the situation, a politically charged comment about a specific process of

---

* This chapter is based on field work conducted in 1993 and 1994 in Marsa Matruh, al-Qasr, and other areas of the steppe west of Marsa Matruh, with appreciated support from the American University in Cairo and the Ford Foundation. The material presented here has been written up in greater detail and is published by the American University in Cairo Press. See Cole and Altorki, 1998.

change that, since the 1950s, has left 'Unayzah more a victim than a beneficiary of development.[1]

More recently, we engaged in a second joint research project on change and development in another part of the Arab World—in the arid steppe of Egypt's northwest coast, in the Governorate of Matruh. In 'Unayzah, strict gender segregation had meant that we conducted our joint field work separately; but in Matruh we were able to sit together with men in their *majalis*, or 'gatherings.' Thus, we often found ourselves with men who were not that different from those the anthropologist had sat with in 'Unayzah, although the Arabian men were more *hadar*, 'urban,' in background and tended to be much better educated than the Egyptians, who were from the *badiyah*, 'Bedouin.' And, as had happened in Arabia, the issue of the categorization of a community came up during discussion in a *majlis*.

One of us asked about the definition of *'badiyah.'* A man of about thirty years old replied, while a brother, several paternal cousins, and an elderly paternal uncle listened in apparent agreement. He is from a prominent extended family from Awlad 'Ali, resides near Marsa Matruh in al-Qasr settlement, holds a technical diploma in electricity studies, is a government employee in Marsa Matruh, runs a small dairy project in al-Qasr, markets fresh cow's milk in Marsa Matruh, and has a share in the ownership of a farm in al-Qasr. He said,

> The *badiyah* is the desert. Al-Qasr is rural *(rif)*. It is urban *(hadar)*. It has electricity. This change does not mean that the *badiyah* is over, finished. For us here in al-Qasr, the *badiyah* is not over because we are outside of the city. And it will be a long time before the city links up with us.
>
> In the *badiyah*, people are generous. When you come to them, they give you food without your asking for it. The *badiyah* will continue. Of course, the *badiyah* might change and disappear unless we make an effort to preserve it. Suppose someone had a piece of land and decided to sell it and he got a lot of money for it. This person might decide that he doesn't have to take the opinion of other, of older people, anymore. People watch television and see films that we are not used to. This makes things change a great deal.
>
> We also have those [from the *badiyah*] who now live in the city. In Marsa Matruh. They are of us. But their language has changed. Their food has changed. Their clothes have changed. We eat bread and rice; but they eat differently. Weddings have changed. Marriage has changed. But the Arabs in Marsa Matruh still apply the *'urf* ["customary law"]. The people always like to return to the *'urf*.
>
> The *badiyah* is dying. Life is changing and the *badiyah* is changing. Since they intermarry with others, Awlad 'Ali will probably not be here any more. My uncle married a woman from Alexandria. When I speak to my cousins, they answer in the dialect of Alexandria.

here any more. My uncle married a woman from Alexandria. When I speak to my cousins, they answer in the dialect of Alexandria.

The *badiyah*, as this man tells us, is both an environment or habitat (the desert, *sahara*) and the people who live there. Yet, those who are of the *badiyah* are much more than just desert-dwellers. They are people who adhere to and make use of the *'urf* and who are generous. They are associated with linguistic, sartorial, and culinary markers. They are also threatened: by men marrying non-*badiyah* women; by land sales; by television and its 'strange' films. In seeming contradiction, the *badiyah* is changing, dying, and will continue, while the *badiyah* settlement of al-Qasr is rural and also urban.

Anthropologist Gerald Obermeyer conducted research in al-Qasr in the early 1960s and wrote of the community as having an "in-between quality" and as being a "sedentary Bedouin society which is not quite tribal and not quite peasant." He attributed this ambiguous status to change that had begun around 1900 and that was increasingly drawing al-Qasr "into the political and economic life of the Egyptian national community" (1968:18). Obermeyer, no doubt, never imagined that thirty years after his field work a young man from a family he knew well would echo his ambiguous characterization of al-Qasr, except that in the 1990s "tribal" and "peasant" are replaced by "rural" and "urban."

Obermeyer also wrote of al-Qasr as epitomizing "a post-tribal or pre-peasant stage of social change" (ibid.:vi). Thus, he seems to have expected al-Qasr to become a peasant community, a transformation that presumably would involve major sociocultural assimilation. But to become what? A part of one version or another of rural Egypt? By contrast, the young Awlad 'Ali man in al-Qasr indicates change but not assimilation from this to that. He suggests a bricolage, a complex mix of elements that are, or appear to be, contradictory but that coexist in the culture and the society as lived by individuals, at least in his part of the northwest coast. This mixture, of course, is not idiosyncratic, although differences exist among individuals and between genders, the old and the young, the sellers' of land and the buyers of land, and so on.

Based on her extensive and rightly well-known research among Awlad 'Ali in Burj al-'Arab,[2] anthropologist Lila Abu-Lughod introduces issues of identity related to Awlad 'Ali, and Bedouin generally in the northwest coast. She writes that after the 1952 revolution the Egyptian state's goal concerning these people changed "from political control to assimilation," as the government became interested in "integrating the Bedouins into the Egyptian polity, economy, and national culture." However, after about twenty-five years of numerous achieved." She further writes that Awlad 'Ali still contrasted themselves in strong distinction from "the Egyptians or peasants." They knew something of national and international politics, but "their passions are aroused only by tribal affairs." Moreover, "[b]lood, in the sense of genealogy, is the basis of Awlad 'Ali identity" (Abu-Lughod 1987:42–44).

Based on our research among other Awlad 'Ali in another part of the northwest coast, we agree that "assimilation has not been achieved;" and we recognize as 'factual' the various aspects of identity mentioned above. We stress, however, that changes have occurred and continue, although we do not view this change as either assimilation, or hybridization, to use a more fashionable terminology. Also, our interpretation underscores the existence of strong ties between the region's local people and other people and institutions in Egypt.

We address, in the companion paper in this volume, aspects of economic change that, in our interpretation, show powerful and changing links between the regional and wider national and inter-Arab economies. Meanwhile, we focus here on selected features of socio-cultural change that reflect changing relations between Awlad 'Ali and wider Egyptian domains. Specifically, we briefly summarize (some) Awlad 'Ali presentations of self through the use of oral history, indicate how Awlad 'Ali shaped a major sedentarization program to their own wishes and perceived needs, and show interactions of state and tribe within the context of Egypt's local government system.

For this presentation and analysis, it is important to note that Awlad 'Ali are the most prominent local people in the northwest coast, but they are not the only people there. Also existing within the region's society are other Bedouin, many migrant settlers from the Nile Valley, and others. If the scope of reference is the northwest coast, then our concentration on Awlad 'Ali reflects a bias—but of time and space, rather than a myopia. Moreover, the 'Egyptian' other from a northwest coast perspective lacks the homogeneity and hegemony often attributed to it. As an Awlad 'Ali senior man put it, "The *fallahin* are like us; but those who come from Cairo are strange." Of course, the rest of Egypt—like its northwest coast—has a complexity, the details of which far exceed the boundaries of this paper.

## Awlad 'Ali's Presentation of Self Through History

Awlad 'Ali men, in our experience, usually introduce themselves as a people by noting the arrival in the northwest coast of Muslim ancestors from Arabia—usually the Bani Sulaym "in the fourth century people by noting the arrival in the northwest coast of Muslim ancestors from Arabia—usually the Bani Sulaym "in the fourth century after the hijrah" or, more vaguely, with the *fath al-Islami*, "Islamic conquest." These grandfathers, they say, went on to Libya and then to 'green' Tunisia, Algeria, and al-Andaluz before returning to settle down (as nomadic pastoralists) in eastern Libya.

Then, "recently, about three hundred years ago," Awlad 'Ali found themselves exhausted from a war with the Harabi (close agnates) in Libya. They received an invitation, or request, from the Jumi'at in the northwest coast to come to their aid against the Hanadi (also close agnates). So, Awlad 'Ali returned back into Egypt, defeated the Hanadi, and subsequently provided protection to the Jumi'at without requiring payment of tribute.

Awlad 'Ali then rapidly engaged as active participants in events that mark the beginnings of modern Egypt. As Arabs, "known to ride horses and to fight wars," Awlad 'Ali fought against the French infidel invaders in battles near Alexandria and at the Pyramids of Giza. Soon, thereafter, they assisted Muhammad 'Ali Pasha and defeated the Mamluks and/or, according to another version, helped him put down a rebellion in Upper Egypt. They say they fought alongside Ibrahim Pasha during his campaigns in the Sudan and then accompanied him to Arabia to assist the Ashraf, "because Egypt did not want the Wahhabiya."

Muhammad 'Ali Pasha, widely considered the founder of modern Egypt, is often mentioned by Awlad 'Ali. Indeed, one senior told us that his father had told him that Muhammad 'Ali Pasha was a Turk only because of his upbringing. He was really an Arab, he said, whose father "or maybe it was his grandfather" came from al-Sagia al-Hamrah (in Libya), from among the Masamir. A powerful tribe of *murabtin bi-l-baraka* status,[3] the Masamir are matrilateral relatives of the patrilineage of the senior who recounted this connection. Thus, Muhammad 'Ali Pasha becomes not only an Arab, at least from the point of view of these Awlad 'Ali, but a distant relative.[4] Nonetheless, "Muhammad 'Ali Pasha tricked the Awlad 'Ali," a senior in his nineties told us. The Pasha sought to "reward Awlad 'Ali for their support by exempting them from military service; but this was a grave mistake for Awlad 'Ali." Keeping them out of the army, he explained, meant that Awlad 'Ali were cut off from involvement in the affairs of state, which contributed to their marginalization within contemporary Egypt.[5]

Although the Sanusiya religious movement is known to have been active in the northwest coast during the late nineteenth and early twentieth centuries (see Evans-Pritchard 1949), Awlad 'Ali we know state administration into the area, they skip to Khedive Abbas Hilmi II at the beginning of the twentieth century. They like him a lot, we were told, this Abbas whom "the English banished." They say he introduced development *(al-'amar)* to the region: the railroad, police stations ("with Arab police and with Sudanese *hajanah* ['camel corps'] with scars on their cheeks"), and schools. He had maps drawn up and also visited the area—the first time ever for a ruler of Egypt since Alexander the Great. "Abbas, he was the one who opened up the desert." Meanwhile, the British appeared on the scene and offered to create a province *(wilayah)* separate from Egypt for the "people in the desert." Awlad 'Ali rejected the offer: "Our grandfathers said, 'No. We are Egyptians.'"

Awlad 'Ali continue on with long stories about World War I battles in the area and about their support for Muslim and Arab causes, especially as organized from within Libya by Sayid Ahmad al-Sanusi. In 1919, they did not rise up alongside Egyptian peasants and urbanites to counter the British, because the battle at that time, Awlad 'Ali say, was in the Nile Valley and no longer in the desert as it had been in 1915 or so. Colonialism figures prominently in their discourse, as elderly seniors describe in minute detail how the colonial–military administration of their desert territories operated. They also speak of their resistance to colonialism. For example,

> There were many English people here, and the Arabs stole from them. And it was not bad to steal from them. We hate the English. And the person who steals from him is not a thief. In fact, we tell him "thank you."

Also, in the words of another,

> We did not benefit from the English. That was colonialism. And no benefit can come from colonialism. The English had a grand political strategy: make use of the Arabs but let them keep their customs and don't interfere in their affairs as long as they stick to their own business. The English kill you without your noticing it.

Then, there was World War II, which persists as a nightmare for those who experienced forced relocation and loss of all or almost all property and possessions. Many suffered serious wounds and/or lost loved ones from the ubiquitous land mines left behind by the foreign armies. Finally, the rebuilding of shattered lives after the war begins the current phase of their existence in the northwest coast. This phase, we were told, especially began in 1959 when military administration of the area was replaced by a civilian local government system.

## An Interpretation of Awlad 'Ali Presentation of Self

Barring Muhammad 'Ali's ancestral ties to the Masamir and al-Sagia al-Hamrah, all of the above happenings are parts of recorded history. However, Awlad 'Ali who recounted them to us did not read about them in books. "This is what our fathers and grandfathers told us," we often heard them say; and some, perhaps all, of this history exists in their poetry.

This brief outline of what they told us shows that the northwest coast and its people are certainly not without history. Human life there has been much more complex than is suggested by images from the outside of tribes or of nomadic pastoralists rhythmically migrating according to the dictates of the seasons. However, we present this material not only to call attention to this complex and varied past but especially to stress that this discourse reflects how Awlad 'Ali, or at least some Awlad 'Ali men, identify themselves as an entity within a complex and varied wider system of relations.

Ties to the *fath al-Islami* and to the Bani Sulaym indicate noble ancestry and, also, that descent forms an element in their identity. These ties provide strong links to historical Islam and to Arabia and Libya, and also proclaim their presence in the region for a thousand years or more. Their return to Egypt "three hundred years ago" implants the Awlad 'Ali firmly in the northwest coast and identifies an existing ambiguity in their relationship with the Jumi'at, whom they protected without demanding payment of tribute—unlike the recalled situation for other groups in the region. Their warfare with the Harabi and the Hanadi also shows that common descent need not translate into brotherly relations and shared common interests.

Their recall of fighting against the French stakes a powerful claim to being Egyptian, Arab, and Muslim patriots. Participation in this defense and, later on, in the military activities of Muhammad 'Ali and of his government of Egypt were far removed from the domain of tribal conflicts within their own local systems. Indeed, their participation was as a category of specialists within a complex division of labor in which they fought but did not work as corvee labor in the digging of canals, a duty which fell on others who did not fight. Moreover, this military involvement within the then newly developing Egyptian state system strongly suggests that adjectives such as 'remote' or 'marginal' would not have been applicable to them in the past. Their marginalization, we argue, was more a result of their exemption from the army and of other state policies than of their tribal identity per se, or of their occupation of an arid steppe beyond the borders of the Nile Valley.

Their presentation of self through oral history brings into play powerful forces other than their own tribal selves: Islam, the state, colonialism, and twentieth century world wars are subjects that recur frequently in their talk about themselves. This does not mean that they do not also have identities that employ the idiom of kinship and follow a pattern of segmentation of groupings divided into smaller and smaller units. Genealogies and the names of larger and smaller segments provide information that is of major internal importance among Awlad 'Ali. Yet, kinship alone is not the essence of their identity. Also existing in their sense of self is the *'urf*, a remembered history, and ties to communities much larger and more complex than the tribe, clan, and lineage. One of those communities is Egypt—of which country they are citizens and in whose armed forces their sons now serve on an equal footing with other citizens. "Gamal 'Abd al-Nasir brought us back into the army," an elderly senior said.

## Tribe, State, and Development

People in the northwest coast were not 'immune' to the transformational changes of the 1950s and 1960s that reverberated throughout the Arab world. Thus, a list of changes from this period for the area includes, but is not limited to, the following: replacement of military administration by a civilian system of local government; the issuance of state identity cards to Awlad 'Ali and other Bedouin; active political organization by the Arab Socialist Union; sponsorship and organization of development programs and projects by the general desert development organization (*'Ta'amir al-Sahari'*); the introduction of local agricultural cooperative societies; the setting up of public schools and health care centers, along with the expansion and/or upgrading of physical infrastructure; rapid urbanization of Marsa Matruh and other towns, with settlers coming from both the steppe and the Nile Valley; expansion of trade and waged labor activities, both within the region and between it and neighboring Libya's new oil-revenue based economy; and modest development of summer holiday facilities for use by vacationers from Egypt's main cities.

These changes emanate strongly from the state and from market systems, and have also involved international development organizations such as the World Food Program (WFP). These changes employ the languages of locality and citizenship, of trader, laborer, employee, and capitalist owner, of cooperative societies, of boards of directors, and of elections. Yet, in describing these changes and their involvement in them, we often heard Awlad 'Ali say, "We are *qaba'il* ['tribes;' 'clans']." Our response to this apparent contradiction is that Awlad 'Ali accepted change from the outside but usually on their own terms and, sometimes, on the basis of converting—indeed subverting—the change itself to fit their own perceived needs and aspirations. Two examples of this phenomenon, each briefly sketched, will have to suffice.

The sedentarization of Awlad 'Ali and other Bedouin in the northwest coast was strongly supported by the Egyptian state in the 1960s, motivated by the state's need to control them. Other concerns also existed; among these is what we conclude to have been a genuine desire on the part of state officials to introduce modern community social services, such as schooling and health care, among this component of Egypt's population. Thus, a housing program for the nomads was introduced in the early 1960s, with contributions by the WFP and with subsidized loans with very easy repayment terms from the government of Egypt.

Individuals from among the *badiyah* who wished to build a house were encouraged to submit their applications to the authorities and, if approved, the government extended loans when the foundations of the houses began to be built. Food aid was provided, as we were told, when one started to construct the frame; "and people take the food to the market, sell it, and use the money to complete the house." Wooden beams, window frames, a door, and a gate were provided free of charge. Meanwhile, the nomads designed the houses as they wished and combined their own domestic labor with that of hired workers, mainly Upper Egyptians, for construction. They made their own decisions about where to locate the housing—almost always within their lineage territories and near or on patches of land where their fathers and grandfathers had planted barley and/or other crops.

Thereby emerged a dispersed settlement pattern of isolated homesteads and of small clusters of houses scattered about the steppe. This settlement pattern accords well with the region's ecology and also with the segmentary system of lineages and clans of Awlad 'Ali and other Bedouin. However, this type of settlement hardly facilitates the provision of social services. Children very often have to walk for several hours across rough terrain to get to a school, while school teachers feel lonely in the remote locations and are said to have high rates of absenteeism. Still, if the goal of sedentarization was to settle the nomads in permanent housing, then that goal was achieved. Indeed, this nomad sedentarization project was one of the Arab world's most successful attempts at state-sponsored sedentarization.

Whether the state gained the control it wished is questionable, especially since illegal trade and smuggling flourished during the heyday of this state-sponsored sedentarization. However, closure of the border with Libya in the early 1970s brought an end to the smuggling of that period; and, as we were told, "People returned and then everybody settled down." The smugglers had challenged state authority; but they returned to Egypt and invested their money in housing, in new agriculture, and in other development activities in the northwest coast that the state also supported. Some of yesteryear's smugglers now figure prominently among the region's leading businesspeople. Scattered around the steppe in comfortable housing within their lineage territories, such people remain Awlad 'Ali or other Bedouin; but the cleavage of economic differentiation increasingly severs the bonds of common descent that link them to the majority of their kindred. Nevertheless, "We are Awlad 'Ali; we are *qaba'il*."

In al-Qasr which we were told is both urban and rural, while remaining Bedouin, we visited with the head of the community's village council in his *majlis*. He explained the formal structure of Egypt's local government system, with elected popular councils and appointed executive councils at the levels of the village, district, and governorate.[6] Marsa Matruh has city councils; and at the level of the nation there is the People's Assembly, with elected representatives from the governorate. Thus exists one chain of ties that links the small settlement via Marsa Matruh to a powerful but seemingly remote state that remains highly centralized in Cairo.

According to this man who is from Awlad 'Ali and in his sixties, al-Qasr's village council is derived from a unit set up by the Arab Socialist Union in the early 1960s. He said he had joined the socialist union as a young man and noted with pride that his tribe, 'Ali al-Ahmar, had been the dominant tribe in the socialist union in Matruh. He recalled that, when the socialist union established the unit in al-Qasr, people from his lineage (*'aylah*) had eagerly joined but were annoyed when they learned that others from outside their lineage could also participate. They invited the governor to lunch and told him they wanted to limit membership in the unit to their lineage mates, "because we don't like those other people." However, the governor explained that divisions based on kinship did not accord with the principles of socialism, and they had to accept others into the unit.

A police station was located in al-Qasr in 1964. But, as we were told, "The police never received a single complaint. Not one disturbance. So they packed up and left after several years." That the police heard no complaints and encountered no disturbances is not due to any lack of conflict among people in al-Qasr. Indeed, the head of the village council and many others mentioned numerous disagreements about land boundaries, trade agreements, and water rights. Some of these escalated into conflicts involving violence. But, "We are very effective at solving problems before they get bigger and bigger." Even problems that explode into violence are usually quickly brought under control and then solved through the *'urf*, without recourse to the police.

The solving of 'problems' is a passion among many Awlad 'Ali men and a highly developed skill among a few, especially older men. Avoidance of problems is also considered wise and is given as a main reason for not holding elections, if at all possible. In fact, we were told that in al-Qasr the elected members of the local council,

> Do not become members as a result of elections. We have lineages here; and each lineage sends members according to its weight [size]. Each lineage decides who it will send. About voting, I believe in democracy ... [But] to tell the truth, elections only bring us problems. For us, it is a big problem if a person is nominated by a lineage and does not win in an election. We are relatives. Voting brings disagreements, even quarrels between people. We Awlad 'Ali do not have elections. We are *qaba'il*.

A similar process of selection is said to operate at the level of the governorate council. The relative sizes of the various tribes and of the community of Siwa were determined after an election in the 1960s "exploded with problems." The proportional representations of 'Ali al-Ahmar, 'Ali al-Abyad, and Sinayna from Awlad 'Ali, the Jumi'at, and the people of Siwa were agreed to, along with a provision for a system of rotation in case "a tribe has to be left out for some reason during a term." Additionally, Awlad 'Ali say they entered into a "famous secret agreement" with President Sadat to exempt Bedouin of the northwest coast from elections. As the head of the village council put it, "Awlad 'Ali agreed among themselves and made Sadat agree to it. I don't know the exact content of that agreement; but they have it in the governorate."

In addition to the local government system, Awlad 'Ali and other Bedouin also serve on the boards of local agricultural cooperative societies and on the board of directors of the central cooperative society. Almost always, the board members are selected by *tazkiya'*, 'nomination;' 'endorsement,' by lineages or clans or, in the case of the central cooperative, by tribes, happens as in the local government system. Selection by consensus on the basis of kin accords well with ancient sentiment and reinforces tribal and sub-tribal structures in a contemporary setting. Having largely crafted this selection system themselves, Awlad 'Ali and other Bedouin are quite pleased with it, at least in principle.

However, outsiders are blocked from breaking into the system; and opposition is stifled. Moreover, an oligarchy of seniors tends to dominate the popular councils and the boards of the cooperatives, as many of the same men serve in both sets of institutions. Increasingly, a few younger men have ventured to challenge the hold of seniors on these positions. Louder challenges are voiced by many of the Nile Valley migrants in the northwest coast who deeply resent the monopoly of Awlad 'Ali and other Bedouin on the local government system. To which complaint an Awlad 'Ali answer was,

> We elect representatives to the People's Assembly in Cairo to represent our interests and to discuss important issues. How can someone from Alexandria go and represent us in the national parliament? These migrants may have been here since 1914. They have a vote, but they don't win elections. They have a place reserved for them on the city council in Marsa Matruh. Also, the governor is a migrant. And all the people who work in the governorate are migrants.

Is this a voice of tribal resistance against Egyptian intruders from the Nile Valley? Although spoken by a young Awlad 'Ali man in anger and directed against Nile Valley migrants, his is more a cry of frustration about the status of the governorate and its development within the context of Egypt and, since they are near the border, in comparison with Libya. Back in the 1960s, anthropologist Abdalla Bujra (1967) expected that most positions in the government sector in Matruh would be filled by local Bedouin by the mid-1970s. This expectation has not been achieved, a phenomenon that is not due to any particular fault of the Bedouin. Younger and better educated Awlad 'Ali and others often spoke to us of their desire for a governor from the region and for a governorate system firmly based in the region. Generally, they feel that the governorate represents the state and its interests and, increasingly, the interests of Nile Valley capitalist investors with little concern for the interests of the local people—be they Bedouin or migrant settlers from elsewhere.

## Concluding Remarks

Is the northwest coast a part of rural Egypt? Perhaps it is more appropriate to think of the northwest coast, the governorate of Matruh, as a part of provincial Egypt—the Egypt of the *muhafazat* (governorates) outside the great metropolitan centers. In the past, the area was *badiyah*—in the classic Arab sense of a steppe and its people devoted to nomadic pastoralist production and some dry land farming, and organized mainly on the basis of tribes, but also with connections to settled communities and markets beyond the domain of the range. That *badiyah*, that past, has almost totally vanished except as a memory and as a proud identity of—in our experience—a lawyer, a pharmacist, a veterinarian, a deputy director of a bank, a farmer, and of many others.

The population of the northwest coast, according to the 1986 census, numbered about 162,000 and was divided almost equally into what the census classified as 'urban' and 'rural' components. Most of the half that is rural is from the *badiyah*, while we reckon that the urban population is divided roughly into one half from the Nile Valley and Siwa and the other half from the *badiyah*. Differences exist between Marsa Matruh, the smaller towns, and the dispersed settlements and homesteads on the steppe. Nevertheless, within the region all of these are tightly linked to each other: travel deep into the steppe to visit someone, and he is not present—"gone to Marsa Matruh;" ask a migrant settler in Marsa Matruh from among those long resident there about the region's development potential and he will mention, among other things, the condition of the range and the prevailing situation concerning the export of livestock.

Matruh, as a governorate, has its specificities but is comparable to similar entities. Certainly, meaningful comparisons can be made with Egypt's other 'frontier' governorates and also, perhaps, with smaller governorates of the Nile Valley. Too often the contrast has been between the 'desert' and the 'town,' between Awlad 'Ali and Egyptians, between Bedouin and peasants. Those dimensions exist; and one would not be surprised if a conference on rural Egypt did not include reference to desert Egypt. Yet, we are here—not quite content to include Awlad 'Ali and other Bedouin among the rural, but searching for connections that may transcend the dichotomy of rural and urban, a dichotomy that all too often distorts by imposing an overly hard internal border and that also wrongly excludes the *badiyah* as being too much of the outside.

## Notes

1 Concerning 'Unayzah, we have been astonished that non-Arabians who have read our book, *Arabian Oasis City*, often ask questions or comment about the 'village' we studied. Do people think of the community as a village because it is an oasis and has significant agriculture in its vicinity? Is it because they think cities don't exist in Saudi Arabia? Or that if anthropologists do not study tribes, then their work must be about villages?

2 The Burj al-'Arab part of the northwest coast was severed from the Matruh governorate in the early 1990s. Major land reclamation dependent on Nile water has taken place in the area, while New Burj al-'Arab is an example of Egypt's new cities in the desert. The area is now incorporated as a district in the urban governorate of Alexandria.

3 *Murabtin*, the 'tied' ones, constitute an important part of the diversity that prevails in the northwest coast, as well as in eastern Libya. They claim a

multiplicity of origins in terms of descent, usually have not engaged in warfare, and normally are not expected to provide refuge *(nizalah)* as set forth in the *'urf*. By contrast, Awlad 'Ali and many others share descent from the same woman ancestor, Sa'ada, have a 'traditional' specialization as warriors, provide refuge, and have extended protection to murabtin. The *murabtin b-il-baraka* are distinguished by their religious associations and are usually accorded high social status.

4 According to Obermeyer (1968), Awlad 'Ali in the 1960s often claimed Gamal 'Abd al-Nasir to be a kinsman.

5 In some Arab countries, Bedouin were central to the military, and thus also to affairs of state.

6 For a relevant and detailed comparative perspective on the local government system in the rural Nile Valley, see Radwan (1994).

## References

Abu-Lughod, Lila. 1987. *Veiled Sentiments: Honor and Poetry in a Bedouin Society.* Cairo: American University in Cairo Press. (first published 1986).

Altorki, Soraya, and Donald P. Cole. 1989. *Arabian Oasis City: The Transformation of 'Unayzah.* Austin: University of Texas Press.

Bujra, Abdalla Said. 1967. "A Preliminary Analysis of the Bedouin Community in Marsa Matruh Town." American University in Cairo, Social Research Center. (report).

Cole, Donald P., and Soraya Altorki. 1998. *Bedouin, Settlers, and Holiday-Makers: Egypt's Changing Northwest Coast.* Cairo: American University in Cairo Press.

Evans-Pritchard, Edward E. 1949. *The Sanusi of Cyrenaica.* Oxford: Clarendon Press.

Obermeyer, Gerald J. 1968. "Structure and Authority in a Bedouin Tribe: The 'Aishaibat of the Western Desert of Egypt." unpublished Ph.D. dissertation. Bloomington: Indiana University.

Radwan, Hanan Hamdy. 1994. "Democratization in Rural Egypt: A Study of the Village Local Popular Council." *Cairo Papers in Social Science* vol. 17 (1).

# III

## CULTURAL REPRESENTATION: CONSUMPTION

# 7

# Television and the Virtues of Education: Upper Egyptian Encounters with State Culture

LILA ABU-LUGHOD*

## Representing the Sa'id

In 1997, first on Nile TV, the new satellite channel, and several months later on the main government channel, a dramatic serial called "Dream of the Southerner" (*Hilm al-janubi*) was broadcast. The opening episodes, set in and around Luxor, reproduced common images of rural Upper Egyptians (*Sa'idis*). There were violent and dumb peasants, some who refused to pay the rent for the land they were farming, and others who were loyal henchmen of important men. There was a wealthy but illiterate local man who had worked in tourism but had become rich by digging beneath his house and unearthing Pharaonic antiquities (a figure the scriptwriter insists was based on a real person he had heard about as a boy, but that this happens is a common perception of the people living near Luxor). A poorly informed tour guide with bad English misled tourists about ancient inscriptions, and another character—who would become the real villain of the serial—had just returned from the oil-rich Gulf states, bringing gifts for the unprincipled school principal to get his teaching position back. The actors all attempted Sa'idi dialect, using characteristic pronunciations and words; mostly, however, they

---

\* I would like to thank the National Endowment for the Humanities, the John Simon Guggenheim Foundation, and New York University (Presidential fellowship in 1993 and a Challenge Fund Grant in 1995–96) for research support. I am also grateful to Hania El-Sholkamy, Rema Hammami, Nick Hopkins, Tim Mitchell, Malak Rouchdy, Reem Saad, and Boutros Wadi' for comments on an earlier version of this paper; to Siona Jenkins and David Sims for generously sharing their knowledge and help with logistics; and to the many individuals in the village who have shown me hospitality and friendship over the years but whom I cannot name to preserve their anonymity. Small portions of this paper were previously published in Abu-Lughod (1997).

thought to make themselves into Sa'idis by speaking gruffly.

These stereotypical characters were pitted against Nasr, a unique individual. He is a cultured local teacher who lectures his students on the history of the great civilization of ancient Egypt, although it is not in the curriculum, and spends his afternoons studying his archaeology books in Karnak Temple. He defends the rights of the sons of poor men to have an education, in one case loaning the money to cover the school activity fees. The boy whom he helped had retorted to the principal's threat to expel him with a defense of the state. "Education," he says, "is free in Egypt."

As is true of the best Egyptian television serials—and this one had an unusually complex set of social themes, exciting footage shot on location, colorful characters, and nice dramatic tension—claims to social verisimilitude were made. The writer boasted that he wrote about what he knew and had lived.[1] He himself was born there, near Qina (though he has spent most of his life in Alexandria, the other setting for "Dream of the Southerner"). Yet despite grains of ethnographic truth in the serial, including the use of genuine Sa'idi entertainers in a wedding celebration scene, the writer had deployed many of the stock themes of rural backwardness and Upper Egyptian violence. Not only were there the stupid and angry locals, but also the worn theme of arbitrary patriarchal authority. This was expressed most often in the control over women and the institution of forced arranged marriage, both part of the plot of "Dream of the Southerner."[2] Also, like so many serials since the 1993 media policy of 'confronting extremism,' this one included a group of closed-minded and intolerant religious extremists.[3] They were hoodwinked into mistaking the protagonist's scholarly interest in Egyptology for idol worship and so set fire to his house, burning his precious collection of scholarly books and a papyrus document that was the key to the location of Alexander's lost tomb. (This papyrus was presented as a priceless national treasure that our hero had refused to return to the self-interested tomb-robber who found it. Nasr was horrified that this ignorant man had wanted to sell it to foreigners.) When the producers of "Dream ..." were challenged about the accuracy of Luxor as a setting for such militant groups, the writer defended his script by arguing that all around Luxor, from Armant to Nag' Hammadi, were the sugarcane fields in which terrorists hid.[4] The actor who played the lead role quickly added that geography was not the issue anyway. It was the danger these groups posed that the drama wanted to convey. The serial reproduced and reinforced the common northern association of religious violence with the marginality of Upper Egypt.[5]

All that seemed missing at first was the vendetta (*tha'r*), the long familiar trope for Upper Egypt. To the writer's credit, this image was self-consciously mocked when the owner of an Alexandria apartment building did not want to rent to our noble hero because he was a bachelor from the Sa'id. She worried that he might be involved in a vendetta and did not want trouble. "You know the way you Sa'ayda are," she apologized. But the plot, gripping and passionate as it was, eventually did come to turn on revenge. Our hero's most dangerous foe became his former colleague from the school, the returned migrant, who married the tomb-robber's niece (for her money) only to discover that she was in love with the cultured teacher. Out of wounded pride he joined his in-law, bent on revenge for the financial loss of the precious papyrus. So the violent vendetta was there, but cheapened by being rooted not in grief and the fierce love of family but in competitiveness, pride, and greed.

Unlike many television serials, "Dream ..." balanced these negative figures with good Sa'idis who were able to join forces with honest and patriotic urban Alexandrians—most educated—in a black and white morality play. There were two simple but loyal and honest servants: one a country bumpkin, and the other distinguished by his integrity in friendship. And there was the young woman—the love object—who wanted to defy custom and ended up bravely saving the day. But the two main protagonists were Sa'idis who had been redeemed by true education. Nasr had differentiated himself from others around him by his love of learning and selfless devotion to his civilization and nation. His main protector and friend was a wise, retired judge, whose cultural taste and knowledge were symbolized by the framed reproduction of the Mona Lisa hanging in his home.

In such representations, "Dream ..." followed the pattern of many television serials: the educated, cultured individual represents the good, the law, culture, national responsibility, and pride in the greatness of the nation's heritage.[6] An article in *Majallat al-idha'a w-al-tilifizyun*, which described the serial as a "television ode to the love of the nation," quoted the scriptwriter as saying that the serial was not so much about the theft of antiquities as the larger question of the integrity or authenticity of the Egyptian character (*asalat al-shakhsiya al-Misriya*).[7] In a seminar sponsored by the same magazine after the serial was broadcast, he explained that he had tackled five dangerous elements: religious extremism, foreign power, the class driven only by personal interest, government corruption, and personal envy. He had done so, however, and perhaps unthinkingly, by glorifying true education and patriotism.

## Rural Citizens as Subjects of Education

The actor who played the role of Nasr defended the Manichean morality of the serial on the grounds that, "Television drama is important, dear to people, and the teacher of the new generation."[8] What "Dream ..." and numerous other television serials teach is the value of education and devotion to the nation. The same lessons are taught in the schools. They are part of what might be called state culture. For many rural and uneducated Upper Egyptian villagers, encountering state culture means being put in one's place as inferior (as these television characters show and the outside examiners who visit Upper Egyptian schools make the secondary school students feel); as people who at times are unsophisticated enough to need television to show them things; and as people who have little access to the kinds of lives depicted in school books or on television, particularly nowadays with the explosion of television advertisements for water heaters and toilet bowl cleaners. State culture positions the rural and uneducated as people who must be taught the most basic things in the name of national development.

The families living on the west bank of the Nile across from Luxor with whom I have spoken and watched television appreciate the fact that television serials, produced for state television and approved by censors, are didactic. People talked about how "television shows people things." It shows people principles such as good and evil (*khayr wa sharr*), how things work (bribery is given as an example), and that the government is always there. The latter was expressed especially in relation to a favorite documentary program called "The Confrontation" (*al-Muwajaha*) in which criminals are interviewed/interrogated. As village women excitedly told me about various people who had appeared on this program ("none from around here—they are all from Giza, Asyut, Minya and other places" they quickly pointed out) they explained that the show taught people that if they did wrong, the government would find them out. As examples, they described a woman who had drowned two children because she was angry with the family. She tried to make it look as if it had been a robbery: "But the government knew immediately." They also recounted the story of a man who had murdered someone and then tried to destroy any traces by putting the body in a rubber tire which he set on fire with kerosene. But he forgot the gloves he was wearing at the scene of the crime. "The government" found them, fingerprinted all the neighbors, and caught him. The women were amazed ("*subhan Allah*," they exclaimed) at how the government could track down the culprits

Many viewers also remarked on the educational value of television. One man explained that through television "people become aware *(wa'yin)*." His wife agreed: "The importance of television is that people like us learn things from it." When she says "like us" she means Upper Egyptian peasants who are not educated or well-traveled. This echoed the sentiments of her similarly unlettered sister-in-law who had compared the present to the past. "People like me," she said, "are angry with our parents for not giving us an education. Now, after schools and television, people know a lot more."

This is certainly the intention of many involved in writing and producing for television. Their discussions are often couched in the language of "making people aware." The interviews with the writer of "Dream ..." and some of the actors who participated in it are typical. One actor described how newspapers uncover each day crimes by people who care only to make themselves rich by destroying the Egyptian heritage. He concluded, "The serial has an important role in making people aware of our history and our priceless antiquities." The scriptwriter was even more ambitious. By means of this serial on antiquities theft, he said he wanted to expose all the problems blocking the progress and potential of Egypt.[9]

The most socially concerned television writers see television as a means to both educate and communicate the value of modern education. They do not work alone. Adult literacy classes, for example, are seen in the same way. The textbooks produced for these classes, which have recently gained new momentum, are intended to teach people to read and write. They also exemplify the efforts of state culture to promote certain values. In the Upper Egyptian village I know best, literacy classes for women were begun in 1995. Some local women, unemployed graduates of technical institutes, were hired as teachers. In one class that I attended, of about twenty-five students, mostly adult women in their twenties and thirties (with a sprinkling of younger girls who never had an opportunity to go to school), the teacher drilled them using the same techniques of sing-song repetition used on school children. She worked with a text whose intention of teaching basic citizens' rights alongside literacy was in many ways admirable but whose condescending presumptions about the students' simplicity were distressing and whose obvious messages could be read as state propaganda, given today's realities.

Entitled, "I Learn and Become Enlightened" (*Ata'allam wa atanawwar*), the book begins with lessons that place individuals first as citizens. One is called "My Identity Card."

My name is on my identity card.
My occupation is on the card.
On my card is my place of residence.
On my card is a number.

It also teaches women some basic rights, as in such lessons as, "The Marriage Contract."

> Marriage is God's way.
> The family comes into being with the marriage contract.
> For the contract you need two witnesses.
> This contract exists with the bride's consent.
> The consent of the bride is a precondition of marriage.

Later lessons build vocabulary while promoting certain ideas about hygiene and health. They do not miss the opportunity to push family planning, a value, like education, crucial to ideas about making Egyptians modern and developed that can end up devaluing rural women.[10] Lesson 8 is not subtle.

> Kamil loves his family.
> Habiba is Kamil's wife.
> Kamil loves his wife and Habiba loves her husband.
> Tariq is Kamil's son and Samah is Kamil's daughter.
> Tariq and Samah are Kamil's children.
> Kamil's family is small.
> Kamil's family is small and happy.

At the bottom of the page, in small print, the aim of the lesson is spelled out for the teacher: "To deepen the feelings of love among family members and to grasp the connection between the small number of family members and their happiness."

Finally, the textbook directly affirms the value of education. It links individual and national needs, as in the following lesson:

> Illiteracy is dangerous.
> Illiteracy is a threat to production.
> Illiteracy is dangerous for people.
> Illiteracy is dangerous and a big waste for all.
> I am fighting illiteracy ... I am getting educated.
> I am getting educated ... I am fighting illiteracy.

In principle it is difficult to argue with the virtues of literacy and education, or knowledge of the rights and responsibilities of citizenship, even when couched in the overbearing language of national development. However, in what follows I want to explore some of the problems posed by the subjection of rural villagers to such educational messages and messages about education in a national context in which quality education, like other resources, is not equally available to all citizens. I will first show how little these cultural productions reflect of the actual lives and problems of late twentieth-century rural Upper Egyptians. Then I will try to suggest some of the silencing effects on villagers of such well-meaning but condescending discourses. However, I will also argue that the most significant impact of these discourses and the images they support is on those who have the power to reshape the lives of the rural poor.

## Texts and Lives

Do the women in these literacy classes—so eager to learn and write (and to spend their afternoons together working away amidst jokes and chat, escaping the daily chores of the household and the tired company of their families)—juxtapose what they memorize and what they actually know? I never heard anyone make fun of the lessons, even though the picture of Egyptian society and what the government provides for its citizens must strike them as idealized. The lesson on the right of all citizens to free health care (something USAID is working hard to end) must seem hollow to women who often complain that when they go to the under-financed government clinics the wait will be long and the 'free' medicines more likely than not unavailable.

Even more farfetched are the rosy lessons about Egypt's new cities and communities in the desert. One lesson brags about the work opportunities in these new communities, going on to explain the equal rights of male and female workers and the role of the union in defending workers' rights. The teacher who led the chanting repetition of the lesson knows how few work opportunities there are generally, having explained to me in another context that only those with connections can possibly hope to get the secretarial jobs for which she is trained. All the women in the class have brothers or cousins who have graduated from technical schools or colleges and sit unemployed, waiting for seven or eight years to be assigned to positions. As for the less educated men in their families, the lucky ones get waged employment in restoration or guarding Pharaonic temples. Their salaries are LE120 ($36) per month. If fortunate enough to have some land, they work it in the afternoons, plowing, planting, irrigating, and harvesting. These can treat the salary as a helpful cash supplement—something to help cover children's school expenses and medicines. Village women simply do not work outside their households. Girls who have graduated from the local agricultural high school lose touch with their friends, staying at home to help their mothers until it is time to get married. How relevant is the next lesson in the textbook that teaches students how to fill out the form requesting a vacation? There are no vacations from getting fodder for the sheep or sweeping, cooking, or child care.

The text teaches reading and writing through essays promoting notions specific to a modern capitalist economy. One of these is about savings accounts. As one lesson reads:

> Did you know,
> That opening a savings account is free?
> That you can open a savings account at the Post Office with one pound?
> That your money in the account increases?
> That the savings account helps protect your money from confiscation?
> That a savings account is tax-free?
> That in a savings account your money quickly grows and that saving is a security for the family and society?

This lesson, transcribed dutifully into school notebooks, is for women many of whose families have difficulty even keeping up with the monthly expenses, often having to borrow until they can sell a calf or goat. These are women who may have some savings in their gold necklaces and earrings but who invest, if they have anything extra, in livestock. The advantage of livestock is that they increase, even if they require a lot of care. Many women spend their mornings cutting berseem (clover) or corn for their sheep and goats. Morning and evening they take them to graze on the stubble or grasses that grow on the edge of the desert. They get water for them to drink. At the end of each day they move them from outside pens to the safety of indoors. Some of these women also care for the family water buffalo or cow, looking forward to calves that can be sold for cash and to the supply of milk that will nourish their children and nieces and nephews.

Even the messages about education are unrealistic. Lesson 11 echoes the message of the television serial, "Dream ...". It declares the dogma of the state and the values of intellectuals who link development and education:

> Education is the right of all.
> Education is the right of every citizen.
> Education is the duty of every citizen.
> I am getting educated.
> I am progressing.
> I am becoming enlightened.
> I am going to continue learning.
> I am going to continue learning for free.

It is true that the literacy classes are more or less free, though students must provide their own notebooks and pencils. But that education more broadly is free is simply not the case, as every village family knows. Parents are so convinced that education will provide a future for their children that they deny themselves much to be able to afford it. They forfeit the children's labor, in some cases completely. In other cases, the children have to help before they leave for school or after they return, depending on which shift they are on. Especially at the start of the school year, parents feel the cost of schooling. They will endlessly count and recount the expenses—for new clothes, for notebooks, pens, book bags, books, and daily allowances for snacks or transport; not to mention the private lessons, as later in the year it becomes apparent that their children are failing. Multiply these costs by the number of children—usually no fewer than three and up to six or seven—and you have some staggering figures, given household incomes.

Is it really worth it, given how understaffed and under-financed the schools are and how few children can actually succeed in such schools? Even if the family has sacrificed to send them to an institute or college, they will most likely remain unemployed, especially now that the government has ended its policy of guaranteed employment for graduates. No one asks. They see no other way, given how little land there is. Those lucky families who have any land, find it split more and more ways with each generation. They say that even the most basic jobs now require a diploma. And they have been taught, by television, that to be a hero, one must be educated, and so they want the social capital that education provides in the local community and marriage market.

Only Zaynab, a sharp woman with eight children whose husband had migrated to Cairo, expressed any doubt.[11] She once asked me, "Why is it that even though I never learned to read or write I understand most things? More than my children who are in school?"

## Cosmopolitans in the Countryside

Zaynab's remark brings us to the second problem with the literacy textbooks and television serials. The villagers I know are all more sophisticated than urban intellectuals imagine. Their knowledge comes from their close involvement in the management of daily life in their households and wider families, their detailed knowledge of the experiences of many neighbors, relatives, and other more distant subjects of gossip and discussion, and, it must be admitted, their exposure to television. I have elsewhere described many of the village women I know as cosmopolitans.[12] These are not the kind of people we usually consider cosmopolitans—AUC professors or Cairene business people equally at home in English, French, and Arabic, people who shop in London and at the Cairo World Trade Center shopping mall, and often disdain state television. Nor are they television writers who study international film and participate in conferences on Arab intellectual trends. These village women illustrate other varieties of cosmopolitanism—ones not recognized in the cultural projects of the state but found in many rural areas around the postcolonial world.

For many rural villagers, poverty impedes full access to the consumer culture and commodification of signs so conspicuously a part of a modern cosmopolitan's life. Yet, someone like Zaynab is not untouched by this culture. Television advertisements insistently traffic in such signs as their jingles, written by advertising firms with names like Americana, entice people to buy brand name shampoos and yogurt. For a variety of reasons, Zaynab remains fairly unmoved by, even resistant to, these advertisements. Yet she is forced to enter consumer culture through her children. The little ones cry for 'Chipsy' potato chips, while the older ones insist on particular brands of running shoes, and her eldest daughter, Sumaya, dreams of Tefal cooking pots.

Zaynab also seems far from cosmopolitan in the way her life is anchored by economic constraints in her house, family, and village. The aspiration to educate her children is the only modernist national ideal somewhat within her reach. Yet she has great knowledge of other worlds, gleaned not just from television but from relatives and foreign friends. It is not only that Zaynab's husband, like many local men, has migrated to Cairo. More important, the hamlet she lives in has seen many European and North American archaeologists, folklorists, journalists, political scientists, tourists, and aging divorcees enamored of young local 'husbands.' Zaynab has even spent time in Cairo, getting medical treatment for her son. There she stayed in a Canadian folklorist's apartment decorated with Egyptian antiques, folk art, Bedouin rugs, transcribing machines, and books. However, Zaynab's subaltern relationship to this metropolitan world—related to her poverty and her lack of education—is symbolized by what she wore in Cairo. Despite her versatile knowledge, she wore the only clothes she had and felt comfortable in—clothes that announced her regional and rural origins.

This is in contrast to the form of cosmopolitanism that characterizes her wealthy neighbor, Fayruz, the daughter of the largest landowner in the village and married into another wealthy family. She lives in a house that looks quite different from Zaynab's. There is a mud brick house adjoining a concrete and brick house, complete with balcony. The latter is the sort of 'villa' people with money now aspire to build. When I first met Fayruz, she lived in the mud brick house. Like all village women, she baked bread in her outdoor oven. But her house looked cleaner because she did not need to keep animals to boost the household income. When I returned in 1996, she had moved into the adjoining structure, with its stone floor tiles and bright blue ceramic tiled bathroom, complete with toilet and bathtub. She proudly showed me around the house so I could see all the furniture—beds, wardrobes, couches, armchairs, and side tables. The new 'modern' house had been prepared for Fayruz's younger brother-in-law. But when he finally found a bride, a girl from another wealthy local family, she refused to live there, preferring an apartment near her sister in Luxor.

When Fayruz unlocked her wardrobe and started pulling out dresses to show me, I understood better how her wealth enabled a different form of cosmopolitanism than Zaynab's, while her lack of education and her location in the provinces still differentiated her from urban cosmopolitans. She showed me amazing dresses of chiffon with sequins, silk with gold buttons, all long and with long sleeves—only the urban upper classes and movie stars would nowadays wear anything more revealing. Nevertheless, some of the dresses had surprisingly curved bodices and extravagant flounces. I was surprised because around the village she wore the usual black head covering and an overdress only slightly more sophisticated than most other women's.

This ornate wardrobe full of extraordinary dresses out of a lavish television serial reveals something about urbanity, class distinction, and the national context of these for a provincial. When Fayruz had gone to Cairo, to get medical treatment for her migraines, unlike Zaynab, she had stayed in a part of town with few foreigners, near business contacts that her brother-in-law had developed through attending the business school run as part of the parallel educational system by Al-Azhar. Whereas Zaynab, despite her contact with foreign cosmopolitans, had worn her village clothes, Fayruz, whose knowledge of other worlds came from Upper Egyptians with urban experience or aspirations, or from television, plucked her eyebrows, wore makeup, and put on some of the more modest dresses she had in her wardrobe. She also replaced her black head cloth with the *higab*—the head covering associated with modest Islamic dress—thereby erasing her village identity. This adoption of the *higab* is not surprising. For rural Egyptians, like urban lower- and middle-class women since the 1980s, to become 'modern' and urbane has, in most cases, meant taking on a more identifiably Islamic look and sound.

We can read in these differences the contrast between the cosmopolitanisms of the more national and middle-class frame of an up-and-coming provincial and the sharp juxtapositions produced for a poor woman by the intersection of neocolonial travel by folklorists and tourists, postcolonial nationalist modernization projects, and television. Fayruz's participation in the nation, with its power centers in the cities, will be intensified if she continues with her literacy classes. Fayruz is attending more from wounded pride (and loneliness) than any desire for better citizenship. When her brother-in-law's new bride refused to stay in the household with her, she had put on airs because of her education. Telling me the stories, Fayruz had fumed, "Is she better than me?" Look at who my father is, she would add. Yet the bride's claims to superiority rested in part on her school diploma. In the national context where standards are set by the urban, Fayruz realized she could not rely only on wealth and family name for status.

Zaynab's eldest daughter Sumaya illustrates yet another type of rural cosmopolitanism, one characteristic of the new generation that has grown up with schools and television. Sumaya has the education Fayruz lacks while not the wealth that enables Fayruz to live in a 'modern' house and have a wardrobe full of dresses that cannot be worn around the village. Because of her education (she has completed agricultural secondary school) she, too, wears a version of the *higab* when she goes to school or dresses up, replacing the locally tailored gowns she wears ordinarily with a bright polyester store-bought outfit and high heels. She saves up to buy face creams she has seen advertised on television and she knows how to bake 'cakes' because of her home economics classes. She sometimes reads the newspaper and plans to have a small family. Sumaya's first gift to me bespeaks her generation's form of cosmopolitanism. Shyly, she had presented me with a color postcard framed with green and blue twisted yarn. The postcard, out-dated, printed in Italy, and of the type widely circulated across Egypt, portrayed a European bride and groom gazing into each other's eyes. The frame was her own handiwork, a design no doubt learned at school. It was a home-grown amalgam of elements originating in various communities and places, expressing her romantic fantasies, fantasies encouraged by television, and signifying her modern state-initiated vocational education.

I have described the complex situations, cultural knowledges, code-switching abilities, and imaginative possibilities of these three village women to suggest that the kinds of ignorant rural Egyptians imagined as subjects and citizens by state officials and urban intellectuals, including television and textbook writers, do not exist.

## To What Effect?

What effects do such inaccurate images of the rural and uneducated and such unrealistic messages about the values of education and national development have? This question has two parts. First, one must consider those to whom they are directed. Then, one must ask about those who already share these values and are in a position to enact policies affecting the lives of rural villagers. My argument is that the ubiquity, authoritativeness, and the pleasure association of these images work together in a political process that keeps rural Egyptians in their place as inadequate and inferior citizens whose rights and needs come second, but who cannot articulate opposition.

As my descriptions of village women's acceptance of the textbooks and the general belief that television is good because it 'increases awareness' suggest, people who are disadvantaged do not seem to articulate the criticism that the gap between the messages they receive and the lives they live might be expected to generate. It is surprising to me, for example, that the faith in education is so widespread given that there is so little decent employment for the educated, and that the overtaxed educational system is so poor (with underpaid teachers forced to make ends meet by offering private lessons in the afternoons and evenings to students who learn nothing in overcrowded classrooms). Yet, no one questions the value of education.

In part, this absence of a critical discourse based on the knowledge of the gap between state rhetoric and everyday experience must be related to television. Television upholds these linked values of education and development, not just obliquely through dramas like "Dream ..." and many others with educated protagonists, but directly.[13] A classic example is a program called "100 percent." Intended to encourage 100 percent literacy in Egypt, the program hammers home the value of education in part by shaming those who are not going to school. One evening the host set off to the car mechanics' street in Cairo. He interrogated garage owners about whether they hired under-age labor. They all denied it. Then, just as belligerently, he interviewed young mechanic's apprentices about why they had dropped out of school. In most cases, the boys cited 'circumstances.' When pressed, they explained that financial circumstances in their families had forced them to leave school and begin working. They explained that they gave their wages (most said they made LE6 [less than $2] per day) to their mothers. The interviewer then taunted them: Don't you think you would make more money if you were educated? Aren't you just being lazy? Just because you didn't like school doesn't mean you shouldn't try. What kind of future do you think you will have?

Yet it is not just bombardment by authoritative discourses by more educated northerners associated with the government that prevents the development of critique. I think a more subtle process—in part psychological—is at work. It reveals itself in the failure to openly resist the mischaracterization of rural lives. I have heard of only two communities, one in Sinai and another in Upper Egypt, who have raised lawsuits against television serials for defamation of character. In the second case, according to Muhammad Safa' Amir, the writer of the serial in question ( "The Mountain Jackal," *Dhi'ab al-jabal*) the case was dropped as soon as people actually saw the serial.[14] As he described what happened, a group of Hawwara from Upper Egypt had gathered from the media that a serial about them was being filmed, and had protested. They were, however, happy with their representation in what turned out to be an extremely popular serial widely praised by ordinary people across Egypt as authentic. Those villagers with whom I have watched serials set in Upper Egypt have never voiced objections to the disfigurement of their dialect or the negative depiction of their fellow Sa'idis. The dialogue prompts them to discuss the differences among dialects from village to village. And the negative characters are simply hated for being bad people, like any villains. People enjoy recognizing places or bits of clothing and are glad to be included in the television world they love. Many told me excitedly about the film that was shot in their villages in the late 1980s and about others shot more recently. One filmed in the temple of Madinat Habu in the fall of 1996 included scenes of some local women imitating funeral laments, just as "Dream . . ." had included women singing wedding songs.

Nevertheless, serials like "Dream . . ." place villagers in a double bind. Ordinary villagers easily distance themselves from tomb robbers and materialistic teachers, interpreting serials with such moralistic messages as useful because they show viewers the difference between good and evil. They readily identify with morality and integrity. And yet, uneducated or undereducated villagers must find it hard to identify with the cultured and educated history teacher of "Dream . . ." The serial thus positions them to identify with the hero, a position they accept because they see themselves as good people, but when they try to identify with such a protagonist, with all the other values s/he represents, they must realize their own inadequacy as people who have not achieved the protagonist's level of education, culture, and commitment to the nation. Serials like "Dream . . ." must thus force them to feel their inferiority, even as they encourage new values. And because this whole process takes place in a context of pleasure—since they genuinely enjoy watching television serials—it is difficult to be critical either of the didactic messages or the misrepresentations of themselves.

To suggest that as they identify with the good they are stifled from developing a critical alternative is not to say that they are defenseless against the ideological onslaught. In fact, people seem to resist the most insulting of the representations by simply continuing to go about their lives as if they had value. The pride in being a Sa'idi still exists. It is revealed in comments like that of a woman who watched my four-year-old son vigorously weeding in a field. She complimented him by saying: "He's a real Sa'idi!" Manhood, toughness, and skill were all implied. Moreover, people often suggest that Sa'idis are more moral than their northern or urban compatriots—both for the behavior of women and the virtues of poverty and hard work.

What strikes me as best revealing that, despite their lack of cynicism about the messages of state culture, such villagers escape some of the negative entailments for their sense of self is the very fact that they persist in being fully involved in the unfolding events and social life of their own community. They continue to use a language of good and bad that is their own. They may identify with some of the morality of television serials when these exonerate authentic ordinary Egyptians—people with integrity, generosity, and old-fashioned values. But they do not, in their own interactions, immediately appropriate for their own use the values of being educated and cultured, presented in serials such as "Dream ... ." Instead, they judge educated individuals, like anyone else, by their behavior. Nor do they necessarily suspect those uneducated who have suddenly become wealthy, even though these are the favorite villains of many television serials. Zaynab, for example, once praised a neighbor whose family had succeeded fabulously in tourism. She whispered about the briefcases stuffed with money that one son brought home every day from his concession at Karnak. But she insisted on what a good woman his mother was: she always said yes if you asked her for a loan and when you came to repay it she would ask with concern, "Are you sure you don't need it anymore?" This was a woman, Zaynab implied, who understood the plight of her neighbors.

## Images and Policies

There is evidence that state officials and urban intellectuals do not share this rich woman's concern for her rural neighbors. I would argue that their seeming insensitivity to the plight of the rural poor is related to the unchallenged way in which they represent rural people even in sympathetic serials like "Dream ... ." In other words, the most consequential effect of the ways that Sa'idis and other rural and uneducated people are placed by condescending or negative discourses is that officials and educated intellectuals end up colluding in projects that, sometimes inadvertently, have painful consequences for such people.[15]

A good example of this is the project now underway in Luxor that is creating real-life drama for the villagers: the plan to remove the population living in the village of Gurna adjacent to, or on top of, Pharaonic ruins. This project of the Luxor City Council is supported by the Supreme Council for Antiquities as well as by many urban intellectuals who write in the press.[16] The project is defended in the name of many of the same values expressed in "Dream ... ." The residents of Gurna are accused of tomb-robbing and illegal trafficking in antiquities. They are also accused of destroying the archaeological sites that are not just part of the wider national heritage but world heritage (even though tourist buses that spew exhaust, and tourists who breathe inside the tombs also cause serious damage to the monuments). Their desire to live in their own houses, on their own land, and in their old community is represented as selfish and individualistic. In the interest of the wider good of preserving the antiquities and making them attractive to the public, the villagers are being asked to move far away from their fields, their palm trees, and their work and, for the residents of the hamlet near Madinat Habu, the rest of the village of which they are a part. They are being asked to resettle in small half-built houses in an exposed and barren area at the edge of the desert, away from their relatives and everything they have known.[17]

It is difficult to separate patriotic concern for the preservation of Egypt's heritage from desires to increase tourism and the income it generates for the state and private investors.[18] The plan to relocate the villagers is in line with proposals of an earlier 1970s World Bank scheme for the development of tourism in Luxor and other plans going back to the 1940s. As the Minister of Tourism Mamdouh Al Beltagui states regarding the plan, "This goes again with the development of archaeology in Egypt. It is a very good project to make Luxor into an international museum for everyone."[19]

There is no doubt that the preservation of Egypt's extraordinary treasures is important, and the problems of balancing this goal with the needs of ordinary people who live near them are thorny. But that their needs are so easily brushed aside cannot be unrelated to the ways in which such people are perceived. Their removal has been openly justified in terms of the kinds of backward lives these villagers live. Such villagers do not present to the outside world, especially to the millions of foreign tourists who visit Luxor to see the Pharaonic monuments, the right image of Egypt. They live in shabby houses, they ride donkeys, they take their water buffalo to the irrigation canals to bathe, they look poor. "Dream ..." reconfirms that many are stupid and uneducated, crudely sucking sugarcane and unable to read Arabic, even less appreciate Pharaonic inscriptions. Worst of all, dressed in filthy rags, they beg. The best thing is to get them out of the way so that no one will have to see this embarrassing face of Egypt.[20] One rumor is that the plan is to preserve some of their houses as artists' studios, while in others actors dressed in Pharaonic costumes will reenact the lives and ways of the ancient Egyptians. A clue to the priorities is that the only locals to be allowed to remain will be the manufacturers of objects like alabaster vases and painted papyrus for sale to the tourists.

Like the makers of "Dream ... ," many involved in this project of relocation are sophisticated and socially concerned. They may even be sympathetic to the locals. Yet they cannot help seeing the solution in terms of a particular set of values and priorities, tied to a vision of national modernity that has a long history in twentieth-century Egypt.

Television, literacy classes, and other forms of state culture try to promote and encourage these values of education and national modernity. The problem is, as this chapter has tried to show, that unless the basic structures of economic and political life that could sustain such values are put into place more universally in Egypt, the values themselves come only to symbolize a lack on the part of many rural villagers: their inability to measure up to the ideals. This has consequences for their own self-images as well as for wider policies affecting them.

## Notes

1 Khidhr (1997:20).
2 Interestingly, these themes also figured in another serial about Egyptian life that was being broadcast at the same time. Called "Our Folks" *(Ahalina)* and written by the brilliant television writer, 'Usama Anwar 'Ukasha, it was particularly striking for the contrast between the broad sympathy and subtlety with which ordinary urban Cairenes were represented and the crudeness of the portrayal of rural people. These rural characters included a psychotic nouveau riche Bedouin from Sallum (near the Libyan border), accused of being 'ignorant,' despite his education, and a closed-minded elder brother of the protagonist family. This elder brother, still living in the countryside, refuses to sell the land and share out the family inheritance, despite the desperate financial needs of his brothers, and attempts to force his educated niece to marry her cousin. He had previously cut off ties with his sister when she had insisted on a love marriage.
3 For more on this policy of confronting extremism with media, see Abu-Lughod (1996).
4 Seminar sponsored by *Majallat al-idha'a w-al-tilifizyun*, May 16, 1997. Partial transcription in *Al-Idha'a w-al-tilifizyun*, May 24, 1997, pp. 8–15.

5 For a detailed examination of the tropes by which the Sa'id is represented in the literature and political discourse of the north, see Rieker (1997).
6 For more on this, see Abu-Lughod (1993, 1995).
7 Khidhr (1997:21).
8 Seminar sponsored by *al-Idha'a w-al-tilifizyun*.
9 Khidhr (1997:21).
10 Family planning is another value supported by television through its spots on birth spacing and a gentle masculinity in programs like "Crowds," and even a serial ("The Nile Flows On"). These were produced by the Information, Education, and Communication Center of the State Information Service, with some assistance from foreign donors, such as USAID, and with collaborators such as the Johns Hopkins Center for Communication Programs.
11 This and the names of other villagers are pseudonyms.
12 See Abu-Lughod (1997). For more on the concept of discrepant cosmopolitanisms, see Appadurai (1996).
13 A series of ten television spots entitled "Egypt's Heroines" is being produced now as part of a literacy campaign targeting women in Upper Egypt and jointly sponsored by the Egyptian government and the British Council. Made by the film maker Attiyat al-Abnoudy, the series "spotlights Egyptian women talking about how learning to read has enriched their lives" (Abbas 1997:14).
14 Personal communication.
15 For another persuasive argument that images of the peasant are put into service to justify policies detrimental to their lives and livelihoods, see the discussion of the role of representations in the press of tenant farmers in the debate on the change in tenancy laws (Reem Saad, 1998 [b]).
16 An exception is Nawal Hassan who began in 1997 a campaign to save Gurna, using the argument of preserving vernacular architecture.
17 For more on the relocation project, see Siona Jenkins (1996a, b).
18 See Mitchell (1995).
19 Larter (1997:2).
20 See Reem Saad (1998 [a]) for an insightful discussion of the way in which Egyptian intellectuals try to censor work that represents poor people in Egypt because it is a 'shame.'

# References

Abbas, Dalia. 1997. "Upper Egypt's Ongoing War Against Illiteracy." *Middle East Times*. May 16–22. p. 14.

Abu-Lughod, Lila. 1993. "Finding a Place for Islam." *Public Culture* 5(3):493–513.

———. 1995. "The Objects of Soap Operas" in Daniel Miller, ed. *Worlds Apart: Modernity Through the Prism of the Local*. London: Routledge. pp. 191–210.

———. 1996. "Dramatic Reversals" in Joel Beinin and Joe Stork, eds. *Political Islam*. Berkeley: University of California Press. pp. 269–82.

———. 1997. "The Interpretation of Culture(s) After Television." *Representations* no. 59 (Summer 1997). pp. 109–34.
Appadurai, Arjun. 1996. *Modernity at Large*. Minneapolis: University of Minnesota Press.
Jenkins, Siona. 1996a. "Lifting Roots and Moving Home." *al-Wakalah*, March. pp. 36–37.
———. 1996b. "Letter from Egypt." *Guardian Weekly*, September 15. p. 25.
Khidhr, Faris. 1997. "Hilm al-janubi: qasida tilifizyuniya fi 'ishq al-watan." *Majallat al-idha'a w-al-tilifizyun*, January 18. p.20.
Larter, Christopher. 1997. "Tourism has a Bright Future after a Boom Year: Interview with Tourism Minister Mamdouh Al Beltagui." *Middle East Times*. January 19–25. p. 2.
Mitchell, Tim. 1995. "Worlds Apart: An Egyptian Village and the International Tourism Industry." *Middle East Report* 196. pp. 8–11, 23.
Rieker, Martina. 1997. "The Sa'id and the City: Subaltern Spaces in the Making of Modern Egyptian History." Unpublished Ph.D. dissertation, Temple University.
Saad, Reem. 1998 [a]. "Shame, Reputation and Egypt's Lovers: A Controversy over the Nation's Image." *Visual Anthropology* 10(2–4): 401–412.
——— 1998 [b]. "State, Landlord, Parliament and Peasant: The Story of the 1992 Tenancy Law in Egypt" in Alan Bowman and Eugene Rogan, eds. *Agriculture in Egypt from Pharaonic to Modern Times*, Proceedings of the British Academy 96:387–404.

# 8

# Conflict or Cooperation: Changing Gender Roles in Rural Egyptian Households

KAMRAN ASDAR ALI

This paper explores how changing landholding patterns, recent history of male out-migration, removal of food and agricultural subsidies, and high unemployment rates are experienced by women and men in rural Egypt. I will further consider how women adjust to the changing social and economic conditions reflected in the volatile male employment market. Based on field work in a village in Lower Egypt, this article will finally suggest ways to rethink gender relations and the domestic sphere in rural Egypt.[1]

Most studies take the unequal gender relations as a given, seldom questioning how they are maintained, perpetuated, or changed in relation to the social changes in society. In opposition to the dominant representation of Middle Eastern gender relations in anthropological and social science, I would argue that the separation of the male and female sphere, with the dominating patriarch, is an exaggerated depiction of lived experience. Inequalities certainly exist between the genders, but analysis needs to move toward understanding their dynamics; how these differences are maintained and undermined within constantly shifting social contexts. Cooperation and sharing between genders exist simultaneously with male practices and rhetoric that seek to generate power and authority. Therefore, to understand the socialization processes through which gender asymmetry is maintained we must examine the experiences of both sexes.

## Women, Development, and Autonomy

Recent literature on women, gender, and development links women's autonomy and independence to their access to wage labor in different societies. Such formulations cross culturally gauge women's status linked to the concepts of free choice and women's autonomous decision-making ability. These culturally neutral and seemingly universal concepts of free choice and autonomy thus become indicators for the emancipation of women from more 'traditional' sets of constraints. Development literature celebrates these concepts as they enable women to make independent decisions without reference to local, familial, and communitarian context.

This complex process of movement from traditional control into the liberating arm of state relations, a journey, as it were, from the household to the factory, has been documented by anthropologists in different cultures. For example, Aihwa Ong (1988) shows how changing Malaysian socioeconomic conditions have increased women's access to wage labor. She documents the depersonalized work relations in a multinational computer chip industry in Malaysia where female workers with "manual dexterity" are put under exhaustive work regimes. These women leave rural households to enter strict regimes of disciplined capitalist production and the world of modern consumption patterns where choice plays a major part in their individual self-fashioning.

Similarly Patricia Fernandez-Kelly (1983) shows how exploited female *maquiladora* workers in Mexico anticipate the traditional roles of motherhood and prospects of marriage to opt out of the wage market. For the Middle East, Fatima Mernissi (1982) analyzes the negative impact of capitalist development on Moroccan peasant women, while Soheir Morsy (1990) ethnographically demonstrates how women's household and outside work responsibilities have increased with the advent of labor migration from Egyptian villages.

Such studies force us to complicate the straightforward narrative of emancipation linked to wage labor. Clearly the issues are complex and varied and much research, especially in the Middle East, needs to be done on women's work and its linkage to class and the larger social, economic, and cultural context in which this work is available and performed.

## The Context

Qaramus is approximately one hundred kilometers northeast of Cairo and about five kilometers from the town of Abu Kabir in Sharqiya governorate. Zagazig, the capital of the governorate, was founded by Muhammad Alı Pasha in 1836–37, as a market town for the cash crops of the region. By the 1860s with the development of agricultural infrastructure, deepened canals, barrages, railway connections, cotton gins and workshops, and the settlement of foreigners, Zagazig along with the province of Sharqiya had become the center of cotton trade for the region (Baer 1962; Wilson 1934). The area was a major producer of cotton, and landholdings were primarily large estates owned by the ruling elite.

At the time of the revolution in 1952, the land around Qaramus belonged to the Crown Prince Muhammad 'Ali Tawfiq. During the turbulent period preceding the revolution, the peasantry participated in anti-landlord revolts and action all through the Delta region. Villages around Qaramus revolted against the managers of the Crown Prince's estate. After the revolution, almost all land in the area was expropriated and redistributed as land reform parcels to the peasantry.

In the last forty years, the village has grown from a hamlet dependent on the *'izba* owners into a small town of ten thousand inhabitants. It is administratively linked to the district of Abu Kabir, which is a major market and commercial center for the region. Today, Qaramus can be reached by service taxi, bus, and railway from Cairo. A two to three hour journey through the Delta brings you to Abu Kabir, and from there a commuter truck takes you to the village for twenty-five piasters. The village itself is divided by the central main road into two distinct parts, both surrounded by agricultural land. Like most villages in the Delta, its most noticeable sights are the mushrooming new constructions due to the inflow of remittances and the investment in housing by returning migrants. Informants told me of the rapid expansion of concrete housing replacing the older adobes or mud brick family compounds. Elders in the community describe the growth since the 1970s as extremely brisk, and attest that almost a quarter or a third of the village has been built on agricultural land during the last two decades.

There is a main market with two pharmacies, a clinic, a few grocery stores, and stores for machinery repair. A weekly market dominated by women sellers is held every Sunday. Villagers buy weekly supplies of vegetables and meat there. The sellers are themselves *fallaha* (wives of peasants or peasant women), but the products they sell are not necessarily grown by them. They buy fresh vegetables in the marketing center of Abu Kabir or Hayya, another nearby town, and follow a weekly route to smaller towns and villages of the region.

## Agriculture

Almost all of the land surrounding Qaramus is incorporated in the land reform cooperative and organized around the crop rotation patterns of the system. Qaramus was historically the mother village of the larger estate, and a number of *kafur* (plural of *kafr*; hamlets) surround it. Older informants remember the times when the area was controlled by the supervisors of the royal prince. One elderly farmer talked of those days with anger and frustration:

> The people lived in abject poverty. Whenever they, the Turks, wanted to beat someone, and take things away, it would not bother them. The revolution was a godsend. Living conditions were deplorable. Two families with their adult married children lived in a single, small home ... .

Such memories suggest an appreciation of Nasir and the land reform. In conversation, people would generally thank Nasir for the grant of land and opportunities of education denied to their kind before.

The major crops grown are cotton, corn, and rice in the summer, and wheat and fodder (berseem) in the winter. Vegetables and fruits are grown interspersed with these crops, and some beans are also produced on excess land. Almost twenty-four hundred feddans of land is registered at the land reform cooperative office for the area. This land is distributed among 750 registered land reform beneficiaries. The largest of these landholdings are in sizes of two to five feddans.

The holdings are divided among family members, especially if there are adult sons in the household. This division fragments the holding into smaller plots. To avoid this fragmentation, families sometimes assign one member to take care of the land and draw most of the profit from it. This member may then supply fodder to the others for their cattle, allow them to grow vegetables, and also share some basic staples that are not sold in the market. The scarcity of land and the small size of holdings has led most landowning farmers to obtain government or other jobs to supplement their earnings from farming.

Actual holdings may be larger or smaller than the landownership records show. Nicholas Hopkins (1987) suggests that landholdings should be understood as landownership plus the land rented in subtracted by the land rented out. These patterns of renting land are present in the village but details about them are hard to come by. The small landowners fear discussing money matters and agricultural profit. This should be seen in the context of how people respond to the long history of regressive taxation by the Egyptian state.

Those who have emigrated to the city or the Gulf states have rented out the little land that they owned, in order to guarantee a family income in their absence. Others who are gainfully employed with the government or in the private sector and possess very small holdings of a few qirats frequently tend to rent-out their share of land. Similarly, women who do not have their spouses at home or are widowed often participate in this practice.

Farmers who rent-in land may have additional incomes from adult members of their families with non-farm incomes. These farmers control sizable amounts of land due to their access to finance through their relatives. For example, a farmer who tilled eight feddans of reform land, comparatively a large holding in the village, had three sons in Cairo who worked as mid-level government employees and two in Kuwait. He had rented-in four feddans of land and also managed a poultry farm of 250 birds. His credit dependency on the state or private sources was minimal as he had access to money directly from his sons, who were compensated through the agricultural earnings.

In June of 1992, a new agrarian law was passed by the Egyptian People's Assembly (Hinnebusch 1993).[2] This law raised the land rent from seven times the basic tax to twenty-two times for an interim period of five years.[3] In 1992–93, the basic tax was LE33 per feddan per year for the area. The going market rate of renting a feddan was somewhat higher than the new changes would allow (24 x 50 or LE1200 as opposed to 22 x 33 or LE726 with the new rent ceiling). In changing the rent ceilings, the state sought to bring the renting rates for the reform land nearer to the going market rate. Similarly, the sale price of one qirat of agricultural land was approximately LE1200. For house building purposes, it ranged from LE4,000 to LE7,000 per qirat, depending upon its proximity to the main road that passes through the village. As most of these transactions are illegal, the nature of sales and renting arrangements are very difficult to ascertain. Peasants fear being taxed over and above their normal dues. Only in conversation, with some slips here and there, can one start comprehending the breadth of these practices.

The recent changes in agrarian policy have started to affect other aspects of life in Qaramus as well. The state recently lifted subsidies on fertilizers and other agricultural inputs. Concurrently it released price controls. This may be linked to a further concession to the middle- and large- landowning peasantry that can afford inputs but were burdened by these controls. For small landholders, the burden of procuring fertilizers from the open market, however, is an added expense along with the increase in other costs.

The long term effects of the new agricultural policy could be toward accumulation of land in the hands of fewer landholders. Robert Springborg (1990b) in an analysis of the 1982 agricultural census data[4] argues that a consolidation rather than a fragmentation of land has already taken place at the expense of smaller landholders. This led to the bifurcation of the agricultural sector into a growing and well capitalized subsector and a diminishing, impoverished peasant sector.

The economic liberalization of the 1970s did not substantially change the legacy of the agrarian reform, yet allowed for some private accumulation of land by the owners gaining control of the rented land. The process dispossessed farmers, who increasingly sought off-farm work, and in some cases sold their remaining plots to the larger holders.[5]

## The Effects of Wage Employment on Gender and Family

As changes in agriculture have intensified, the increase in off-farm employment has become a major issue for the young men of the village. Some who have access to land tend to stay in the village and work on the family farm. Those who are somewhat educated or have learned a trade, such as masons or electricians, seek jobs in the construction sector in nearby towns like Zagazig, or even Cairo. In the last two decades, many emigrated to the Gulf Arab states and to Jordan and Iraq. People told me that a member from each family was away at sometime during the last ten years. The migration years increased real estate value as people primarily invested their remittances in constructing brick houses, either by improving their older adobe ones or buying new land for construction, leading to encroachments on agricultural land.

The flow of wealth due to migration during the 1980s meant a change in living styles. Older informants would occasionally talk about growing up in a household compound where the whole family slept in the same room. As sons grew up and got married they would construct extra rooms in the same compound. The kitchen and the bathroom/toilet would be shared by all members. Migration money has thus meant an increase in separation of households over the last twenty years.

For those who could afford it, money saved through remittances was invested in the construction of new living quarters. Married men who lived in separate households would continuously talk about how amicably this separation had proceeded in their case and how their parents were content seeing them happy with their immediate families. Women sometimes told me how they could feel free in their own homes and not worry about what they wore, for the sake of modesty, as the only people in the house were their husbands and children. They said that they could talk freely to their husbands and feel comfortable in doing what they pleased without their in-laws interfering in their lives.

These exchanges on the benefits of one's own house and amicable nature of separation occurred repeatedly in my conversations. They may reflect not only the general satisfaction that people feel in this process of change, but also the anxieties that are latent in a changing environment where new and different kinds of relationships and living patterns are being tested and given precedence over older established ones. There is also a notion of privacy and private space that arises here and takes the form of domestic areas that are shared by some and not by others. A modern sensibility towards certain sections of the house is cultivated in which a bedroom becomes a private domain for the married couple and the bathroom is only shared within the immediate nuclear family living in the same house. Whenever I was invited to see a new house, invariably I was shown the bathroom with its internal plumbing and a modern style commode. The link between accumulated wealth and the creation of certain modern private spaces, like toilets with running water, created distinctions between these informants and those who still lived with their whole extended family in a compound with outhouses used by many. Becoming modern in this case was reflected in becoming more enclosed, private, and individualistic about personal habits like washing oneself. The availability of running water and a modern commode itself may change the way bodies become trained to perform ablutions under the influence of different ideas of hygiene and cleanliness. I seek to suggest that the introduction of modern household architecture along with increased wealth and education is perhaps also changing the way people think about self and body. I would argue that in talking about change, transformation, and the impact of modern values, it is sometimes the mundane and ordinary habits that give us the important clues to these processes.

After the Gulf war of 1990–91, there was a return migration. The decrease in remittances due to declining emigration has led to stagnation in the construction sector, the one area where jobs were plentiful in the past several years. Men who were previously in the Gulf states have come back to diminished job opportunities. Educated but landless returning migrants now work as low-level government employees. They may have saved enough to build a house, pay off their loans, accumulate luxury goods like a television or a VCR, but they may still feel trapped in their salaried position without access to land. They complain that those who have agricultural land and a job are better off as their food bills are partially subsidized. Therefore, individuals with two or more feddans of land are envied in the village, as they are thought to possess some level of security.

As economic disparity increases in urban and rural areas, families struggle to manage under increasing adversity. Women are forced to seek employment outside their homes to help pay for maintaining households and the increasing costs of educating and rearing children. In urban areas, women in poorer neighborhoods are seeking employment as domestics and as factory laborers. The excursions of wives outside their household cut through the rhetoric of idealized domesticity. Men grudgingly agree to their wives working because of the need for the additional income. Yet they also complain that their wives neglect domestic duties, including the proper training of the children. The fact that their partners need to work to support the household destabilizes men's roles as providers and challenges their authority within the family. Men also fear competition from potential female applicants in an already shrinking job market. Mustafa, a primary school teacher in the village, complained about women teachers in these terms:

> Why should they work? By working they just lose their house and husband. Anyway the inclusion of women teachers has meant less work for all of us and also less salary. Men can do all the work that these women do and we should be paid double what we get.

Hence social problems are deflected into the realm of gender tensions within the family and in society. Rapid socioeconomic changes are not only undermining traditional male power; the process as a whole may be extremely painful for those who are experiencing it. Even for women, the economic insecurity of their male partners undercuts the benefits of the 'patriarchal bargain' (Kandiyoti 1988) that they enjoyed. Recent data show that the ill effects on nutrition and health linked to structural adjustment are worse for women and children (Nassar 1994). Old support structures are disappearing and new forms have yet to evolve. It is a time of much apprehension and uncertainty for the underprivileged in Egyptian society.

Friends of mine with college education who had gone to Jordan or Iraq came back to a somewhat changed world, partly created by the inflationary tendencies set up by remittances of people like themselves. For example, Idris, a forty-year-old university graduate, had spent most of the 1980s in Jordan. The son of a peasant, he had sent money home so that his younger siblings could be educated and their house could be constructed better. Coming back after the Gulf War in the early 1990s meant living on his savings, as he was without a job for almost six months. He is now working for the agricultural cooperative office as a low-level employee. "I have friends who are university graduates who are *'ummal* (workers)," he said one day, frustrated at his inability to earn a decent living and also at not having enough resources to get married. "I do not have enough land to support the whole family," he continued, "and I am the only breadwinner now. My younger brother is learning the electrician trade, and after military service we will try to send him to Kuwait, but it is getting difficult as the papers are very expensive."

The anxieties of men over employment opportunities are also reflected in the nature of the marriage arrangements they face. The economy and the changing nature of society were occasionally blamed by my unmarried friends for their inability to marry even into their thirties. The accumulation of wealth and the accessibility of consumer goods has also changed marriage patterns and expectations in the village. Whereas older male informants would tell me that they were married by presenting only a silver bangle to their brides, the recent shift is towards gold bangles and jewelry along with other household items, such as washing machines and televisions. Although these practices are inherently favorable to women, they also mean a delay in marriage for a high percentage of couples. Such high expenditures partly explain why men like Idris, who were educated and did not consider themselves as *fallah*, have not been able to get married. He cannot afford the marriage expenditure in light of all his other responsibilities toward his family.

Marriage patterns are generally changing for women too. Women would tell me that the tradition of parents arranging matches was giving way to men and women choosing each other. They insisted that all this was done within the parameters of modesty, and not like in the city, where men and women were without any shame. Even this discretion was criticized by the older generation. An older woman complained about the situation in the following terms:

> We are *fallahin*, and should marry among ourselves, but now these girls go to school and want an educated *muwazzaf* (government servant). They are now all choosing for themselves. *Wallahi* [I swear] I was married for just thirty pounds.

Migration, however, remains the only hope for a number of educated and uneducated young men who seek to create a better future for themselves and their families. I occasionally would hear of men who were even trying to migrate illegally to European countries like Spain or Germany. Mustafa, another friend, went to Cairo for three years. He worked in a falafel restaurant as a short-order cook earning LE10 a day. The year I did my field work, Mustafa came back to the village and started to live with his parents. His father, who works for the local police as a constable, found him a job with the bus company in Abu Kabir. Mustafa asserted that, "I would like to be independent and live on my own with my wife and daughter, but I cannot imagine it on the pay I receive." When I inquired why he had not thought of bringing his wife to the city instead of returning home, he replied that in the city, the expenses were very high and he could not support a family, although he was earning almost LE200 a month.

These examples point toward a sense of anxiety, especially among those who do not have enough resources like land or a well-paid job. Although these men are still lucky to have a job, inflationary tendencies and changing expectations for better living are major challenges for the future. It could be said that those who have not migrated are biding their time waiting to leave. Unequal distribution of income is an important incentive for many of the most productive Egyptians to contemplate leaving their country (Ajami 1982).

## Women's Work and Presentation of Self

This section will ethnographically illuminate how changing landholding patterns, the recent history of male out-migration, removal of agricultural subsidies, and high unemployment rates are experienced by women in rural Egypt. I will discuss how these larger socioeconomic changes impact the household level and especially the women in Qaramus.

In the last two decades, migration by large percentages of rural men has also increased the numbers of the rural female labor force. Historically, women in rural Egypt have always worked along with their family members in the agricultural sector. Yet it is at times of shortage of male labor that their presence becomes more obvious to policy makers.[6] Emigration patterns have resulted historically in a labor shortage, with an increase in wage rates in some cases, but essentially a feminization of agriculture in most areas (Springborg 1990a; Toth 1991; Dethier 1989). James Toth argues that gender has traditionally been used in the agricultural sector to divide the labor market and reduce labor costs, while increasing profits for employers (1991: 231). The rates of daily wages in Qaramus were LE3.5 for women compared to LE5 for men in the farming sector. This discrepancy in wages has long been used to depress wages for male daily workers as well. At times of surplus labor, especially, men have been forced to do traditional female jobs to make a living.

Although men in Qaramus would at times deny the involvement of their womenfolk in agricultural labor, it was common for peasant women to look after the cattle, work on vegetable patches, cut berseem for the market, and effectively be employed along with their children during the cotton picking month. The denial may reflect a rhetoric of masculinity and self-sufficiency that is perpetuated by men in economically unstable times. It also underscores how people tend to represent their community as opposed to others. Therefore, the assertion that women in Qaramus did not work was meant to indicate that the village was wealthy and honorable, and there was no need for its womenfolk to work for a living. I was given names of other villages where men were not able to adequately provide for their families and hence their women had to work. Through this exercise, my informants constructed a geography of the region depending on which villages allowed their women to work and which did not. This was a kind of a spatial analysis of where people like themselves lived opposed to less honorable people. Such maps also served in arranging kin relationships and marriage arrangements. These views were articulated perhaps more to convey the hopes of these men (and sometimes women) of being able to live with dignity in a social environment that did not force them to labor extremely long hours throughout the year to help make ends meet.

Lynn Freedman (nd) analyzes the consequences of structural adjustment on the rural labor of third world women. She shows that as cash crop production with better wages is introduced into local economies, women are forced into subsistence agriculture. Comparably, mechanization in Egyptian agriculture has resulted in men taking the more highly paid jobs of transport and machine operating while women have been pushed into the less well-paid mundane chores (Hopkins 1983).

In this regard, studies on women left behind by male migration in Egypt rarely emphasize the increased responsibilities and labor that overwhelm women in the absence of their male partners. Literature on male labor migration in Egypt has looked at its impact on the household in breaking down the authority of the extended family and the senior female member of the family (mother-in-law). Hind Khattab et al (1982) have argued that the enhanced economic status of migrants' wives, due to the remittances they receive, has also given some of them a higher status in rural communities. Fatma Khafagy (1984) presents a similar argument by showing that women gain power in the public sphere by being responsible for negotiating terms with cooperatives and making other decisions for the household in the absence of their male relatives. Mona Abaza (1987) partially agrees with this analysis, but also contends that as women get more access to decision-making in the agricultural sphere, their work becomes socially devalued as peasant work by men. So as women become seemingly independent, the work itself is denigrated as being of a lower status.

The complexity of familial relationships and household structures also forces us to look more closely at the lives of women in the absence of their menfolk (Morsy 1990). A recently married woman in a somewhat prosperous joint-family household may not be able to exert as much 'autonomy' compared to an older woman in a less well-to-do family.

Fatima, a high school graduate from Cairo, was married to her mother's brother's son in a nearby village a year before I started my field work. I knew her as a receptionist at the government clinic and also as the sister-in-law of one of the clinic managers. One day, while sharing a taxi ride with her to Cairo, she informed me that this was her first trip back to the city after her wedding and she had not seen her natal family in over a year. Fatima's in-laws had three feddans of land, most of her brothers-in-law had government jobs, and her father-in-law/uncle ran a general store in the village. They had one of the largest brick houses in the area and were considered a wealthy family. Her husband had left for Saudi Arabia three weeks after their wedding. It was only when her husband came back for his yearly vacation and then left again that we shared this taxi ride. This trip materialized as her husband had given her permission to visit her relatives. She was traveling alone and was, as an educated woman who had grown up in Cairo, interestingly enough, trusted by her family to navigate the city by herself. Fatima was very matter-of-fact on this issue. Her structural position in the household did not allow her to make decisions independently, although she had access to some of her husband's remittances, and led a comfortable life.

Even those women who may have the social space to make independent decisions feel burdened by the increasing work load of single-handedly taking care of the farm, raising children, supervising house repair or construction, and maintaining familial responsibilities. Women spoke to me about feeling quite exhausted by all these responsibilities, especially when other male kin were also away from the village.

Another aspect that is often ignored in representations of women left behind by their migrating spouses is the emotional loss that women may feel when their husbands are away for long stretches of time. Seldom does literature on women or gender in the Middle East address the issue of affection between husbands and wives and how bonds of mutual support and caring are constructed within households. Lila Abu-Lughod's (1986) work on the Awlad 'Ali helps us to see how women in this community use poetry to convey very strong emotions. She analyzes these poems as sub-discourses of resistance by the socially weak. However, these poems also give us a window into the private lives of these women and inform us about their romantic desires and their relationships with their husbands. The affective linkages that the women invoke binds both sexes into a single, symbolic bond and hence undermines the sharp representations of public and private spheres.

Similarly, some women in the village spoke to me of the loss they felt when their husbands were away. Hala worked as an employee in a government facility in the village. Her husband had been away for over two years in Saudi Arabia. She had a teenage daughter and one third of a feddan of land which she rented out. As an uneducated rural woman married to a poor, almost landless, peasant who had gone abroad to make a living, Hala suffered from taunts and jokes from her coworkers about how her husband had left her alone with her daughter and would never come back. Hala was always anxious about the well-being of her husband and felt alone and tired in dealing with life by herself. "Duktur," she would say to me, "Could you not get my Ibrahim here through your *mashru'a* [project; meaning my work]. Why does he have to work so hard there when he can get some guineas (Egyptian pounds) here?"

Hala's direct lament was an interesting episode in my understanding of how some peasant women talk about general life situations. Depictions of gender relations in rural Egyptian households always portray women as oppressed without ever mentioning relationships of kindness, sharing, and mutual love between husbands and wives. These representations may follow a long history of how the 'Arab' family is historically placed in a classification of themes. Some of these repeated themes are: the non-consensual marriage where men are dominant and the family is more important than the individual; the cross-cousin marriage patterns; women's honor; the social powerlessness of women; and the threat of polygyny dangling like a sword over women's heads (Tucker 1993:196–99). I do not seek to locate 'love' as a Western-influenced concept within the *fallah* household in order to 'humanize' the subjects of this ethnography, but to question the terms in which relationships within these households are portrayed. The representation of women in rural Egypt as gaining independence, autonomy, and power within the household only when their men are away is, I think, also based on the above-mentioned conceptual and Orientalist models of Middle Eastern households and gender relations.

Women's work needs to be also rethought with regard to their contribution toward their families' welfare. The economic adjustment programs being instituted in Egypt have drastically diminished social subsidies. Rising inflation and a deteriorating job market for male labor away from the farm has increased the precariousness of poor households in the village. The desire to educate children, which is evident in most households, has meant the added expenditure of after school lessons. Parents especially want their boys to succeed in the competitive exams so they can be placed in better universities or high schools. Work by both parents in these circumstances becomes crucial for the level of household income. Women who opt to work in their husband's presence or absence do so because the added income is a necessity for the economic survival of their families. Given an option, many women, considering the lower wages they receive, may not want to engage in hard, day-long labor. Rasha, a peasant wife who worked the full ten days of the cotton picking season on LE3 a day, along with her two children and husband, was very clear on this issue when she said, "If my husband was a primary school teacher getting a monthly salary, maybe I could have stayed home and raised some poultry, but now I need to work if my children are to go to school."

Egyptian rural statistics show that the number of family members employed in farm labor is lowest for the smallest and largest landowning groups. This indicates that very small landholders need to find off-farm work while the large ones can employ others to do their work (Springborg 1990b:38). In Qaramus, women whose husbands were educated and had well-paying jobs, were landowners with better incomes, or were rich migrants had opted out of the rural job market.

This may also help us understand the veiling patterns among women. Peasant women wore the traditional *hijab* that does not cover the face. These women, at times, found those who were taking on the more restrictive veil, the *niqab*, that covers the whole face, not only cumbersome but religiously incorrect. However, their criticism took on less of a moral and more of a socioeconomic emphasis. Zaynab, a peasant housewife, one day saw one of her relatives donning the *niqab* for the first time. She complained to her husband that since her relative's husband had come back from Saudi Arabia with lots of money, the relative had started wearing the *niqab* and not working outside the home. Also, Zaynab stressed, this man had joined the *sunniyin* (meaning the Islamists, by reference to their beard—they follow the Sunna or the teachings of Muhammad). What I propose is that the ability to refuse work in the village is linked to the socioeconomic status of the individual family. Hence, the practice of wearing the *niqab* may be partially connected to the enhanced wealth of some women and their families.

The argument on veiling cannot entirely be made on a socioeconomic basis. The issue of correct practices of behavior and dress are imminently important in today's Egypt, as the Islamist political forces gain acceptance as an important voice on defining Islamic norms. Those in the village who belonged to the Islamic groups not only formed political connections with other parts of the Islamic world, but demonstrated how the body itself was similarly disciplined across borders. The regulation of correct practices of how one prayed, washed oneself, wore clothes, veiled, kept a beard, cut hair, and behaved in public and private spaces was important to link them to larger groups of Muslims in other parts of the world.

In Qaramus, the acceptance of these tendencies was never very clear cut. Men were at times admonished, in front of me, by relatives of their wives for forcing them into more restrictive veils. Women among themselves would caution young girls not to associate with the more Islamist women who might lead them astray. This caution may be due to the prevalent fear spread by the state. Peasant families, forever cautious, may not want to get into any trouble by associating with people who are considered on the wrong side of the law. Yet people also had definite opinions, in opposition to the Islamist interpretations, on what was correct practice in Islam and what they regarded as exaggeration or unnecessary.

It may be argued that recent increases in wealth for some families have prompted them to confine women's labor to the household (Morsy 1990:143). The control of female movement may be linked to the reassertion of Islamic norms in the community. These formulations may be correct, yet we need also to look at how women themselves may be party to these decisions. Contrary to the literature that argues that rural Egyptian women became more active in the public sphere through access to remittances, I would argue that the options are varied and open at this stage. Some women may have decided to show their 'autonomy' by shunning the public place. Rather than work for wages, some may have opted out of the wage economy sector altogether. What does this mean to liberal notions of autonomy of women and their control over their work situations? In such formulations, are there spaces for those who opt not to work for wages? Following these questions we may also want to consider the choice made by women to put on the more restrictive veil, the *niqab*. Do such choices have a space in the liberal formulations of choice and autonomy? The questions need to be answered through further understanding of these women's life experiences—a task I am not able to perform in this study.

## Conclusion

Starting with Ester Boserup's (1970) now classic work, social scientists have argued for a more complex understanding of productive roles by women, in relation to those of men, across different cultures. This article has not only emphasized the productive contribution of women in rural and urban settings but has attempted a more realistic assessment of female work in social reproduction.

Hence, autonomy and work need to be, at least in the case of my informants, thought about within the parameters of how the social, economic, and cultural changes impact their lives in rural Egypt today. Class differentials, access to off-farm employment, remittances, household formations, and competing moral ideologies shape the experiences of women and men. Women's work should be understood with reference to these experiences and not in abstract formulations. As support structures for independent female-headed households are increasingly diminishing, the available options for some women may be to survive within the structure of their families. Further, questions about how power and resources are negotiated within rural Egyptian households need to be discussed beyond the models of conflict between genders. Rather, I would suggest that these issues should also be addressed in an understanding of the caring and mutual support that may exist between spouses.

## Notes

1 The field work in Egypt was supported by a doctoral grant by the Population Council and by the anthropology department at Johns Hopkins University. I thank the participants in the conference on "Rural Egypt at the End of the Twentieth Century" for their valuable comments. Special thanks to Nicholas S. Hopkins and Kirsten Westergaard for their close readings and suggestions. However, I remain responsible for the final shape of this article and any shortcomings therein.
2 For more details, see the introduction to the book.
3 Egyptian law prohibits renting or selling of agricultural reform land. However, systematic renting and selling of this land goes on unofficially. The new owner takes on the government installment and debt and abides by the crop rotation schedule. In the year that I was doing field work, the market rate for renting one *qirat* of land (175 square meters) was about LE50 per year.
4 This analysis is based on data accumulated a few years after the beginning of the Sadat era *Infitah* (economic opening). Ireton in this volume analyzes more recent figures.
5 Hopkins (1983) shows that farmers owning less than one feddan are forced to look for off-farm work to supplement their household income. It is estimated that more than one third of a feddan is needed to support one resident dependent on agriculture. Members of families with very small holdings have less than a tenth of a feddan each, while those with small holdings have 0.28 feddans each. According to figures analyzed by Springborg (1990b:38), there are 1.9 million Egyptian families in these

categories. He argues that almost 70 percent of the Egyptian rural population may be living below the level of subsistence, forcing a large percentage of these to seek labor outside the agricultural sector (Springborg 1990b).

6 James Toth (1991) in a review essay on labor in rural Egypt, gives the example of the 1961 critical crop failure in Egypt. See also his paper in this volume.

## References

Abaza, Mona. 1987. "The Changing Image of Women in Rural Egypt." *Cairo Papers in Social Science* Vol. 10(3).

Abu-Lughod, Lila. 1986. *Veiled Sentiments*. Berkeley: University of California Press.

Ajami, Fouad. 1982. "The Open-Door Economy: Its Roots and Welfare Consequences." in Gouda Abdel-Khalek and Robert Tignor, eds. *The Political Economy of Income Distribution in Egypt*. New York: Holmes and Meier Publishers. pp. 469–516.

Ammar, Abbas. 1942. *A Demographic Study of an Egyptian Province*. London: Percy Lund Humphries and Co. Ltd.

Baer, Gabriel. 1962. *A History of Landownership in Modern Egypt. 1800–1950*. Oxford: Oxford University Press.

Boserup, Ester. 1970. *Woman's Role in Economic Development*. New York: St. Martins Press.

Dethier, Jean-Jacques. 1989. *Trade, Exchange Rate, and Agricultural Pricing Policies in Egypt*. Vols. 1 and 2. World Bank Comparative Studies. Washington D.C., The World Bank.

Fernandez-Kelly, Maria Patricia. 1983. *For We Are Sold, I and My People*. Albany: State University of New York Press.

Freedman, Lynn P. nd. "Women Health and the Third World Debt: A Critique of the Public Health Response to Economic Crises." unpublished manuscript.

Hinnebusch, Raymond. 1993. "Class, State and the Reversal of Egypt's Agrarian Reform." *Middle East Report* no. 184. pp. 20–23.

Hopkins, Nicholas. 1983. "The Social Impact of Mechanization. in Alan Richards and Philip Martin, eds. *Migration, Mechanization and Agricultural Labor Markets in Egypt*. Boulder: Westview Press. pp. 181–97.

———. 1987. *Agrarian Transformation in Egypt*. Boulder: Westview Press.

Kandiyoti, Deniz. 1988. "Bargaining with Patriarchy." *Gender and Society* 2(3):274–90.

Khafagy, Fatma. 1984. "Women and Labor Migration: One Village in Egypt." *Middle East Report* no. 124. pp. 17–21.

Khattab, Hind Abou Seoud, and Syada Greiss El Daeif. 1982. "Impact of Male Labor Migration on the Structure of the Family and the Roles of Women." *The Regional Papers of the Population Council*. Cairo: The Population Council.

Mernissi, Fatima. 1982. "Women and the Impact of Capitalist Development in Morocco." *Feminist Issues* 2 (2): 69–104.

Morsy, Soheir. 1990. "Rural Women Work and Gender Ideology. A Study in Egyptian Political Economic Transformation." in Seteney Shami et al., eds. *Women in Arab Society*. Oxford: Berg/UNESCO. pp. 87–159.

Nassar, Heba. 1994. "The Impact of Adjustment Policies on Nutrition in Egypt." in S. Heidhues and B. Knerr, eds. *Food and Agriculture Policies under Structural Adjustment*. Frankfurt: Peter Lang. pp. 517–32.

Ong, Aihwa. 1988. "The Production of Possession: Spirits and the Multinational Corporation in Malaysia." *American Ethnologist* 15(1):28–42.

Springborg, Robert. 1990a. "Agrarian Bourgeoisie, Semiproletarians, and the Egyptian State: Lessons for Liberalization." *International Journal of Middle East Studies* 22:447–472.

———. 1990b. "Rolling Back Egypt's Agrarian Reform." *Middle East Report* no. 166, pp. 28–30, 38.

Toth, James. 1991. "Pride, Purdah, or Paychecks. What Maintains the Gender Division of Labor in Rural Egypt." *International Journal of Middle East Studies* 23:213-36.

Tucker, Judith. 1993. "The Arab Family in History: Otherness and the Study of the Family" in Judith Tucker, ed. *Arab Women: Old Boundaries, New Frontiers*. Bloomington: Indiana University Press. pp. 195–207.

Wilson, Ella M. 1934. "Zagazig: A Cotton Market." *The Geographic Review* no. 24.

# 9

# The Vision of a Better Life: New Patterns of Consumption and Changed Social Relations

KIRSTEN HAUGAARD BACH

Consumption practices in rural Egypt, as well as in many other parts of the world, have changed radically during the 1980s and 1990s. This paper describes and discusses change processes in a village in Sharqiya governorate over the ten-year period from 1983 to 1993. It is based on findings from three field work periods, supplemented by shorter visits in the village.

I argue that new opportunities for money income and new patterns of consumption since the mid-1970s have affected the division of labor and social relations in the village by encouraging a more individualistic direction, compared to the previous more subsistence oriented livelihood. Family and community spheres of social identification and cultural outlooks are complemented by new social encounters and new social networks. Education and work abroad, as well as television and radio provide new flows of information and cultural norms. New experiences have influenced indicators of status and aspirations for consumption and have led to a growing dependency on money income. The paper discusses how the introduction of new consumption practices and the prevalence of new levels of education in the village have affected social relations both within and between the families. New indicators for social distinction have developed with an impact upon people's practices and behavior.

The new consumption practices appeared gradually during this period and differ highly from family to family. They include adoption of new types of housing, clothes, furniture, and equipment for work and leisure. They are primarily, though not exclusively, embraced by the younger villagers, particularly the formally educated ones. I will employ villagers' own distinction of themselves in the paper as *muta'allimin* (educated) or *fallahin* (peasants). I conceive the two categories as social fields in Bourdieu's sense of the word (Bourdieu 1984, 1988:544, 1990; Bourdieu and Wacquant 1992). Each one includes spaces of objective relations between social positions in a hierarchy of specific species of various forms of capital (economic, social, and cultural). I shall analyze differences in consumption norms between the two fields from a capital-oriented perspective.

In 1983, villagers expressed a relative optimism for the future and a belief in economic growth through the new types of income. In 1993, this optimism had been replaced by an apprehension, particularly among the younger generation, and a fear for the future. They stressed the difficulties of finding a job locally or abroad and the insufficiency of land for cultivation compared to the size of the paternal holdings that their fathers had inherited. The period I describe in the paper thus refers to a period of expansion of consumption of commodities that is now being challenged by new national policies and by the unstable situation for work abroad.

## The Village and its Population (Farming, Migration, and Income)

In 1983, the village, which I will here call Kafr, included 237 households and about two thousand inhabitants. In 1993, ten years later, after partition of several families into two or more households, there were 284 households. Emigration and immigration to the village balanced each other over this period.

A considerable part of the population lived in three generation households. One family had managed to keep all their five married sons as an economic unit, and in a few families brothers remained together as a joint household after the death of the parents. However, the proportion of extended households in Kafr appears to have declined over the ten-year period. In 1983, extended households composed 52 percent in a sample of half of the village households. In 1993 they made up only 36 percent of a larger sample of 83 percent of the households.

Most of the extended households were split at the death of the elder generation. The majority of the nuclear households consisted of middle-aged couples with their adolescent or adult but yet unmarried children. Some couples separated early from the paternal household due to lack of space within the compound or due to conflicts between members of the household. Few, if any, newly married couples established an independent household straight after marriage.

The majority of the families in Kafr had income from farming. The major part of the land was organized in the village agricultural cooperative, but some of the villagers cultivated agrarian reform land outside the village *zimam* and were organized in a reform cooperative located in the nearby subdistrict village. Other villagers owned land in neighboring villages which they had inherited or purchased. Several such purchases were made in the ten-year period 1983–93 using savings from labor migration. The large rate of labor migration in the village compared to its neighbor villages led to uneven prices for land in the area. It had become cheaper to acquire land outside than inside the village. Three villagers bought plots of ten or twenty feddans in a land reclamation area 50 kilometers away. These purchases expanded the area that was under cultivation by the villagers in the research period from 459 feddans in 1983 to 510 in 1993.

Most families had small holdings of their own. The prevalence of landownership has been increasing since the 1950s when the land reforms eased the economic conditions of the tenants by introducing rent ceilings and reduced prices for purchase of rented land. In 1983, 44 percent of the families in the village owned pieces of land, and in 1993 the share had increased to 49 percent (all these figures cover holdings inside and outside the village). The portion of cultivated land owned (rather than rented) by the cultivators rose from 36 percent to 42 percent in the same period. Tenancy decreased within the period, particularly in the form of cash tenancy *(igar)*. The share of households who rented in land decreased from 56 percent in 1983 to 33 percent in 1993. As much as 29 percent combined ownership with renting of land. Some individuals held land under three or more types of land tenure. Holdings with mixed tenure were on the average larger than holdings of 'mono-tenure,' whether they consisted of owned, rented, or agrarian reform land. All the largest holdings consisted only of owned land, while half of all ownerships were smaller than one feddan. Although the number of holdings rose within the period, the share of total village households which owned land declined from 87 percent to 77 percent.

The average size of villagers' holdings of land thus decreased within the ten-year period in spite of some farmers' purchase of land outside the village. Holdings greater than five feddans decreased from 8 percent of the holdings in 1983 to 6 percent in 1993, and medium-sized holdings of between two and five feddans declined from 47 percent to 27 percent, whereas holdings below the two feddan mark increased rapidly.

Most landownership originated in relatively cheap purchases of *igar* land from absentee landlords. Prior to the land reforms, three families in Cairo[1] had owned practically all the land in the village. A former small-scale farmer who had inherited his father's position as an overseer for the landlords gradually managed to buy almost a quarter of the land registered with the village cooperative. In addition to land in Kafr, this rich landowner also possessed land outside the village. In 1993, he stated that he had a hundred share cropping families inside and outside the village to cultivate his land. Today, four more families possess more than ten feddans each, following purchases of relatively cheap land outside the village. Parallel to these families' successes in increasing their landholdings by purchases of land, there was a continuous fragmentation of landholdings in the village. This was almost exclusively a result of the division of paternal holdings among heirs.

Landlessness has also grown. In 1983, landless families constituted only 13 percent of all village households. In 1993, their share had increased to 23 percent. However, only a fifth of the landless households were employed in agriculture. Almost all landless agricultural laborers were younger generation families who had separated from a landholding paternal household and who were expecting to inherit land at the death of their parents. The large majority of landless household heads were employed outside agriculture. They included those who were self-employed within a craft or trade, as well as public employees *(muwazzafin)*. Most of the latter belonged to the young, educated generation who had separated early from parental farming households. A few elderly *muwazzafin*, such as the two *imams* in the village, renounced their share of paternal holdings for the benefit of farming brothers.

Most of the larger landholdings (above two feddans) were held by extended households, whereas the nuclear households made up a larger percentage of the small landholdings. The increase in the share of small holdings of less than two feddans within this period primarily happened through a division of larger holdings between many heirs (in a few cases between as many as six sons).[2] Few farmers had reduced their holdings by sale of land in the period, due to the relative affluence in Kafr from work abroad. The majority of the sellers were non-farmers who wanted money to build a red-brick house. There were, however, farmers who had sold land in order to invest in the purchase of a tractor or to expand their possessions by purchase of cheaper land outside the village.

Labor migration and local non-farming employment became increasingly important in the village after the mid-1970s. In 1993, full-time farmers constituted only half of the total household heads in the village. They included 20 percent who were farmers on their own holdings and 33 percent who also worked for others in the village as agricultural laborers. The remaining 48 percent of household heads in the village worked abroad or had other occupations locally. Some of the full-time farmers had access to non-agrarian income through *muwazzafin* sons with monthly salaries, whereas others had no household income other than farming.

Compared to other villages in the area, many people from Kafr worked abroad. At the peak of emigration, almost a hundred villagers were abroad at the same time. However, the importance of work abroad declined after this period. Between 1986 and 1993, there were between seventy and eighty migrants annually. The share of migration was highest among relatively newly established small-scale farmers who would otherwise have been forced to supplement their income by low-status work as agricultural laborers in the area. A growing number of the migrants were unemployed *muta'allimin* who had not yet been appointed to a government job. Many of them were sons of full-time farmers with holdings greater than two feddans. In 1993, a total of 215 men had worked abroad on average for periods of almost five years (interrupted by various lengths of holidays at home). By then, as much as 62 percent of total village households had experienced the migration of one or more of its members, compared to 49 percent of the households in 1983.

Education in Kafr began in the 1930s, when relatively affluent farmer or trader families were able to send sons away to formal institutions of education in Zagazig and Cairo. The graduates (*muta'allamin*) were employed in Cairo or in the provincial capital of Zagazig, and they displayed new cultural possibilities and outlooks for the village. Their learning endowed the whole family with prestige and respect. The prestige of the *muta'allamin* was strengthened during the Nasir period, when the local power of absentee landowners was transferred to state authority, administered by public employees, *muwazzafin*. This prestige still appeared to play a role in 1993 in encouraging farming families to push their children through the educational system.

## New Types of Consumption

When I first came to Kafr it appeared a densely clustered unit of gray–brown and yellowish-colored mud-brick houses surrounded by green fields. There were but six newly built red-brick houses. Most houses were of one floor with stores on the roof for grain, straw, berseem, and other products. Women in flowing cotton outfits were washing dishes and clothes at the canal bank, while men and young boys riding donkeys passed me on the narrow path. I had got off the pick-up taxi at the asphalt road in a nearby village and had walked the remaining half kilometer along the canal. Being of farming origin and having grown up in a village, I felt at home with the bright green color of the fertile fields, and I enjoyed the peacefulness compared to noisy Cairo, where I had spent half a year preparing for my field work.

During the decades prior to my arrival, Kafr had undergone substantial processes of structural transformation via land reforms, expansion of education possibilities, provision of public health, and, since the mid-1970s, the opportunity to work abroad. Compared to the situation before the land reforms, the economic condition of most villagers had improved markedly, and new patterns of consumption and sources of income had developed. This development has gradually led to an increasing dependence upon money income, compared to the previous subsistence dominated household economy in the village. The further procurement and expansion of such an income has been challenged in the 1990s by the abolition of employment guarantees for graduates with high school diplomas or university certificates, by decreased salaries and demand for Egyptian labor abroad, and by a new tenancy law which abolishes rent ceilings on rented land, and which, after October 1997, gives landowners the right to expel tenants.

In the childhood and youth of the present middle-aged and elderly part of the population, purchased consumer goods were a luxury, available only to the most affluent villagers, large landowners or traders and, particularly, to categories outside the village who represented power and authority. New patterns of landholding after the land reforms, as well as education and income from work abroad have since allowed new patterns of consumption.

The most obvious and probably also the most far-reaching differences in consumption styles are the new standards of housing, which have had a marked influence on patterns of social relations. In 1983, only a few rich farmers and traders, as well as one or two public employees *(muwazzafin)* families lived in red-brick houses. In 1993, ten years after my first arrival, the housing pattern had changed and a third of the houses were red-brick. They were generally adopted as signs of affluence, and they signaled a high educational level in the family (that is, the presence of sons and daughters who are high-school or university graduates). Several of the new houses were multi-storied, some included four floors, providing space for separate flats for married sons or brothers. Most of the new houses were built on the outskirts of the village, but it was not unusual to demolish an old mud-brick house to build a new prestigious red-brick house. The red-brick houses complemented and, in some cases even surpassed, the importance of landownership in determining social distinction in the village, in particular among the educated. Thus, findings in 1993 showed that a few small-scale farmers with uneducated, farming sons had also used their savings from work abroad to build such houses instead of buying land for farming.

Most of the mud-brick houses included an open air courtyard inside the house where many of the daily activities of the women took place, where food was prepared and eaten, and where the big oven for baking bread was located. The courtyards of the larger houses were surrounded by rooms, some for sleeping, others for domestic animals. They could be converted to rooms for sleeping and vice versa according to the changing size of the family. The mud-brick houses were usually built by the family itself, assisted by neighbors or relatives, and from materials taken from the fields and the stable. This building material easily reverts to soil again when the house is demolished.

The new red-brick houses displayed a more urban style of housing. They were not built by the family but by specialists hired from another village in the district. The bricks, cement, and the iron bars that constituted the supporting pillars of the house were bought from outside the district. None of these materials can be returned to nature easily. On the other hand, the villagers expected that, compared to the mud-brick house, the structure would last much longer and would require a minimum of repair and maintenance.

The amenities characteristic of the two types of housing varied significantly. The mud-brick house was designed to serve farmers' purposes, and included a space for animal husbandry and a storeroom for products from the field. The traditional oven, the *furn*, was centrally-located in the inner courtyard and had a previously important role in cooking. The oven reflected the subsistence-oriented way of life and was heated by leftovers from farming: *gilla* (dried cakes of dung and straw) and stalks and straw from the fields. It had largely been replaced by kerosene or butagas cookers for daily cooking but continued to play a vital role in baking the local type of large dry baladi bread. At the time of my first stay in Kafr, this bread constituted a very basic part of the family diet. It was made from locally produced grain, in most cases from their own fields, and was ground at the village mill a few days before the bread was baked. Baking occupied four to five women for a whole day, but supplied the family with bread for up to four or even six months. It was one of the most important activities for exchange of labor, *zamala*, among women. The women of the family were usually assisted by women neighbors or by married daughters whose in-laws allowed them to assist. Baking was hard work, but was also an occasion for women to strengthen social links between themselves and to enjoy each others' company for a whole day. The fresh bread attracted visitors, and part of it was given as gifts in small portions to neighboring friends and relatives, and sometimes also to needy people in the village.

Most of the red-brick houses included a modern-style, *ifrangi*, kitchen, different from the simple equipment of the open air kitchen used by most women in the mud-brick houses. In 1993, the trousseau of young *muta'allim* brides was assembled in anticipation for future residence in a red-brick house. It commonly included a refrigerator and a Western-style gas cooker, with a small oven, fit for modern types of bread and cakes but far too small and unsuitable for baking the traditional bread.

The spread of the red-brick houses and their mass-produced appliances expressed the spread of a monetary economy in the village during the ten-year period Cash became increasingly necessary for covering basic needs, compared to the situation at my first field work visit in 1983, when consumption was more subsistence-based. In 1993, all sorts of commodities were common, such as food, clothes, electrical equipment, and means of production, such as irrigation pumps. Subsistence-based production has increasingly been relegated to the supply of daily food, but even here practices have changed, as the increasing sale of ready-made bread has indicated. Purchased fruit and vegetables from the weekly market in the nearby village and meat from the district town became a regular component of peoples' diet during the 1980s.

## Social Relations, Division of Labor, and New Practices

Villagers complained that mutual aid was no longer what it used to be: "Everything now has to be paid for by money, nobody helps each other any longer." Men's mutual aid groups, *zamala*, had already disappeared in 1983. Ten years later, women's *zamala* was still practiced in such activities as baking bread. Men's work was integrated earlier into a national and transnational economic framework (through production of cash crops, public employment, and work abroad) whereas women's work, until the mid-1980s, was confined to farming and household activities.

Women's division of work in 1993 was affected by the 'new times.' In 1983, very few women worked outside the house. The first year-group of diploma-holding young women had only recently graduated and were on the point of being appointed to jobs. Over the research decade, education of daughters multiplied. The graduates' entitlement to a job as *muwazzafin* had made education popular both for sons and daughters. Many young, educated women benefited from employment guarantees and in 1993 worked as secretaries or teachers, both inside and outside the village. It became normal practice to educate daughters, and few women tried to make their daughters leave school in order to help them increase family income by dairy activities. Girls were busy at school and with private tutoring after school, resulting in some women no longer having *fallaha* daughters or daughters-in-law to relieve them of their work burdens. A few affluent women with educated daughters and daughters-in-law had started to hire less affluent women from the village to help them in their domestic duties.

However, the effect of the growing unemployment among young graduates on the economy of the individual families was marked. Many of the newly graduated women stayed at home in a kind of waiting position, neither bringing home income as they were expected to do because of their education nor fully taking part in farming activities. Having succeeded in the educational system, the *muta'allim* women did not expect to carry out traditional farming work, such as dairy farming or raising of poultry, tasks that were vital for household income in many families. Many educated women expected to live a 'modern' life, with a government job as a secretary or teacher, and their trousseaus of modern kitchen equipment reflected this aspiration. They took part in 'clean' household work, but not in work in the fields such as a *fallaha* daughter-in-law would do. The unemployed, educated young generation was thus becoming an increasing burden to the household economy.

This burden was articulated by some elderly Kafr women who complained that their unemployed diploma-holding daughters-in-law refused to make cow-dung cakes, *gilla*, as fuel for the bread ovens. Two women had threatened their educated daughters-in-law with divorce over this issue. In village discussions over the matter, their standpoint was opposed by younger women who argued that nobody could any longer demand such work from a woman. Some young women even considered it a sign of distinction that their mothers had not taught them such an old-fashioned *fallaha* activity. The issue provided an arena for testing of power in some households, in particular for demarcation of the status of educated women within less affluent households and for a definition of work duties and spheres of authority between the two generations. However, the increasing unemployment among younger graduates weakened their attempts to redefine patterns of authority. It has become increasingly difficult for them to enhance their status and independence in the extended household compared to the women who were educated in the mid-1980s. The power and authority of the elder generation may thus have been strengthened once again, at least temporarily.

In one of the conflicts, the bride had married her maternal cousin (mother's sister's son). She was the mother-in-law's own choice and the couple had also married out of love. The son worked in one of the desert cities for a relatively modest income but was unable to support his wife and small baby there. He returned to the village on weekends while his wife stayed with his parents, next door to her own parents. Both families lived in small, comparatively newly built mud-brick houses. The daughter-in-law had not yet been assigned a job and she helped her mother-in-law in the house. Toward the end of my stay in the village, she quarreled with her mother-in-law and refused to make *gilla*. The in-laws threatened to divorce her and she left the house and moved back to her own parents. On a short visit to the village three years later, in 1996, the young couple was still married. The husband had found his young wife a job in the company he worked in and they now stayed together in the desert city, returning to the village on weekends, just to see their child, who stayed with the maternal grandmother.

Another case followed a different course. It was also a marriage of love, but between non-relatives, and, unlike the first example, both the son and the daughter-in-law were unemployed. When the bride moved back to her parents after quarreling with her mother-in-law, the in-laws and her husband were slow in asking for her return. They finally came and after some negotiations she returned to them. However, on my next visit to Kafr in 1996, the bride, now with a small baby, was once again staying with her parents. The couple was close to a divorce. The young husband had lost hope of ever getting a government job and worked now with his father on the small family holding. In order to gain some independence from the parents he had begun part-time trading involving the repair and reuse of sacks, but without much success. He was not able to financially support his small family. The young wife had no prospects for a job, either. Neither of them had been appointed to a *muwazzaf* job and were unlikely to get one due to the cancellation of the employment guarantee.

In neither of the two cases had the brides grown up in a red-brick house and both knew well how to make cow-dung cakes. As a recognition of their distinction as educated women, both had been equipped with trousseaus of modern gas cookers with small size ovens, suited for a different type of bread than the one made in the traditional *furn*. The brides regarded making dung cakes as *fallaha* work and they felt humiliated when their mothers-in-law asked them to make cakes. In their own self-conception they were *muta'allimat* and they aspired to settle accordingly in a red-brick house with modern furnishings and light household work. Their inadequate income made this dream difficult, however, especially when the husband was unemployed. The mothers of the husbands, on the other hand, had worked hard[3] with dairy products to help finance their sons' private lessons and the costs of a *muta'allim* wedding and equipment. They now wanted their daughters-in-law to provide them some ease in their own life.

New technology also affected men's and children's work. In particular, children's farm work was lightened when the waterwheel, the *saqiya*, was replaced by electric water pumps. The *saqiya*, which was still in common use in 1983, was chiefly guarded by children, whereas the water pump, which in 1993 had become dominant, was handled by men. Fertilizers partly replaced the need for child labor, too, in the transport of silt from the canal border to the fields. Pesticides reduced the importance of children's collection of cotton worms. In other words, farmers were no longer dependent upon a large number of sons to assist them in daily work. New means of production and the small size of holdings made it easier to spare children and send them to school. It has become possible, too, to combine farming with government jobs or work abroad.

Not only have relations within the family been affected by the new means of production and consumption. Social relations between families have also been influenced. New styles of housing and equipment have promoted new types of privacy and reduced traditional spaces for social intercourse between villagers.

The wide entrances of the old houses provided a space where the residents of the house could enjoy the coolness of the evenings during hot summer days and the social company of villagers who would pass by on the street. Straw mats, *liblib* (sunflower) seeds, tea, or a water pipe provided visitors with an open invitation to sit down for a chat. The entrance complemented the privacy of the inner courtyard with a sense of community, of being 'one family,' and a demonstration to outsiders of sociability and hospitality. The wide gate of the mud-brick house which was designed to allow entrance of buffaloes and cows has been replaced by a much more narrow door in the red-brick house, often elevated from street level by a two- or three-step staircase. An open door to the street, or a verandah in front of the house, might have indicated an open invitation to visitors, but the staircase expressed a distance compared to the intimacy with the street of the mud-brick house. The staircase signaled the privacy of the entrance room, the *sala*, from the public sphere of the street. Inside the *sala*, a door has instead been opened to a larger world, via the TV. Social closeness has been replaced by national and global orientations.

Kafr was electrified a few years before my first stay in 1983 and most families had already connected their houses to the grid by then.

Electricity boosted a desire for TV and radio cassettes, which gradually became common over the ten-year period. They constituted a popular commodity among the first labor migrants and facilitated direct access, even for illiterates, to news and entertainment from the outside world. The programs included Cairo and even Hollywood plays, the latest songs, advertisements of mass-produced consumer goods, political speeches by national leaders, public messages, and Quranic interpretations. The importance of literacy in getting information about political events, life, and culture outside the village has declined with the new media, which has democratized access to knowledge and information for the large number of elder-generation illiterates.

Television has opened new doors of identity but may also have affected social intercourse between families in the village. Some families have consciously used television to keep themselves apart in order to avoid conflicts which living in close proximity might otherwise make common. A poor widow with many children told me that she had bought the TV for the children's sake. She wanted them to stay at home because there was always a lot of trouble with neighbors when they played on the street. The TV made it easier to keep them at home. She herself rarely watched it. Another family who did not have a TV emphasized this as a mark of their poverty and complained that their children were less able to succeed at school, as they could not follow educational serials as most other children in the village did.

Another example of the new frameworks for social life coming as a result of new technology comes from the extension of access to piped water to the compound. In 1983, the canal bank provided a female meeting place for exchange of news and gossip. Drinking water was collected from public standpipes and the canal itself provided a huge basin for washing and cleaning. Very few houses possessed piped water. Young daughters as well as married women fulfilled their domestic duties of washing at the canal bank while they enjoyed the social company of other women and girls. Three years later, during my second field work stay, water was installed street by street by the villagers' own efforts, *maghud zati*. In 1993, almost all houses had water taps inside the house and most had access to a simple sewage system, too, which had also been organized by *maghud zati*, under the direction of one of the villagers who worked as an official in the water company in the district town. Underground sewage pipelines were established in most streets to carry waste water from the houses to a big drainage ditch behind the village. The sewage system made it possible to furnish houses with *ifrangi* bathrooms, and showers, water hoses, and water closets have become common in most of the larger red-brick houses. Semi-automatic washing machines also multiplied after 1986.

Women play an important role in social networking in Middle Eastern societies, which has been overlooked in many studies which focus on men's political role in the community. This role was under transformation at the time of the 1993 study. Young girls and women no longer used the canal bank as a common meeting place for a chat. Ritualized visits of politeness, for instance when somebody was ill, for the occasion of a weddings, after child birth, or when a son or a daughter graduated from school, were still practiced, and some women visited each other almost daily. The space for casual encounters with distant relatives or friends from childhood where people could keep up with each others' lives has become more limited, but new forms of social encounters have emerged. A weekly market has opened in a nearby village and has facilitated meetings among younger women. Children attended school outside the village and villagers worked abroad or in government offices. This new pattern has directed the previously much more family- and village-based orientation for social intercourse towards new sets of trans-village and even transnational social relations. These relations were created on a more personal basis than the former social relations, in which the person tended to represent a family rather than an independent person. New personal friendships and loyalties were being created across old boundaries. Because of their orientation to the home, women were more vulnerable to the individualizing effects of the new means of production and consumption than men and children.

Men's social life in Kafr appeared less affected than women's by the new means of production and consumption practices. Men met each other for daily prayers (or at least on Fridays) in one of the two mosques in the village. Farmers met at the weekly cattle market in the district town or at work in the fields, and many shared a meal under the shadow of the trees on the canal bank during the working day. *Muwazzafin* (mostly still men) saw each other while waiting for transport to the district town. Young men and boys often met in the *nadi*, the club for various male recreational activities which was established in the early 1980s with support from a local politician and the Ministry of Youth.

## New Types of Income and Consumption as Social Distinction

Possession of expensive consumer items was regarded with some ambivalence in the village. They were opportunities for jealousy and the evil eye.[4] On the other hand, they have become a means for social distinction. They signaled affluence (that is, economic success and ability) as well as modernity, education, and urban attitudes compared to the more subsistence-oriented consumption patterns of the *fallahin*. The new sources of income that appeared outside the community in the 1970s and 1980s implied that economic success was less likely to have been acquired at the expense of co-villagers than previously. Government jobs were acquired as a general entitlement on the basis of education. Economic progress became "open to all" who were active. Such progress became a mark of the intelligence and hard work of the individual student and therefore brought prestige. Income from work abroad, too, was a signal of individual capability and strength to endure the hard life away from the family. Affluence and its display through new types of consumption, which previously demonstrated landlords' power and cultural superiority over the peasants, no longer implied exploitation of other villagers. The competition for the goodwill of the landowner (or his representative), which was implied in the pre-revolution tenancy system, became transformed into the legal rights of inheritance of rented land during the land reforms in the 1950s and 1960s. Open signs of wealth through consumption have gradually become more accepted and consumption competed with traditional prestige-giving behavior, such as generosity and hospitality. Both types of behavior tended to generate symbolic capital.

Bourdieu's analysis (1984) of consumption practices in France includes an identification of distinct taste and behavioral patterns in various social classes. Though inspired by his writings on consumption and social distinction, I have not related my analysis of consumption to a class analysis but to a distinction separating villagers into *fallahin* and *muta'allimin*, each of which I regard as sociocultural fields, representing specific types of economic, social, and cultural capital. The two categories include distinctive arenas for fulfillment and demonstration of selfhood in the village. Practices of consumption and spending of resources depend not only upon economic factors, such as income and affluence, but also on those cultural factors for selfhood and status that are honored in the village, such as family roots and education.

Family roots and kinship networks were expressed as being important indicators of social capital among the *fallahin*, whereas level of education and personal connections to a network of colleagues in the public administration and services were considered an important characteristic of the social capital of the *muta'allimin*. Cultural capital among the *fallahin* was identified as personal experience, wit, generosity, and hospitality. The *muta'allimin*, on their side, had expanded their farmer background with *adab* (culture), signaled by their standards of living (red-brick houses or specific styles of clothes and furniture), which distinguished them from other people inside and outside the village, and their familiarity with urban ways and fashions.

Family labor and possession of land, preferably as ownership, were elements of the economic capital of the *fallahin*. They tended to spend possible savings on purchasing land to secure the family rather than on building a red-brick house. The *muta'allimin*, on the other hand, were not dependent on land but on education and personal connections for their income. During the 1980s, several educated people gave up inherited land to build a red-brick house. They invested in standards of living that raised their position among the other *muta'allimin* and secured them a distinctive *muta'allim* bride.

Many villagers belonged economically, socially, and culturally to both fields at the same time. Some *muta'allimin* were part-time farmers, their salaries being insufficient to support a family. Almost all *muta'allimin* were the first generation to be educated and had grown up with norms of distinction similar to those of their *fallahin* relatives. The *fallahin*, on the other hand, were constantly exposed to the norms and values of the *muta'allimin*. Many of them shared households with educated sons and daughters or brothers and sisters, and TV socialized both the educated and the farmers into new norms and values.

The number of *muta'allimin* and *muwazzafin* in the village grew rapidly in the research period. Commodities gradually became marks of status and success throughout the whole village. When farmers got access to cash income through work abroad after the mid-1970s they, too, bought electrical equipment as gifts to relatives and friends. However, after their first years of working abroad they spent most of their subsequent savings on purchases of land for farming, not on building a red-brick house (Bach, 1984). This pattern has become increasingly difficult to maintain. Due to greater purchasing power, land has become more expensive and difficult to acquire. A number of *fallah* labor migrants have built red-brick houses, particularly to provide housing for *muta'allim* children, signifying that the latter have raised the social status of the family in the village. Some men have worked abroad for years, not only to provide tutoring for children but also to establish a *muta'allim* daughter with a suitable trousseau.

The two fields thus coexisted in the village and interacted with each other in a dynamic way. Their relative status and strength in the village changed over time due to developments in economic conditions and political interventions, and to flows of shifting cultural discourses at national and transnational levels. However, after a period where education and consumption became common indicators for status, it is likely that landownership will become more important as a secure basis of income at the end of the 1990s. The recent abolition of the employment guarantee rendered education less useful, and the new tenancy law may reintroduce the great difference between tenants and owners that prevailed previously.

The repeal of the employment guarantee has not affected village spending attitudes and strategies for social reproduction. In at least two recent cases, *muta'allim* families living in big red-brick houses used their savings to purchase land. This may be due to habit, influenced culturally from growing up in a *fallah* family and living in a *fallah* environment. They themselves referred to it as an investment—security for children who will grow up and need money for a proper marriage, and who will want to supply their own food and thus be independent of relatives and neighbors in basic foods such as rice or *berseem* or poultry. A combination of land and public employment has become increasingly necessary for support of a family, both for *muwazzafin*, due to the low salaries in government jobs, and for *fallahin*, due to the small holdings.

A villager expressed the changes in his society by saying: "Previously family roots and landownership were indicators of status and power, then it became education and government jobs, now it is more and more becoming money."

## Notes

1 The families were of Greek/Turkish origin and had never lived in the village but had acquired the land in the nineteenth century when farmers were unable to pay their taxes.
2 This also applied to the inheritance of reform land, in spite of formal restrictions on partitioning of holdings on this type of land. In most cases, daughters inherited land from landowning parents. In some cases, daughters also inherited reform land, but never rented land.
3 In the first case, the father of the young husband had worked abroad and the mother had been 'alone' with several children, not without difficulties.
4 The spending pattern of migrants mitigates jealousy among close relatives. The first year's savings from work abroad is generally spent on gifts within the social network as an acknowledgment of norms of generosity; whereas the savings from later years are spent according to the migrant family's own decision.

## References

Bach, Kirsten. 1984. "Agrarian Transformation, Socio-economic Conditions and External Labor Migration in an Egyptian Village." Copenhagen: Centre for Development Research.

Bourdieu, Pierre. 1984. *Distinction: A Social Critique of the Judgement of Taste*. Trans. R. Nice. London, Routledge.
———. 1988. "Flaubert's Point of View." in *Critical Inquiry* 14:539–562 (1988).
———. 1990. *In Other Words: Essays Towards a Reflexive Sociology*. Trans. M. Adamson. Cambridge, Polity Press.
Bourdieu, Pierre, and Loïc J.D. Wacquant. 1992. *An Invitation to Reflexive Sociology*. Cambridge, Polity Press.

# IV
# HEALTH

# 10
# Being Sickly or Eating Well: The Conceptualization of Health and Ill-Health in an Upper Egyptian Village

HANIA SHOLKAMY

> Disease belongs to culture, in particular, to the specialized culture of medicine. And culture is not only a means of representing disease, but is essential to its very constitution as a human reality (Good 1994:53).

## Introduction

This paper addresses the definition of children's health and well-being as well as that of ill-health and its causation within the parameters of village relationships and resources in rural Upper Egypt.[1] The study establishes the relationship between everyday processes, experiences, and values which color and shape villagers' social, economic, and political lives as well as their concerns, conceptualizations, and experiences of their own and their children's health and ill-health. In particular, I address two concepts here, that of *batlan,* 'being sickly,' and that of good health as it is linked to diet.

In the village of Rihan,[2] modern medicine coexists with other medical cultures. However, while modern medicine is powerful, it is not always convincing. In its shadow lie other intellectual traditions which interpret physical experiences and construct health and ill-health in different and more diverse terms than the strict biomedical model does. These intellectual traditions transcend health and ill-health as limited physical experiences and construe and construct them as social and historical categories which are the vocabulary of an epistemology of health and ill-health. This paper describes the processes by which the health of children in Rihan is conceptualized by their families and how such processes of conceptualization and articulation reflect the social, culture, and material circumstances of villagers and of the village.

I do not include important information on the material conditions of children and on the role of the confluence of deprivation and desperation in the construction of diseases, ill-health, and their experiences. Instead, I suggest that disease and hardship are painful, potentially mortal, and persistent realities created by poverty and powerlessness, and they are also symbolic expressions constructed by 'culture.' My focus here is on the definition of health and ill-health and how both are described and experienced with reference to locally significant symbols and values so as to reassert and not to challenge people's material experiences of health and ill-health. Thus I hope to insert meaning into the political economy paradigm of health and ill-health.

In relating health and ill-health to the ethnography of rural Egypt, I present some of the discourses through which children's health and ill-health are represented as indicators both of the situation of children's health in a village in Egypt and of an aspect of village life and concerns which is often confined to the literature on health and rural development and less often integrated into the ethnography of rural Egyptians and of villages. The paper concludes with some reflections on children's health and on the village studied.

## The Study of Rural Egypt and the Relevance of Health

Rihan is a small hamlet in the district of Abnub, one of the most deprived regions of the governorate of Asyut in Upper Egypt. Rural Upper Egypt as a whole is recognized by its persistently "problematic" demographic and health statistics as compared to the rest of Egypt. Average family size in Upper Egyptian rural areas is 6.2 compared with a national average below 5. The governorate also has a higher total fertility rate than the rest of Egypt at 6.7 births per woman, while the national average is 4.55 births per woman (CAPMAS 1993:139). Children in Asyut are significantly worse off than children elsewhere. They are at twice the risk of mortality and malnutrition than are children in greater Cairo (CAPMAS 1993). This dimension of the profile of rural Asyut is the one which interests policy makers, development specialists, and quantitative analysts. The anthropologist has been looking elsewhere.

When I began my field work (1992–94) among the 1,200 people who live in Rihan, I was drawn to the region and village by these facts and figures and by the conviction that there was a richer and more complex potential to the relationship between health and culture. I hoped that health could be translated into the ethnographic mainstream and brought to bear on what we know, or think we do, about the Egyptian villages.

I began my field work with a door to door survey of a partial sample of 123 houses in Rihan.[3] My purpose was to discern some of the broad demographic and socioeconomic features of the village. The survey showed that families are large (average family size is 7.6 individuals), that many girls are still not attending school (57 percent of girls who should/could be in school are not), and that people will choose endogamous marriage when they can (69 percent of men are married to close female kin). My survey also looked at the structures of landownership, male and female income generation, and the organization of labor. The 'economic' peasant, defined by landownership, markets, cooperatives, and crops, is the peasant with the most academic currency. When health is considered then this peasant becomes a victim of disease and a willing or unwilling target of public health campaigns. In the event, my survey proved fruitless in terms of data on health, and a more ethnographic approach was brought to bear.

The language of statistics provoking policy change is the dominant language of discourses on health, particularly those where rural children are the subjects of research and debate. Indeed, there is a detectable disjunction between health and ethnography in the context of rural Egypt. Questions of health are summarily bypassed by ones of production and distribution in researchers' descriptions of social organization, or they are subsumed by issues of gender and perhaps fertility by researchers studying the intricacies of community. Questions of culture, class differentiation, and social relationships are rarely answered with reference to health and disease. This disjunction is problematic if not a pity because:

1. Health, particularly that of children, is a major preoccupation which takes up a substantial amount of time in the lives and peasant men and women.

2. Health is a major item of expenditure for many village households, and for all those with small children, which, if one looks at family size, fertility rate, and age structures, are the majority of rural households.

3. Health, disease, hygiene, and products of medical technologies are idioms in an often fractured but essential discourse between people in villages and the media, the public and private spheres, development agencies and other NGOs, and the state.

4. The conditions that favor health and the services to restore it are human and civil rights of which rural areas are being deprived; instead, health services have long been commoditized by the proliferation of private health care and by schemes to make the peasants and others pay.

5. The language and social relationships of health, ill-health, and of well-being are an integral, little understood, and rich part of the daily life, culture, and history of Upper Egypt.

Just as health has been the missing category from rural Egyptian ethnography, so has "culture" been the problematic category in studies of medical anthropology, where the practical and the symbolic have been artificially separated (Morsy 1993). Dominant paradigms of spirit possession, indigenous medical therapies, and the practice of humoral principles of medicine are realms of interest for anthropologists. On the other hand, we find the worthy realm of action and intervention researched and monitored by NGOs.

In this essay, and the larger study from which it is taken (Sholkamy 1997), I attempt to resurrect culture without resort to culturalism by looking at health as a socially constructed, materially affected ideal from which experiences of disease, accidents, and villagers' health-seeking behavior can be better understood.

## Being Sick and Being Sickly

*Batlan, marid,* or *'ayan* are analogous words which all mean to be sick. These are words used to describe the condition of a child or adult who has been unwell for a protracted period of time, which could last for months, even years. The child who is *batlan* may regain health, but will very soon become sick again, and so good days and bad days merge and form weeks, months, or even years of anxiety, expenditure, and uncertainty.

Short-term afflictions, such as the occasional flu, headache, sunstroke, diarrhea, or minor accidents leading to cuts and sprains are distinguished from the condition of being sick. A child suffering from any of the above is said to have a headache, a runny nose, a broken arm, *latshit shams* (sunstroke), or *biyitmasha* [feminine: *bititmasha*] (has a runny stool and defecates frequently), all words which specifically describe the condition.

Children born with congenital problems or those who suffer disabilities are not described, nor do they describe themselves, as *'ayan,* or 'sick.' 'Arafat was left deaf by measles and has consequently been unable to master speech. 'Ula was born with a mental and physical disability. Zaynab is severely mentally handicapped. None of these children are thought of or described as being 'sick.' Congenital and chronic conditions are accepted as the way these children are. 'Ula's mother told me "hiya kidah" ("This is how she is"). 'Arafat is also accepted as being mute and deaf; this is "how he is."

*Marid* and *'ayan* both mean to be ill or sick. *Batlan*, however, is the word most commonly used in Rihan, and in Upper Egypt in general. The term literally means 'unwell,' and implies weakness and lack of energy. When a child or an adult is described as *batlan*, it does not just mean being sick, but also intimates being sickly. Physicians at the general hospital in nearby Abnub, at the clinic in 'Arab Mattir village, and at the government clinic in al-Hamam all expressed their frustration at this category of ill-health. Adults bring their children and when asked for symptoms they say that he or she is *batlan*. The physician is then obliged to go down a whole list of possible symptoms to diagnose the case. What is most frustrating to them is that they sometimes cannot diagnose a particular condition and wind up prescribing expensive vitamins so as to avoid the embarrassment of prescribing nothing in particular.

In fact, the word is not just a generic, glossing term. When used in retrospect it implies a series of illnesses which affect the general well-being of a child. When used in the present it means that a person is generally incapacitated. The condition of being *batlan* affects appetite, energy, the physical body, and perhaps even the mind. Muhammad 'Abd al-Bassat is a typical case of *batlan*.

> Muhammad is a three-year-old boy. Since he was born he has been weak, refused to eat properly, and has had bouts of diarrhea. His parents have taken him to several private doctors who prescribed medications. A few weeks after their last visit to the doctor, he had a severe bout of diarrhea and vomited. They took him to the hospital in Abnub very late at night. From there he was transferred to Asyut where he spent eight days accompanied by his mother and father. There he was put on an IV drip before being released. Two days after his discharge his mother found his feces mixed with blood. His father then took him to another private doctor in Abnub, who gave them a cure for dysentery. But he keeps vomiting and defecating blood from time to time. Every three weeks or so he is taken to the doctor. The last visit yielded a prescription which would have cost LE16 had his father bought all of it. They do take him to the government clinic from time to time where oral rehydration salts have been prescribed. He refuses to take them, and the other private doctors have told the parents that he is a weak child who needs medication and vitamins. He has in the past suffered urine retention, acute respiratory tract infection, and several nasty falls.

The above is a summary of the condition of a boy who is described as *batlan*. Although I knew of days when Muhammad was well, I could see why these days did not figure much in the minds of his parents, since overall he had been *batlan* for most of six months.

During the intervals when his parents were not visiting hospitals and clinics, his mother was consulting relatives, neighbors, and spiritual healers. She sent his *riha* (an item of his clothing which is then used by a *khatib* [spiritual healer and shaykh] to diagnose his condition) with his father to 'Arab Mattir. There he was told by the spiritual healer that his son is *manzur* (the victim of an envious/evil eye). This explained why he was not getting well and did not conflict with, nor interrupt, resort to government and private clinics.

One could well ask if Muhammad was *batlan* because he is sick or sick because he is *batlan*! While some children are thought to suffer the cumulative effect of successive bouts of ill-health and thereby become sickly, others are defined as sickly and consequently expected to be in continuous ill-health. The distinction between the two groups lies in their structural position in the community and in their biological, social, and political heritage.

"Only the precious get sick," announced the local midwife and village sage. Some special categories of children, such as only sons, boys with many sisters, children born into grief or family strife, or those who become afflicted by some spiritual agent may have a weak disposition to begin with. Such a child is prone to being *batlan* and is expected to be sick. This in turn alters adult expectations of this child's physical condition and affects health-seeking behavior and recourse to therapy. These children are either overprotected, as in the case of only sons, or neglected as they are condemned to their poor health. In either case, this weakness may last until these children are five or six years old. In general, if they have survived these bouts, they will be able to survive their childhood. Children who are born strong to fertile couples and who have many brothers and sisters are expected to be well and to be able to overcome ill-health with ease. Families with strong, healthy children, who do not expect them to be at risk, may pay a price for their confidence, as did Mahasin who tells of her son's death:

> He was four years old and in good health. His face was round and red and he was such a good boy. He was playing up on the roof on a hot day. Then a playmate struck him on the head and he fell. He came inside and I was so scared because he was shaking. His grandmother said it was *latshit shams* and, after rubbing a cloth with salt to draw the heat, she tied it around his head. He did not get any better and vomited. It was only after three days or so that we took him to the doctor. He said that he had meningitis and gave him medication and said to take him to the hospital. We brought him back so that his father could see him and take him to the hospital. We all went, and I stayed with him, but he died that very night. He had been crying from his head. He was not *batlan* or anything; he just died. Now I know that it was the ignorance of his grandmother who did not let me take him to a doctor.

Mahasin was justifying the family's reluctance to take her son's condition seriously by the fact that he was not *batlan* to begin with. In his case, she was expecting him to overcome his headache because he was a healthy boy.

The definition of a child as healthy or not also affects the expectations of recovery that parents and relatives have. Medications are viewed as palliatives which do not address the root of the problem. In some extreme cases, children are considered to be in a structural disposition of being sickly. But because these children are not expected to recover promptly, their therapy is not seen as an issue of urgency. There is no purposeful neglect, as described by Scheper-Hughes (1992) in the case of children in north-east Brazil. As far as some children are concerned, families accept a certain degree of ill-health which verges on being detrimental to the child's health.

Being *batlan* marks a split in levels of exegesis and interpretation. On one level, the sickness event is addressed; on another, the context in which these events take place is confronted. Thus families may seek immediate therapy for the particular bout of vomiting, diarrhea, fever, or whooping cough at hand. But they also address the perceived root cause for the child's general condition. In one case, Muhammad was *manzur* (subject to the evil eye). In a second case, 'Izz, another small boy who suffered from repeated bouts of diarrhea, fainting spells, and other afflictions, was born into a structural disadvantage: he was born the day his brother died, which affected his mother's milk and ultimately condemned him to ill-health.

Adham is also *batlan*. His mother says that his father used to beat her a lot when she was pregnant with him and that he had been born *madrur* (a very weak baby) as a result of these beatings. Moreover, she had become pregnant with his younger brother straight away so he did not breast feed enough. The problem was not that he had been nutritionally deprived, but that his early weaning had instilled in him a jealousy of the younger brother who had "taken his milk," and this jealousy was the cause of his frail disposition.

The important distinction to make here is that *batlan* is not a diagnosis, it is a disposition which endows children's experiences of ill-health with meaning and shapes the responses of adults who are responsible for these children. It shapes these responses in seemingly contradictory ways. In some cases it leads people to address root causes as they perceive them, such as the evil eye, malevolent spirits, *khar'a*,[4] or bad feelings in the family, to the neglect of other more immediate remedies and therapies. In others, it makes people wary of any deterioration in a child's condition and they become aggressive in their pursuit of therapy for particular sickness events. *Batlan* describes the actuality as well as the potentiality of disease and affliction.

## Risk as a Vicious Cycle

Once placed in this position of risk, it is very difficult for children to escape it. Children who have been sick in successive bouts for long periods of time are at times said to be caught up in a drug use cycle. They are taking as much medication as their families can afford and consequently suffering from their side effects and addiction. As the village midwife put it, *"al-dawa kayf"* ("medication is an addiction"). All the mothers who had children with chronic conditions, or whose children felt sick, often were under the impression that their children were addicted to the medication (Melrose 1992).

> Insaf believes that her three-year-old son, 'Abd al-Fattah, is addicted to the prophylactic medication the doctor prescribed for his bronchial asthma. He consumes a bottle of Zaditen every week, at a cost of LE8.10 ($2.50). She stopped the Zaditen in Ramadan because they needed the money. His father says that the medicine is making his chest better but making him *batlan*. "Medications are strong and small children cannot bear them, but you have people here coming and going to the doctor, and bringing medication that their children are becoming addicted to *("yighwah")* and fall sick if they do not have it. He has become addicted to this medicine that he has been taking for years!" asserted his father. The more medications prescribed, and the more their families buy for them, the more dependent they become, and the weaker they are if deprived of these medicines. That is how families explain this cycle of addiction, which they perceive as one of the main problems of a child who is *batlan*.

Dysentery is another condition which places children in a vicious cycle of risk. Dysentery is endemic in Rihan and very few households are free of it. Those children who have dysentery and who frequently defecate blood are rarely treated for their bouts of diarrhea. When they become dehydrated, they are taken in for rehydration. But none of the parents whose children had dysentery thought that dysentery could be cured. Moreover, they feared that continuous episodes of bleeding would just weaken the child and make even temporary recovery impossible. These children are accepted as ones who are at risk and less healthy than others.

Sickly children also tend to eat less. Because they have less of an appetite, they are expected to be able to eat less than other children. Consequently they are often offered less food. 'Abd al-Bassat's mother lamented that she could not afford to make him special foods or give him more meat because they were a poor family. She admitted that because they were so poor, she was unable to offer 'Abd al-Bassat special foods, like eggs and meat, knowing that he would not eat them.

If I give him a morsel, I know he won't eat it, and I wind up having it anyway, so sometimes when the other children are hungry, I just give them the foods and buy him a soft drink as compensation, as he likes these drinks very much.

Other women concurred that it is pointless to offer children food when they are too sick to eat. Meat was mentioned as the food that both gives health and needs health as it is a heavy food and difficult to digest. Mothers strive to give their weak children what they want, rather than what they need. Sweets, carbonated soft drinks, savory snacks, and the like are given whenever there is enough money to buy them. These foodstuffs gladden the hearts of children and help them overcome their distress and discomfort.

But children are not condemned to being sickly all their lives. Time, events, and growth may make them one day healthy again.

## The Description of Health

The term *batlan*, by opposition, stresses well-being as a core concept for people in Rihan. Even if a child is not diagnosed as suffering from a clinically defined condition, but s/he is not well, not energetic, or not eating as much as s/he can lay their hands on, this is cause for comment and concern. To describe a healthy child, women and men put the thumbs and index fingers of both hands together to make a circle which they hold up say, "the face was/is like this." To do this is to bring the evil eye on the child being described. It is only acceptable to do so in the past tense, to describe how a child was before he became *batlan* or even, God forbid, died. In addition, such a healthy and round countenance is usually described as being red. In this case, red may refer to fairness as well as to the wide-spread ideal of 'rosy cheeks.'

Healthy children are active to the point of being rowdy and disobedient. They should have a robust appetite and be able to overcome minor mishaps or health problems without falling victim to a vicious cycle of sickness and weakness. The generic word 'healthy' is therefore not a residual category. It is a positive definition of a state of well-being and not a negative one that describes the absence of disease.

### *The Sturdiness of Girls*

There is near consensus in the village concerning the sturdiness of girls. Girls are in general healthier than boys. When small, they are hungrier, have better immunity, and are much stronger than boys. The list of assumptions concerning the health of girls is a long one.

Whenever it is the topic of discussion, exceptions are made and stories of fragility come up.

There seem to be genetic factors which favor girls, and so create a situation where female infant mortality is lower than that of males in Egypt (and elsewhere). However, this small advantage that girls have is offset by cultural factors which favor boys, and so female under-five mortality rates are higher than those of males.[5]

Um Hasan compared her own daughter and son:

> The girls are strong and that is why they survive, while the boys don't. My daughter Rida, who is four years old, only once got a bit of diarrhea from mixing food when she was weaned, but she took some medication and became well. But my small son is always sick. They live in the same house and eat the same food but one is strong, and one is weak. This is how God made us, otherwise, how would we be able to bear the pain of childbirth.

Two-year-old Mona gets sick often and her mother always takes her to the private clinic. Mona is always given as an example of a girl who is *batlana*. Once she had itchy genitals and was taken by her mother to a private clinic where she was given a long prescription that cost her LE23 ($7), including the visitation fee. Sometimes, gossip-mongers would wonder if it was because her father was making a lot of money in Saudi Arabia that she was so often sick.

But the rule is that girls are *shudad* (singular, *shadida*), meaning that they are both healthier than boys and healthy in general. The mother of Adham, mentioned above, likes to remind people that she once had twins: "...the boy died and the girl lived," she marvels. Now this daughter is in her fifth year of primary school and has never been sick a day in her life. As Salma jokingly likes to say, "Girls are such devils; even their own *qarina* [sibling spirit] can't kill them."

## Eating Well

Healthy children can eat anything and indeed should be hungry all the time and eat a lot. Having good food is part of being healthy. Ideally, children should have red meat at least once a week. This is the practice of most peasant households who look forward to Thursday nights when meat bought earlier in the day is cooked and consumed with maybe some left for lunch the next day, Friday. Red meat is a delicacy which supplies strength and energy. Because of scarcity and poverty, the meat that is bought often contains more fat and bone than muscle fiber.

Milk and meat are the important ingredients which children need to grow. If they are not getting enough of either then they are expected to become sickly and eventually become sick. Sick children should be given meat, broth, and ghee made with fresh milk to revive their energy. The same prescription applies to weak children who need special protection from sickness. The belief in the efficacy of meat and ghee is universal in rural Egypt. In the good old days, wealthy Egyptians used to have chicken on their non-meat-eating days. Now, with the soaring price of red meat, chicken is considered a replacement. The following account is typical of Thursday mornings in Rihan when families are getting ready for the meal of the week, the meat meal:

> Ramadan knocked at the door as Ni'mat was skimming the morning's milk. He said that he had bought a goat from the market and wanted to slaughter it and share the price. The practice that is common in Rihan is for a man to buy a goat or sheep and to offer to slaughter and cut it up in return for the normal fee of the skin and head. The rest of the carcass is sold off without obvious profit. Some people buy meat, while others who cannot afford meat buy bits of bone, fat, or entrails. These local part-time butchers do not slaughter the animal until they have pre-sold all of it. They can neither afford to treat their own households to the unsold meat, nor do they have the means of storing it and selling it later. They must be wealthy enough to make the down payment for the animal in the first place, but they can rarely afford not to be repaid in full, including their transport to and from the market. If the animal is not pre-sold then it is kept until there is enough demand.
> 
> "I have already sold three quarters of it," he said. He wanted Ni'mat to pledge to buy a kilogram or two. She refused, saying that her husband was buying meat on his way back from Asyut. "You have a refrigerator, you can keep the rest," he challenged her. "Don't you eye my refrigerator! Even so, where can we get twenty pounds for more meat," she replied.
> 
> Ramadan began to plead with her, saying "Are our children to starve? They'll be sick. Mine haven't tasted meat for weeks. They'll forget the taste." But Ni'mat would not budge. She suggested that he ask her aunt who might be interested.
> 
> Ramadan knocked on Aunt Salma's door and explained the situation. She refused, saying that her husband was away and she was alone. "Treat your two grandsons," he suggested, "They need meat." She still refused, saying that the boys eat with their mothers in their fathers' homes. He then joked, "Then feed your granddaughters." As he left she ran after him and asked if any one had bought the neck. He said no one had. She then told him that she would ask her daughter whose husband was also away if she would share the neck with her: "Let the children eat," she said.
> 
> Ramadan then continued his round but failed to find buyers. "This village cannot afford meat on a Thursday, this is how poor we are. Now all of those who had promised their children meat will give them a can of sardines instead."

The next morning, I saw his elder son Sha'ban in the street. The first thing he said was that towards the afternoon, his father had sold the rest of the animal and had slaughtered it. "We had meat and broth and my father ate all the head," he said with a huge grin. Then he added, "Even my sister took a share just like mine."

Sometimes the children get bones with no meat on them. When chicken or pigeon is on the dinner *tabliya*, the task of distribution becomes an intricate one, where meat, entrails, skin, and bones all figure in calculations of equity and entitlement. For example, when the family of Awad Allah sat down for a dinner that included a chicken and two pigeons, the babies in the family got bits of fried liver and kidneys, while the older children got the bones which they cracked and munched to an indigestible mass.

While all food comes at a cost, villagers make the distinction between *"illi min al-bayt"* (from the house) and *"hagat bara"* (things from the outside). The former are goods produced by household members from their land and livestock. These are foods for which the family does not pay money. The latter are items which cost hard-to-come-by cash. Many families cannot spend money on food and try to make do with what they can produce themselves.

Some vegetable and fruit merchants in Rihan specialize in rotten produce. One merchant explained, "In this village they cannot afford the top quality stuff so we go to the market and buy some good stuff for the few who will buy it and we collect the rotting stuff which is what people can afford." Some families buy a mixture of rotting and good tomatoes and put them together in the evening salad so that the plate is affordable and not too offensive.

Children who live in a house with a water buffalo or cow are guaranteed a supply of fresh milk, cheese, and ghee, as well as money from the sale of these. "Izz comes up to the *magur* [clay container] while I milk in the morning, and licks the milk from it like a cat," says Um 'Izz of her toddler son. She says that it is the only proper nutrition he gets and without it he would be even sicker than he is. When their water buffalo was pregnant she had to buy milk from the nearby dairy farm owned by the government. However, this milk is often adulterated with water. The milk was expensive and not as nutritious as that of the house. She stopped buying it and relied on the generosity of neighbors who offered 'Izz the occasional early morning cup until the buffalo had her calf. "Then I distributed *sarsubiya* [milk from first milking] to all those who kept 'Izz well with those sips of milk," she said.

It is not an exaggeration to say that the provision of meat to the house and family is one of the main roles of the head of the household. Meat has nutritional, near medicinal, social, and economic significance. 'Adila, for example, would often say that before her beloved Sayid died of cancer she had tried to keep him strong with meat and broth. When his head ballooned into twice its size because of the tumor growing inside it, she used to "... bring him meat to gladden his heart, and books because he was so intelligent, and Pyrosol (insect repellent) so that he could sit in cleanliness." Now she only has 'Abd al-'Al and his sisters. She laments that she cannot give them the food they need to be well. I once innocently suggested lentils as an alternative source of protein to 'Adila. With tears in her eyes, she repeated, "Yes, I can give them lentils, but no meat; my children can only eat lentils; we poor people can only eat lentils." For 'Adila, lentils are poor food. She could not strip the different foods down into their nutritional values. For her, foods are more than calories masquerading as proteins or carbohydrates. Meat is more than the sum of its calorific content. Meat is a good energy-giving, satisfying, and tasty symbol of well-being. Lentils are lentils.

## Conclusions

These accounts of children's health, fortunes, and misfortunes in Rihan illustrate the relevance of culture, society, and history to the definition of ill-health and the recognition of health and its pursuit. They also illustrate the extent to which health and ill-health are central to other village discourses. Poverty, powerlessness, gender, food, and other dimensions of social life are not isolated from discourses on disease, ill-health, and good health.

In the introduction, the separation of health discourses from their natural context was criticized as a practice undertaken by those who research health and those who research social life and organization. Health researchers focus on practice and isolate narrow domains in which their interests lie. Even language is separated from its philosophical and cognitive foundations. Public health campaigns trying to instill changes in the behavior of village dwellers frame public health messages in the street talk of Upper Egyptian villages to convince women why they should vaccinate their children or insert intrauterine devices (IUDs). The language of the messages is altered in terms of vocabulary and pronunciation, but the content remains the same, so the message is not fully adapted to local understandings. Village dwellers are deprived of their experiences of daily life, relationships, and social and moral structures, and left with only a dialect.

Children are also the instrument of preference that the establishment uses to encroach on the daily lives of villagers. They are the subjects of an on-going debate between peasants and the state, each trying to assert its own view on how children should be brought up, educated, protected, and cured. The international discourse on children has somewhat standardized the definition of children's health (Boyden 1990:184–90). Charts to plot weight, height, and head circumference in accordance with a percentile average have become part of model pediatric and public health practice. While from a human rights perspective, all children have the right to the same high quality services, the best possible care, and the opportunity and circumstances to grow and prosper, these global views on children's health nevertheless promote the abstraction of health and children from history and from social contexts.

Health services should, and must, be universal, but this does not mean that people are not entitled to realizing wider and deeper health ideals which may posit social justice alongside vaccines, and the integrity of the environment alongside head circumferences. There is a cultural construction of child health, in which kinship, everyday life, ideas and ideals about the physical and metaphysical world, and emotions, are articulated. Villagers also want healthy children. But they have a definition of health which in part coincides with, and in part transcends the current biomedical model.

The ethnography of rural Egypt has only recently incorporated health into relationships of power and gender and the practices of everyday life (Morsy 1993). Here, I extend this argument by emphasizing the centrality of children's health, in particular, to village daily life, and to its dwellers' perceptions of their past, present, and anticipated future.

I have argued that health and the structures and institutions which challenge, maintain, and restore it are an essential part of understanding society as a whole. Health and healing are not reflections of, nor reactions to, biology and society. They are generative components on the conceptual systems which shape the intellect, culture, and experiences of individuals and of society. In investigating the medical culture of villagers in Upper Egypt as it relates to the health of young children, I hope to have contributed to a better and deeper understanding of rural Egypt, as well as to the appreciation of the health and ill-health of rural children.

I am not trying to construct an essentialist, culturalist model, but to discern a logic of practice that people in Rihan find meaningful. This logic has been fragmented by the anthropological gaze itself. The medical culture of child health and ill-health in Egypt is more than a product of the confluence of hardship and poverty. It is a cacophony of practices which have a contextualized coherence.

Rihan, like other villages, has witnessed dramatic changes in the recent past. Villagers have modernized themselves at a rapid pace, learning to cope with the change in their own lives and environment and with the upheavals going on in the world around them, and those enacted by the people of Rihan themselves. Their health, ill-health, and health-seeking behavior have changed along with the turbulent context and content of their own and their children's daily lives.

One of my goals has been to try to say as much about village dwellers in Upper Egypt as has been said about children and their health. *Al-ard* ('the land') and *al-'ard* ('honor') are the two commonly recognized essential values of rural life in upper Egypt and have great, real and symbolic significance in the context of Upper Egyptian culture. The third important value is *al-wild* ('children'). Children mean as much to a man as does land and female sexual integrity. They mean even more to a woman. Their significant absence may be due to a male bias in ethnography, even that which focuses on women. Children and their well-being are a priority for families. Children are also the source of many parental anxieties and frustrations, especially when they are sick.

The conceptualization of children's ill-health demands an understanding of the social and material, as well as the phenomenological construction of health. I have described how the health of children is conceptualized, restored, and protected in a poor Upper Egyptian community. In doing so I have drawn attention to the importance of family world view and self-perception as essential determinants of health.

## Notes

1 This study derives its content from field work conducted by the author in a small hamlet or satellite village in the district of Abnub in the governorate of Asyut in Upper Egypt.
2 The name of the village is a pseudonym.
3 This is about two-thirds of the whole.
4 Sickness by fright, equivalent to *'susto'* in Latin America. It is a condition of general weakness, and in the case of children wasting away. It results from shock, such as falling into a well, off a bed, in a dark alley, or stream, or being frightened by seeing a terrible thing, such as a fatal accident or a rotting corpse.
5 Between the ages of one to five years more girls than boys die. Before the age of one, during early infancy, the male mortality rate is higher than that of girls (CAPMAS 1993).

## References

Boyden, J. 1990. "Childhood and the Policy Makers: A Comparative Perspective on the Globalization of Childhood" in A. James and A. Prout, eds. *Constructing and Reconstructing Childhood*. London: Palmer Press. pp. 184–216.

CAPMAS. 1993. *Egypt Maternal and Child Health Survey 1991*. Cairo: Pan Arab Project for Children and Development, League of Arab States.

Good, B. 1994. *Medicine, Rationality and Experience: An Anthropological Perspective*. Cambridge: Cambridge University Press.

Morsy, S. 1993. *Gender, Sickness, and Healing in Rural Egypt*. Boulder: Westview.

Scheper-Hughes, N. 1992. *Death Without Weeping: The Violence of Everyday Life in Brazil*. Berkeley: University of California Press.

Sholkamy, H. 1997. "Children's Health and Well-Being: An Ethnography of an Upper Egyptian Village." Ph.D. thesis in social anthropology, London School of Economics.

# 11

# Health Units in Rural Egypt: At the Forefront of Health Improvement or Anachronisms?

SOHAIR MEHANNA and PETER WINCH

## Introduction

When the World Health Organization, UNICEF, and other international organizations were established at the end of World War II, the most important causes of morbidity and mortality in countries such as Egypt were malnutrition and acute infectious diseases affecting young children, such as measles, dehydrating diarrhea, pneumonia, and malaria. It was natural therefore that ministries of health, international organizations, and bilateral donors chose to target these problems, first with vertical disease eradication program of the 1950s and 1960s, followed by the primary health care and child survival programs from the 1970s to the present day (Habicht 1987; Walt 1993). The structure of many ministries of health reflects this history; various divisions and departments have often been established when external funding for disease control programs is terminated, and donors request that the government absorb their personnel, equipment, and control strategies (Justice 1986).

Rapid changes are occurring in the pattern of diseases that affect the population of Egypt, and most other low- and middle-income countries. Chronic and degenerative diseases occurring in adults, such as diabetes, high blood pressure, heart disease, and cancer are replacing acute infectious diseases among children as the major sources of morbidity and mortality (Mosley, Jamison and Henderson 1990; Omran 1982). One cause of this shift is improvements in child survival as a result of increasing levels of maternal education and the diffusion of medical and public health interventions, such as immunization, oral rehydration therapy, and antibiotics (Millard 1994; Mosley and Chen 1984). In addition, decreasing fertility rates have resulted in children constituting a lower proportion of the overall population, especially in Latin America and Southeast Asia. An increasing proportion of the adult population are exposed to risk factors for disease that previously were uncommon, such as high-fat diets, cigarette smoking, and air pollution (Mosley, Jamison and Henderson 1990).

Decreases in the impact of infectious diseases, such as dehydrating diarrhea (Miller and Hirschhorn 1995; Rashad 1989) and schistosomiasis (Michelson et al. 1993), are also being documented in Egypt. While these conditions continue to merit attention, concern is now shifting to problems such as maternal mortality, environmental contamination, and the chronic degenerative diseases. This paper will draw on the authors' experiences in a project on the epidemiology and control of schistosomiasis in an area of ongoing land reclamation from the desert, fifteen kilometers southwest of Isma'iliya (Mehanna et al. 1994; El-Sayed et al. 1995). We will argue that the rural health care system, in its current form, is in a poor position to confront these problems, and that rural people prefer to use private sector services, rather than the health units, even when transport is a major problem. We will then discuss the implications of these findings for efforts to improve health in rural Egypt.

## Characteristics of the Study Population

Al-Manayif is an area of reclaimed desert, 159,333 feddans in size, straddling the Cairo–Isma'iliya highway, and is part of Isma'iliya governorate. This article is based on the study of the part of al-Manayif to the east and south of the Cairo–Isma'iliya highway, six kilometers directly southwest of the center of Isma'iliya. This part contains twenty-eight hamlets, or *'izba*s. The *'izba*s closest to the Cairo–Isma'iliya road are located on land which has been reclaimed for more than twenty years. As one moves south toward the desert, the *'izba*s are located on more recently reclaimed land. Four hamlets, or *'izba*s, were chosen for intensive study. All four are close to the edge of the desert, and therefore more recently reclaimed. They are all served by one government health clinic.

The population of the area is a mixture of *fallahin* from the Nile Valley and recently settled Bedouin. The *fallahin* come from all parts of Upper and Lower Egypt, but principally from the governorates of Isma'iliya and Sharqiya. Some Bedouin originate from the Sinai Peninsula and others from the Arabian Peninsula. There is minimal social interaction, and no intermarriage at all between the Bedouin and the *fallahin*. There are extremely high rates of migration. Reasons for migrating into the areas include the availability of land

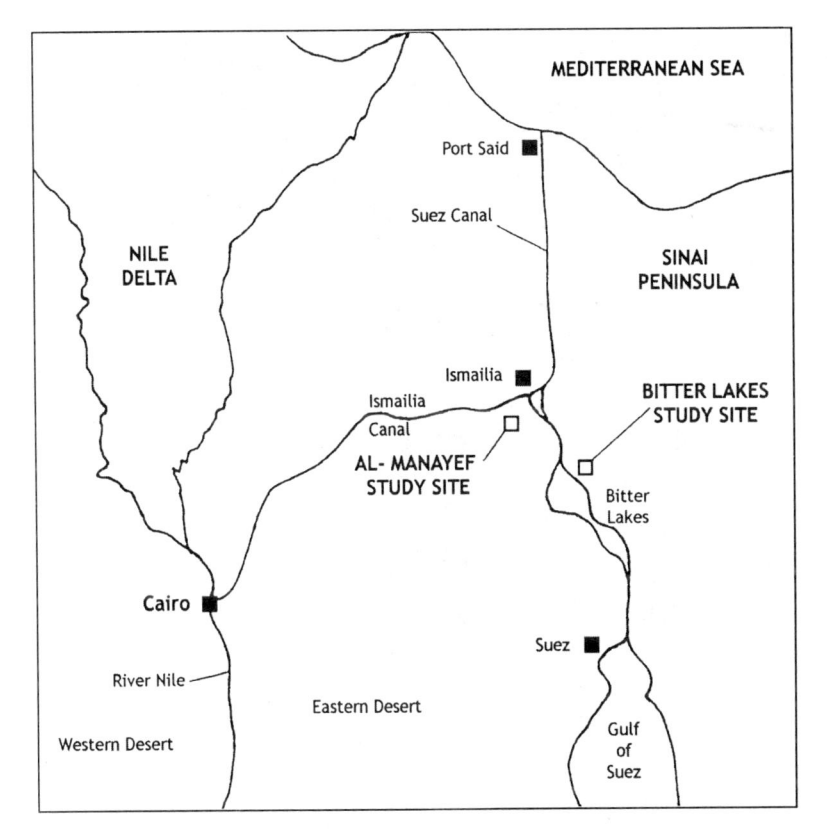

Figure 1 *Map of the Suez Canal Zone Showing al-Manayef*

and the opportunity to escape social pressures in one's home village and to be anonymous. Reasons for out-migration include seasonal migration to the Nile Valley to work as laborers during planting and harvest periods, migration to Isma'iliya or Cairo to work in industry, migration to oil-producing countries, such as Saudi Arabia, and migration with flocks of animals in search of better grazing.

In al-Manayif, of the 820 adult males, 46.8 percent work in agriculture, 36.6 percent are either students or serving time in the military, 7.3 percent work as industrial laborers, 4.7 percent are retired or unable to work, and 4.5 percent work in a service industry or small business, in the civil service, or as professionals. The proportion working in agriculture rises to 74.4 percent in men over the age of forty (See Table 2). Among 786 adult females, 22.9 percent are in school, and all but six of the others are engaged in a mixture of housework, care of children, and care of domestic animals and agriculture.

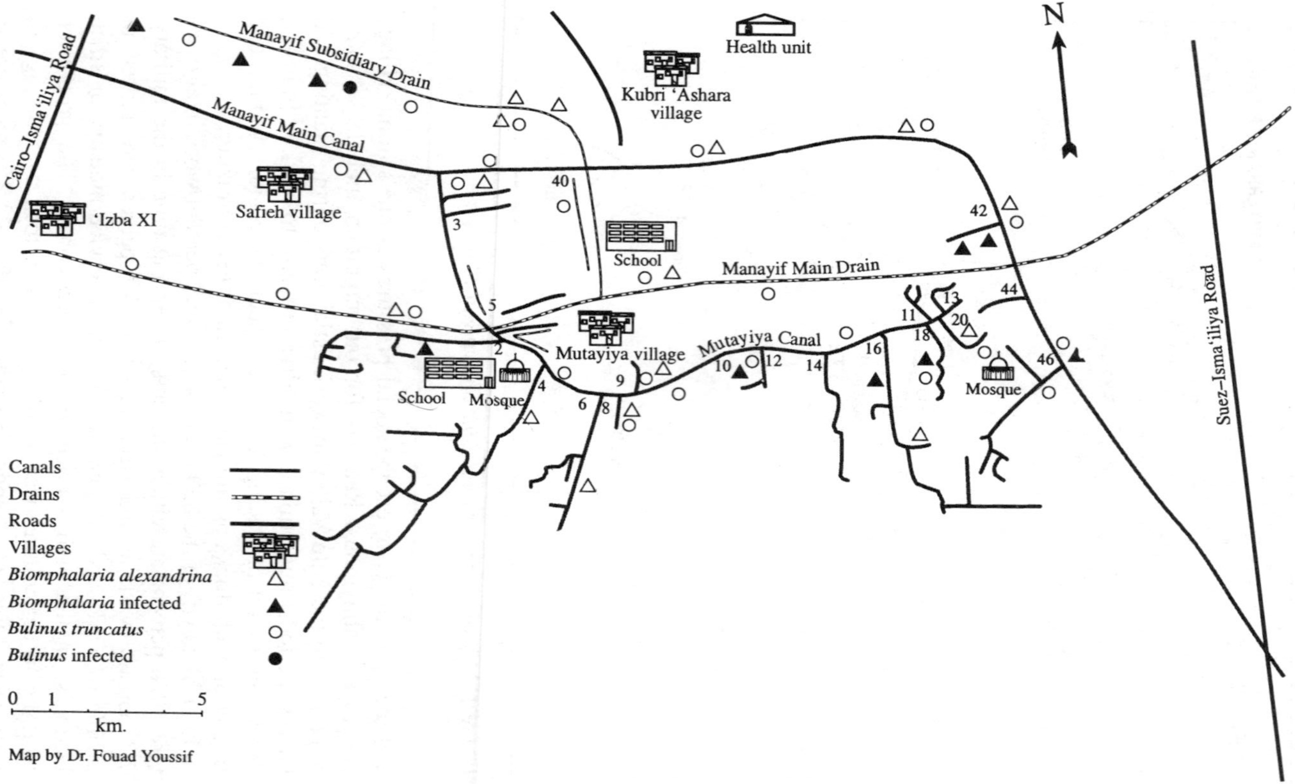

Figure 2 *Map of Al-Manayef*

The number of people working outside of the village is 110. Of these, 20 percent work in a village or town in the Isma'iliya governorate, 36 percent work in Isma'iliya, 32 percent work in another governorate, usually Sharqiya, and 15 percent work outside Egypt, primarily in the Arab oil-producing countries.

Crops cultivated in the summer include rice, peanuts, sesame seed, corn, and summer vegetables, such as tomatoes and squash. Winter crops include wheat, barley, clover (berseem), beans, and vegetables (tomatoes, green pepper, potatoes, and peas). The main types of animals raised by residents are cattle and sheep. A few of the Bedouin also have camels.

Demographic and socioeconomic characteristics of the population are summarized in Tables 1 and 2. The majority of both males and females are under eighteen years old (Table 1). Rates of illiteracy are still unacceptably high, but show signs of improvement. While 97.1 percent of the women over forty years of age are illiterate, this figure is considerably lower, 46.2 percent, among women between fourteen and nineteen years of age. Despite the proximity to employment opportunities in Isma'iliya, agriculture is the predominant occupation among men of all ages and a significant proportion of women. The vast majority of both men and women work in their village or an adjacent village in the same *markaz*. Work outside of Isma'iliya governorate is only common among men in their twenties.

In al-Manayif, the prevalence of urinary schistosomiasis is 3.3 percent, while the prevalence of intestinal schistosomiasis is 49.3 percent (El-Sayed et al. 1995). Diseases that most affect children, such as intestinal parasites, anemia, diarrheal disease, and pneumonia are all common and coexist with the chronic diseases among adults, such as urinary stone disease (El-Sayed et al. 1995), diabetes, hypertension, and cardiovascular disease.

Table 1: *Characteristics of al-Manayif: Population (1992 Census)*

| Age Group | Males | Females |
|---|---|---|
| 0–13 Years | 460 / 43.9% | 447 / 44.4% |
| 14–19 | 172 / 16.4% | 173 / 17.2% |
| 20–24 | 83 / 7.9% | 78 / 7.7% |
| 25–39 | 161 / 15.4% | 173 / 17.2% |
| 40 & Over | 172 / 16.4% | 136 / 13.5% |
| TOTAL (all ages) | 1048 / 100% | 1007 / 100% |

Table 2: Characteristics of al-Manayif Population: Education, Marital Status, Occupation (1992 Census)

| | 14–19 | | 20–24 | | 25–39 | | 40 & Over | |
|---|---|---|---|---|---|---|---|---|
| | Male | Female | Male | Female | Male | Female | Male | Female |
| **Marital Status** | | | | | | | | |
| % Married | 0% | 9.8% | 20.5% | 64.1% | 86.3% | 94.2% | 94.8% | 69.9% |
| % Divorced or widowed | 0% | 0% | 0% | 1.3% | 0.6% | 3.5% | 4.1% | 25.7% |
| **Education** | | | | | | | | |
| In school | 41.9% | 20.2% | 7.2% | 0% | 0.6% | 0% | 0% | 0% |
| Illiterate | 12.2% | 46.2% | 22.9% | 59.0% | 45.3% | 88.4% | 72.7% | 97.1% |
| Primary or less | 36.7% | 23.1% | 37.3% | 20.5% | 34.2% | 8.7% | 25.0% | 2.2% |
| Preparatory or above | 9.3% | 10.4% | 32.5% | 20.5% | 19.9% | 2.9% | 2.3% | 0.7% |
| **Occupation** | | | | | | | | |
| Prof/business/industry | 4.1% | 0.6% | 15.7% | 1.3% | 28.6% | 1.7% | 16.9% | 0.7% |
| Agriculture or fishing | 48.8% | 11.0% | 44.6% | 10.3% | 67.7% | 2.3% | 74.4% | 1.5% |
| Student or military service | 11.6% | 19.1% | 15.7% | 15.4% | 5.0% | 21.4% | 8.1% | 20.6% |
| Not working outside home | 42.4% | 20.8% | 36.1% | 0% | 1.9% | 0% | 0.6% | 0% |
| | 4.7% | 67.6% | 3.6% | 88.5% | 1.9% | 96.0% | 8.1% | 97.8% |
| **Work Location** | | | | | | | | |
| Same village or *markaz* | 91.9% | 97.7% | 71.1% | 97.4% | 83.9% | 97.7% | 91.9% | 99.3% |
| Capital (Isma'iliya) | 5.8% | 1.2% | 6.0% | 0% | 8.1% | 0.6% | 4.7% | 0% |
| Outside Isma'iliya governorate | 2.3% | 1.2% | 22.9% | 2.6% | 8.1% | 1.7% | 3.5% | 0.7% |
| **Sample Size** | 172 | 173 | 83 | 78 | 161 | 173 | 172 | 136 |

## Sources of Care

According to residents questioned in a series of open interviews, there are six sources of advice and treatment for illness episodes: the home, pharmacists, the government health unit or clinic, hospitals, private doctors, and sheikhs who practice traditional Arab medicine.

The first source of advice and treatment in any illness episode is the home. Treatments in the home can be either medical or non-medical. If someone shows symptoms for an illness previously treated, they may either take medicine left over from a previous episode or go to relatives to see if someone has that medicine. Non-medical home remedies include cold compresses for sunstroke and high fever and a variety of teas and other hot drinks containing various herbs for cough and influenza.

The next category are the pharmacists. If the individual has had the symptoms before, they either take the prescription from the previous episode to a pharmacy and buy the same medicines, or simply ask the pharmacist for the medicine they took the last time. If they have not had the symptoms before, they describe them to the pharmacist, and request that the pharmacist provide them an appropriate medicine. Pharmacists not only dispense pills and syrups, but also perform injections. In al-Manayif, there is one pharmacy on the opposite side of the Cairo–Isma'iliya highway, in the village of Kubri Saba', fairly close to the study villages. Residents also travel into Isma'iliya to go to the pharmacies there. People seldom finish a prescription, but instead save tablets for future use. Furthermore, medicines are frequently shared between neighbors and family.

Most people have made use of the government health unit or clinic at some point. The rule is that patients could be examined at the village health unit for a nominal fee of fifty piasters (half an Egyptian pound) between 9 a.m. and 12 noon. After midday, the physician is free to examine the patients privately for a fee of LE3–4. Despite the higher cost, most people prefer the private examinations, since they feel that the physician gives them more attention and a thorough examination. In al-Manayif, there is one health unit in Kubri 'Ashara, and another just outside the study area in the village of al-Samakin. The clinic was built in 1986. In addition, residents make use of the government general hospitals in Isma'iliya, such as the fever hospital and the chest hospital, for operations and X-rays. People from both areas consult private doctors located in Isma'iliya, Bilbas, Zagazig, and Cairo. These doctors are consulted as a last resort, since they cost the villagers a great deal of money, between LE7 and LE30. Nevertheless, some people feel they are worth the money, and have regular appointments with them. One man, for example, said that he went to Isma'iliya for check-ups although free treatment was available at the health unit much nearer to him:

> I had bilharzia six times in my life. The first time I was fifteen years old and took the injections, but I was reinfected because I work on the land and cultivate different crops. Now I go each year to Isma'iliya for a check-up and if I find that I have bilharzia I take the pills. I know that it is a dangerous disease.

The final category of sources of medical advice and treatment are specialists in traditional Arab medicine, almost all of whom are Bedouin. They may be paid with money or in kind (two kilos of sugar or two packs of tea). One informant described them as follows:

> There are people here who know the Arab medicine. The sheikh asks for a piece of cloth which belongs to you, then puts it in a pan of water and reads it, then throws it away and tells you what ailment you have. He then prescribes either burning [cauterization] or, if he knows that you're possessed by spirits, some herbs, because he knows that spirits cannot tolerate the burning. The fee he gets is LE10 to LE30, depending on your ability to pay.

In addition, Arab practitioners perform *zar* rituals for those possessed by spirits. These practitioners tend to be a last resort for the non-Bedouin; for example if the drugs from the pharmacy do not work. Some of the Bedouin, in contrast, rarely go to the health unit or a private doctor, as illustrated in this quote from a Bedouin man:

> We seldom go to a doctor. Unless we are extremely sick and can't move or eat, we will not go to a doctor. They say, "Why go to the doctor, everything to him is a dangerous disease and requires extreme care."

## Transportation and Health Care

From the perspective of informants in al-Manayif, the problem of health care is intimately linked with the problem of transportation. Traveling to clinics, pharmacies, or hospitals is costly in terms of both time and money. People must first walk a long distance to get to the paved road where they can flag down a truck or a bus. There are private trucks which charge fifty piasters per person to take them to the highway where they can board either a bus for thirty-five piasters or a private taxi, which is heading for Isma'iliya, for LE1.50. If someone is sick and needs to have a taxi come to pick him up from the house, he or she pays a fee of LE10. The cumulative effect of the cost and inconvenience of transport, medical care, medication, and the fact that other problems have a greater priority than health, is to dissuade many people from seeking treatment for bilharzia and other illnesses compatible with clinical schistosomiasis. One informant from al-Manayif stated:

> A lot of people here have bilharzia because they are *fallahin* but they do not care to go for urine and stool analysis. I have known someone who died of bilharzia but the people do not care—they have to work on the farms.

## Hierarchy of Resort for Different Illnesses with Abdominal Symptoms

We will now examine what the hierarchy of resort is for different illnesses, and what characteristics of the illnesses affect the hierarchy. We might expect that people would go first to the government health unit because services are available there free of charge and the health unit is much closer to people's homes than the private practitioners. The cost of the private practitioners includes not only physicians' fees and drugs, but also the time and cost of travel in a taxi or bus, or on foot. We would therefore expect that people would only go to private practitioners in cases where they had visited the health unit, but had been unable to have their problem diagnosed, or where the recommended treatment was not available. In fact, what the data suggest is that most people go first to the private practitioners. The health unit is only used if it is known that free treatment is available for the specific condition the person thinks s/he has.

This section will present data from a survey conducted in 1993 of 814 adult residents of al-Manayif. We discuss health-seeking behaviors for four locally-defined illnesses affecting the abdomen: *bilharsiya* (bilharzia or schistosomiasis), *didan* (intestinal worms), *ta'niya* (nausea, diarrhea, pain on defecation), *kila* (kidney stones), and *safra* (jaundice, liver disease). Data is only available for conditions affecting the abdomen, because it was collected as part of a larger study on intestinal schistosomiasis. One question the study addressed was the degree to which people can distinguish between intestinal schistosomiasis and other illnesses, and factors that affect knowledge of the symptoms of schistosomiasis (Mehanna et al 1997).

Table 3 shows the symptoms commonly ascribed to each of the five conditions with abdominal symptoms, the percent of respondents who reported having had the condition previously, and the source of treatment when they were sick. *Bilharsiya* is the only condition where the majority of respondents reported seeking care at the health center, and intestinal worms are the only other condition for which the health unit is the most common source of care. This is despite the fact that both

Table 3: *Knowledge and Treatment Practices in al-Manayif Related to Five Locally-Defined Illnesses Affecting the Abdomen (Cross-sectional Survey, 1993)*

| Illness | | Bilharsiya | Ta'niya | Kila | Didan | Safra |
|---|---|---|---|---|---|---|
| | Approximate translation | Schisto-somiasis | Nausea & diarrhea | Kidney stones | Intestinal worms | Jaundice, liver disease |
| Symptoms most frequently stated to always occur | | Weakness, burning & blood on urination, abdominal pain | Weakness, nausea, go to bathroom continuously | Flank pain | Worm in stool, always hungry, stomach pain | Yellow eyes, yellow urine |
| Respondents who report having condition before | | 531/814 65.2% | 589/814 72.4% | 234/814 28.7% | 230/814 28.3% | 66/814 8.1% |
| Source of treatment | Private doctor | 77/531 14.5% | 107/589 18.2% | 114/234 48.7% | 43/230 18.7% | 31/66 47.0% |
| | Pharmacy | 2/531 0.4% | 218/589 37.0% | 7/234 3.0% | 26/230 11.3% | 1/66 1.5% |
| | Health unit/hospital | 307/531 57.8% | 94/589 16.0% | 47/234 20.1% | 79/230 34.3% | 14/66 21.2% |
| | Folk treatment | | 96/589 16.3% | 11/234 4.7% | 28/230 12.2% | 17/66 25.8% |
| | No treatment | 9/531 1.7% | 40/589 6.8% | 52/234 22.2% | 47/230 20.4% | 2/66 3.0% |
| | Other | 136/531* 25.6% | 34/589 5.8% | 3/234 1.3% | 7/230 3.0% | 1/66 0.1% |

\* Mostly from the research project

private pharmacies and private physicians are located just outside of the study area.

Consulting a private physician requires more time and money for both services and transport. One might predict that residents living in close proximity to the health unit would be more likely to seek care there. Convenience does not appear to have a strong influence on use of the health unit. Table 4 shows that residents of the village where the health unit is located (Kubri 'Ashara) were more likely to prefer the health unit to private doctors than residents of the other villages (53.2 percent as against 40–47 percent), but the effect was not large. In Kubri 'Ashara, 41.1 percent of survey respondents still preferred to consult private physicians, despite the fact that there is a five kilometer walk to the road involved in order to catch a bus or taxi.

Table 4: *Relationship between Preference for Health Unit or Private Doctor and Location of Health Unit in Village*

| Village: | Kubri 'Ashara | al-Mataya | al-Safih | 'Izbet Hid 'ashar |
|---|---|---|---|---|
| Health unit in village? | Yes | No | No | No |
| Preference stated by respondent — Health unit | 53.2% | 40.5% | 47.0% | 44.4% |
| Preference stated by respondent — Private MD | 41.1% | 56.1% | 50.6% | 51.4% |
| Preference stated by respondent — No preference | 5.7% | 3.4% | 2.4% | 4.2% |
| Sample size | 314 | 262 | 166 | 72 |

Table 5: *Preference for Health Unit or Private Doctor and Reasons for this Preference*

| Preference stated by respondent | Free treatment | Treatment available | Proximity | Quality of care/doctor | Other answers |
|---|---|---|---|---|---|
| Health unit N=383 | 176/383 46.0% | 36/383 9.4% | 101/383 26.4% | 62/383 16.2% | 8/383 2.1% |
| Private MD N=397 | 16/397 4.0% | 0/397 0% | 1/397 0.3% | 294/397 74.1% | 86/397 21.7% |

In a further set of questions, reasons for preferring the health unit or private doctors were investigated. Table 5 demonstrates that those who prefer the health unit primarily do so because of the availability of free treatment and its proximity, while those who prefer private doctors do so because of the quality of care provided and the quality of the doctors. If respondents are considering quality, they overwhelmingly choose to consult private physicians. Table 6 shows that younger respondents are more likely to prefer private doctors over the health unit. The implications of Table 6 are that successive generations are less likely to prefer the health unit. In some ways this is counterintuitive. The health units traditionally are more oriented toward control of the acute infectious diseases that affect younger people, while private practitioners have the technology and treatments available for chronic, degenerative disease, such as heart disease and cancer. We might expect a decline in the preferences for the health unit among those currently under twenty years of age as they grow older and develop chronic diseases.

Table 6: *Association between Preference for Health Unit or Private Doctor and Age*

| Preference stated by respondent | 12–13 | 14–19 | 20–24 | 25–39 | 40 and over |
|---|---|---|---|---|---|
| Health unit N=383 | 33/82 40.2% | 98/220 44.5% | 44/98 44.9% | 104/222 46.8% | 104/192 54.2% |
| Private MD N=397 | 49/82 59.8% | 113/220 51.4% | 50/98 51.0% | 109/222 49.1% | 76/192 39.6% |
| No preference N=34 | 0/82 0% | 9/220 4.1% | 4/98 4.1% | 9/222 4.1% | 12/192 6.3% |

Age group shown across columns.

Table 7: *Association between Preference for Health Unit or Private Doctor and Governorate of Origin*

| Preference stated by respondent | Cairo or other city | Lower Egypt/ Nile Delta | Middle or Upper Egypt | Desert (Sinai, Marsa Matruh) | Isma'iliya governorate |
|---|---|---|---|---|---|
| Health unit N=383 | 10/30 33.3% | 69/155 44.5% | 12/20 60.0% | 18/32 56.3% | 272/574 47.4% |
| Private MD N=397 | 19/30 63.3% | 79/155 51.0% | 6/20 30.0% | 12/32 37.5% | 280/574 48.8% |
| No preference N=34 | 1/30 3.3% | 7/155 4.5% | 2/20 10.0% | 2/32 6.3% | 22/574 3.8% |

Table 7 shows that respondents who have migrated to al-Manayif from the more densely populated and urbanized governorates (Cairo and Lower Egypt) are more likely to prefer private doctors. This is to be expected, as health units have been the only source of care in many rural areas in the past, so that people migrating into al-Manayif from other rural areas would be expected to show a preference for health units. The continued urbanization of Egypt is yet another factor that will accentuate the growing preference for private practitioners.

## Discussion: The Future of the Rural Health Units in Egypt

This paper started with a discussion of the epidemiological changes occurring in Egypt, with the emergence of chronic, non-infectious diseases such as cancer, diabetes, and cardiovascular diseases as major public health problems, while social and environmental conditions continue to favor the transmission of infectious diseases such as schistosomiasis and dysentery. Data on social and economic conditions in a rural area near Isma'iliya were then presented. The population is fairly young, most work locally in agriculture, transport is poor, and rates of illiteracy are high. These characteristics might appear to favor treatment-seeking at the government health unit, as it is both close to where people work and inexpensive relative to the consultation of private practitioners. The data presented demonstrate, however, that despite the time and expense in seeking health care in the private sector, residents appear to prefer consulting pharmacists and private doctors, except where the health unit offers specific advantages such as free testing and treatment for schistosomiasis. In some senses, health units have become nothing more than sources of free drugs. When quality of care is an issue, people go to the private sector.

There are two paths that Egypt might follow in planning the future of rural health units. One path would be for the public health system to no longer aspire to providing a wide range of services for the entire population. The private health system would be the main provider of services, with the public health system serving a regulatory function, providing some highly specialized services, and perhaps serving as the care provider of last resort for those who cannot afford to seek care from the private sector. A second path would be for the role of the public health system to evolve to include prevention and treatment of chronic diseases, at the same time as it improves the quality of its infectious disease control activities. The first path will require research on how best to regulate a diverse array of private practitioners, as well as provide continuing education that fits the needs of the practitioners and of the population.

The second path, that of a renewed and perhaps expanded role for the public health system, may be more desirable in terms of equity and effectiveness, but it would require a thorough reassessment of the current system. Health units are reasonably effective at delivering drugs and vaccines for infectious diseases, but are not currently equipped to provide the long-term follow-up and to promote changes in behavior, such as tobacco cessation and diets lower in fat that will be needed for Egypt to confront the emerging epidemic of chronic disease (see El-Katsha and Watts 1995). In addition, many infectious diseases, such as trachoma, diarrhea, and schistosomiasis still require more control efforts as the conditions that favor them, such as poor water and sanitation, remain unchanged (see Watts and El-Katsha 1995).

The present situation offers several clues for how the health units might evolve. First, there will need to be an emphasis on quality in the care provided and in patient–health worker communication. Second, television may be able to play a role in both educating people about emerging diseases, as well as creating appropriate expectations among both health personnel and residents of rural areas regarding how health units operate and the services they provide. To some extent, the mass media have created what health units are. Television spots not only inform people about the health unit, but to some extent create the image of the health unit, portraying it as a facility for immunization, oral rehydration therapy, family planning, and treatment of endemic diseases. The TV spots affect both the health workers and their clients. Given the infrequent training and supervision of staff in many health units, one of their major sources of information about what the health unit is and what they are supposed to do as health personnel is the mass media.

## References

El-Katsha, S. and S. Watts. 1995. "Schistosomiasis Control through Rural Health Units." *World Health Forum* 16:252–54.

El-Sayed, H. F., N. H. Rizkalla, S. Mehanna, S. Abaza, and P. J. Winch. 1995. "Prevalence and Intensity of Schistosoma Mansoni and S. Haematobium Infection in Two Newly Reclaimed Areas of Egypt." *American Journal of Tropical Medicine and Hygiene* 50:29–33.

Habicht, J. P. 1987. "Strategies in Primary Health Care." *American Journal of Public Health* 77(11):1396–97.

Justice, Judith. 1986. *Policies, Plans, and People: Culture and Health Development in Nepal*. Berkeley: University of California Press.

Mehanna, S., N. H. Rizkalla, H. F. El-Sayed, P. Winch. 1994. "Social and Economic Conditions in Two Newly Reclaimed Areas in Egypt: Implications for Schistosomiasis Control Strategies." *Journal of Tropical Medicine and Hygiene* 97:286–97.

Mehanna, S., P. J. Winch, N. H. Rizkalla, H. F. El-Sayed, and S. M. Abaza. 1997. "Factors Affecting Knowledge of the Symptoms of Schistosomiasis in Two Rural Areas near Isma'iliya, Egypt." *Tropical Medicine and International Health* 2(11): Supplement, pp. A36–A47.

Michelson, M. K., F. A. Azziz, F. M. Gamil, A. A. Wahid, F. O. Richards, D. D. Juranek, M. A. Habib, H. C. Spencer. 1993. "Recent Trends in the Prevalence and Distribution of Schistosomiasis in the Nile Delta Region." *American Journal of Tropical Medicine and Hygiene* 49:76–87.

Millard, A. V. 1994. "A Causal Model of High Rates of Child Mortality." *Social Science and Medicine* 38(2):253–68.

Miller, P. and N. Hirschhorn. 1995. "The Effect of a National Control of Diarrheal Diseases Program on Mortality: The Case of Egypt." *Social Science and Medicine* 40 (10 Supplement), S1–S30.

Mosley, W. H., D. T. Jamison, and D. A. Henderson. 1990. "The Health Sector in Developing Countries: Problems for the 1990s and Beyond." *Annual Review of Public Health* 11:335–58.

Mosley, W. H. and L. C. Chen, eds. 1984. "An Analytical Framework for the Study of Child Survival in Developing Countries." *Child Survival: Strategies for Research.* (Supplement) *Population and Development Review* 10:25–45.

Omran, A. R. 1982. "The Epidemiologic Transition." in J. A. Ross, ed. *International Encyclopedia of Population.* New York: Free Press. pp. 172–75.

Rashad, H. 1989. "Oral Rehydration Therapy and its Effect on Child Mortality in Egypt." *Journal of Biosocial Science*, Supplement 10:105–13

Walt, G. 1993. "WHO Under Stress: Implications for Health Policy." *Health Policy* 24:125–44.

Watts, S. and S. El-Katsha. 1995. "Changing Environmental Conditions in the Nile Delta: Health and Policy Implications with Special Reference to Schistosomiasis." *International Journal of Environmental Health Research* 5:197–212.

# V
# VILLAGE HISTORIES

# 12

# Change and Continuity in the Village of Batra: Family Strategies

MALAK S. ROUCHDY

It is difficult to grasp the contemporary historical development of agrarian relations in rural Egypt given the complexity of the socioeconomic and political relations they entail in general, and the regional specificity that shapes them at the micro level. Moreover, the lack of detailed documentation at the village and national levels, based upon written and oral sources, renders the task even more complicated.

Not being myself a historian, but concerned with the process of socioeconomic diversification and differentiation in the village of Batra[1] in the context of the changing national economic policies of the 1980s, I have tried to reconstruct the history of the village. My initial questions revolved around the manner in which socioeconomic change is generated through the forms of access to land, irrigation, and markets, and through the various forms of organization of agricultural production. The focus on the historical background of the village emerged from the necessity to understand the reasons behind the persistence of various forms of agrarian relations, particularly the persistence of non-commodity relations within a highly commoditized economy.[2]

This is the framework I used to conduct my study in Batra, focusing upon production and market relations. However, what concerns me in this paper is to present one aspect of this work which touches upon the social mobility of certain families who assumed significant roles in the historical development of the village. I will present the case of two families, both established in the early twentieth century, who adopted two different forms of agricultural production which were reflected in their socioeconomic relations and development in Batra.[3] By no means do the two examples illustrate the village structure or the prevalent relations. They simply reflect two different trajectories in time with different repercussions on socioeconomic relations at the village level.

In order to situate the two families economically and socially, it is important to locate Batra in its region, and to illustrate its territorial features, which will represent my main references in locating the two families.

## A Brief Description of the Territory

Batra is located on the west side of the Damietta branch of the Nile, fifteen kilometers north of Mansura, and forty-five kilometers south of Damietta. The population of Batra is estimated at around sixteen thousand,[4] and its territory covers nearly 2,897 feddans. The territory of the village is bordered on the south by the Damietta branch and on the north by the railway joining Shirbin and Bilqas centers.[5] The main road that joins Mansura and Damietta divides the territory into two distinct sectors. In addition, the two main sources of irrigation for the territory, al-Sahil Canal and the Damietta branch of the Nile, run parallel to the main road; together they constitute a demarcation line between the various sectors of the territory. The ecological diversity of the territory is largely determined by the location of the land in relation to the source of irrigation, which has partly determined the quality of the soil and consequently the type of cultivation and the quality of the crop. The schematic map of the territory shows that it can be divided into three distinct sectors.[6] Sector A, represents 55 percent of the total territory comprising 1,600 feddans, sector B represents 25 percent covering 735 feddans, and the remaining area, 550 feddans, constitutes sector C, located directly on the main branch of the Nile (Figure 1).[7]

## Historical Background

In attempting to draw the borders and define the spatial contours of the village, I realized that there was a gap between the official cadastral maps, dated 1917, and the territorial and spatial changes that have taken place since that time. The spatial transformation was directly reflected in the direction of the urban expansion and in the crop distribution and rotations over the territory of Batra (Figure 1). To understand the nature of spatial change, I tried to trace the process by which the inhabitants of this village acquired land for agricultural production. The few contracts of ownership I consulted showed that these properties were acquired at the turn of the century from individuals or from companies working on reclaimed agricultural land. However, these indices were not sufficient to establish the development of the forms of access to land. I also had to rely on a few published sources in order to draw a rough schematic description of this development.

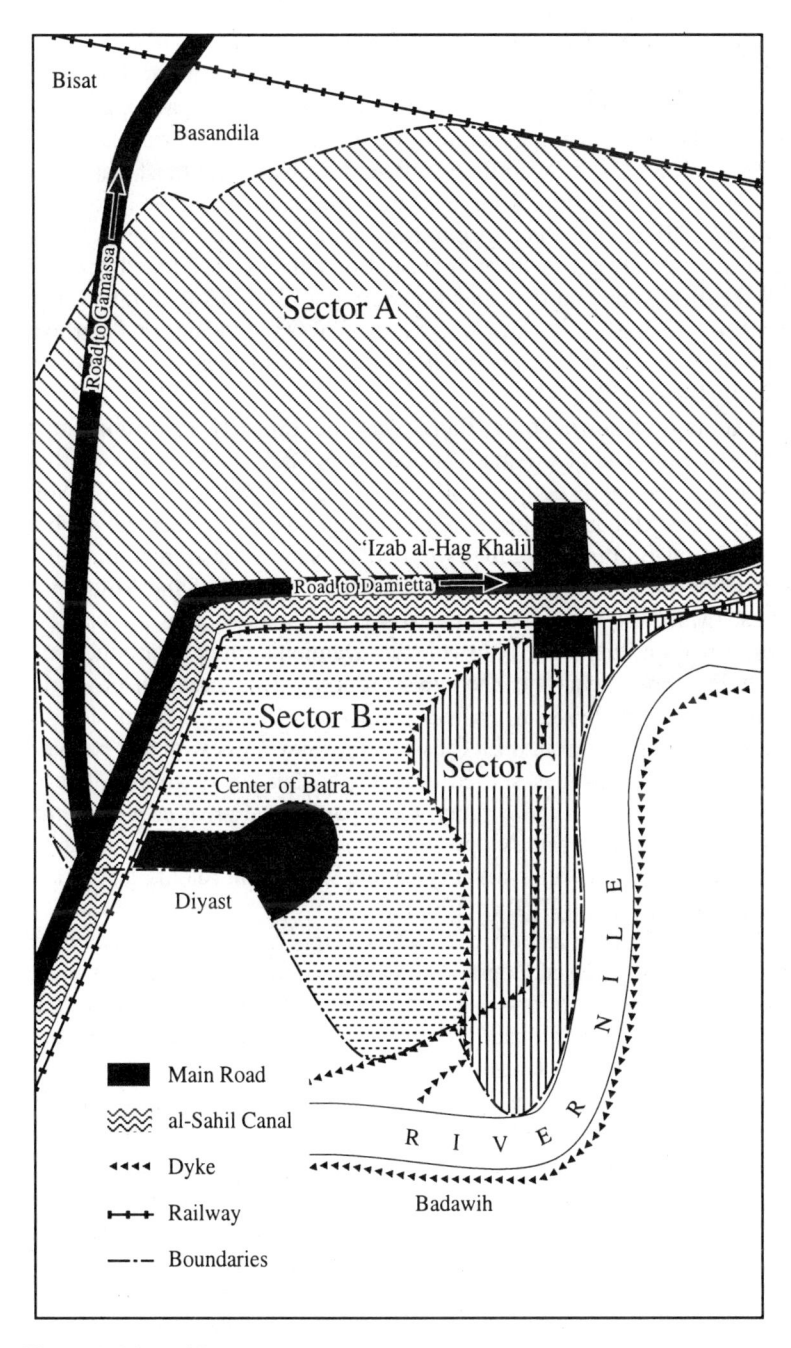

## Change and Continuity in the Village of Batra 239

Figure 1 *Map of Batra*

In his monumental work, *al-Khitat al-tawfiqiya al-jadida* (1886), 'Ali Mubarak[8] counted the number of irrigation pumps in Egypt. In Batra he counted one mobile irrigation pump with a capacity of sixteen horse power, registered in the name of *jiflik* Batra (Mubarak 1886, vol. XIX:41). According to Baer, "Probably the most important factor in the formation of large estates last century was the institution of *jiflik*".[9] Baer adds that, "A number of contemporary sources ... state that the greater part of them consisted of villages abandoned because of the heavy tax burden and transferred to the royal family." The property of the ruling family covered 370,000 feddans in Gharbiya province, to which Batra was administratively attached until the early 1940s (Baer 1962:17–18).

The region surrounding Batra was the property of Muhammad 'Ali's family. Khedive Isma'il (ruled 1863–1879) had a palace with a large garden and cotton mills in Talkha (Mubarak 1886, Vol. XIII:33).[10] Mubarak adds that the village of Bisat, located on the borders of Batra, was called *jiflik* of Bisat; he also mentions the existence of *jiflik* al-Hisa, shared between Batra and the village of Bisat (Mubarak 1886, Vol. XIX:14–41). This shows that a considerable area on the west bank of the Damietta branch, around and including Batra, was the khedive's property. This situation probably continued until 1878, when the economic deficit of Egypt led to European control through La Caisse de la Dette. A new distribution of large landed properties started, due to the burden of foreign debts. "Towards the end of the century, then, part of the great estates of the Khedive and his family passed into the hands of new large landowners, in particular wealthy people who could readily afford the large outlay necessary" (Baer 1962:28).

Some of the new landowners were foreigners whose interests were protected by the Mixed Courts[11] and also by the foreclosure measures, as most of the creditors were foreigners. According to Baer, the province of Gharbiya had the third largest number of foreigners owning agricultural land. The creation of land companies by foreigners was one of the means of expanding the market of agricultural land (Baer 1962:66–67).[12] According to property contracts and to the statements of landowners in Batra, until the end of the nineteenth century and the beginning of the twentieth century, parts of the agricultural land was owned and controlled by foreigners through the Société Anonyme d'Irrigation dans le Béhéra, created in 1881.

The former *shaykh al-balad*, Hag Guda Gawdat, an elder in the village and an authority on local history, told me that landownership and tenancy were not common practices among peasants during the first and second decades of this century. Peasants could not have paid the high rents nor the expensive purchase prices. But of more importance was an article in the contract stating that the Sublime Porte had the right to confiscate landownership for public use if needed in exchange for a compensation (see Mursi 1936:219). This clause represented a threat to the peasants who were neither rich nor powerful enough to protect their property from such a decree.

It should be noted, argued Hag Gouda, that peasants did not begin to own land until the middle of the 1920s and the beginning of the 1930s.[13] The largest estate reached seven hundred feddans in sectors A and B, and a hundred feddans in sector C, mostly owned by absentee landowners and cotton traders.

In the following section, I will examine in detail the development of the landholdings of two families, and the emergence of new groups of landowners in Batra before and after the agrarian reform of the 1950s. The first family is the Hag Khalil family, which established itself in sectors A and B, and the second is the Fakhri family, which established itself in sector C. These two families followed different trajectories, and established different relations with the village and its authorities.

## The Hag Khalil Family

The history of Hag Khalil's family is closely linked to the engineering works conducted by the Beheira Land Company in the region of Batra. In the early 1910s, when the Beheira Land Company started constructing al-Sahil Canal, Hag Khalil, originally from Minya in Upper Egypt, was hired by the company as a contractor to dig the canal. During his stay in the region, around the 1920s, he bought a large plot of land in the sector for LE30 to LE40 per feddan,[14] some of which was in compensation for his work on the canal. The property extended around the canal to cover both sectors A and B. Hag Khalil was residing then in Batra, but got extensively involved in public works with the Beheira Land Company and with cotton plantation and marketing.

By the end of the 1940s, Hag Khalil owned seven hundred feddans. The property covered a large area of sector A and extended into sector B. He did not farm his land directly, instead, given the large scale of the property, he brought peasants with their families from neighboring villages who hoped to find better working conditions. These laborers first developed the land, then became sharecroppers on the estate. The property was divided into small plots, and each family household sharecropped a plot on which they grew cotton, wheat, rice, and berseem. At that time, sharecropping was a form adopted by most landowners of large properties cultivated in cotton and requiring intensive labor. The owner controlled the workers and their families by rendering them totally dependent on him and his capital for their survival. This form of relations led gradually to the establishment of the *'izba* system[15] on the estate of Hag Khalil, and the settlement was named administratively 'Izab al-Hag Khalil.

Thus, the peasant households and their subsistence economy were directly linked to the estate and its owner. Sharecropping was an oral agreement that was inherited from one generation to the next; the peasants and their families were entirely dependent on the owners for their social and economic survival. Thus, the sharecropper's family was present only as long as it provided the necessary labor in exchange for a share of the product of the land.

## Yusif and Yasin Families: A Gradual Ascension

In the lifetime of Hag Khalil, two families of laborers, among those who were brought from other villages, progressively gained the confidence of the landowner and became the labor supervisors on the property. The Yusif family is originally from the village of Badawih, and the Yasin family moved from the village of Dikirnis. Both families settled where they were hired by Hag Khalil to install a water pump on his property. On the death of Hag Khalil, these two families held important positions among the peasants of the *'izba*. In the absence of the owners, the two families offered to rent the land from the absentee landowners on the basis of three-year contracts. Starting from that time, they expanded their activities in the region, and became the largest families in the sector, competing with each other in marketing crops from the sector.

These two families progressively controlled the peasants who remained sharecroppers on the land, providing them with inputs and capital, if needed. At the end of the agricultural season, they collected the crop from the peasants, sold it to merchants in the cities; less than half of the crop was distributed to the sharecroppers. Under the system of sublease, the peasants suffered a great deal from this monopoly. Many cases of theft were reported, as peasants could not live off their share of the crop, and the inhabitants of this part of the territory were known in the village to be the least privileged groups.

After the promulgation of the agrarian reform law and the abolition of agricultural sublease, the owners had to manage and directly control the works on their property. This period coincided with a government monopoly on cotton marketing, which affected tremendously the cotton merchants and prices. By that time, the Yusif and

Yasin families had accumulated great wealth and had reoriented their activities toward the marketing of other crops, mainly cereals and vegetables. Under these conditions, and with the constraints imposed by the agrarian reform laws, the Khalil family was unable to manage their property directly and so they started to sell out. The price of the agricultural land in this part of Batra is known to be very low[16] as compared to the value of land in sectors B and C. The price of a feddan reached LE 500 at the most, and the peasants used to pay by installments as they could not afford to pay in cash.

A considerable part of the Khalil property was bought by the Yasin and the Yusif families, and the rest was sold to the peasants who had been sharecroppers on the land. The Yasin family bought part of the property which extended into sector B, and built a large house in the area for their family. Similarly, the small peasants who bought land in this area built their houses in this extension. Thus, a new *'izba* was added bearing the name of the family who owned the largest part of the area. These two families became the leaders of 'Izab al-Hag Khalil, and asked for the separation of the *'izab* from Batra. Their claim was based on the argument that the *'izab* are located on the periphery of Batra, which made it harder for them to reach government agricultural, civil, and administrative services. They argued that the inhabitants of Batra were systematically abusing their rights and appropriating their quota of services. This claim was eventually used by the Yasin and Yusif families during the parliamentary elections of 1987. They promised the villagers' votes to one of the candidates in their constituency in exchange for supporting their independence from Batra. This promise was redeemed only in the early 1990s, when the National Democratic Party member of parliament was able to promote the *'izab* into a separate independent village from Batra. Today the village of Hag Khalil includes several *'izab*, with an independent infrastructure and administration.

This itinerary shows that over the last eighty years, the Khalil family flourished and prospered but disappeared progressively from the political and social scene once they cut their ties with the village and migrated to cities. However, while they were retreating from the community, their successors were gaining ground, thus taking over property, capital, and power in the community.

## The Fakhri Family

The Fakhri family followed a different strategy from the Hag Khalil in order to survive and adapt to developing political and economic conditions.

The historical development of ownership in sector C finds its origins in the distribution of agricultural land by the Beheira Land Company. Sector C was a fallow region, covered by reeds, and inundated annually by the flood. It was not until the early twentieth century, when the company established its works in sector A by digging al-Sahil Canal, and by the purchase of land for improvement, that the works for the adjustment of land and the creation of irrigation and drainage networks began in sector C. When the development was completed, the company sold the reclaimed land to absentee landowners. According to a contract of a property division, dated February 24, 1914, signed by the company and four buyers, an area of 351 feddans was sold by the company to an Egyptian living in Disuk, a Greek living in Mansura, an Egyptian living in Cairo, and a Jewish person from Alexandria holding French citizenship. Most of them were businesspeople and absentee landowners investing in agricultural land and in the marketing of crops.

As compared to sector A, the purchase of agricultural land in sector C took place on a smaller scale, not exceeding plots of a hundred feddans at the most. Because there was a limited area of reclaimed land, and cotton cultivation was not possible, investments in agricultural production and in marketing had to be based on other crops. Under these conditions, the forms of access to land in this sector followed a different course than in the other sectors. They were related to the cultivation of newly introduced vegetables and fruit.

It is in this context that 'Abd al-Raziq Fakhri started to establish himself in sector C. Originally from Disuk, a region whose economy was based on the cultivation of cotton, rice, and wheat, he was one of the first buyers of agricultural land in the sector. The purchase of land in reclaimed regions was not only related to investments in agricultural land, but was essentially related to the cultivation of potatoes, since that was becoming an important commercial crop by the early twentieth century.[17]

Cotton and tobacco remained the most lucrative crops until the end of the nineteenth century. However, with the further orientation of the Egyptian economy toward cotton plantation and exports, tobacco producers were subject to high taxation on their production, and many had to abandon tobacco in favor of cotton. 'Abd al-Raziq Fakhri, a tobacco producer, decided to find an alternative crop to tobacco, while maintaining his area devoted to cotton in Disuk. Together with another tobacco producer, they traveled to France, where they imported adequate varieties of potato seeds in an attempt to reintroduce potatoes in the Delta. In the beginning, it was an experimental project, but it proved to be successful. By 1914, with the beginning of World War I and the increasing number of British troops based in Egypt, a new market for potato producers emerged and 'Abd al-Raziq Fakhri became one of the first suppliers of potatoes to the British army (Sirki nd:20).

With an increasing demand for potatoes, 'Abd al-Raziq Fakhri purchased 175 feddans of agricultural land in Batra: around a hundred feddans were located in sector C, and the rest was located in sector B. This was the origin of the Fakhri family estate in Batra. The new property was cultivated with summer potatoes, vegetables, and bananas. In 1930, citrus fruit were introduced to the inner side of the al-Gizira sector to replace a variety of vegetables, such as artichokes. In spite of the very high organization of production and the diversification of crops, cultivation in sector C was not without serious difficulties. Every summer, the annual flood of the Nile submerged the river banks for almost two months, rendering summer cultivation almost impossible. However, measures were adopted to reduce the effect of the flood on the plantations. The property was divided into small sections, each protected by two small dikes parallel to the Nile and at different levels. Water pumps were installed on the banks of the Nile to pump out the excess water during the flood.

All these measures required a large number of wage laborers, working night and day, to control the dikes and the water overflow. It also required a high capital investment to cover the high costs of production and the very meticulous management and accounting systems. Therefore, a managerial organization was developed and was directed in a hierarchical manner. A *nazir*, a *katib*, and a *khuli*[18] were permanently engaged. Consistent bookkeeping records were elaborated and a comprehensive control system was adopted. Thus, under a very complex managerial system, and despite high production costs, the quality of the land allowed a substantial margin of profit as productivity was considerably increasing and marketing was successful.

'Abd al-Raziq Fakhri had a daughter and three sons, one of whom was in charge of the land in Batra, while the other two were in charge of the land in Disuk. After his death in 1932, the land was distributed among the heirs. Ali, the son in charge of the estate in Batra, concluded an agreement with his sister and brothers to concentrate his inheritance of agricultural land in Batra, and thus he inherited the largest part of the land there, while his sister and two brothers owned an average of twenty feddans each.

Ali was a highly educated man, who had pursued his studies in Switzerland, and who worked as the director of a Belgian bank in Mansura. Married to the daughter of a prominent large landowner from Mahalla al-Kubra, a neighboring district, he resided for a number of years with his wife in the village. His social and professional connections were quite important in the region, and he invested in them to maintain solid relationships with the notable families of the village and the surrounding areas. The *'umda* and the *shaykh al-balad* families were important figures on whom he relied. Equally important were the families of merchants, on whom he depended extensively for the marketing of his crops. But he also offered many facilities through his position in the bank, which at that time offered financial support for the production and the marketing of cotton.

In the course of the second half of the twentieth century, the agricultural production of the property was intensified and diversified according to marketing conditions. Citrus fruit and banana plantations expanded gradually to replace potatoes, as peasants became acquainted with their cultivation, and as they proved to be highly profitable on the market. Yet they were only cultivated in the inner parts of the property protected by dikes, as the flood would have destroyed the trees. However, banana cultivation was conditioned by its market price, so that it was not cultivated on a regular basis like orchards. Thus, agricultural production on the property was oriented toward the cultivation of non-administratively priced cash crops based on a diversification of crops according to marketing conditions. On the other hand, the management of the property was highly centralized as the owner supervised the agricultural operations directly. At the same time, many merchants in the village started to orient their activities toward orchards and bananas, and gradually a small group of field merchant families started to establish themselves on the market by selling the crops of the Fakhri estate.

In the late 1940s, Ali Fakhri expanded his property when he purchased around twenty feddans in sector C. In the meantime, he tried to buy the share of his sister, who refused his offer, and instead tried to sell it to 'an outsider.' The matter turned into a severe dispute and was taken to court. Many villagers thought that the sister had no right to sell the land to 'a stranger.' *Shaykh al-balad* told me, commenting on this event, "A sister has no right to disobey her brother and to scatter the family's land. We do not inherit the land, it is the land that inherits us."

Although Ali worked hard to expand and unify his property, and to increase its productivity, the agrarian reform laws shattered his dreams. In 1965, Ali sold fifty-five feddans under tenancy to forty-six peasants who were originally holders of the plots. The price was paid in installments, and the value of the land was reduced by half because it was already occupied by tenants. In an attempt to avoid the expropriation measures, as the size of the holding still exceeded the ceiling fixed by the agrarian reform laws, he tried to register the plot acquired from a late brother in the name of his daughter and son. But the administrative procedures for the registration took more than one year, which allowed the expropriation committee time to investigate the matter and to claim the right to expropriate the land.

Finally, the landholding was reduced to eighty-five feddans, located in sector C, and cultivated with citrus fruit and bananas. Before his death in 1969, Ali registered his property in the name of his son and daughter, and the borders of the farm were defined both administratively and territorially. When his son took over the management of the property, the family was no longer able to maintain the large house they owned in the center of the village, nor were they able to expand their agricultural investments. The family house and its dependencies were subdivided and sold to peasants working on the property, and the family moved into a more modest house built in the middle of their property. The residential area, the dependencies of the farm, and the property were, for the first time, gathered into one single basin (section), with clear boundaries separating it from the rest of the village.

Despite efforts at maintaining the property under direct management by the owners, one feddan out the eighty-five feddans owned by the Fakhri family has remained under tenancy until the present time. The renting-out of this one feddan took place under specific conditions due to ecological factors. Every summer, a large part of the bank of the Nile was flooded by water. During this time, the land was planted in bananas, with the exception of a long narrow strip which was planted in vegetables. This specific area was annually submerged with water as it is lower than the rest of the area. After a high flood one summer in the early 1950s, Ali Fakhri decided to rent this plot to the gardener of bananas, Nigma, who was in charge of the entire area. The idea was that Nigma would rent a feddan parallel to the Nile that would be long enough to border a large part of the property, so that when the floods arrived, he would take the necessary measures to protect his own plantation, and would consequently protect the land located behind it. In other words, it was a means of ensuring a regular and permanent protection from the flood without undertaking the necessary work.

However, as the effects of the High Dam were felt after the agrarian reform laws, the owner did not pay attention to this rented feddan located in the middle of his holding. Meanwhile, the children of Nigma inherited the right to rent the plot and begun to switch from a rotation cycle based on potatoes to banana plantations. However, the

Fakhri family did not attempt to evict the tenant, Hag Latif Nigma, who was also the field merchant who marketed the Fakhri's produce, and thus mutual interests were involved.

Despite the partition of land due to inheritance and despite the agrarian reform laws which compelled the owners to sell their excess land under threat of expropriated, the Fakhri estate remained concentrated in one area as owned land, and was farmed by them directly, using hired wage labor. Only some tenancy was maintained, on a very limited scale, under specific circumstances pertaining to ecological conditions in the beginning, and later because of mutual social and economic interests between the tenants and the landowner. The organization of agricultural production based on the intensification and diversification of crops, seasonal wage labor, and high capital investment allowed the Fakhri family to comply with market forces. Under this system, the family acquired a high margin of flexibility which allowed them to adapt to political and economic changes at the national level.

It was under the agrarian reforms and afterward that the Fakhri family most needed their social relations and contacts to overcome the period they refer to as 'the crisis.' They relied on their ties with village notables, merchants, and village administrators to sort out their property and to appeal to the various expropriation and agrarian reform committees.

Under these conditions, and during this period, several small merchants and peasants emerged in Batra as important and influential figures. The conjunction of several economic and political factors, both at the national and local levels, allowed them to surface and gain more power over the marketing channels and over the administrative system. Hag Latif Nigma, who emerged as an influential field merchant through the Fakhri property, is only one among several such figures.

## Hag Latif Nigma

Hag Latif Nigma was among those who purchased agricultural land in sector C from the Fakhri family. He was the son of Nigma, the gardener of bananas on the Fakhri property, and his activities expanded to include the marketing of fruit. The purchase of agricultural land in sector C, cultivated in vegetables, was a means of acquiring one of the best plots of land in the territory, and a way of expanding his lucrative business. Through the purchase of land in this area, Hag Latif Nigma ensured his regular presence on Fakhri property, the largest estate whose crop he traded.

The location of his land near the Fakhri estate was an important factor in his commercial affairs, allowing him to maintain his relations with the owners through, for example, irrigation, or other aspects of agricultural production that bind together the interests of the holders in the same section. Likewise, being in the neighborhood of the property allowed him to be informed of what was happening on the property concerning the production, sale, or marketing of the crop. Although this factor may seem unimportant, it must be considered in view of the tight competition between the small number of field merchants monopolizing the fruit market and controlling the small number of large properties cultivated in orchards.

In the late 1960s, Hag Latif Nigma bought nearly ten feddans suitable for vegetables from the Fakhri family. The land was bought with the capital raised from the marketing of bananas from the Fakhri property, and, like the rest of the purchasers, he was given payment terms.

Beginning in the 1970s, Hag Latif Nigma annually bought the entire production of the Fakhri property and, thus, over the years he monopolized the marketing of their crop. Given the large size of the property and its high production, Hag Latif Nigma could not afford to pay the total price of the merchandise on his own. Through his connections with the small peasants in Batra, he collected enough cash to buy the crop. At the end of the season, each person contributing in the capital received an appropriate proportion of the share in the profit. Through marketing and commerce, Hag Latif Nigma expanded his holdings, which at the present time amount to thirty feddans located in sectors C and B, cultivated in non-administratively priced cash crops. Furthermore, in the early 1980s, he started investing in food security projects promoted by the village bank. On two feddans of agricultural land located in sector B, he constructed a cattle station for meat and dairy products, in addition to a large poultry station. These projects were financed through loans provided by the village bank with his land as collateral.

Hag Latif Nigma has become one of the village's largest field merchants, on whom many small peasant and peddler households depend for their survival. Through his connections in the village institutions, the job opportunities offered to many landless peasants, the marketing possibilities presented to peddlers from the remainder of his merchandise, and the marketing channels provided to small peasants involved in non-administratively priced cash crops, he has acquired an important position in the village. Many peasant families are devoted to him and his family, in exchange for his financial and social support.

After fifteen years of monopolizing the marketing of the crop produced on the property, Hag Latif Nigma began to interfere in the management of the farm. He started to gather the permanent workers around him, to gain their support, and they became his informers. Similarly, he started neglecting the work he was supposed to do, and began to store his merchandise on the farm. Thus, the agricultural operations following the harvesting were delayed, which affected the state of the farm. He was able to gather around him most of the small peasants who have access to irrigation from the Fakhri farm. He gained power on the farm through his relations with the permanent workers there, the labor contractor, and the small peasants whose interests were related to the farm. In return, he offered his financial support, his social protection in the village, and his presence in cases of emergencies. Gradually, the owners felt that their authority over the management of the farm was threatened, and that they had to put an end to Hag Latif Nigma's monopoly over the marketing of their crop. As an expression of their presence, their right over the management of their land, and of the fact that Hag Latif Nigma was, finally, a merchant who could be replaced by another, the owners decided to change their merchant.

The Fakhri family signed an annual contract to sell the crop for a year to the al-Nil Company, a government company for the export of citrus fruit. In fact, the Fakhri family accepted a lower selling price offered by the company, rather than the one offered by Hag Latif Nigma and other merchants who knew about the breakdown of relations. The following year, Hag Latif Nigma offered an even higher price, above the market rate, his idea being to regain his position on the farm; but the owners refused and sold the crop to the company. The third year, the same scenario took place, and Hag Latif Nigma started to feel the effect of this loss on his commercial activities. It was difficult for him to replace the advantages of the location, size, and quality of the crop. Not only did the company buy the crop of this farm, but they also bought the crop of another farm in a village located north of Batra, from which Hag Latif Nigma used to buy his merchandise.

The same year, several accidents of sabotage took place on the Fakhri property: the pipes of pesticide machines were broken, furniture from the house was thrown into the Nile, a warehouse was set on fire, and anonymous threatening letters were sent to the permanent workers on the farm. Investigations did not reveal the perpetrator, while the opinions of the workers on the farm, and those indirectly concerned, were divided. One party accused Hag Latif Nigma, as their loyalty was to his rival Hag Lutfi, another influential field merchant in Batra, on the grounds that he was the only one sufficiently motivated and capable of such actions. Meanwhile the other party, whose members depended on Hag Latif Nigma in many aspects, defended him vigorously, praising his merits and his good intentions.

The Fakhri family did not give in to the pressures, and the crop was never again sold to Hag Latif Nigma nor to members of his family. Since this dispute, the Fakhri family has made it a point always to sell to a field merchant who is not from the village, even if they must compromise on the price. On another front, Hag Latif Nigma is currently refusing, by all legal and illegal means, to return the rented plot to the Fakhri family after the promulgation of the new law on tenancy.[19] A new round of conflicts has started between the two parties.

In spite of these conflicts, the Fakhri family maintains regular ties with the villagers to ensure village support and loyalty, without which the family cannot operate in the village. They contribute financially to community projects, such as the construction of schools and the installation of sewage systems. They are always present in person, or through a representative, at important village meetings and major social events. They also maintain a habit of inviting village notables and workers for *iftar* in Ramadan. This habit maintains the ties between them and the village community. The Fakhri family has understood that it cannot survive and expand both production and property unless it has the support of the community.

## Conclusion

From the foregoing account, it is clear that the Hag Khalil and Fakhri families followed two different itineraries in the village. The conditions that drove them to settle in Batra and purchase agricultural land were different. Both families relied on community relations to establish themselves, and each of them was speculating in a different direction. The ecological differences of the territory partly determined the direction of investment and expansion for both families. Hag Khalil, an entrepreneur of public works, directed his capital and investments to the most lucrative crop of the time, cotton, while Damietta, a potential market, was only forty-five kilometers away from Batra. 'Abd al-Raziq Fakhri, a landed bourgeois from Disuk, was speculating in an unknown area, where the investment was high and the profit uncertain. To a large degree, he succeeded in his speculation, and he and his heirs were able to ensure continuity in the village.

As the Fakhri family was consolidating its property, the Hag Khalil family was losing ground, and other villagers were emerging on the scene. The latter gained considerable access to agricultural land, power over market channels, and, finally, power on the village political scene.

Although most of them are not official figures occupying political positions, they remain the most influential agents in the community. At the present time, it is with the authority and approval of the Yusif and Yasin families that any major decision is taken in the village of al-Hag Khalil, although they may not occupy official positions. It is also with the approval of influential families, such as the Nigma,[20] the Husnani,[21] and other families, who do not officially hold power, that important decisions are taken in the village of Batra. These families delegate their power to those who are in official positions, such as the *'umda* or *shaykh al-balad*, or to those running in political elections. They delegate their power to their agents who act upon their directives.

It is in this context of power distribution that the Fakhri family survived in the village, by siding and allying with the various families in power, adapting to periods of crisis, and reemerging when conditions were favorable. However, it is their skill at maneuvering and linking their city relations with those of the village that ensured their continuous presence in the village for three generations.

Thus, the story of the Khalil and Fakhri families is only one example of how social and economic relations evolve, determined by a number of complex factors, and influence the course of social development in a village. The ecological conditions, in conjunction with national economic policies and changing power relations, play a determinant role in the process of social mobility and differentiation.

In reality, the complexity of studying agrarian relations lies in the fact that both commodity and non-commodity relations are adopted in different forms in order to ensure the process of survival and accumulation by the various social categories under changing national policies. Further, the case studies discussed above are a historical illustration exhibiting one aspect of the socioeconomic mobility that is taking place in the village of Batra. At present, in the 1990s, newly emerging classes of entrepreneurs and merchants are gradually taking over the positions of the old field merchants who established themselves during the era of Gamal 'Abd al-Nasir and under Anwar al-Sadat's open door economic policy. An ongoing process of socioeconomic mobility is occurring through market relations, and an ongoing empowerment of entrepreneurial activities in various fields is being consolidated. In this process, notably with the economic structural adjustment program and the changes in tenancy laws, a further differentiation will take place, reinforcing market relations. Its impact on agrarian relations can only be understood if studied in the context of historical development on national and international levels.

# Notes

1. This paper is derived from a larger study conducted on Batra between 1985 and 1989 (Rouchdy 1990).
2. Non-commodity relations refer to unpaid work, exchanges of services and land, kinship ties, local arbitrage in disputes, and so on, all of which contribute directly to the processes of survival and accumulation.
3. It should be pointed out that all the names used in this article are pseudonyms.
4. The Central Agency for Public Mobilization and Statistics, 1986.
5. Shirbin and Bilqas centers are located in the Governorate of Daqahliya.
6. This division is based on four criteria: a) The location of the land in relation to the source of irrigation, b) the quality of the land, c) the type of crop rotation, and d) the access to the market centers and the center of the village. It is beyond the scope of this study to examine in detail the characteristics of each sector. It is sufficient to say that each sector has a different market value for agricultural land, which can vary by a factor of two.
7. Sector C is called *al-Gizira* land, that is, the land of the island. The strong movement of the Nile during the flood period erodes land from one bank and deposits it on the other bank, creating a large lower flood plain called *'al-Gizira'* (Mursi 1936:110).
8. 'Ali Mubarak (1823-1893) was an administrator in the government and the author of a number of books advocating the modernization of Egyptian institutions. He occupied several political positions, such as minister of public works and minister of education. He was also the founder of *Dar al-'Ulum*, the 'House of Sciences.'
9. The etymology of the word *'jiflik'* is traced to a Persian name and "[I]t eventually came to mean land given to the ruler, beginning in Egypt with Muhammad 'Ali himself to members of his family" (Baer 1962:17–18).
10. Talkha is the administrative center to which Batra is affiliated.
11. The Mixed Courts were created in 1875 with the consent of the Powers, to try and defend cases involving foreigners.
12. Baer argues, "The interest shown by foreigners (and also to some extent by Egyptians from towns) in acquiring land increasingly took the form of investment through land companies, a considerable number of which were founded in the 1880s and 1890s. The main business of these companies eventually came to be the improvement of land with a view of re-selling it, but they seem at first to have tried to work the land themselves" (Baer 1962:68).
13. This period corresponded to the economic depression between the two world wars. During this time, large landowners faced considerable losses on the world market with the drop in cotton prices, to the extent that the Egyptian government had to intervene on the spot market for cotton to save the investments of the landowners and the merchants (Rouchdy 1990).
14. This price is average if compared with the prices of the agricultural land

purchased in sector C, which reached LE90. This will be discussed in the following section of the paper.
15 Georg Stauth defined, in a historical context, the socioeconomic development of the *'izba* system as being a vestige of the large estates of the end of the nineteenth century, where the production unit was separated from the village economy and was based on peasant wage labor (Stauth 1983:288–87). However, in this particular case, wage labor was not the dominant form of relations, instead sharecropping relations dominated.
16 The value of land in sector A is lower than in the two other sectors because it is located far from the source of irrigation, the Nile. Further, this sector was, and still is, predominantly cultivated in cotton, whose market value remains by far lower than any other market crop. Together, these factors contributed to the decrease in land value, which until recently was very low, amounting to around LE60,000, compared to an average of LE120,000 per feddan in sector C.
17 Potato cultivation, introduced in the early nineteenth century under Muhammad 'Ali, was not a successful crop at that time, as the plants were affected by many diseases (Sirki nd.:15).
18 The *nazir* is the general supervisor of the farm and is directly accountable to the owners. The *katib* is the accountant of the property, and reports to the *nazir*. The *khuli* is a labor contractor, supplying daily wage laborers, and is responsible for the accounts of workers. He reports daily to the *nazir* and the *katib*. This hierarchy is not unique to this farm, but is the general system adopted on large properties, where bookkeeping represents the main system of management. Until the present time, the Fakhri family maintains a strong hierarchical system of management, and has kept consistent documentation since the establishment of the property.
19 In 1992 an amendment to the tenancy law was promulgated stating, among other clauses, that the owner has the right to terminate the rental contract with the tenant if the owner so wishes. This clause came into effect as of October 1997. On the basis of this law, the Fakhri family is attempting to recuperate the feddan rented to Hag Latif Nigma. It is beyond the scope of this article to discuss the new laws on tenancy but for further details, see 'Abu Mandur (1992:33–34), and *al-Ahram al-iqtisadi* (1992:54–56).
20 Over the past few years, Hag Latif Nigma's commercial activities have considerably declined as a consequence of several financial crises and poor health. None of his family members have taken over his role.
21 The Husnani family is one of the most important field merchant families in Batra; they have held the position of *'umda* for several generations.

# References

'Abd al-Tawab, Mu'awwad. 1984. *al-Wasit fi-l-tashri'at al-zira'iya min al-nahiya al-jina'iya wa-l-madaniya*. Cairo: Dar al-Fikr al-Hadith.
'Abu Mandur, Muhammad. 1992. "al-Qanun bayna al-hulul al-shamila w-al-muwagaha al-juz'iya." *al-Ahram iqtisadi*. July 6. pp. 33–34.

al-Ahram iqtisadi. 1992. "al-Ta'dilat al-jadida li-ba'd ahkam al-qanun raqm 178 li-sana 1952 bi-l-islah al-zira'i." *al-Ahram iqtisadi.* July 20. pp. 54–55.
Baer, Gabriel. 1962. *A History of Landownership in Modern Egypt 1800–1950.* London: Oxford University Press.
Croutchley, A. E. 1938. *The Economic Development of Modern Egypt.* Great Britain: Longman, Green & Co.
Mubarak, 'Ali. 1886. *al-Khitat al-tawfiqiya al-jadida.* Cairo: al-Matba'a al-Amiriya al-Kubra, 20 Volumes.
Mursi, Muhammad. 1936. *al-Milkiya al-'aqariya fi Misr wa tatawuriha al-tarikhi min 'ahd al-fara'ina hata alan.* Cairo: Nuri Press.
Rouchdy, Malak S. 1990. "Peasants and Merchants in Batra. The Process of Economic Diversification in an Egyptian Village." Ph.D. thesis presented to the University of Durham, UK.
———. 1992. "Représentations et transformations socio-économiques d'un village égyptien: Batra." *Egypte, Monde Arabe* no. 8. pp. 63–86.
Sirki, Muhammad 'Ala' al-Din. nd. *Intaj al-batatis.* Cairo: al-Gama'iya al-Ta'awuniya li-Muntij al-Batatis.
Stauth, Georg. 1983. "Capitalist Farming and Small Peasant Households in Egypt." *Review* 7(2). pp. 285–313.

# 13

# Spaces of Poverty: The Geography of Social Change in Rural Egypt

DETLEF MÜLLER-MAHN

## Introduction: Changes in Society and Social Space

Egypt's villages are changing rapidly, both in their physical appearance and the socioeconomic conditions of their inhabitants. The rural settlements in the Nile Valley have grown to be three or four times as large as they were in the 1950s. During the same period, their material substance has been renewed and changed to a great degree, and life in the village has become more and more influenced by urban examples. Yet, new houses do not necessarily mean that the conditions of life in the village have improved for everyone. From the perspective of social geography, the deterioration of the conditions of the rural poor deserves special attention, especially in Upper Egypt.

Rural Egypt has always suffered from poverty, but the situation seems to be continuing to deteriorate these days.[1] In 1997, more than 800,000 *fallahin* lost their landholding titles which allowed them to cultivate land on the basis of permanent rent contracts dating from the agrarian reforms of the 1950s and 1960s. During the implementation period of the new counter reform laws between 1992 and 1997, there was much speculation about the reaction of the dispossessed tenants: Will they continue to rent land at free market prices ten times as high as the previously fixed rates? Will they search for alternative incomes in their home villages? Or will they pack and move to Cairo?

What makes the issue so alarming for Egypt's current development is not only the number of affected families—roughly one fourth of the rural population—but the prevailing atmosphere of uncertainty. As late as March 1997, six months before the changeover, most renters were still left completely unsure of how they were going to survive after the passing of the land to the original owners, many of them absentee landlords with little experience in farm management and agriculture. Scholars also need more information. This includes information about the tenants themselves, especially with respect to their social background, their economic conditions, and geographic distribution. This paper will present a case study of a village in Minya governorate that attempts to link an analysis of the social history of the village with an assessment of the impact of present economic reforms.

Change affects many levels. There are alterations in the geography of the villages that happen more or less on the surface and can be observed directly, and there are the underlying changes in the social structures and the living conditions of the village people. The question to be discussed in this paper is how these two levels are related to each other, that is, how socioeconomic changes are being reflected in geographical structures and their transformation. The interest is not in the structuring of space as such, but in the social meaning of spatial phenomena. Space, as seen here, has a double significance: on the one hand, it has been created by society, which has left its imprints on the geographical surface of the cultural landscape; on the other hand, space itself plays an essential role in the structuration of society because it is part of the framework for social action.[2] The study of geographical structures aims at a better understanding of the social history and present conditions of villages in Egypt. The paper is based on field research in selected villages of Gharbiya and Minya governorates, conducted during intermittent periods between 1992 and 1997.[3]

## The Eviction of the Small Tenants and its Regional Impact

The main effect of Gamal 'Abd al-Nasir's agrarian reforms was not so much the redistribution of land, but the regulation of agricultural wages and land rents.[4] Rent contracts were fixed on a permanent basis and at an annual rate of seven times the tax paid by the owners. The establishment of permanent titles *(hiyaza)* was of great benefit for the tenants because they were inheritable and allowed their holders to profit from the services of the agricultural cooperatives, as well as to take subsidized credits. Despite the annual rents that still had to be paid to the original owners, most tenants felt as if the land was theirs.

The ending of permanent rent contracts was decreed on June 28, 1992, when the Egyptian parliament passed Law no. 96, which contains new regulations governing the "relationship between landowner and tenant." The law declared a five-year transition period until the end of agricultural year 1996/97, during which the rent of the land would be gradually increased until it reached the rates of the free market. At the end of the transition period, the owners regained full control over their property, including the right to cultivate the land themselves or to let it to anyone who is willing to pay the rent demanded.

The changes made by Law 96/92 is part of Egypt's structural adjustment program. Economically, the termination of rent control aims at a restoration of the old, prerevolution large estates, an expansion of market-oriented production and—so it is hoped—a modernization and intensification of land use. The social consequences of the agrarian counter-reform points to an eviction of the masses of agricultural small holders and an increase in rural poverty.

The impact of the expulsion of tenants will significantly vary from region to region, as can be seen in Figure 1. The map contains two pieces of information about the situation of holdings before the realization of the present reform: the first is the number of farms per governorate, which is expressed by the size of the circles, and the second is the percentage of different types of landholdings (ownership/permanent rent contracts) per governorate, expressed by the sectorial differentiation of the circles.[5]

The map shows a significant difference between the governorates of Lower and Upper Egypt with respect to the relative importance of holdings with permanent rent contracts. The highest percentage of tenant farms in this category lies in the Bani Swayf and Minya governorates, where more than 50 percent of all farms depend on holdings based on the *hiyaza*-type rent contracts. With the implementation of the new law, these tenants are losing their land. That means that in these two governorates, about half of all the peasants who previously had had a 'secure' economic base will have to look for a new economic base.

Before coming to the question of how landless peasants try to cope with the situation, their social history and geographical differentiation are analyzed in the following case study of a village in Minya governorate.

## The Historical Development of Irrigation and Settlements in Minya Governorate

The emergence of a class of landless peasants is closely related to the development of irrigation and landownership during the nineteenth century.[6] During the same period, a particular settlement pattern was established with the creation of two new types of villages for agricultural laborers and nomads. The hamlets of the laborers (*'izba*; plural, *'izab*) in general are much smaller than the old 'mother villages' to which they belong. They were founded on large estates as geographically separate units outside of the existing settlements, but for administration and services they depend on the 'mother' villages. In contrast, the nomad settlements on the edge of the cultivated land are

Spaces of Poverty 259

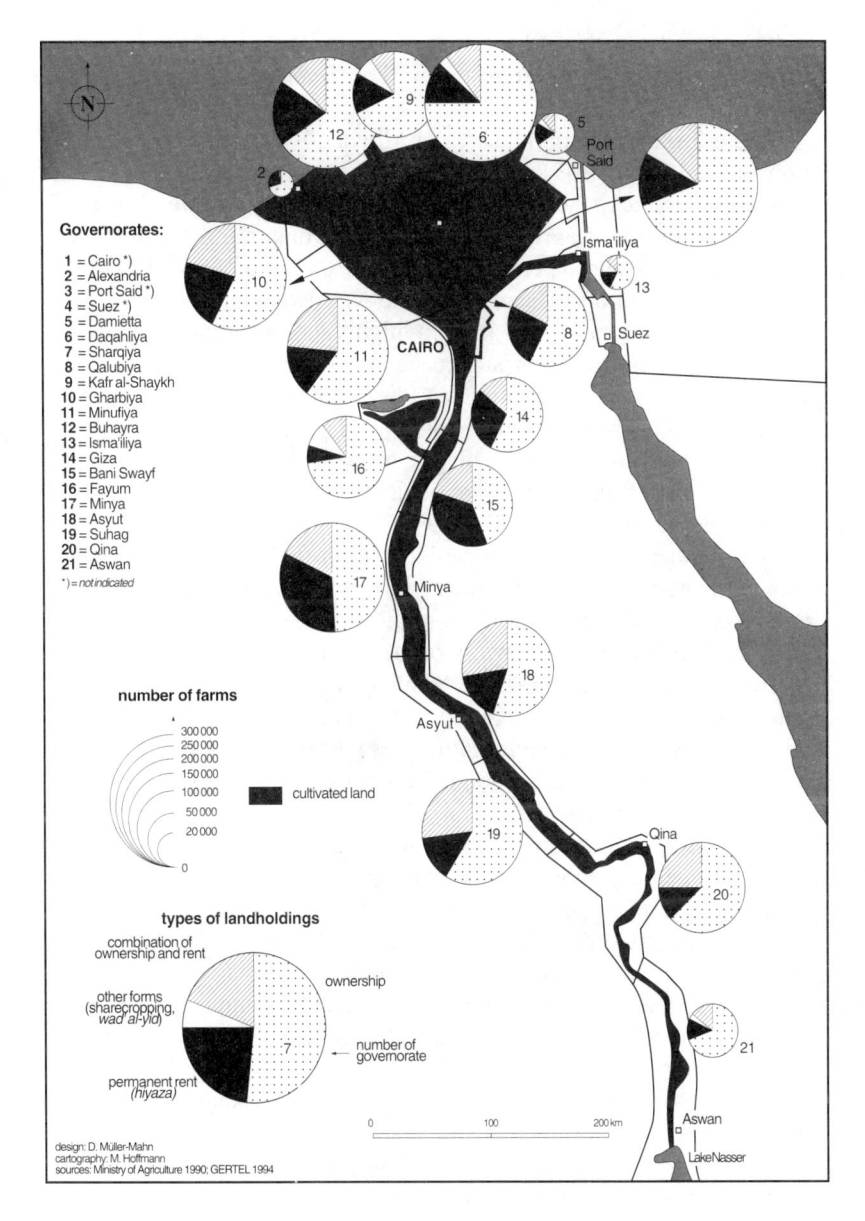

Figure 1 *Types of Landholdings in the Governorates of Egypt, 1990*

independent from the old villages of the valley, and their dispersed layout is distinctly different from the *'izab* and villages of the *fallahin*.

Figure 2 shows the middle area of Minya governorate and the situation of land use in 1891.[7] Here it can be seen that at the end of the nineteenth century, the Nile Valley was divided into three zones of different intensity of agricultural production: only the first zone, west of the Nile, was under perennial irrigation, and was dependent on the newly built Ibrahimiya Canal. This land was owned primarily by large landowners who exploited it in a highly commercialized type of agriculture. Large areas of sugarcane were cultivated in the area of Bani Mazar. As shown on the map, the sugarcane was transported to the factories by narrow-gauge railways. The large number of *'izba* settlements outside the old villages is evidence of the massive in-migration and settlement of agricultural laborers in the areas of commercial farming.

The number of agricultural settlements in the second zone, which was cultivated using the traditional form of basin irrigation until the end of the nineteenth century, is significantly lower. The region is not connected to the railroad network of the intensive cash crop farms.

The third zone, beyond Bahr Yusif, is a pasture land for Bedouin herds. It is not even demarcated on the map of the British colonial administration because the irrigation and pasture land of this zone was clearly only of marginal economic importance. Just a few old villages and irrigation basins (*hawd*; plural, *ahwad*) lie directly on Bahr Yusif.

The differentiation in the land-use patterns at the end of the nineteenth century shown in the map no longer exist because all the land has been under perennial irrigation since the building of the High Dam. Nonetheless, the social distinctions that parallel the division of the Nile Valley into distinct zones exist until the present day.

In the course of the nineteenth and twentieth centuries, a gradual sedentarizing of nomads has occurred in the third zone, which is the region that borders the desert on both sides of the valley. The results of these processes are shown in Figure 3, which shows the ethnic differentiation of the contemporary settlement pattern in the same geographic area as the previous one.[8] Rural settlements fall into two distinct groups according to the *fallahin* or Bedouin origins of their inhabitants.

The majority of the settlements shown are of the *'fallahin*-type' in the areas of zones one and two described above. Beside them, on the western edge of the Nile Valley, and less numerous on the eastern edge, is a chain of smaller settlements of a distinctly different type. Considering their names and population composition, these villages

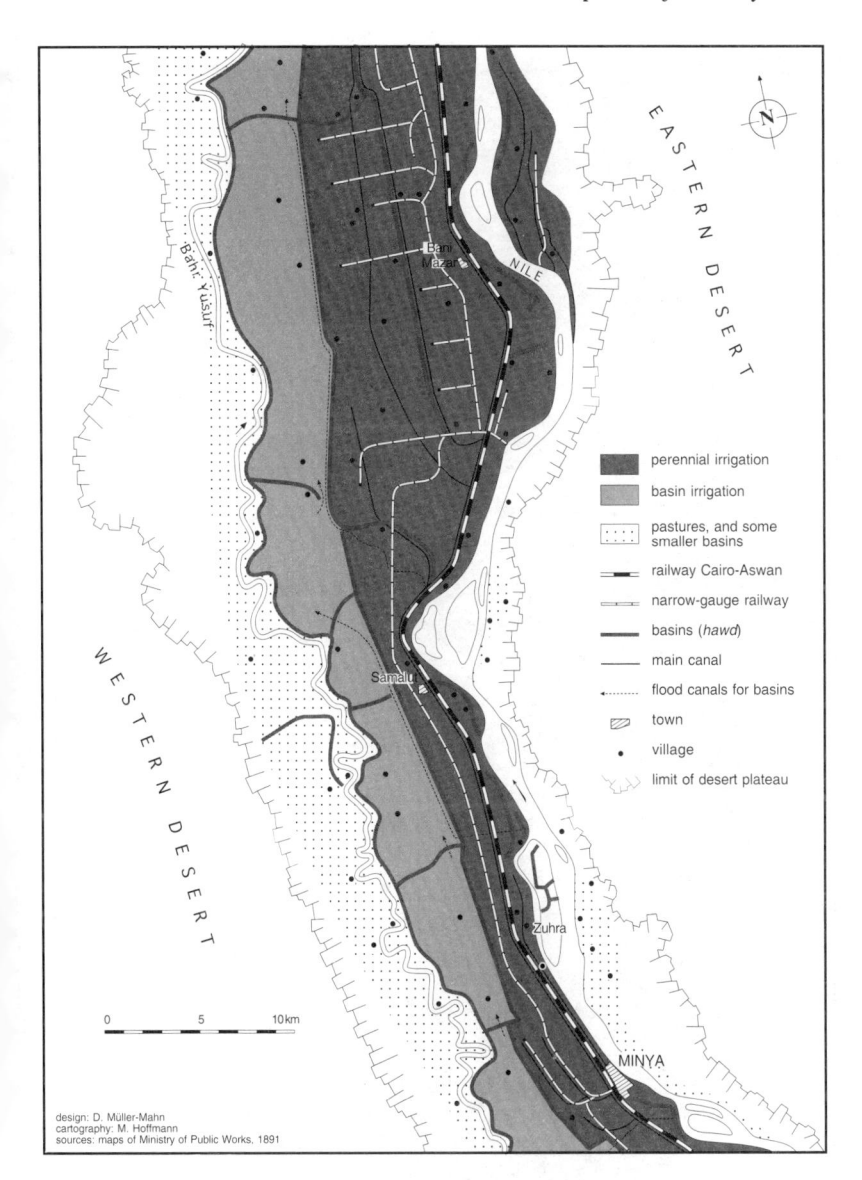

Figure 2 *Irrigation Development in Minya Governorate, 1891*

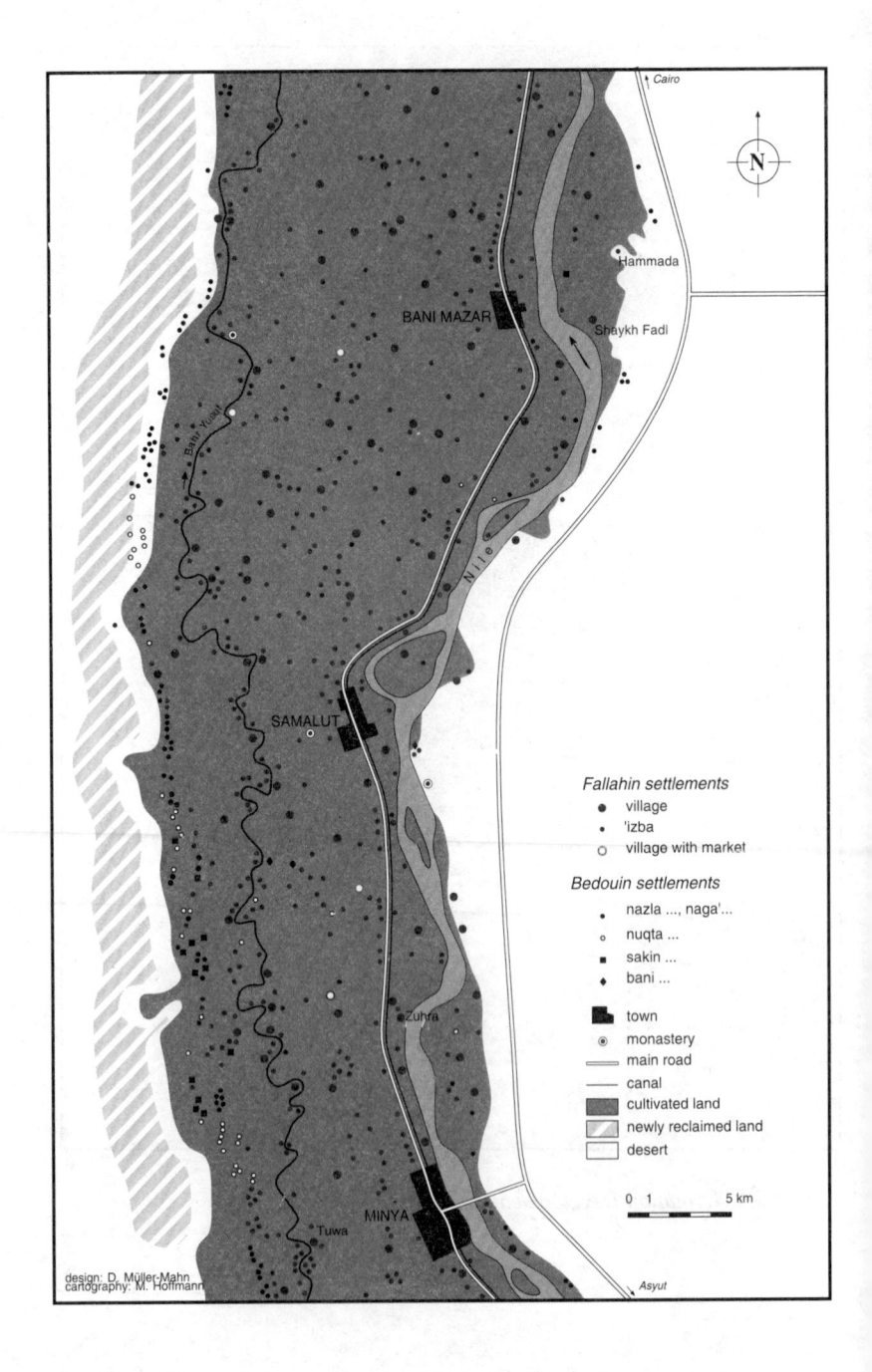

Figure 3 *Settlements of* Fallahin *and Bedouin in Minya Governorate*

trace their roots back to the nomadic settlement and sedentarization processes of the last half of the nineteenth and the first half of the twentieth centuries.[9] The first cartographic evidence of settlement in this region is to be found on a British map published in London in 1807, and updated in 1816.[10]

The places that may be counted among the 'Bedouin settlements' bear terms in their names that reveal the Bedouin or nomadic origins of their founders, as do the composition of their present-day populations. Five segments of the settlement names can be distinguished, of which the first three indicate a clear semantic reference to the sedentarization process:

> *nazla* (settlement, camp); *naga'* (Bedouin settlement); *nuqta* (camping place, small settlement); *sakin* (residence, sometimes in a context such as *sakin al-'arab*); *bani* (sons of ...).

The most common of these designations found on the sector shown in the map is *nazla*, which appears 105 times. The next most frequent is *nuqta*, appearing thirty-eight times. The settlements of the sedentarized nomads consist of more-or-less scattered, isolated houses, and generally lack the density and narrowness of the clustered villages of the *fallahin*. A second characteristic of the Bedouin settlements is the social organization of the inhabitants, who usually belong to the same tribal groups. They are not necessarily relatives though, because the major tribes of *"arab'* origin have incorporated other groups of inferior status. Sedentarization has been accompanied by a disintegration of tribal organization. This process is more advanced among the descendants of the nomads of the Western Desert, while the members of the Ma'aza tribe of the Eastern Desert, who settled completely only a generation ago, still preserve their traditions to a great extent.

The historical, ethnic distinctions exhibited among the denizens of the Nile Valley are significant to the present time. They are not only reflected in the shapes of the villages, but can also be correlated with the economic strategies of the inhabitants.[11] Families of Bedouin origin tend to rely more on animal husbandry, and the ones on the east side of the Nile especially depend on labor in quarries or the oil fields in the desert.

During the agrarian reforms of the 1950s and 1960s large properties, especially in the zone along the Nile, were distributed among the peasant population. Yet, from the case studies conducted in Minya governorate, it seems that most of the reform land was given to members of the 'old' village families, whereas the descendants of Bedouins, or former migrant laborers in the *'izba* settlements and on the edge of the old villages did not benefit from land distribution to the same degree. Consequently, the social contrasts are still markedly apparent here, as we shall see in the case of the village of Zuhra in the following section.

## The Interplay of Spatial Development and Social Differentiation at the Village Level: The Example of the Village of Zuhra

The village of Zuhra, which has a population of around 8,500, lies about ten kilometers north of Minya on the west bank of the Nile. In the following section, three maps are presented and interpreted with respect to what the geography of the village reveals about its spatial development and social history. Figure 4 shows the horizontal expansion of the village over the past three decades by indicating the age of each single house. Figure 5 gives an interpretation of some of the historical–geographical features in the layout of the village. Figure 6 finally shows the distribution of family groupings within the village. By comparing these three maps and interpreting the information they contain on different levels, the interplay of spatial development and social differentiation in the village will be analyzed.

The layout of the village, as shown in Figure 4, reveals some features that are typical for most villages of Middle Egypt: the circular locus of the ancient settlement lies within a 'ring road' which marks the *dayr al-nahiya*, that is, the boundaries of the village at the end of the nineteenth century. Inside the *dayr al-nahiya*, the alleyways are narrow, irregularly shaped, and mainly characterized by dead ends. The oldest part of the village lies about two meters higher than the area that was built up later. This observation was already mentioned in 1836 by Edward Lane in his *Manners and Customs of the Modern Egyptians*:[12]

> Most of the villages of Egypt are situated upon eminences of rubbish, which rise a few feet above the reach of the inundation, and are surrounded by palm-trees, or have a few of these trees in their vicinity. The rubbish which they occupy chiefly consists of the materials of former huts, and seems to increase in about the same degree as the level of the alluvial plains and the bed of the river.

In a comparison of Figures 4 and 5, one can see how the network of streets and alleyways of the village developed out of old footpaths, irrigation ditches, and field boundaries. The broadest of the radial roads leaving the *dayr al-nahiya* of Zuhra once connected the village with the river in the east. Another narrow street, which heads north from the *dayr al-nahiya,* developed out of a footpath that once linked the village with the small hamlet, 'Izba Tadrus Ibrahim—named after

Spaces of Poverty 265

Figure 4 *Spatial Development of Zuhra Village (Governorate of Minya, Egypt)*

its last owner, a Christian—about three hundred meters to the north. The *'izba* has by now become part of the growing village.

The more recent extensions to the village over the past thirty years are quite different from the old part because the streets here follow straight, parallel lines, and houses generally have a rectangular shape. The reason is that the new houses were built on plots obtained from the parceling of long strips of agricultural land, so that the pattern of village streets is like a blueprint of the fields that were transformed into building land. The sale of land for construction was highly profitable for landholders who owned fields next to the houses. The money gained from such business was primarily invested in new houses. In some cases, however, landowners who had originally refused to give up their land were eventually forced to dispose of their fields because the expansion of the settlement made irrigation and cultivation too troublesome. The fruit garden of the al-Rifa'i family, for example, which is shown in Figure 5, had to be sold for construction purposes after it was finally cut off from its water supply.

In Zuhra, it was possible to collect information about the process of the settlement's development and the change in the living conditions of its inhabitants for a period of about the last hundred years. This was achieved by means of interviews with elderly residents. Any attempts to explore oral history deeper into the past were not very successful, especially when attempts to inquire about the biographies of specific families were made. Therefore, another approach had to be applied by using the interpretation of the geography of the village as an additional source of historical information.

Figure 5 presents some spatial characteristics from the cadastral maps of 1936,[13] which have left their traces in the present day layout of streets and houses of Zuhra. Two observations from this map reveal particularly interesting geographical information about the history of the village. The first shows that the village center, within the circular structure of the *dayr al-nahiya,* has to be further differentiated, because an older and much smaller nucleus can be discerned in its middle. The second observation relates the expansion of the village to the migrations of agricultural laborers.

As for the first geographical observation about the area inside the *dayr al-nahiya*, the land registers prove that in 1936 four cemeteries lay within the limits of the village. They no longer exist today, because they have subsequently been built over. Three, however, are still visible in their contours. Two of the abandoned graveyards have been used by the government for the construction of a cooperative and a youth club. In one case, the tomb of a holy man *(wali)* was simply integrated into the courtyard of a house. What is important about the

Spaces of Poverty 267

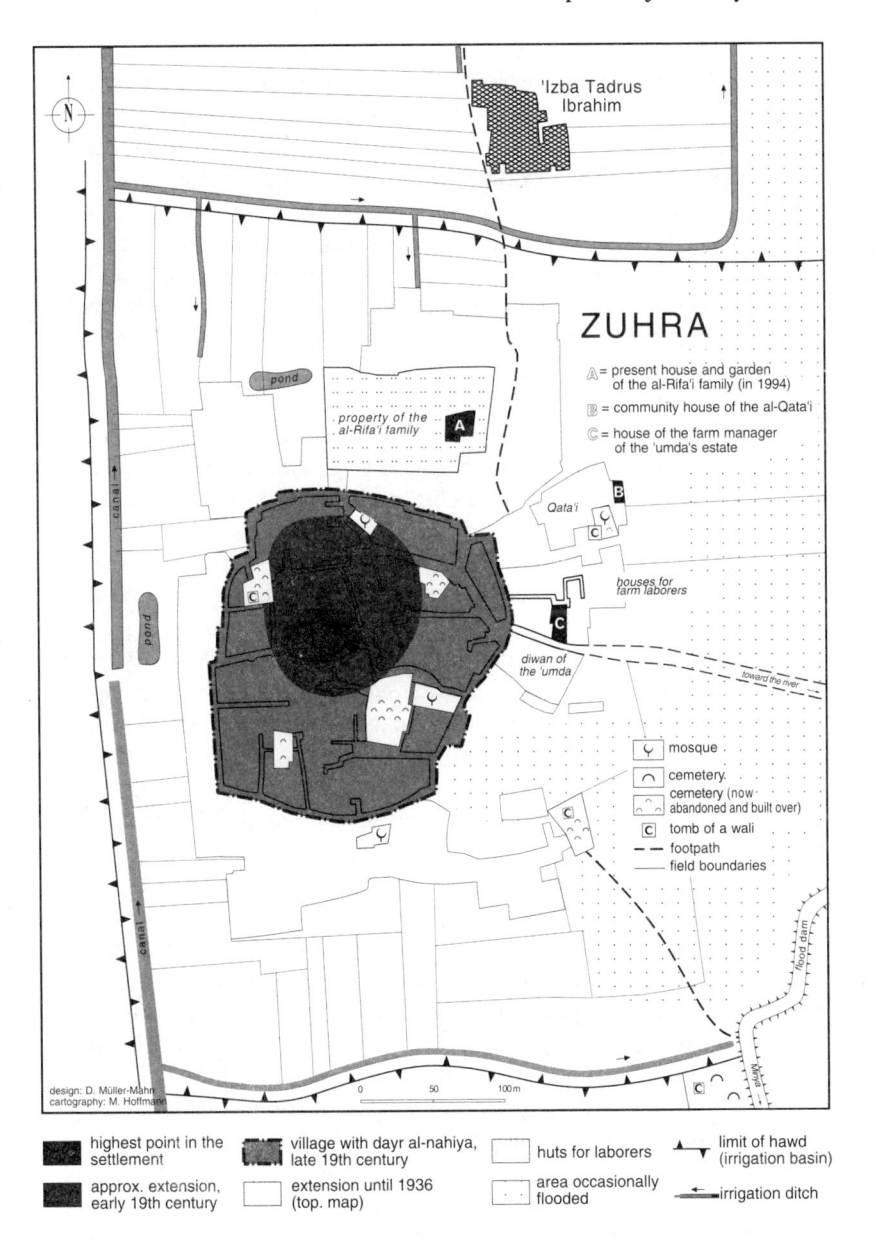

Figure 5 *Spatial Development of Zuhra Village (until 1936)*

location of the old cemeteries is that they mark the four corners of an older nucleus of the village. Between them, a small area of about fifty by a hundred meters is to be found. This area lies, once again, one to two meters higher than the rest of the village, and there is good reason to assume that is the most ancient nucleus of the village. It will be discussed later why this information may be important.

The second piece of historical–geographical information that can be read out of the cadastral maps of 1936 concerns the relationship between settlement development and migration. The maps show a belt of expansions that were constructed before 1936 outside the *dayr al-nahiya*, and three areas with huts on the eastern edge of the village near the house of the *'umda*. The huts and the still-existent cul-de-sacs, with their identical tiny houses, were clearly built to house laborers. According to narrations by several elderly men from this area, their forefathers came to Zuhra around the turn of the century, most of them from Suhag governorate.

The development of capitalist agriculture in the nineteenth century was based on peasant wage labor.[14] It resulted not only in the establishment of the *'izba* system, with numerous small *'izab* lying apart from the older settlements, but also led to agricultural laborers from other regions of Egypt settling on the edges of the existing villages. There is reason to assume that the expansion of the village of Zuhra outside the *dayr al-nahiya* was the result of a massive in-migration of laborers from Upper Egypt who found work in the great sugarcane and cotton plantations of this area. A wave of migration that brought a large number of new inhabitants into the village is confirmed by many narratives of elderly residents.

The questions remain, however, in which part of the village the immigrants settled, how they were integrated into the community, and where their descendants live today. In this respect, the historical interpretation of the village's physical situation proves to be of great interest when it is compared with the social structure of Zuhra's contemporary population, as shown in Figure 6. The village's families are organized in large groups, whose spatial distribution in clusters is clearly recognizable.[15] Family-based neighborhoods are a common phenomenon in many villages in Egypt.[16] In a study of some villages in the Delta, Berque calls it the *"zoning familial,"* and describes its transformation into a *"zoning économique"* in the course of present developments.[17]

As can be seen in Figure 6, the population of Zuhra belongs to nine different groups. Six of them claim that their internal relationship is based on kinship (Salhiya, Naghamsha, Hamili, Sa'adna, Shahabiya, and Qati'i). The other three groups, that is, the *"aylat al-'umda,"* the

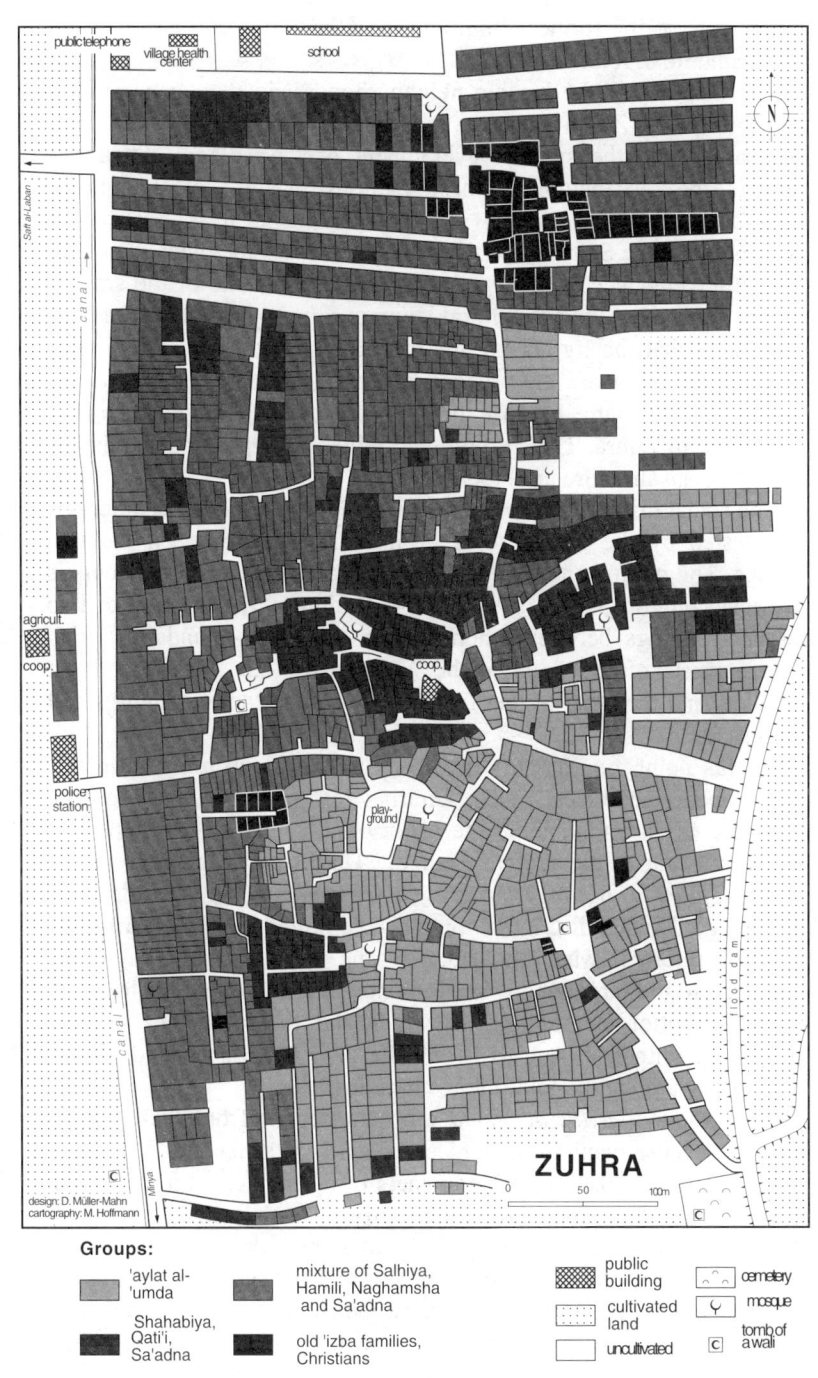

Figure 6 *Spatial Distribution of Kinship Groups in Zuhra Village*

inhabitants of the former *'izba*, and the Christians, consist of neighbors rather than relatives.[18]

The analysis of the kinship neighborhoods and their geographical distribution in Zuhra becomes particularly interesting when it is compared with the spatial development of the village. When one regards the distribution of these factions in light of the above-mentioned historical analysis of the settlement, it is possible to conclude that the Salhiya and the Naghamsha own the older section of the settlement, whereas the *'aylat al-'umda* and some of the smaller groups live where the agricultural laborers formerly resided. It may be concluded that the former are the original inhabitants of the village, whereas the latter are the progeny of the in-migrants. The *'aylat al-'umda* bear this name because they depended on the *'umda* when they first came to Zuhra. Their origin determines their position within the village social structure until today.

The social distance between the old families and the 'newcomers' is manifested by the low number of intermarriages between the two groups. The mixing and dissolution of factions that currently occurs is restricted only to the old families. It is leading to the creation of two larger groupings between whom—as in the past—boundaries exist. One consists of the Salhiya, the Naghamsha, the Hamili, and the Sa'adna, and the other of the *'aylat al-'umda* and the remaining small groups.

At this point, one has to come back to the initial remarks in this paper about the effects of the agrarian reform and counter-reform. How are explanations about the history and social differentiation of Zuhra relevant to the present changes? Until today, members of the 'old' families do not regard the *'aylat al-'umda* as 'full' residents of the village. Hidden discrimination played an important role during the agrarian reforms, when the lands to the west of the village that belonged to the large landowner Muhammad Sultan were distributed. The distribution committee, on which the local notables exerted significant influence, saw to it that the land was distributed almost exclusively among the 'old' village families.

Even so, the *'aylat al-'umda* did also benefit from the agrarian reform, because many of them received a *hiyaza* as tenants. This gave them a status similar to the landowners of the village, and closed the economic gap between old and new groups in the village. Yet with the recent changes to the tenancy laws, the descendants of the migrant workers are again dispossessed and the historical cleavages are resurfacing. New differences between the economic foundations of the families are developing, because the tenants who have lost their land will have to look for alternative sources of income. The following section gives an example of a strategy of survival for the rural poor.

## Spatial Differentiation of Economic Activity Strategies: The Example of the Brick-Making Industry in Zuhra

With the last example of maps about Zuhra, we turn to present economic activities of the inhabitants of the village. Fewer than half the households in Zuhra own agricultural land. The percentage of landless families and small farmers with holdings of less than two feddans is higher in Zuhra than elsewhere in the governorate. This can probably be attributed to the relatively high influx of agricultural laborers, as mentioned above.

Of the total of 1,070 *ha'izin* who are registered with the local agricultural cooperative, approximately one third (327) are tenants who lost their use rights with the termination of their *hiyaza* in 1997. Three quarters of all *ha'izin* have less than one feddan of owned land at their disposal, and cannot provide for their families from agriculture alone. This means that, with the increased fragmentation of landholdings and the dismissal of the tenants, more and more individuals will have to look for income sources outside agriculture.

There are two sources of income available to the people of Zuhra outside farming. Almost a third of all households depend on jobs in the public sector, primarily in the neighboring city of Minya. Beyond this, the main source of employment and income, especially for the lower-income groups, is the brick-making industry, which has a long tradition in Zuhra. An estimated two hundred to three hundred families live from this industry in the so-called informal sector. It is, however, particularly prone to risk because it is susceptible to vacillations in demand, and is also illegal.

The spatial organization of the brick-making industry in 1993/94 is shown in Figure 7, which illustrates three important points with respect to production activities, soil mining, and land prices. First, it is obvious that this activity is most preponderant in the areas where the brick-makers live and work. The bricks are made of mud, to which sand or sawdust is added, and set in a simple wooden frame. In Zuhra, this task is most commonly performed by women. Adequate space for drying the freshly made bricks is available on the edges of the village, and especially in the largely uninhabited houses in the southeast part. Several of the alleys in the latter districts actually have the look of mini-industrial areas. The kilns in which the dried raw bricks are fired to create the red bricks used for construction are situated in the same parts of the village as the production facilities.

272  DETLEF MÜLLER-MAHN

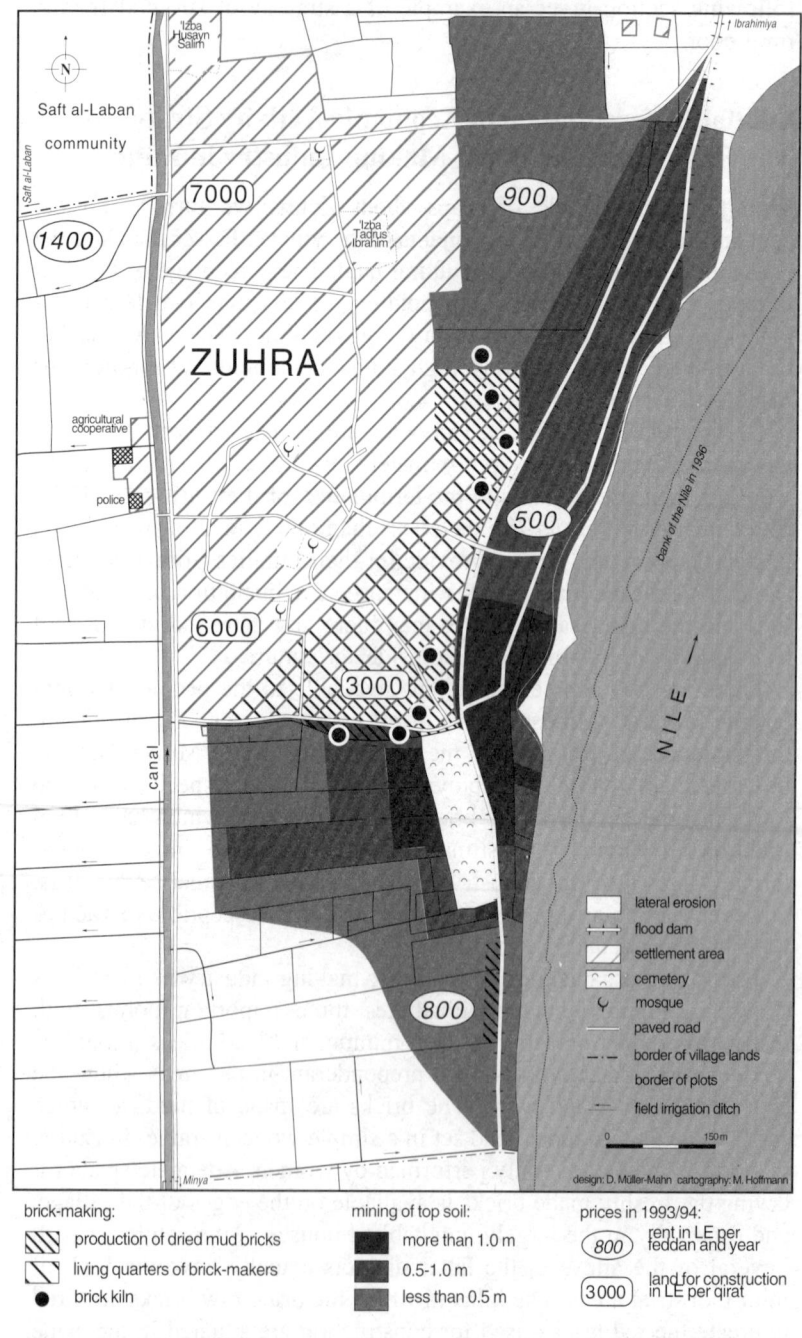

Figure 7  Brick-Making, Soil Mining, and the Value of Land in Zuhra Village

Secondly, one can see in the map that large areas are devoted to soil mining, from which the raw materials for the bricks are taken. In a few small parcels on the sloping bank of the Nile, more than two meters of topsoil have already been dug away, rendering this land unfit for agriculture. The commodification of the land adjacent to the Nile, in particular, is viewed as economically justifiable by the landowners because of the exacerbation of lateral erosion since the completion of the Aswan High Dam. The *fallahin* hope to convert this resource to cash in the short run, before it is lost to the Nile, as it definitely will be, in a few years. On most plots, however, the earth is only scraped away in thin layers after the harvest and then used for brick production.

Soil mining affects a clearly defined area in the southeast of the village. The spatial concentration of soil removal can be attributed to several factors: viewed geomorphologically, these areas provide the most suitable sandy clay; through the proximity to the production sites, transportation costs are minimized; and the soil in this area is less fertile. The lower productivity is reflected in lower lease prices.

Thirdly, the influence of the spatial organization of the brick industry is reflected in a differentiation in the price of both construction plots and the yearly leases of agricultural fields, as indicated in Figure 7. Prices (in 1993/94) are highest, about LE7,000 per qirat, for construction plots on the asphalt road that links the village to the neighboring city. In most of the village, one qirat is around LE6,000; in the vicinity of the brick-production areas, however, it is only about LE3,000 per qirat. These prices reflect perceptions of the difference in the quality of life associated with the various areas. In the areas that surround the brick kilns, with their smoldering oil fires that pollute the air, only those reside who cannot afford anything better.

The analysis of the spatial organization of the brick industry in Zuhra sheds light on the background of the history of the settlement's present-day social structure. It is members of the *'aylat al-'umda* who are principally involved in work in the informal sector. Most of them are landless or tenant farmers. With the termination of the long-term leases in 1997, the village of Zuhra may witness yet another massive flow of laborers into the brick-making industry.

## Conclusion

The examples presented above illustrate the pivotal role spatial structures play in rural development. Consequently, an analysis of geographical features may help us to understand social and economic differentiation processes better. In so doing, two aspects of space have to be considered, one referring to the past, and one to the future.

As for the first, spatial structures such as villages, can be taken as the physical results of the previous actions of the people who lived in these villages in former times. Space is like an archive full of traces of historical developments. An interpretation of such 'imprints' of previous actions may help to explain the present.

The second aspect of space is that it provides part of the framework within which people organize their lives and within which they act today. In dealing with the link between space and agency, geography presents some analytical tools that can bring about a sensitivity to the spatial aspect of social phenomena.

This paper has offered several examples of how social and economic differentiation of the population of rural Egypt has been translated into geographical differentiation, expressed in the different types of settlements, or the social and economic 'zoning' in the village of Zuhra. Poverty in Zuhra is related to the origins of the different groups within the village. The agrarian reform decreased the economic differences between the 'old groups' and the descendants of labor migrants who had settled in the village a century ago. The agrarian counter-reform, and especially the eviction of the small tenants, may reemphasize the old cleavages in the village. The informal sector activity of brick-making is a strategy to survive without land, but this type of development cannot be considered sustainable.

## Notes

1 The collection of papers in this book supports a rather critical view with respect to the current economic liberalization and its effects; see especially the contributions of Ray Bush and Tim Mitchell.
2 Giddens (1984).
3 Müller-Mahn (forthcoming).
4 Abdel-Fadil (1975).
5 Ministry of Agriculture, 1990. The 'official' figures need some interpretation: seasonal or annual rent has not been included. The information about sharecropping seems to be incomplete for some of-the governorates. The number of *hiyaza* holdings is not necessarily equivalent to the number of farms, since micro-holdings of close relatives are often combined in one farm. Despite such reservations, the figures give an impression of the general situation.
6 Baer (1962); Brown (1990); Cuno (1992); Hopkins (1987).
7 The basis of the illustration is a map from the Ministry of Public Works published in Cairo in 1891.
8 The map was developed by means of an interpretation of the names of the settlements in topographic maps.
9 see: Awad (1954); Müller-Mahn (1989).

10 Royal Geographical Society. 1807, updated 1816. *Map of Upper Egypt.* London: Royal Geographical Society.
11 The most recent settlement area of nomads in the region belongs to the Ma'aza tribe, east of the Nile. In another case study undertaken here as part of the research project, it was possible to observe the differences of economic strategies as compared to those of the *fallahin*. An example is the economic importance of the neighboring desert, particularly for the poorer members of the tribe.
12 Lane (1963:22–23).
13 The cadastral maps provided by the survey of Egypt present the area of the villages in outline sketches, but nonetheless contain a great deal of illuminating information, including data regarding Zuhra. In all cases where they were applied, they proved to be of great reliability for the purpose of the study. The old bench marks mentioned in the maps were still in the fields and facilitated the identification of particular places.
14 Stauth (1983).
15 There are some uncertainties in this map, which are due to the method applied to collect the information presented here. Distribution of kinship groups was mapped with the help of guides from the village, but not in house to house interviews. Difficulties result from the fact that the different factions have begun to mix within the village society, and also because it was not always possible to achieve a completely clear picture of membership in a specific family during the field work.
16 Several papers in this book mention the relationship of community and space, or of social and geographical entities, see the papers of Malak Rouchdy, Kirsten Bach, and Ahmed Zayed. Reem Saad in her case study on a village in Upper Egypt gives an interesting account of the somewhat misleading attempt of a development project to supply these 'tribal' clusters with new street names.
17 Berque (1978:333).
18 In the newly built northern quarter of the village, it was not possible to differentiate the families, because people here are a mixture of Salhiya, Naghamsha, and Sa'adna.

# References

Abdel-Fadil, Mahmoud. 1975. *Development, Income Distribution and Social Change in Rural Egypt (1952–1970): A Study in the Political Economy of Agrarian Transition.* Cambridge: Cambridge University Press.

Arab Republic of Egypt, Ministry of Agriculture and Land Reclamation. 1990. *Nata'ig al-ta'dad al-zira' 'an al-sana al-zira'iya 1981–1982.* Cairo: Ministry of Agriculture.

Awad, M. 1954. "The Assimilation of Nomads in Egypt." *Geographical Review* 44:240–52.

Baer, G. 1962. *A History of Landownership in Modern Egypt, 1800–1950.* London: Oxford University Press.

Berque, J. 1978. *De l'Euphrate à l'Atlas: (1) Espaces et moments.* Paris: La Bibliothèque arabe, Éditions Sindbad.
Brown, N. J. 1990. *Peasant Politics in Modern Egypt: the Struggle against the State.* New Haven: Yale University Press.
Cuno, K. M. 1992. *The Pasha's Peasants: Land, Society, and Economy in Lower Egypt, 1740–1858.* Cambridge: Cambridge University Press.
Giddens, A. 1984. *The Constitution of Society. Outline of the Theory of Structuration.* Cambridge: Polity Press.
Hopkins, N. S. 1987. *Agrarian Transformation in Egypt.* Boulder: Westview.
Lane, E.W. 1963. *Manners and Customs of the Modern Egyptians.* London: Dent [first edition, 1836].
Müller-Mahn, D. 1989. *Die Aulad 'Ali zwischen Stamm und Staat. Entwicklung und sozialer Wandel bei den Beduinen im nordwestlichen Ägypten,* Berlin: Abhandlungen–Anthropogeographie 46.
———. i.p. *Fellachendörfer. Sozialgeographischer Wandel im ländlichen Ägypten.* Stuttgart, Erdkundliches Wissen.
Stauth, G. 1983. "Capitalist Farming and Small Peasant Households in Egypt." *Review* 7(2):285–313.

# VI

## DEVELOPMENT: THE ROLE OF THE MARKET AND DEVELOPMENT PROJECTS

# 14

# Farmers and Cooperatives in the Era of Structural Adjustment

MOHAMED H. ABDEL AAL

## Introduction

Since the inception of the first agricultural cooperative society in 1910, Egyptian agricultural cooperatives and farmers alike have been sailing in unpredictable political waters. Recent striking changes include the implications of the structural adjustment policies (ERSAP) and the liberalization laws.

A review of the agricultural cooperative movement in Egypt shows clearly that cooperatives started as a popular movement and ended up as a parastatal instrument. Cooperatives passed through a period of over-promotion, but have been almost completely neglected in recent years. Government promotion, farmers' perceptions of the cooperatives, and the nature of the power structure of the Egyptian village are among the important elements in the process of revitalizing the role of cooperatives. This paper tries to assess some of the variables that account for farmers' attitudes toward the services of the cooperatives and toward the cooperatives' 'elected' boards of directors.

The main theme of the paper is to explore farmers' opinions about cooperatives following several years of the implementation of structural reform policies. The importance of the study stems from the fact that it was conducted in an area dominated by sugarcane, the only crop still subject to controlled delivery to the state-owned sugar mills (Rady 1996). In other words, cultivators in this part of the country are interacting with two contradicting economic systems: free market and central planning.

The paper has two main objectives:

1) To clarify farmer opinions regarding the following: Their relations with cooperative boards of directors; their participation in cooperative elections; the change in inputs: sources, prices, and source

preferences; the change in, and their satisfaction with, cooperative services; and the future of the cooperative.

2) To identify some of the variables contributing to farmers' attitudes toward cooperative services and cooperative boards.

## Brief Review of the History of Cooperatives: From Over-promotion to Neglect

The agricultural cooperative movement can be viewed from three perspectives: (a) the series of legislation aimed at channeling cooperatives into the mainstream of state policies; (b) the constant change in governmental supervisory bodies; and (c) the uneasy relation between cooperatives and credit institutions.

### Cooperative Legislation

The popular movement started by 'Umar Lutfi led to the establishment of the first agricultural cooperative in 1910, which was at that time called the agricultural syndicate (al-Rafi'i 1914).

The increase in the number of cooperatives and their membership motivated the state to intervene to 'regulate' the sector. Between 1914 and 1983, a series of laws was enacted to achieve this purpose (El Imam et al. 1983). In 1914, the government enacted the first law, which (along with other laws) was soon suspended due to the eruption of World War I. The first law to be practically applied, enacted in 1923, was considered highly progressive, in view of the sociopolitical conditions of that time. In 1927, the movement encountered another legislative change, allowing for the formation of cooperative unions, which resulted in the forming of the Supreme Council for Cooperatives. In 1944, another law was promulgated. With that law the 'Cooperation Authority' *(Maslahat al-Ta'awun)* was formed to act as the governmental supervisory body. The law granted the authority rights to inspect, control, and audit the financial performance of the cooperatives. After the land reform law of 1952, another law was enacted in 1956. This law was concerned primarily with the functions and structure of multipurpose and specialized cooperatives, which increased enormously in number after the land reform laws. The cooperative law of 1969 clearly geared the cooperatives to the general framework of state policy. According to that law, cooperative financial assets started to be treated as public assets, "cooperative officers and members of the board and supervision committee members" as public workers, and records, papers, and stamps as official.

## Government Supervision

Since the very beginning, state supervision over agricultural cooperatives has shifted from one governmental body to another. According to the 1923 law, the responsibility was first assigned to the Ministry of Agriculture, then moved to the Ministry of Finance in 1937, then to the Ministry of Social Affairs in 1939, then reassigned to the Ministry of Agriculture once again in 1960, where it remains to this day.

## Cooperatives' Financial Difficulties

The question of the financial situation of cooperatives dates back to the establishment of the first agricultural cooperative. The struggle of cooperatives to establish their own financial institution has, until now, failed. The 1944 law allowed cooperatives to establish a 'cooperation bank,' but there was no real support from the government. Instead, in 1948, the government changed the name of the Egyptian Agricultural Credit Bank to the Egyptian Agricultural and Cooperation Credit Bank in order to allow for the cooperatives to have shares in the bank. By 1961, cooperative membership became mandatory for farmers. Credit to individual farmers became restricted to cooperative members only. In 1976 the Central Agricultural Cooperation Union (CACU) was dissolved, and village banks were established as branches of the Principal Bank for Development and Credit (PBDAC). The financial and credit activities—which used to be performed by cooperatives— as well as the storage facilities which belonged to the cooperatives, were all taken over by the new village banks. Many writers claim that the events of 1976 marked the start of the decay of agricultural cooperatives. Some even went further to claim that the widening food gap in Egypt was among the indirect consequences of the weakening of cooperatives at the end of the 1970s.

# Cooperatives within the Structural Adjustment Programs

Agricultural cooperatives in many developing countries, and not only in Egypt, shared a common past, and they are also sharing a common present situation within the context of structural adjustment program policies. Gibbon, in his discussion of African agriculture under structural adjustment (1992:87), concluded that, "Cooperatives ... in most parts of Africa are state-instituted and state-organized bodies which have somehow escaped the agenda of reform." He went on to say that, "there has been unholy compromise to maintain a polite silence over co-operatives, between donors wanting to secure the abandonment of single-channeled marketing organization and governments wishing to retain control of economically and politically important functions."

The prolonged dominance of the state over cooperatives in Egypt, along with the inefficiency of cooperative boards, have led farmers to deal with cooperatives and their boards as two separate matters. They have viewed the cooperative as a state body in charge of handling and/or enforcing agricultural matters. The cooperative board, meanwhile, is seen as subject to and emerging from the pattern of the power structure. The cooperative board, like other organizations at the village level, is easily dominated by the rich peasants and important village leaders, especially where direct government influence is limited (Adams 1986). In Qina and Aswan, with the influence of tribalism *(qabaliya)*, the dominance of members of big families on cooperatives is more obvious than in many other parts of Egypt. The responses of the majority of farmers during the field work for this study reflect their perception of board members as another expression of the natural leadership structure, which grants the elite and large landowners unquestioned rights to hold posts on the board, whether they have an effective influence on the performance of the cooperative or not. The law also enhanced the control of rich farmers over the cooperative boards. According to the cooperative laws of 1952 and 1961, 80 percent of board members were supposed to be peasants holding less than five feddans, but with the promulgation of Law 51/1969, this condition was relaxed (Baker 1978:213; Dyer 1991:86).

The 1993 World Bank Report on Egyptian agriculture in the 1990s proposed the actions needed to be taken to restructure various areas of the agricultural sector. The report named cooperatives among those areas, and referred to the efforts needed to reform cooperatives as including: a review of existing cooperatives; the introduction of new legislation; the provision of cooperative education and training; and freeing cooperatives' access to finance. While much evidence supports the fact that efforts aimed at reforming other sectors of agriculture were satisfactorily realized, there is no evidence available to show that any efforts were made to extend the reform activities to cooperatives.

Any attempt to look at the conditions of cooperatives in the context of structural reform must consider a number of factors. First, although the state has practically abandoned the cooperatives, this has not yet been officially declared; on the contrary, the supervisory role of the state is still fully—yet ineffectively—maintained. Second, farmers' relations with cooperatives have never been completely terminated. Farmers are still tied to cooperatives for several administrative services, and for inputs, such as seeds. Third, along with continued state supervision, the elected cooperative boards—whether they are effective or not—will continue to affect the context of the cooperatives.

## Types and Sources of Data

The current paper is based on data collected for a larger study on "The Organization of Work and Production in Qina and Aswan Governorates." The data were gathered during the summer of 1995. The study settings included thirty-five villages, nineteen of which are in Qina, and sixteen in Aswan. Probability samples of owners, tenants, and agricultural workers were selected for interviews. The records of the agricultural credit and land reform cooperatives were used in randomly selecting farmers. Key informants were used to identify persons working as agricultural wage laborers, and the required numbers of workers were then sampled. The total sample yielded 2,664 respondents, among whom were 1,840 credit cooperative farmers, 391 land reform farmers, and 433 agricultural workers. Data used for this analysis is a sub-sample consisting of the farmer members of the agricultural credit cooperatives (n = 1,840). The sub-sample also includes 113 cooperative board members.

The findings presented in the current paper are divided into two parts: Part One is descriptive, dealing with the first objective of the paper. It presents the relations between the farmers and the cooperative boards, and farmers' assessments of the change in the provision of and accessibility to agricultural inputs. This part serves as an interpretative background for part two. Part Two is analytical, aimed at assessing the variables associated with farmer attitudes toward both cooperative services and cooperative boards. Operational definitions and dependent variables are explained in Appendix A.

## Analytical Approach

To explore the effect of the selected independent variables on the dependent variables, we used logistic regression, since conventional regression techniques are not appropriate in the case of categorical dependent variables. Logistic regression was used to produce two models. Model I explores the contribution of the independent variables in explaining (or predicting) the attitude toward cooperative services using the whole sample (n = 1,840). Model II explores the contribution of the independent variables in explaining (or predicting) the attitude toward cooperative boards. In Model II, board members were excluded from the cases (n = 1,727).

# Findings

PART ONE

## 1. General Characteristics of Farmers and Cooperative Boards

As shown in Table 1, cooperative board members range in age between twenty and eighty-five years old, with a mean age of 51.6. The age of farmers ranges between fifteen and ninety-one, with a similar mean age of 51.2.

Table 1. *Comparison between Farmers and Board Members*

|  | Farmers (%) | Board (%) |
|---|---|---|
| *Age* | | |
| Minimum | 15.0 | 30.0 |
| Maximum | 91.0 | 85.0 |
| Mean | 51.2 | 53.6 |
| *Education* | | |
| Illiterate | 44.2 | 24.8 |
| Literate | 12.0 | 13.7 |
| Primary | 22.9 | 45.3 |
| Secondary | 21.0 | 16.2 |
| *Landholding Size* | | |
| less than 1 feddan | 24.3 | 14.5 |
| 1–3 feddans | 40.2 | 37.6 |
| 3–5 feddans | 16.3 | 12.8 |
| 5 feddans + | 19.2 | 35.1 |

With regard to education, 24.8 percent of board members are illiterate (although the cooperation legislation puts literacy as one of the conditions for board membership); 13.7 percent can read and write; and 61.5 percent have a school certificate. Among farmers, 44.2 percent are illiterate; 12.0 percent can read and write; and 43.9 percent have a school certificate. These figures indicate that board members generally have a higher level of education than farmers. Also, board members generally hold more land than farmers. Board members with less than one feddan are only 14.5 percent, while farmers in the same category are 24.3 percent. In the 'five feddan or more' category are found 35.1 percent of the board members and 19.2 percent of the farmers.

## 2. Relations between Cooperative Boards and Farmers

The frequency with which farmers seek board members' help in solving farming problems was used as an indicator for the relations between the two groups. Findings reveal that 42.7 percent of board members reported that farmers "never" sought their help, while 31.6 percent and 22.2 percent respectively reported that farmers seek them "usually," or "often." From the farmers' side, over half (56.8 percent) reported that they don't seek help from board members. Figures clearly indicate that farmers do not generally consider board members as among the sources they use in solving their farming problems. Farmers' reasons for not seeking board members help were grouped into six categories, as shown in Table 2.

Table 2. *Farmers Reasons for not Seeking Cooperative Board Help*

| Reasons | No. | % |
|---|---|---|
| Have no problems | 430 | 43.6 |
| Board incapability | 250 | 25.3 |
| Seek other means | 105 | 10.6 |
| Distance | 123 | 12.5 |
| Non-availability | 51 | 5.1 |
| Negativism | 6 | 0.6 |
| No data | 22 | 2.2 |

The reason reported by the largest number (43.6 percent) of those who do not seek the board members' help was that they do not have problems or that their problems cannot be solved by (seeking) board members. About 25.3 percent of the farmers attributed their decision not to turn to the board to the inefficiency or incapability of its members. Expressing their opinions in their own words, farmers said of the board:

They cannot solve any problems.
They are not suitable for their jobs.
They have no authority for solving problems.
They have no activity in the village whatsoever.

The reasons related to distance (12.5 percent), reflect either the physical distance, "live far from the cooperative," or a psychological one:

I feel distant from board members.
I do not know the board members.
They are big farmers, we are small farmers, where can one go?

Some farmers (10.6 percent) seek sources of assistance other than board members. Non-availability of board members (5.3 percent) means that board members are not easy to find when needed. Only a tiny percentage (0.6 percent) reflect the opinion that board members are not supportive to small farmers or treat them badly.

### 3. Satisfaction with the Existing Cooperative Boards

Farmer satisfaction with the existing cooperative boards was assessed in three ways: satisfaction with the existing board; intention to elect the same board in forthcoming elections; and personal willingness to run in the cooperative elections. The majority (63.2 percent) expressed satisfaction with the existing board, while only 29.2 percent expressed dissatisfaction. The percentage changed slightly when farmers were asked if they intended to elect the same board; 55.5 percent reported they would reelect the members of the existing board, while 36.1 percent reported that they would not. The tendency among respondents to run for cooperative elections is relatively low, as only 9.5 percent of cooperative members expressed their willingness to run in the coming cooperative elections.

### 4. Farmers and Voting in Cooperative Elections

When asked to report whether they vote in cooperative elections or not, 51.2 percent of farmers reported that they vote, while 48.8 percent reported they do not. Table 3 shows the reasons reported by those who do not participate in elections.

Table 3. *Reasons for not Participating in Cooperative Elections*

| Reasons | No. | % |
|---|---|---|
| Lack of time | 346 | 45.1 |
| Lack of knowledge | 194 | 25.3 |
| Mistrust | 82 | 10.7 |
| Personal deficiency | 50 | 6.5 |
| Age reasons | 39 | 5.1 |
| Cooperative membership | 39 | 5.1 |
| Distance | 18 | 2.3 |
| **Total** | 768 | 100.0 |

Among the major reasons for non-participation was mistrust, which was expressed in various ways, including lack of time. Nearly half (45.1 percent) cited lack of time as the main reason for not participating; this in fact represented a disguised response of mistrust in cooperative elections. In the farmers' own words:

Cooperative elections are a waste of time.
I have no time to spare for elections.

Various forms of mistrust, such as mistrust in the election process itself, mistrust of the results of the elections, and mistrust in the entire performance of the cooperative, were reported by 10.7 percent of the sample. Some of the farmers' own words better express these reasons:

They select ( support) each other.
Nomination is restricted to certain individuals.
Some persons are preferred [to be always in the board] over others.
There is no real election or voting.

About 25 percent of the non-participants in elections reported that they did not have proper information or knowledge either on the date of the election, or on the existence of elections in the cooperative:

I do not know when elections are held.
There is no election in the first place.
We never heard of any elections held in the village.
They do not inform farmers about elections.

Other reasons, although in small percentages, help to explore farmers' images about the cooperative and themselves. Age-related reasons (5.1 percent) group together opinions of those who reported they are too old or too young to participate in cooperative elections. Personal deficiency (6.5 percent) refers to illiteracy, or to inability to engage oneself in election situations. Farmers expressed these feelings in the following way:

I do not participate in elections to avoid pressure and embarrassment.
My holding is too small.
I am a new member in the cooperative.
I do not have any experience with elections.

Distance, reported by 5.1 percent, refers to the situation of being out of the village during elections or living far from the cooperative.

## 5. The Change in the Situation of Agricultural Inputs

The most compelling among ERSAP measures implemented in the agricultural sector was the removal of input subsidies and lifting of restrictions on the private sector to handle distribution of agricultural inputs. These measures created a new reality in the agricultural scene. Three aspects related to the inputs issue were examined: 1) sources of agricultural inputs; 2) input prices in various sources; and 3) reasons for preference of sources.

## 5.1 Sources of Agricultural Inputs

As figures in Table 4 indicate, the private sector controls fertilizer distribution. The majority of farmers (61 percent) seek out the private sector for that input, while 26.5 percent and 13.2 percent reported that they get fertilizer from the cooperative or from the village bank respectively.

Table 4. *Sources of Inputs for Crops (other than Sugarcane)*

|  | Fertilizers | | Seeds | | Pesticides | |
|---|---|---|---|---|---|---|
|  | No. | % | No. | % | No. | % |
| Cooperative | 269 | 26.5 | 327 | 31.4 | 198 | 58.9 |
| Village Bank | 125 | 12.3 | 36 | 3.5 | 25 | 7.4 |
| Private Sector | 620 | 61.1 | 402 | 38.5 | 113 | 33.6 |
| Last Crop | – | – | 234 | 22.4 | – | – |
| Neighbors | – | – | 44 | 4.2 | - | – |
| **Total** | 1014 | 99.9 | 1043 | 100 | 336 | 99.9 |

The private sector and the cooperatives almost equally share the market for seeds. It is important to notice that a considerable percentage (22.4 percent) use seeds from previous harvests. Only about one third of the respondents use pesticides. The cooperative is still the main source of pesticides for the majority (58.9 percent), while about one third look to the private sector.

## 5.2 Input Prices

Most farmers reported an increase in input prices. Among inputs, the high price of fertilizers was the most often noted, as shown in Table 5, where 83 percent held this opinion. Just over half of the respondents considered that the prices of seeds and pesticides were high.

Table 5. *Price of Agricultural Inputs*

|  | Seeds | | Fertilizers | | Pesticides | |
|---|---|---|---|---|---|---|
|  | No. | % | No. | % | No. | % |
| Reasonable | 459 | 43.0 | 131 | 12.3 | 133 | 34.0 |
| High | 554 | 52.0 | 884 | 83.0 | 205 | 52.4 |
| Don't know | 3 | 0.3 | – | – | 2 | 0.5 |
| No data | 50 | 4.7 | 50 | 4.7 | 51 | 13.0 |
| **Total** | 1066 | 100.0 | 1065 | 100.0 | 391 | 99.0 |

## 5.3 Reasons for Preference of Sources

The reasons why farmers prefer one source of inputs over another are shown in Table 6. "Easy deals" was the reason reported by 13.7 percent of those who preferred the cooperative, and 15.2 percent of those who preferred private traders, while the same reason was reported by only 10.6 percent of those who preferred the bank.

Table 6. *Reasons for Preference of Sources*

| Reasons | Cooperative | Credit Bank | Private Sector |
|---|---|---|---|
| Easy deal | 14.5 | 14.0 | 16.5 |
| Quality guaranteed | 18.9 | 23.8 | 2.0 |
| Better prices | 39.5 | 23.1 | 16.6 |
| Nearness | 10.7 | 1.4 | 0.4 |
| No interest charged | 1.1 | – | 14.6 |
| Input on credit | 8.9 | 27.3 | 3.5 |
| Availability of inputs | 3.8 | – | 37.9 |
| Low interest charged | 0.3 | – | – |
| Provide information | 1.7 | – | – |
| Being a coop member | 0.2 | – | – |
| Get loans on crops | – | 7.0 | – |
| Bank financial power | – | 3.5 | – |
| Avoid banks' high interest rates | – | – | 3.6 |
| Clear financial deals | – | – | 5.1 |
| No specific reason | – | – | – |

Farmers have more confidence in parastatal organizations than in private sector for input quality; this reason was reported by 18.9 percent and 23.8 percent of those who preferred the cooperative and the bank respectively, compared to only 2 percent of those who preferred the private sector for quality. The same trend can also be seen in regard to prices, where cooperatives were ranked higher in preference than other sources.

Some reasons applied to two sources, while some others were applicable to only one source. Availability of inputs, and acquiring inputs without added interest were two reasons cited by 3.8 percent of those who selected cooperatives, and 37.9 percent of those who selected traders. It is clear that farmers who preferred the private sector put those two reasons among the most important.

There are reasons specific to cooperatives only and reported by 2.2 percent of those who preferred cooperatives. Those reasons in farmers' own words were:

The cooperative is the guarantee for me, because I do not own anything else.

I am a member in the cooperative, and I pay membership fees, hence I should get my inputs from there.

The cooperative provides me with extension services.

Reasons specific to the village bank were reported by 10.5 percent, and included confidence in the financial power of the bank, and the possibility of getting loans on crops.

Reasons specific to private traders were reported by 8.7 percent respectively and included avoidance of the high interest rates of the village bank, and clarity of financial transactions.

## 6. Farmers' Opinions of the Services, Activities, and the Expected Future of the Cooperatives

In most of the following items, farmers were more or less split into two groups, one defending the cooperative, the other criticizing its conduct.

### 6.1 Cooperative Services

Farmers were asked to give their assessment of the level of services in their cooperative. As figures in Table 7 indicate, only 9 percent of the respondents considered that cooperative services had improved, while 42.7 percent considered that the services of the cooperatives have always been good, and 47.3 percent saw services as either deteriorating or continuing to be as bad as before.

Table 7. *Farmers' Opinions of Cooperative Services*

|  | No. | % |
|---|---|---|
| Better than before | 166 | 9.0 |
| Less than before | 467 | 25.4 |
| As good as before | 785 | 42.7 |
| As bad as before | 403 | 21.9 |
| Don't know | 6 | 0.3 |
| No data | 13 | 0.7 |

### 6.2 Cooperative Activities

Farmers were asked to give their opinion on the change in cooperative activities compared to a period two years earlier. As figures in Table 8 indicate, the majority (68.4 percent) reported that there was no change, while 22.4 percent reported that activities have decreased over this period.

Table 8. *Farmers' Opinions of the Change in Cooperative Activities*

|  | No. | % |
| --- | --- | --- |
| Increased | 148 | 8.0 |
| Decreased | 413 | 22.4 |
| No change | 1258 | 68.4 |
| Don't know | 8 | 0.4 |
| No data | 13 | 0.7 |

### 6.3 Satisfaction with the Cooperative

The same split in opinions was also clear when farmers were asked to express whether they were satisfied with the cooperative. As the figures in Table 9 indicate, most farmers (47.2 percent) reported that they were satisfied with cooperative activities, while 31.0 percent expressed dissatisfaction, and 20.3 percent were undecided.

Table 9. *Satisfaction with the Cooperative*

|  | No. | % |
| --- | --- | --- |
| Satisfied | 868 | 47.2 |
| Undecided | 373 | 20.3 |
| Dissatisfied | 570 | 31.0 |
| Don't know | 5 | 1.3 |
| No data | 24 | 1.3 |

### 6.4 Future of the Agricultural Cooperative

When farmers were asked to give their opinion about the future of cooperatives, responses of the majority revealed a positive position toward the cooperative. As Table 10 shows, the majority (89.2 percent) wanted to keep the existing cooperative, but they asked for certain improvements in activities and services. Other opinions, such as forming new cooperatives or maintaining the status quo, were reported by relatively small percentages.

Table 10. *Opinions Regarding the Future of the Agricultural Cooperative*

|  | No. | % |
| --- | --- | --- |
| Improve the existing cooperative | 1641 | 89.2 |
| Form a new cooperative | 27 | 1.5 |
| Keep situation unchanged | 102 | 5.5 |
| No need for cooperative | 54 | 2.9 |
| Don't know | 3 | .2 |
| No data | 13 | .7 |

PART TWO

The results of the logistic regression analysis of the attitudes toward both the cooperative services and the cooperative board are presented in Table 11. Following is a presentation of the main findings.

**Patterns of Production**

Findings related to the pattern of production set of variables revealed that respondents who cultivate a high percentage of their farm holdings with sugarcane (odds ratio = 1.004 p<0.05) are more likely to have a favorable attitude toward cooperative services, compared to those who cultivate a low percentage.

The increase in operational landholding significantly decreased the probability of having a favorable attitude toward cooperative services (odds = 0.959 p<0.01). On the other hand, increase in operational landholding does not significantly affect the attitude toward the cooperative board.

Farmers who raise animals are more likely (odds = 1.311 p<0.01) than those who do not raise farm animals to have a favorable attitude toward cooperative services. On the other hand, animal holders are also more likely to have favorable attitudes toward the cooperative boards (odds = 1.8823 at 0.001 level of significance).

Respondents who use both family and hired labor are more likely to have a favorable attitude toward the cooperative board (odds = 1.572 p<0.01) compared to those who use family labor only.

'Sources of inputs' has different impacts on attitudes according to the type of input and the source used. The market (private sector) as a source of fertilizers is inversely associated with the attitude toward cooperative services (odds = 0.575 p<0.01). The same inverse association is found regarding the attitude toward cooperative boards but is not significant.

Respondents who get fertilizers from the village bank are more likely to have a favorable attitude toward the board (odds ratio = 2.637 p<0.01), compared to those who get fertilizers from the cooperative.

Respondents who do not use pesticides (odds = 0.6027 at p<0.05) and those who get pesticides from the private sector (odds = 0.4949 at p<0.01) are less likely to have a favorable attitude toward cooperative services compared to those who get pesticides from cooperatives.

Farmers' opinions on the prices of various inputs were used to predict their attitudes toward both cooperative services and boards. Farmers who report seed prices as reasonable are more likely to have a favorable attitude toward cooperative services (odds = 1.3503 p<0.05). It is interesting to find that respondents who consider prices

Table 11. Logistic Regression of Farmers' Attitudes Toward Cooperative Services and the Cooperative Board.

| Sets of Variables | Variables | Status | Model I<br>Attitude Toward Co-op Services<br>Odds Ratio | Model II<br>Attitude Toward Co-op Board<br>Odds Ratio |
|---|---|---|---|---|
| Production Pattern | CANAREA | Continuous variable | 1.0044 ** | 1.0005 |
| | LANDHOLD | Tenant | R | R |
| | | Owner | 1.1407 | 0.9071 |
| | LANDSIZE | Continuous variable | 0.9598 *** | 0.9898 |
| | ANIMLOWN | No | R | R |
| | | Yes | 1.3107 * | 1.8823 *** |
| | FARMLABR | Family only | R | R |
| | | Hired only | 1.1462 | 1.5721 *** |
| | | Family & hired | 1.1071 | 1.2056 |
| Source of inputs | SEEDSORC | Co-op | R | R |
| | | Previous crop | 0.9253 | 0.8232 |
| | | Bank | 1.2028 | 0.6988 |
| | | Market | 1.2283 | 0.9633 |
| | FERTSORC | Co-op | R | R |
| | | Bank | 1.1707 | 2.6372 *** |
| | | Market | 0.5747 *** | 0.9933 |
| | PSTISORC | Co-op | R | R |
| | | Not use | 0.6072 ** | 0.8279 |
| | | Bank | 0.7611 | 0.5982 |
| | | Market | 0.4949 *** | 0.9287 |

Table 11 contd.

| Sets of Variables | Variables | Status | Model I<br>Attitude Toward Co-op Services<br>Odds Ratio | Model II<br>Attitude Toward Co-op Board<br>Odds Ratio |
|---|---|---|---|---|
| Price of inputs | SEEDPRIC | High | R | R |
|  |  | Reasonable | 1.3503 ** | 1.0696 |
|  | FERTPRIC | High | R | R |
|  |  | Reasonable | 1.3558 | 0.5705 ** |
|  | PSTIPRIC | High | R | R |
|  |  | Reasonable | 1.4574 | 1.6782 * |
| Socioeconomic | EDUCTION | No school | R | R |
|  |  | Up to preparatory | 0.7961 *** | 1.3287 ** |
|  |  | Secondary or more | 0.6697 ** | 1.7624 *** |
|  | OCUPATON | Farm only | R | R |
|  |  | Farm/other | 1.2630 * | 1.2608 * |
|  | INCOMSUF | Income not sufficient | R | R |
|  |  | Income sufficient | 1.5004 *** | 1.2138 * |
| Demographic | AGE | Continuous | 0.9986 | 0.9935 |
|  | MARSTATS | Unmarried | R | R |
|  |  | Married | 0.8475 | 1.7076 ** |
|  | FAMSIZE | Large | R | R |
|  |  | Small | 1.0396 | 0.7431 ** |
|  | FAMTYPE | Extended | R | R |
|  |  | Nuclear | 1.0675 | 1.1162 |
|  | CONSTANT |  | 0.3433 | -1.7059 *** |

*** p < .01; ** p < .05; p* <0.1; R = Reference

of fertilizers reasonable are less likely to have a favorable attitude toward cooperative boards (odds = 0.5705 p<0.05).

Several socioeconomic variables significantly affected both the attitude toward cooperative services and boards, as Table 11 indicates. Educated respondents with school certificates are less likely to have a favorable attitude toward cooperative services compared to those who are illiterate or only read and write (odds = 0.7961 p<.01, and 0.6697 p<0.05 respectively). On the contrary, the educated farmers are more likely to have a favorable attitude toward cooperative boards (odds = 1.3287 p<0.05, and 1.7624 p<0.01 respectively).

Concerning occupation, respondents who have other occupations beside farming are more likely to have a favorable attitude toward both cooperative services and boards with almost equal odds ratios (odds = 1.2630 p<0.1, and 1.2608 p<0.1 respectively).

Respondents who report they have sufficient income are more likely to have a favorable attitude (odds ratio = 1.5004 p<0.01) toward cooperative services than those who report insufficiency of income. The same result is also noticeable with attitudes toward cooperative boards (odds ratio = 1.2138 p<0.1).

In regard to demographic variables, only two are significantly associated with the attitude toward cooperative boards. Married respondents are more likely (odds = 1.7076 p<0.05) to have a favorable attitude toward the cooperative board. Small family size is significantly, but inversely (odds = 0.7431 p< 0.05) associated with the attitude toward cooperative boards compared to respondents with large family size.

## Discussion and Conclusion

This paper has attempted to highlight farmers' attitudes toward cooperative services and boards in a time of a major change to the cooperative movement in Egypt.

### Patterns of Production

Concerning the effect of the 'patterns of production' variables on the attitudes under study, we found that the increase of the area cultivated with sugarcane increased the probability of a favorable attitude toward cooperative services. We may recall that the important tools to reform the economies of the agricultural sector were removing subsidies on inputs, freeing crop rotation, cancellation of crop quota deliveries, and also the so-called 'cooperative marketing.' It is quite evident that the impact of ERSAP has diminished the role of cooperatives to a minimum.

Cooperative services to sugarcane cultivators in the study area became essentially limited to providing farmers with the landholding proof certificates required for contracting with the sugar mill, and for obtaining credit from the village bank. The role of the cooperatives may also extend to arranging schedules of cane cutting and shipping in coordination with sugar mills.

According to the initial package of agricultural sector reforms, cooperatives and credit institutions were part of the proposed restructuring efforts. Although the functions of the Principal Bank for Development and Agricultural Credit (PBDAC) were restructured, as were the sugar mills, which were included in the new public enterprise sector, the proposed reform of cooperatives is still suspended.

The findings suggest that cooperatives in sugarcane-dominated areas still perform their previous traditional parastatal roles. Sugarcane cultivators may even become more likely to rely on cooperative administrative services which are vital for interaction with both the village bank, as the main credit provider or seller (monopoly), and with the sugar mills, as the only buyer of cane (monopsony). Sugarcane farmers are entirely locked in a triangle of parastatals (the cooperatives, PBDAC, and sugar mills). Cooperatives represent the weakest angle in that triangle, which consequently weakens farmers' position vis-a-vis the other two).

Increase in landholding size tends to worsen respondents' attitudes toward cooperative services. Farmers with relatively large landholdings, regardless of holding type, are more likely than small landholders to establish access to the new sources of services provided by the new private sector. Large landholders, due to their financial and logistic capabilities, are more able to bridge the gap caused by the withdrawal of the cooperatives from the service of input provision. Under free-market mechanisms, farmers are gaining first hand experience with features such as availability of inputs, clear financial transactions, and easy deals, compared to frequent unavailability of inputs, ambiguity of financial transactions, and bureaucratic performance of staff, which characterized cooperatives for decades. These differences lead large holders to have a poor opinion of the cooperatives' services, and to shift their activities toward the emerging private sector. This explanation is also supported by the findings of the study, indicating that respondents who get fertilizer or pesticides from the private sector have a poor attitude toward cooperative services (see Table 11).

The attitude of small holders toward cooperative services is a question that needs more attention. Findings suggest that small farmers may still hold favorable attitudes toward cooperative services. It is possible to interpret this attitude as a nostalgic psychological state, or as a position based upon direct experience of small farmers with the free market. The two views, in my opinion, are complementary. Field observations suggest that small farmers, whether owners or tenants, were the most harmed by the withdrawal of cooperatives from input provision. Moreover, to small farmers, cooperatives were not just a place to secure inputs when they were needed, but rather they were an integral component of the small farmers' decision-making setting. Small farmers for decades have included cooperatives in the organization of their agricultural production, and in my opinion the weakening of the cooperatives' position has consequently affected small farmers' decision-making abilities.

## Sources of Inputs

'Seed sources' have no association with attitudes toward cooperative services. Sugarcane is a perennial crop that remains in the field up to five years. Farmers' need for cane seeds is not seasonal. Even in the case of new cane cultivation, farmers tend to secure cultivation (seeding) requirements from the last cane harvest. Farmers rely on cooperatives to provide cane seeds only when the government introduces a new variety of cane. For other field crops, especially wheat and maize, cooperatives and other parastatal organizations still play an important role in the provision of seeds, as compared to their role with regard to other inputs (Goletti 1996).

## Socioeconomic and Demographic Variables

The general remark is that most of the variables were positively associated with the attitude toward the cooperative board, rather than with the attitude toward cooperative services. This finding means that this aspect of farmers' profiles is in harmony with the board more than with cooperative services, and it means also that farmers positively accept the board regardless of their attitude toward the cooperative services.

Education is one of the important variables in this set. Educated respondents are more likely to have positive attitudes toward cooperative boards and low appreciation of cooperative services. Educated respondents seems to be more capable than the uneducated of perceiving the changes occurring in the economy in general, and relating the impacts of these changes on the village level, and on the services and functions of their own cooperatives. On the other hand, educated respondents who hold positive attitudes toward the board are more likely to identify themselves with the board members than the uneducated, because they probably see themselves as potential members of the cooperative board.

## Cooperatives and ERSAP

The findings of this study revealed and confirmed some of the features of the situation of cooperatives in the ERSAP era. This context now involves the state, the private sector, the cooperatives, and the farmers. In conclusion, the cooperatives in the ERSAP era can be characterized as follows:

1) The enduring influence of the long period of interdependency between state and farmers;
2) The continuing perceptions of farmers that the cooperative is an input supplier;
3) The clear reflection of the village power structure in the membership of the cooperative board, and its impact on farmer–board relations;
4) The continued function of cooperatives as parastatal organizations; and
5) Farmers' perceptions that the cooperatives' performance and the cooperative boards' performance are two separate issues.

The findings of this study set forth additional evidence to the accumulated literature, showing that cooperatives in most developing countries are facing great difficulties due to the liberalization of markets and the lifting of subsidies and government support.

The ability of the emerging private sector to deliver inputs is questionable. Although some may argue that the private sector, within the new market forces, is capable of providing different kinds of inputs to farmers, it is dangerous to assume that the private sector is able, or willing, to reach and provide inputs and services to small and poor farmers. The majority of farmers, especially the poor, are not yet able to reach and efficiently deal with the private sector, due to factors such as lack of cash, illiteracy, and remoteness from markets.

Development is a complex process, and so is agricultural production. Cooperatives are the means of enabling small producers to cope with new situations and to achieve better deals within the open market. Moreover, cooperatives are more capable than the private sector to handle the complexities of agricultural development.

In times of major economic change, government support to cooperatives is a must in order to achieve equity and social equality. The government is still responsible for empowering, enabling, and supporting farmer associations to assume their responsibilities in the development of rural communities. The promotion of such associations is an integral part of the decentralization process, which is a key element in a meaningful liberalization.

## References

Adams, R. H . 1986. "Bureaucrats, Peasants and the Dominant Coalition: An Egyptian Case Study." *Journal of Development Studies* 22(2):336–54.
al-Rafi'i, 'Abd al-Rahman. 1914. *Niqabat al-ta'awun al-zira'iyah.* Cairo: Matba'at al-Nahda al-Adabiya.
Baker, Raymond W. 1978. *Egypt's Uncertain Revolution under Nasser and Sadat.* Cambridge: Harvard University Press.
Dyer, Graham. 1991. "Farm Size-Farm Productivity Re-examined: Evidence from Rural Egypt." *Journal of Peasant Studies* 19(1):59–92.
El Imam, A. Z., M. Rashad, and A. Abdel Rahman. 1983. *Toward a Unified Co-operative Movement.* 'Umar Lutfi Agricultural Cooperative Training Center, No. 4.
Gibbon, Peter. 1992. "A Failed Agenda? African Agriculture under Structural Adjustment with Special Reference to Kenya and Ghana." *The Journal of Peasant Studies* 20(1):50–96.
Goletti, Franco. 1996. "Private Sector Distribution and Market Pricing of Agricultural Inputs: Fertilizers, Pesticides, Seeds and Machinery." in Lehman B. Fletcher, ed. *Egypt's Agriculture in a Reform Era.* Ames, Iowa: Iowa State University Press. pp. 167–91.
Rady, Abdel-Moneim, Mohamed A. Omran, and Fenton B. Sands. 1996. "Impact of Policy Reforms on Agricultural Income, Employment and Rural Poverty." in Lehman B. Fletcher, ed. *Egypt's Agriculture in a Reform Era.* Ames, Iowa: Iowa State University Press. pp. 149–64.
World Bank. 1993. *Arab Republic of Egypt: An Agricultural Strategy for the 1990s.* Washington, DC: World Bank.

# Appendix

Table 12 *Description of the Variables in the Analysis*

| Variable | Description |
|---|---|
| COOPSRVC | Attitude scale toward cooperative services |
| COOPBORD | Attitude scale toward cooperative board members |
| CANAREA | Area cultivated with cane as percentage of total area cultivated in feddans |
| CROPATRN | Cropping pattern (0 = field crops only, 1 = sugarcane only, 2 = cane and field crops, 3 = combined pattern) |
| HOLDTYPE | Landholding type (0 = tenant, 1 = owner) |
| LANDSIZE | Operational holding in feddans |
| MARKETED | Percent of marketed production except sugarcane (0 = less than 25 percent marketed, 1 = 25 percent or more) |
| ANIMOWN | Ownership or sharing farm animals (0 = not own or share, 1 = own or share) |
| FARMLAB | Type of farm labor used (0 = family labor only, 1 = hired, 2 = both) |
| SEEDSORC | Seeds source (0 = cooperative, 1 = previous crop, 3 = village bank) |
| FERTSORC | Fertilizer source (0 = cooperative, 1 = village bank, 2 = market) |
| PSTISORC | Pesticide source (0 = cooperative, 1 = village bank, 2 = market) |
| SEEDPRIC | Opinion on seed prices (0 = high, 1 = reasonable) |
| FERTPRIC | Opinion on fertilizer prices (0 = high, 1 = reasonable) |
| PSTIPRIC | Opinion on pesticide prices (0 = high, 1 = reasonable) |
| EDUCATON | Level of education (0 = no schooling, 1 = preparatory or less, 2 = secondary or more) |
| OCUPTION | Occupational status (0 = work in farming only, 1 = farming and other) |
| INCOMSUF | Income sufficiency (0 = insufficient income, 2 = sufficient income) |
| AGE | Age in years |
| MARSTATS | Marital status (0 = currently unmarried, 1 = currently married) |
| FAMSIZE | Family size (0 = large family, 1 = small family) |
| FAMTYPE | Family type (0 = extended, 1 = nuclear) |

## The Dependent Variables

Two dependent variables were used in the analysis:

1. Attitude toward cooperative services (COOPSRVC) is a dichotomy indicating whether a respondent has a high or low attitude toward cooperative services. Four items were included in this variable:
   a) Services provided by the cooperative: as bad as before, less than before, better than before, or as good as before. These were coded [0], [1], [2], [3] respectively.
   b) Current cooperative activities in comparison to the past: decreased, no change, or increased; coded [0], [1], [2] respectively.
   c) Satisfaction with cooperative services: dissatisfied, undecided or satisfied; coded [0], [1], [2] respectively.
   d) Future of the cooperative: no need for the cooperative, situation should remain as it is, improve the existing cooperative, or form a new cooperative; coded [0], [1], [2], [3] respectively.

   The total score possible was twelve points. Low attitude ranged from zero to five points and was coded [0];. high attitude ranged from six to twelve points, and was coded [1]. Analysis including this dependent variable was run on the total sample of cooperative members, including board members (n = 1,840).

2. Attitude toward the cooperative board (COOPBORD) is a dichotomy indicating whether a respondent has a high or low attitude toward cooperative board members. Seven items were included in forming this attitude scale:
   a) Participation in elections.
   b) Knowing board head by name.
   c) Knowing board members by name.
   d) Seeking cooperative board help.
   e) Satisfaction with board members.
   f) Likelihood of electing same board.
   g) Likelihood of running for cooperative elections.

   All the above items were coded [0] no, [1] yes, except for, "knowing board member by name," which was coded [0] none, [1] some, [2] all. The total score possible on the attitude scale toward the cooperative board was eight points. The low attitude ranged between zero and four, and was coded [0]; and the high attitude ranged from five to eight, and was coded [1]. Analysis including this dependent variable was run on the sample of cooperative members, excluding board members (n = 1,727).

## The Independent Variables

As the above table shows, twenty independent variables were used in the analysis. The variables are grouped into five sets as follows:

1. Pattern of production, including six variables:
   a) Area cultivated with sugarcane (CANAREA) is a continuous variable indicating area cultivated with cane as a percentage of the total area cultivated, with values ranging 0–100 percent.
   b) Landholding type (LANDHOLD) is a dichotomy indicating whether a respondent is a tenant [0] or an owner [1].
   c) Operational holding (LANDSIZE) is a continuous variable indicating the size of land operated by the respondent measured in feddans.
   d) Farm labor (FARMLABR) is a categorical indicating whether [0] the respondent is using family labor only, [1] using family and hired, or [2] using hired labor only.
   e) Farm animal ownership (ANIMLOWN) is a dichotomy indicating whether the respondent is [0] not holding farm animals, or [1] holding farm animals.

2. Source of agricultural inputs:
   a) Source of seeds (SEEDSORC): [0] cooperative, [1] local source or previous crop, [2] village bank, and [3] market or private sector.
   b) Source of fertilizer (FERTSORC): [0] cooperative, [1] village bank, or [3] market or private sector.
   c) Source of pesticides (PESTSORC): [0] cooperative, [1] do not use pesticides, [2] village bank, or [3] market or private sector.

3. Price of agricultural inputs:
   a) Price of seeds (SEEDPRIC)
   b) Price of fertilizers (FERTPRIC)
   c) Price of pesticides (PESTPRIC)

Each was coded [0] price high, or [1] price reasonable.

4. Socioeconomic characteristics: included three variables:
   a) Level of education (EDUCTION) is a categorical variable, coded: [0] has no schooling, [1] primary level, [2] secondary and above.
   b) Occupation beside farming (OCUPTION) is a dichotomy indicating whether the respondent is working in farming only [0], or working in another job besides farming [1].
   c) Income sufficiency (INCOMSUF) is a dichotomy indicating whether respondent's income is insufficient [0], or sufficient [1].

5. Demographic characteristic variables included four variables:
   a) Age (AGE) is a continuous variable which ranged from fifteen to ninety-five.
   b) Marital status (MARSTATS) is dichotomous and coded [0] currently unmarried, [1] currently married.
   c) Family size (FAMSIZE) is coded [1] small (between one and five persons), and [0] large (six or more persons).
   d) Family type (FAMTYPE) is coded [0] nuclear, and [1] extended or joint.

# 15

# Rural Periodic Markets in Egypt

MOHAMED M. MOHIEDDIN

## Introduction

Periodic markets have been and continue to be a main feature of major Middle Eastern cities, towns, and villages. There is a wide variety of such markets. Some are annual, such as those associated with religious festivals commemorating Muslim sheikhs or Christian saints. Other markets are more frequently held, being held monthly, biweekly, weekly, and even twice or three times weekly.

The theatrical work of the Egyptian poet Salah Jahin, *al-Layla al-kabira*—'the big night'—expresses the interrelation between annual markets and religious occasions very vividly. In fact, pilgrimage to Mecca itself is considered to be both a religious and a commercial event. In this regard, the Quran states,

> And proclaim unto mankind the pilgrimage. They will come onto thee on foot and on every lean camel; they will come from every deep ravine. That they may witness things that are of benefit to them, and mention the name of Allah on appointed days over the beast of cattle that He hath bestowed upon them. Then eat thereof and feed therewith the poor unfortunate. (Sura XXII. "The Pilgrimage," Verses 27, 28: 243–44, Pickthall translation).

In both rural and urban areas, some of these markets are highly specialized, such as the livestock markets described by Hopkins (1988:152–53), which are held in provincial towns, and even in Cairo itself. The used-car markets that litter the Cairo suburbs of Ma'adi, Madinat Nasr, and other quarters of the city are another example (Mohieddin 1997b). Other weekly markets are more diverse in terms of the commodities they have to offer, and are geared to satisfy the daily, occasional, or seasonal needs of the local population. Again, such weekly markets are to be found in both rural and urban areas (Larson 1982, 1985; Fernea 1993; Schuyler 1993).

This paper concerns itself with only one of the above-mentioned types of periodic markets, namely the village weekly markets which are oriented toward satisfying the most pressing consumer needs of the local populations. The paper proposes to describe and analyze the structure, organization, and functions of the village weekly markets in two Egyptian governorates. It further attempts to show that these markets are not merely economic, but they also perform social and political functions for their communities. In so doing, the paper takes notice of such factors as class, gender, and the ways in which these factors affect modes of specialization in traded goods, and how they determine inequality within the marketplace. The data for this research was collected during periodic visits to five markets in the governorates of Minufiya in the Delta, and Minya in Middle-Upper Egypt, between October 1996 and February 1997.

Linguistically, the Arabic language provides some food for thought on the issue of markets. *Al-suq* (plural, *aswaq*) is the place where things are sold, and people are regarded as shopping if they buy and sell. *Al-suwayqa* means trade or commerce, and is also the diminutive of *suq* (Ibn Manzur 1993, Vol. I:640). This linguistic definition is in accord with the substantive definition of the market developed by Polanyi, who states that, "A market may be defined as a meeting of a number of persons desirous of acquiring, and getting rid of, goods through the acts of exchange" (Polanyi 1957:267). Such a definition approximates the idea of a free market, unconstrained by any structural elements. It also presupposes the existence of at least six elements in a market: buyers, sellers, a meeting place, a meeting time, things to be exchanged, and rules and mediums of exchange. There is nothing that is specifically rural about these elements. They apply equally to any market situation, be it rural or urban, periodic or permanent.

The question, thus, is what are the features that distinguish rural markets from other markets? For the purpose of this paper, rural markets are not viewed merely as a geographic category. Rather, they are defined in terms of the goods being exchanged. The majority of goods exchanged in these markets are either in their natural form, or have been subjected to minimal processing. In other words, the value added to the goods exchanged is almost negligible, with the exception of livestock. Second, things are sold in most cases by the direct producers, and thus there is no participation on the part of economic firms in the markets. Finally, these markets are periodic, that is, held at a fixed day and place that is known to the local population, regardless of whether the markets have a permanent physical structure or not.

## Village Markets in Egypt: A Brief Historical Overview

Viewed from a historical vantage point, it is difficult to identify the time when these markets started to constitute a phenomenon in Egyptian rural life. Some have suggested that they date back to Pharaonic times, and certainly to the Roman era. It is not easy, however, to ascertain that they have continued to exist on a regular basis since then.

The available historical evidence indicates that they have been operating on a regular basis for almost the past millennium. Ibn Hawqal, who traveled through Egypt during the tenth century, identified seven sites in Minufiya alone where such markets were being held on a regular basis (1967:138–42). A century latter, Ibn Jubayr (1986:17, 27, 33) indicated the existence of such markets in several villages, such as Qalyub, Giza, which had a Sunday market at that time, and Minya, among other villages. Speaking of Minufiya in the twelfth century, al-Idrisi (1894:151–61) added four other village markets to those mentioned by Ibn Hawqal. Other works of Ibn 'Iyas, al-Ishaqi, and al-Zubaydi, confirm the notes of the above-mentioned authors.

With regard to the last three hundred years, Barbara Larson (1985:494–530) has developed the most comprehensive, and probably the only, theoretical and historical account of rural markets in Egypt. Adopting Carol Smith's model, which posits a connection between the distribution and hierarchical pattern of markets on the one hand, and the institutional framework through which goods and services circulate on the other, Larson argues that Egypt's rural marketing system has undergone significant transformations during the last three hundred years, changing from a predominantly solar-administered market in the eighteenth and early nineteenth countries, then to a dendritic–monopolistic system in the late nineteenth and early twentieth centuries, and finally to a contemporary system which combines elements of both administered and competitive, interlocking markets. Furthermore, she stresses that there has been, over the last three hundred years, a parallel growth and development of the horizontal component of the system, namely, the system of weekly markets and local retail shops catering to local needs. In addition, she notes that the vertical component of rural marketing system has always been dominant, and has set the tone and shape of the system as a whole. Finally, she argues that changes in the overall shape of the system have, by and large, been dictated by the needs and/or the desires of the state for more revenue in pursuit of its political and economic goals (Larson 1985:528–29).

On the strength of the historical evidence, it is possible to argue that periodic rural markets in Egypt are the product of a lengthy evolutionary economic process with very little, or almost no intervention on the part of the state in initiating them. Markets, however, were not far from state interests as a source of revenue. In this respect, we find references in several pages of *Description de L'Egypte* to the taxes levied on markets.[1]

## The Structure and Organization of Weekly Markets

In their physical appearance, village weekly markets in Egypt are very similar. Writing in the mid-1920s, Blackman (1968 [1927]:164–65) notes, "The open-air market was evidently as distinctive a feature of ancient as it is of modern Egyptian life." She provides the following description (1968[1927]:164–65):

> Most villages, and all towns, have a weekly market, where a great variety of goods are for sale. The market-place is usually situated just outside the village, and is either Government property or belongs to some private individual. Every one who brings goods for sale pays a small sum to the owner of the property on which the market is held. There is no more animated scene than a village market.

She goes on to describe how the market is spatially organized, and the various activities that take place in it, such as the bargaining process, the entertainment activities, and the seasonal activities of the *saqa*, 'water carrier.'

Until now, village markets in Egypt have remained largely unchanged, at least in their physical appearance. Typically, a market is held in a designated area that is either privately owned or that falls within the public domain of the village land. However, in some Minufiya villages where such open land is scarce due to population pressure, markets are held in the streets of the village. In both Minya and Minufiya, only government-owned markets are fenced to facilitate the collection of fees. Such markets, however, tend to be concentrated in the district capitals. Almost all village markets are privately owned.

Village markets are usually held on weekly basis, and each village that organizes a market designates a given day of the week as its market day. Thus some villages came to be named after their market day, or the day of the week on which its market is held was added to its name. Hence, in Minufiya, there is found the village of Subk al-Talat, 'Subk of Tuesday.' This phenomenon is not uniquely Egyptian, rather it can be found all over the Arab world. In Morocco, we find the villages and towns of Suq al-Talat and Suq al-Arba'a (Wednesday) on the road between Rabat and Tetouan. In Saudi Arabia, the commercially vibrant city of Khamis Mushayt took its name from its famous Thursday market.

In some villages, markets are held more frequently then once a week. Milig in Minufiya, for example, has a market that is held three times a week. One of these markets is entirely devoted to cheese and butter *(suq al-gibna)*, and nothing else. On the other two days, commodities geared toward the satisfaction of household consumption of foodstuffs and durable goods, such as clothes and kitchen utensils, are sold. The majority of the participants in the cheese and butter market, be it as buyers or sellers, are females. While livestock markets exist in both Minya and Minufiya, no comparable specialized market for cheese was found in the area covered by this research in Minya. The life of the market day is very short. The day begins early and finishes early. Thus, a market starts as early as six in the morning, and by the call for noon prayers it comes to an end. In very few cases do markets continue beyond this point of the day. When they do, the number of buyers and sellers declines, and it does not last for more than two or three hours beyond the noon prayers.

Markets in close geographic proximity are held on different days, and big markets are not held directly in competition with one another. Smaller markets, however, may compete with each other. Table 1 shows the temporal and spatial distribution of weekly markets in the districts of Shibin al-Kom (Minufiya) and Maghagha (Minya) in Egypt. It is clear from the table that only in a few cases do periodic markets compete with one another. In Shibin al-Kom, where land is tight and distances between villages are not that meaningful, there might exist some competition, especially in the north and northwest, where markets tend to be concentrated on Tuesdays and Thursdays. The effects of such proximity may be offset by the high population density which characterizes the entire governorate of Minufiya. By contrast, the district of Maghagha shows a balanced distribution of markets over the week days. In the case of the three markets which take place on Thursday, it appears that distance is an effective factor in reducing the competition between them. The two villages in question, Shim al-Basal al-Bahariya and Bani Wallims, are about fourteen and eighteen kilometers away from Maghagha respectively. At such distances, the cost of transporting goods becomes a major risk factor. Furthermore, compared to the Maghagha market, the markets of these two villages are just '*suwayqas*' of no more than seventy vendors. They are designed to cater to the needs of the locals, who usually do not frequent more than one market, or at the most two.

This periodic and spatial distribution is designed to enable traders

Table 1. Temporal and Spatial Distribution of Periodic Markets in Study Areas (by district or region)

| Shibin al-Kom Village Name | Market Day | Location | Maghagha Village Name | Market Day | Location |
|---|---|---|---|---|---|
| Tanbidi | Thursday | NW | Barabat | Saturday | SW |
| Kafr Tanbidi | Saturday | N | Saqola | Sunday | SW |
| Tukh al-Barakhta | - | - | Aba al-Waqf | Monday | S |
| Bakhati | Thursday | W | Bani Khalid | Tuesday | W |
| Mit Khalaf | - | - | Shim al-Basal al-Qibliya | Wednesday | SW |
| al-May | Thursday | SW | Shim al-Basal al-Bahariya | Thursday | SW |
| Kafr al-Batanun | Tuesday | NW | Bani Wallims | Thursday | SW |
| Zuweir | Sunday | E | Maghagha | Thursday | - |
| Shubra Bas | Tuesday | W | al-Qayat | Friday | W |
| Milig | Friday & Sunday | NE | Tanbidi | Tuesday | W |
| Shanawan | Tuesday | S | | | |
| Dakma | Tuesday | E | | | |
| al-Batanun | Tuesday | NW | | | |
| Mit Musa | Wed. & Friday | N | | | |
| Bitibs | Wednesday | N | | | |
| Shubra Khalfun | Sunday | S | | | |

- = Not reported, but has a market
Source: Shibin al-Kom data from Ghurab, 1989: 99; Maghagha data collected by author.

and vendors to attend several markets every week. In this respect, the rescheduling of market days in the district of Maghagha is telling. The Bani Khalid market, which dates back to the 1940s, used to be held on Sundays. In the mid-1970s, it was rescheduled to Tuesdays to reduce competition with the Saqola market, resulting in part from the dramatic improvement in the means of transportation. There were, and still are, no other markets held on that day in the district. At the time when Shim al-Basal al-Bahariya market was established in 1967, there were no other markets operating on Thursdays in the area, except for the one in the district town of Maghagha.

The majority of markets in Egypt are privately operated or owned. Only the ones in the district capitals of Shibin al-Kom and Maghagha are owned by the government, and are auctioned every year. In 1986, the *iltizam* (rental fee) for Shibin al-Kom market stood at LE28,000 (Ghurab 1989:121). In these governmental markets, the fees charged to peddlers are set officially. Private markets either take place on private or public lands. In the latter case, the village council assumes responsibility for collecting the dues. In the first case, it is the suq owner who assumes such responsibility. Here, fees are arbitrarily set, and are a source of constant disagreement, however minimal the difference is. Other market land may be donated for free, as in the case of the village of al-Qayat (Minya), where land has been donated by the family of al-Qayati.

At first sight, village markets in Egypt look anarchic. On close inspection, however, they reveal a high degree of spatial organization. Each commodity sold in the market has a specially designated area. Vendors are lined in relatively straight rows running parallel to each other. Figure 1 shows the layout of a small *suq* in an Upper Egyptian village. Just outside the marketplace, and on the main road, cluster the donkey haircutters, where waste hair can be easily dumped into the canal, or carried away by the wind blown from passing cars. At the narrow entrance sit the craftsmen and the sugarcane sellers, who can put their slender canes against the walls and not jam the entrance at the same time. Immediately past the entrance, one meets the butchers, who are the centerpiece at the weekly markets. Arriving earlier than the rest, because of the practice of on-site slaughter, they have the advantage of choosing their spot. They place themselves against the walls facing north. With the sun rising from the east and to the south, the butchered beasts stay in the shade for the longest possible time. Right next to the butchers' *sibiya*s (tripods) are located the *tabliya*s (tables) of those who trade in intestinal parts, and who are naturally dependent on the butchers. For the major meal of Thursday, vegetables and fruits are in order, and next to the vendors of vegetables and

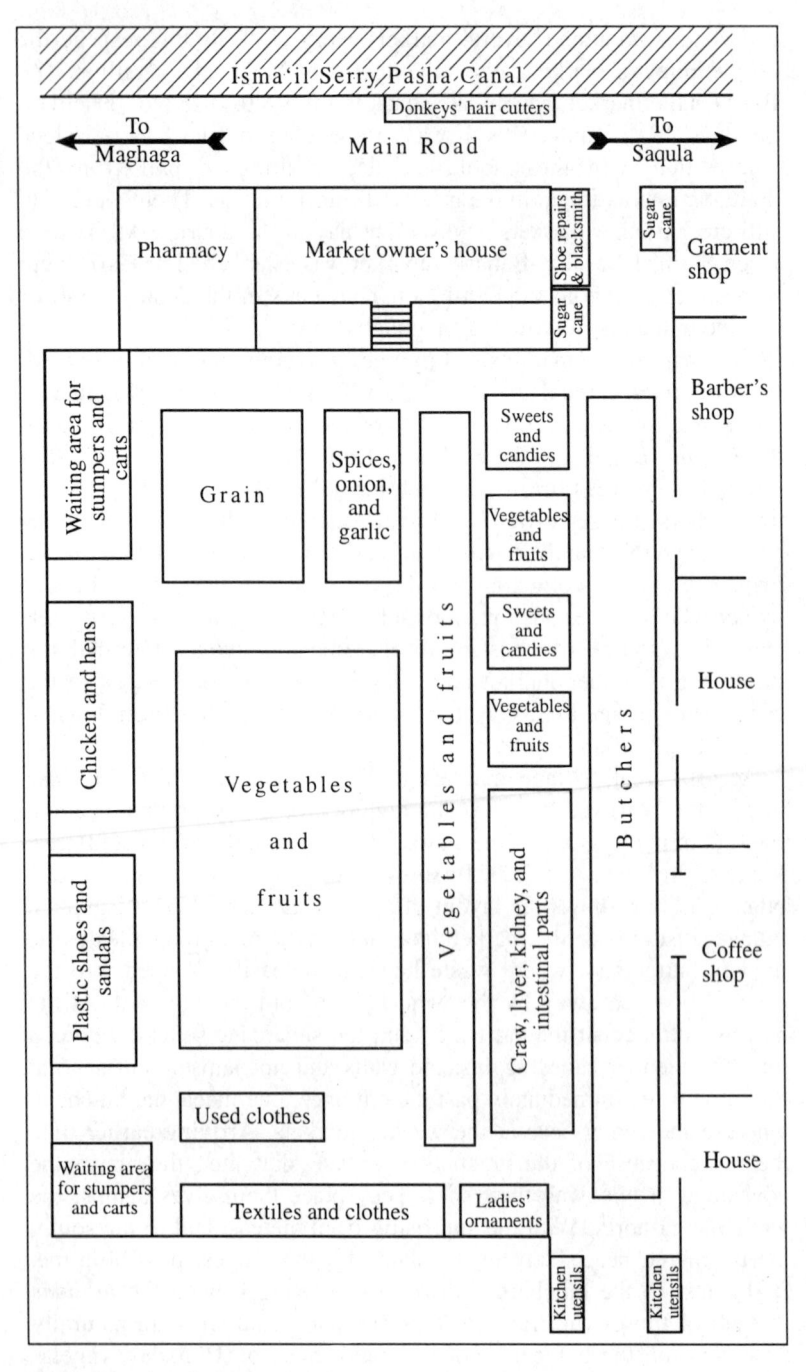

Figure 1  *A Small Village Market* (suwayqa) *in Minya*

fruits sit the spice traders. With their heavy sacks of grain, merchants need their pack animals at close proximity; they are kept in places from which they could not wander away nor be easily stolen. Vendors sell live chickens which are caged and loaded on trucks which have their own isolated spots. Their vehicles are always equipped with umbrellas to protect the birds from the heat. Less frequently demanded goods, such as shoes, sandals, cloth, and textiles have their own niche.

Such spatial organization appears to play two roles. On the one hand, proximity facilitates the job of the buyers, and on the other, the tough competition between vendors works to the best interests of the consumers. A market, however, is not complete without the coffee shop, which finds a lucrative business on market day, offering tea and soft drinks to buyers, sellers, and those who are interested in talking and watching. Other markets appear to have more or less the same pattern of space occupancy, and the overall pattern today seems to be in accord with that given by Blackman (1968:165 [1990:130]) for rural markets in Upper Egypt in the 1920s.

Forms of organization in the market are not restricted to spatial arrangements, but are also affected by other factors. In Egyptian rural markets, there exists also a high degree of specialization along gender lines. For example, while males participate in the grain trade as merchants, females do so as sellers of small quantities, aiming at supplying their households with necessary cash. By the same token, almost all butchers are males. In my investigation of several markets, I ran into only one female butcher, who had inherited the profession from her husband. At the same time, the majority of those who deal in stomachs and other intestinal parts are females. Cheese, butter, margarine, and egg vendors are almost exclusively female. It is, not surprisingly, demeaning in rural Egypt for a man to take up such a profession. Cobblers, blacksmiths, coppersmiths, textile retailers, and vendors of house wares are predominantly, if not entirely male.

Specialization is not confined to vendors and traders, but appears also to cover buyers. In the Egyptian rural markets, for example, buying meat from butchers is for the most part a male speciality. By contrast, females tend to focus their buying activities on vegetables, fruits, chickens and hens, kitchen utensils, and of course cosmetics.

In sum, rural periodic markets in both the Delta and Upper Egypt appear to be highly structured in their spatial as well as temporal organization. Furthermore, they are the loci of gender, social, and economic inequalities.

## The Social, Economic, and Political Functions of the Market

Markets are not merely places where commercial transactions take place. They also perform a multiplicity of functions for their respective communities. Larson (1982) stressed the economic functions of the village markets in contemporary Egypt.

Egyptian markets in the old days used to be the focus of artistic activities: the charmers, storytellers, musicians accompanied by dancers, as well as fortune-tellers were an integral part of big markets (Blackman 1968:168 [1995:130]). Today, these activities are no longer part of the weekly markets, though they are found in the *mulid*s. In the Moroccan context, Schuyler (1993:276–80) indicates the continued presence of this entertainment aspect of the *suq*. Egyptian markets also function as meeting places for prospective couples or actually engaged couples, and sexual harassment is also in existence.

Weekly markets perform several economic functions. First, they provide the peasant consumers and urban dwellers with their weekly needs at cheaper prices. They also provide a limited range of services: repairs of *butagaz* stoves, pots, sieves, bread paddles, leather and plastic shoes, clothes and fabrics, and the like (Larson, 1982:134).

In addition, they make available to the peasant consumers a whole range of mundane, and not so mundane, craft and manufactured items, thereby saving the peasant a trip into town. Despite the developments that have improved the means of transportation and roads in Egypt in the past twenty years, such trips continue to be a bit of a problem. These items consist of such goods as cloth, dishes, pots and pans, pottery, iron implements, agricultural tools, blankets, saddles, and saddle bags (Larson, 1982:134).

Village markets are also major outlets for livestock, both wholesale and retail. In Egypt, the livestock market deals in cows, water buffalo, sheep, goats, and donkeys. Furthermore, they are outlets of livestock by-products, such as milk and cheese, as well as hides. Livestock markets appear to be linked to each other in a hierarchical chain that starts from the small village markets, *suwayqa*s, and continues to the relatively larger ones, such as those of the district capitals, Minuf, Shibin al-Kom, Bani Mazar, and the like, and then to larger markets in big cities, such as Minya, Asyut, and, of course, Cairo. Merchants from Cairo are to be found in these markets. It is a common sight on the main roads of the Delta and the Sa'id to see cows and buffaloes being shipped by truck to Cairo slaughterhouses.

In addition, such markets are in direct relationship with a considerable number of households in big cities in general, and Cairo in particular. This manifests itself in two forms. First, some urban households still prefer to buy their poultry directly from rural markets. This is especially the case where the urban resident has roots in a village near the city where s/he lives. This is usually motivated by two factors: on the one hand, it is usually claimed that the taste of such meat is better than that sold in the urban markets; on the other hand, the perceived and actual price of the meat can be half that in the city, or less for prime cuts.

The second way in which these markets are tied to urban dwellers is related to religious festivals. A month before the *'Id al-Adha*, 'Feast of Sacrifice,' where every financially able Muslim is expected to butcher a beast, village markets experience a frantic trade activity in response to the increasing urban demand for livestock, usually sheep, and prices start to rise considerably. Despite the price increase during this time, the prices of the sacrificial animal in the village of Saqola livestock market are still about 25 percent–35 percent less than those prevailing in Cairo. Each year, the various members of the family of the author place their orders for the sacrificial animal as early as the end of Ramadan, over two months before. Ramadan itself is another time of the year that witnesses such purchases, though to a lesser extent. Judging by personal experience, such practice is not unique to the family of the author, but is widespread.

Finally, such markets provide employment opportunities for the local poor and disadvantaged groups. In Egypt, a good proportion of those who work as vendors do not have access to land or other employment opportunities. In addition, the markets constitute a source of cash for peasant households which allows them to meet the necessities of daily life, as well as the cost of their agricultural inputs and the payment of taxes to the government (Mohieddin 1997a). The market also serves the economic interests of its owner, who charges a fee to the sellers. In one village where I inquired, the owner pays the village council LE30 in local taxes, while his return per week, according to my estimation, was about LE70, on which he probably pays no income taxes.

Prices constitute an integral component of any market situation. Thus, the question of how prices are set in village markets is of central relevance. There are several factors that affect the pricing of commodities in rural markets. First, this largely depends on whether the commodity sold is produced locally, or is imported to the village from other villages or cities. Urban-produced goods are more expensive in the village market than those of comparable quality in the urban markets. The merchants have to add the cost of transporting the goods to the rural market. This does not only apply to goods sold on the free market, but is also true of subsidized ration commodities, such as sugar, oil, rice, and the like, the prices of which are set by the government. The lack of an efficient transportation and distribution system puts the burden of transporting such commodities on the shoulders of the village grocers (see, for example, Mohieddin 1987, Ch. 3). The advantage rural markets have to offer in this respect is that they make available to the peasants cheaper goods, such as kitchen utensils, for example, which are not readily available in the stores of the nearby towns, where only first grade quality is available. Whenever second grade quality is available, rural markets save the peasant the time and cost of making a trip to the town. Pricing has thus to strike a delicate balance between these factors.

Second, the seasonal demand for certain commodities affects price fluctuations. Livestock market prices and their change immediately before the feast, as indicted earlier, is a case in point. It is important here to note that price setting and price fluctuation depend largely on the prices of the inputs in the market, but seldom, or never, include remuneration for labor. In an interview with a female head of household in a village in Minufiya, I asked her how she determines the prices at which she sells a pound of cheese or butter in the market. Her answer was that it depended largely on the price of clover and of milk in the market, and the amount of milk needed to produce a pound of cheese. When questioned if she took into account the time and effort she devoted to produce the cheese and butter, she answered, "How am I going to calculate that? It is part of my duty as a housewife!" It is this factor exactly, that makes the locally produced commodities cheaper.

Third, the network of markets within a given region acts as a web of information flow. Prices of the commodities in the previous daily or weekly market in a neighboring village act as a guideline for setting prices in the next day's village market.

At the micro-level of any given market, another factor that affects pricing is the time at which the process of exchange is taking place. The later in the day the exchange is taking place, the lower the price. This is especially true of commodities with a short life expectancy, such as vegetables and fruit, as well as meat. Other commodities are less vulnerable to such effects. There are also accidental effects, reflecting nature. In one village market, farmers were selling cabbages at twenty-five piasters a head. Later in the day, a peasant who had not planned to sell his cabbages that day, dumped a huge load of cabbages in the market. His cabbages suffered from a dew that had caused the outer leaves of the plants to burn upon sunrise. He was selling his crop at ten piasters a head, and thus forced everybody else to match the price or leave the market.

Periodic markets are not devoid of political functions. They are used as a place to mobilize support for candidates, and to enhance the status of families. In the coffee shop adjoining the market of one village, at a time when elections for the village councils were approaching, I attended a discussion between some educated villagers on the merits of several candidates, and listened to their objections to the *'umda*'s attempts to force the entire populace to vote for a certain candidate. Some vowed not to vote for him.

In the village of al-Qayat, the family of al-Qayati, with its long religious and political history, uses the *suq* as an instrument for enhancing its status. On the one hand, the *suq* is held on a piece of land that belongs to the family. This land is now considered within the residential perimeter of the village, which means that its value is very high. The family does not collect fees from those who sell in the market. A market of comparable size in a nearby village is estimated to yield about LE1000 per week. On the other hand, the day chosen for the village market, Friday, is meant to add religious legitimacy to the family, as vendors and traders would deal, and then pray to get the blessings *(baraka)* of the Sheikh al-Qayati.

Finally, market day is also the day designated by Sheikh Ahmad al-Qayati, who happens to be the member of the people's council for the electoral district, to meet his constituency. Thus, peasants can shop, voice their concerns, and submit their requests and petitions at the same time.

The state announces its presence in the market in various forms, not least of which is the collection of fees when the market is held on government land. In Minya, where religious terrorism is rampant, armored police vehicles roam the big markets of Saqola, al-Qayat, and Maghagha. In some markets, a police station has been established in order to maintain order and keep the large population gathered in the market under control.

In brief, despite the increasing penetration of the state into the countryside, rural markets still retain important social, economic, and political functions for the local population.

## Conclusion

This paper has attempted to describe and analyze the structure and functions of rural markets in Egypt. It has demonstrated that these markets perform, and continue to perform, a multiplicity of functions for their respective communities. At the economic level, they provide consumer goods to the rural populace at lower prices, they provide a source of employment for the rural poor, they also make available to the rural population a wide range of manufactured items, and, finally, they are a major outlet for the sale of livestock.

In addition, markets are also an arena for political activities. They constitute a site for the mobilization of political support for candidates, and are used to enhance the political and social status of families in the villages. On the other hand, they are an arena for the state to demonstrate its presence, and make its existence felt. Markets also play major social functions for their communities and their individual members.

In sum, rural markets continue to be viable economic, political, and social institutions, despite their increasing subjection to state control. Despite the growth of wholesale trade and the wide distribution of retail shops in the countryside, and the relative improvement in transportation technology, rural markets continue to show great resilience and are able to survive the competition. They are likely to continue to exist for some time to come.

## Note

1 See the Arabic translation under the title of *Wasf Misr*, especially vols. 4 and 5, and particularly the study entitled, "The Physical and Administrative Systems in Ottoman Egypt" (vol. 5:49–261). *Description de l'Egypte* was written by the French scholars who surveyed Egypt under Napoleon from 1798–1801, and was published in the early nineteenth century.

## References

Blackman, W. S. 1968. [1927]. *The Fellahin of Upper Egypt: Their Religious, Social and Industrial Life with Special Reference to Survivals from Ancient Times*. London. Frank Cass. [Translated into Arabic by Ahmad Mahmud. *al-Nas fi Sa'id Misr: al-'Adat w-al-taqalid*. Cairo, 'Ayn. 1995.]

Fernea, R. 1993. "Suqs of the Middle East: Commercial Centers Past and Present." in Bowen, D. L., and E.A. Early, eds. *Everyday Life in the Muslim Middle East*. Bloomington and Indianapolis: Indiana University Press. pp. 182–91.

Ghurab, F. H. H. 1989. "al-Aswaq al-Rifiya fi muhafazat al-Minufiya: dirasa jughrafiya." unpublished Ph.D. dissertation. Cairo: 'Ayn Shams University, Faculty for Women.

Hopkins, N. S. 1988. *Agrarian Transformation in Egypt*. Cairo: The American University in Cairo Press.

al-Idrisi, Muhammad Bin 'Abd al-Aziz al-Sharif. 1894. *Sifat al-Maghrib wa Ard al-Sudan wa Misr w-al-Andalus*. Leiden.

Jahin, S. 1992. *al-Layla al-kabira wa khamas masrahiyat*. Cairo: Markaz al-Ahram li-l-Tarjama w-al-Nashr.

Ibn Jubayr, Abi al-Hasan Muhammad Ahmad. 1986. *Risalat 'itibar al-nask fi zikr al-athar al-karima w-al-manask al-ma'ruf bi rihlat Ibn Jubayr.* Beirut: Dar wa Maktabat al-Hilal.

Ibn Hawqal, Abu al-Qasim. 1967. *Surat al-ard.* Leiden: Matabaat Brill.

Ibn Manzur, Abi al-Fadl Jamal al-Din Muhammad Ibn Makram. 1993. *Lisan al-lisan: tahdib lisan al-'arab.* Beirut: Dar al-Kutub al-'Ilmiya.

Larson, B. K. 1982. "The Structure and Function of Village Markets in Contemporary Egypt." *Journal of the American Research Center in Egypt* 19:131–44.

Larson, B. K. 1985. "The Rural Marketing System of Egypt Over the Last Three Hundred Years." *Comparative Studies in Society and History* 27(3):494–530.

Mohieddin, M. 1987. "Peasant Migration from an Egyptian Village to the Oil Producing Countries: Its Causes and Consequences." Unpublished Ph.D. dissertation. University of North Carolina at Chapel Hill.

Mohieddin, M. 1997a. "Bayn shiqi al-raha: asalib baqa' al-usra al-ma'ishiya fi-l-rif al-Misri: dirasa midaniya." Paper under review for publication. Cairo: Arab Research Center.

Mohieddin, M. 1997b. "Urban Periodic Markets in Cairo City, Egypt." Draft.

Pickthall, M. M. (translator.) nd. *The Meaning of The Glorious Koran.* New York: Mentor Books.

Polanyi, K. 1957. "The Economy as Instituted Process." in Polanyi, K., C. M. Arensberg, and H. W. Pearson, eds. *Trade and Market in the Early Empires.* New York: Free Press. pp. 243–70.

Schuyler, P. D. 1993. "Entertainment in the Marketplace." in Bowen, D. L., and E. A. Early, eds. *Everyday Life in the Muslim Middle East.* Bloomington and Indianapolis: Indiana University Press. pp. 276–80.

al-Sha'ib, Z. (translator). 1979. *Wasf Misr.* Vols. 4, 5. Cairo: al-Khangi Publisher. [Originally published 1809–1822 as *Description de l'Egypte, ou recueil des observations et des recherches qui ont été faites en Egypte pendant l'expédition de l'armée française.* 1st ed., 22 vols. Paris: Imprimerie Nationale.

# 16

# Agro-pastoralism and Development in Egypt's Northwest Coast

DONALD P. COLE and SORAYA ALTORKI*

## Introduction

"Smuggling became the source of wealth [in the 1960s]," an elderly *'aqila,* 'wise man,' from the Awlad 'Ali Bedouin told us in al-Qasr village, not far from the Mediterranean coastal town of Marsa Matruh, and about halfway between Alexandria and the Egyptian–Libyan border. More recently, since around 1985, sales of beach front land for summer holiday uses have become the more obvious source of riches in the area of Egypt's northwest coast—for a few local Bedouin businesspeople and for more numerous investors and speculators from outside the region, mainly Egypt's Nile Valley. Meanwhile, the lion's share of Egypt's public and private investment in the northwest coast has been channeled into the development of the tourism sector in Marsa Matruh, and, more spectacularly, into the establishment of about ninety holiday villages along the coast. Also, the Nile's precious and limited water—which sustains Marsa Matruh, other northwest coast towns, and the holiday resorts—has been extended almost to al-'Alamayn for agricultural land reclamation.[1]

Yet, the northwest coast continues to have what botanist Mohamed Ayyad calls Egypt's "most important rangelands in terms of productivity" (1992:2). Dependent on modest rainfall that averages 138mm a year at Marsa Matruh, the narrow (fifty kilometer) but long (five hundred kilometer) steppe along the Mediterranean Sea has, according to geographer Joseph Hobbs, "Egypt's richest flora, with about eight hundred species comprising half of the total number of species

---

* This paper is based on field work conducted in 1993 and 1994 in the Egyptian governorate of Matruh, with appreciated support from the American University in Cairo and the Ford Foundation. The material presented here has been written up in greater detail and is published by the American University in Cairo Press. See Cole and Altorki, 1998.

recorded in Egypt" (1989:39). This steppe, with its coastal plain, plateau area, wadis, and other physical features, and with a complex and rich mixture of habitats, has long sustained a system of mixed dry land farming and range-based pastoral production. However, like other dimensions of the region, this agro-pastoral system has been transformed, especially since around 1960 or so.[2]

After presenting the main features of the area's old system of production, this paper focuses on a process of change which, among other things, has included development of water harvesting and storage systems, introduction of new crops, mechanization of cultivation, expansion of range-based livestock raising, reliance on fodder produced outside the region, and creation of livestock fattening operations. These new land use patterns have resulted in some water erosion and land degradation and have involved increasing use of waged labor and differentiation in size of farm and ranch operations among the region's Bedouin owner-producers. Production is now almost exclusively for exchange value. However, and as local people indicate, numerous achievements in production have been compromised by nonexistent local processing, haphazard supply of production inputs, problems with distribution and marketing of new crops, and other issues, that include conflicts related to land tenure and the development of new class divisions.

We aim to show the overall process of change in production in the northwest coast, although space does not permit full discussion of each of the many dimensions of this complex transformation. We also hold that change in Egypt's desert, Bedouin northwest coast is not dissimilar to that underway in Egypt's rural, peasant Nile Valley—despite major ecological and sociocultural differences.

## The Old, Nomadic Agro-pastoralism

As prologue to the present in the northwest coast, we draw on the discourse of the elderly 'aqila mentioned above. He recalled that, when he was about fourteen years old (in 1928),

> We used to move about, and the land was for everybody. Wherever you wanted to graze, you could graze. Wherever you wanted to plow, you could plow. The land was not for the individual but for the qaba'il ['tribes;' 'clans']. If there was rain in [Sidi] Barrani, people from [Marsa] Matruh would go there and stay as long as they wanted. And [vice versa]. They could stay to plow and to harvest. I used to herd with them close to the border.
> 
> The border between Libya and Egypt existed at that time, when I was fourteen years old. Before that, there was no border. Then, no Egyptian, no

Libyan; just the badiyah ['Bedouin'], and there was the hajanah ['camel corps'].

Our life was very simple. We lived on the rain. We had barley, and the women used to grind it. People lived in tents. There were no permanent houses. We followed the rain. Our anchor was al-Qasr, but we used to move wherever there was rain. There were no cars.

Now, money dominates the world. Before, we did not have so much money, and life was simple. The sheep was for three pounds.

The simplicity of the past, however, should not be exaggerated. The old *'aqila* himself mentioned elements of complexity: traders operating by sea between Alexandria and Marsa Matruh before the railroad reached the latter in 1928, and the presence of forty to fifty Greek shopkeepers in Marsa Matruh, and of many traders from the Magharba tribe of Libya "who were kicked out of Libya by the Italians and came and settled in Hammam and [Marsa] Matruh." One of the old man's sons spoke of how Greek merchants, before World War II, had played a dominant and, in his view, exploitative role in the region's economy. They had lent out money and extended goods on credit, at usurious rates of interest, to livestock raisers, in return for payment in wool and live animals, and, thereby, had converted independent pastoralists into indebted herders of the flocks of others.

Meanwhile, another son detailed a complex system of trade partnerships and the exchange of local produce between the people of Siwa and Awlad 'Ali, who were also the main commercial camel caravan transporters of dates from Siwa, Bahariya, and other Western Desert oases to the Nile Valley. Moreover, Murray noted that Awlad 'Ali, early this century, "chiefly bred [camels] for the markets of the Delta" (1935:113) and that "a busy traffic in [their sheep and camels] goes on weekly in the markets of Hammam, 'Amriya, and the Bahayra" (ibid:277).

The organization of agro-pastoral production out on the range was not overly complex; but specialization and differentiation did exist. At the end of the 1950s or so, most households maintained small-scale herding and crop production activities. What we were told would have been an 'ordinary' household in the 1950s consisted of fourteen people, who kept a couple each of camels and donkeys, six or seven goats, and between thirty and a hundred head of sheep. By contrast, a few 'wealthy' households maintained flocks of between three hundred and five hundred ewes; and some 'poor' households had none or almost no animals.[3] The ordinary household regularly planted a field of barley, and also a few vegetables, and usually some melons. Wealthy households planted more fields of barley—up to a hundred feddans, according to anthropologist Gerald Obermeyer (1968:51)—

and, in some cases, had figs and olives in addition to vegetables.[4] Other households, however, had access to very little or no land that was appropriate for growing crops.

Households without such land included people based in the drier, interior parts of the region. They specialized, or had to specialize, in herding, and were considered to suffer *al-ma'isha wihisha*, 'the bad life,' by people based closer to the coast, who enjoyed what they said was *al-ma'isha simha*, 'the good life.' This ideal way of life was defined as one based on the combination of cultivating barley and raising livestock *(al-sha'ir w-al-mara'i)* (Obermeyer 1968:27). However, within the area of the *ma'isha simha* lived significant numbers of people without sufficient land and/or animal resources to provide their basic household needs. Men from such families contracted to work as sheepherders for households with large flocks and were typically paid annually one lamb for every ten head of sheep herded. "This was good for the sheepherder," an Awlad 'Ali man told us. "With time, he could build up a herd of his own."[5] Other men could, and did, enter into sharecropping agreements, wherein the harvest was divided into equal shares between the 'landowner' (who also provided seeds), and his partner *(sharik)*, who provided all of the labor of cultivation and harvesting.

Hired labor from among the Bedouin was also available in the steppe during the 1950s, as some worked for wages as diggers of cisterns, harvesters of figs and olives, and on other tasks. However, except among the wealthy, most labor for herding and farming was provided by household members. Reciprocal labor parties *(raghata)* composed of relatives and neighbors were also commonly organized to carry out tasks such as harvesting a field of barley or shearing a flock of sheep. Processing and preparing food, making kilims and blankets, and other tasks around the tent were, among poor and rich, the work of household members—which, in this regard, means women.[6]

Concerning that which was produced, households with barley stored it in underground silos *(matmura)* and used the grain for bread, and the straw for fodder. Some of the sheep's wool was kept, as needed, to make blankets and kilims; but most of the wool was sold. Indeed, the sale of wool provided the ordinary household in the 1950s with a major annual source of cash. A household's herd, of course, provided milk, occasional meat, and animals for ritual slaughter, while most of a year's production of male lambs and kids was sold. How many animals were sold depended on how much barley had been produced and stored, the condition of the range, and—for all but the wealthy— whether the household needed cash to meet its basic needs.

## Changes of the 1960s

Aspects of this old system linger today in the northwest coast. However, important changes started around 1960. Marsa Matruh began to expand rapidly, as the new civilian governorate, with the general desert development organization *(Ta'amir al-Sahari)*, and other government institutions opening offices in the town and starting up their activities in the region. Migrants from the Nile Valley increasingly moved in. Summer holiday-making on the beaches blossomed modestly. Marsa Matruh's market expanded rapidly. And Bedouin from outside the Marsa Matruh area began to trickle in. Many of these, according to anthropologist Abdalla Bujra, were "poor people who have no animal stock and therefore cannot live a 'Bedouin life'" (1967:33). Many of them obtained low-skilled jobs in the new government sector or worked in the market.

Meanwhile, Libya's oil-revenue-based economy began to grow, and many younger men from among the region's poor, and the not so poor, began to migrate to Libya to work in trade, or for wages as sheepherders who replaced Libyan Bedouin who had left their own range for cities and towns. Demand for mutton soared in Libya; and Awlad 'Ali and other northwest coast Bedouin shifted sales of live animals from Egyptian markets to more lucrative ones across the border in Libya. Back on the range in Egypt, food and fodder aid from a joint project of the World Food Program (WFP) and the Government of Egypt began to be dispersed to Awlad 'Ali and other Bedouin who joined newly introduced local agricultural cooperative societies. Most of this aid was inappropriate or not needed and was, therefore, sold in the market.

The 1960s' changes had many different impacts, among which was the infusion of a significant amount of cash into the agro-pastoral production scene in the steppe.[7] Although the sale of animals has a long history for the area, monetarization has increasingly dominated both production and consumption since the 1960s. Sheepherders, for example, began to be paid in cash, and no longer in kind, while food purchased in the market began to replace all but a few items grown or produced by the household. Thus, as an Awlad 'Ali livestock raiser living out on the range said, "Now, we buy meat. Before, we used to make bread from our own barley. The children are spoiled. They want white bread."[8]

It is noteworthy that development activities in the northwest coast have often involved foreign and international agencies, including the WFP, the Food and Agricultural Organization, the International Labor Organization, the World Bank, and development bodies of the United

States, German, Dutch, Canadian, and other governments. The aid programs of these various institutions have usually been joint projects with the Government of Egypt, which has contributed significant portions of the aid distributed in the region. Most of the aid programs have been coordinated through the *Ta'amir al-Sahari*, which has played an active and effective supervisory role in the region's development.

Generally, local people praise the work of the *Ta'amir al-Sahari*, and of one of its long-time leaders, an engineer and high-ranking bureaucrat from Upper Egypt, for what they see to have been highly positive contributions. Other government agencies are often ignored and sometimes criticized. However, local people invariably mention the introduction of Egypt's civilian local government system in 1959 as essential for the beginning of the region's development.

## New Crop Production

Development activities initiated in the 1960s by the state in cooperation with international agencies have tended to foster the introduction of new crops, especially olives and figs, but also almonds, peaches, grapes, nectarines, pomegranates, and so on. Some greenhouse agriculture has also been attempted, with mixed results at the time of our field work. The major state and development agency support for this new agriculture has been technical and financial assistance for the construction of a water harvesting system that involves small dams, dikes, and spillways, and some land leveling to control the flow of water through the region's wadis. Support has also been extended to provide cisterns for water storage.

Thus, according to data from the *Ta'amir al-Sahari*, 2,080 dams or dikes were built and 2,959 cisterns were cleaned out or dug under its auspices in the Matruh governorate between 1960 and 1980. Between 1980 and 1993, some 10,415 dams and dikes and 15,185 cisterns were added. To this considerable official support, one must add that local Bedouin beneficiaries also have contributed—through sharing the costs of materials and machinery and through providing some, even most, of the labor. Moreover, an unknown, but supposedly large number of dams, dikes, and cisterns have been built by Bedouin with private funding—often with a Libyan connection.

This new agriculture, as we observed it in Wadi Madwar, Wadi Raml, and elsewhere, is impressive: two thousand olive trees, and 3,500 fig trees on one farm in the desert; a thousand olives and six hundred figs on another, along with thirty or forty each of almond, apple, and pomegranate trees, and perhaps a hundred grapevines. And all dependent on the rain. Awlad 'Ali and other Bedouin farmers rightly exude enthusiasm and pride for their new agricultural investments and achievements. Yet, problems exist.

## Marketing and Other Problems for the New Agriculture

No one owns the land on which the new farms have been developed, as the state fails to grant titles to the 'owners'—despite promises to do so, and despite its own major contributions to individuals to develop the farms. Environmentally, the new agriculture eats into land that was excellent for barley, while that ancient crop—increasingly in demand for fodder—is pushed onto land better left as natural range. Thus, land degradation seriously threatens; and desertification *(tasahar)* is a concern increasingly evoked by some local Bedouin. Also, can the trees survive a severe and prolonged drought, such as that of the early 1950s when no rain fell in four out of five years? Of more immediate concern, however, is the problem of marketing.

In evaluating the new agriculture, local Bedouin producers mention a lack of appropriate technical assistance and advice. Thus, "We learn by experience, and by copying others—which is sometimes wrong." They complain about bottlenecks and other difficulties in obtaining needed, or desired, inputs on time. And, in the words of an Awlad 'Ali farmer about forty years old, a secondary school graduate who has developed new farms in al-Qasr and in Siwa and has traveled to the United States to visit desert farms there,

> We depend on rain for agriculture. However, the basic problem we face is the marketing of what we produce. None of the aid projects has thought about or worked toward solving the problem ... with marketing. The government gives money to cultivate, invests in the development of this new agriculture ... . [But] none of the development projects complete the whole cycle. They focus on production only. The project officials also rely on consultants ... . We see the Egyptian officials; but if the [foreign] representative of [x] had come to me and asked me anything, maybe I would have discussed with him [the problem of marketing], the business of factories, the need to process our products here in the region.

Many issues of direct relevance to the region's development are touched on in this man's short, but perceptive statement. We underscore his recognition of the state's role in this development ("the government gives money" and "we see the Egyptian officials") and take note of his reference to lack of appropriate consultation between the local people and foreign consultants, and other international development project personnel. As he put it in a different context, "The consultants often survey us but they never consult us." Moreover,

## Agro-Pastoralism and Development in Egypt's Northwest Coast

complaints about the marketing of olives and figs abound, and also, in our analysis, reflect ties that link the northwest coast to the rest of Egypt.

The marketing of the region's figs often involves a middle man *(wasit)* who contracts to buy the figs before they are harvested. He pays the cultivator a modest advance and then returns at the time of the harvest to transport the fig production to Cairo for sale by auction in the wholesale market of, at the time of our research, Rud al-Farag. Then, as we were told,

> The middle man deducts the cost of labor, transport, storage; and, sometimes, a five kilogram basket of figs will be no more than one Egyptian pound for the cultivator. That is why some people now are giving up on figs. There seems to be an oversupply of figs on the market.

That both cultivator and trader are Awlad 'Ali, or other Bedouin, who share strong ties of common identity, and even kinship, is hardly of any significance in this operation. We have stressed in the companion paper in this volume that Awlad 'Ali often state that they constitute clans and tribes: "We are *qaba'il*." They also very often say, "Trade is trade." The small-scale cultivator with a farm way off in the steppe somewhere, and without direct or easy access to a distant wholesale market, is thus overly dependent on a few traders more likely to follow the rules of monopsony than those of kinship and tribal solidarity. Meanwhile, a minority of large-scale producers of figs are able to deal directly with a broker *(kumisiungi)* in Cairo; and, after deducting all costs, "We are still making good money. Whatever remains in the end is fine. No problem."

The marketing of olives has followed a different path from that of figs, and of the other more recently introduced fruit crops. Bedouin farmers, since the late 1960s or so, have delivered their olives to the public-sector Egyptian Vineyards Company in Marsa Matruh, and then later on received payment from the central cooperative society in Marsa Matruh. The olives are said to have eventually reached the Gianaclis public-sector company, which converted them into olive oil for sale under its label.[9] Thus, the sale of this crop has also confronted a monopsony, though from the public rather than the private sector. Farmers complain bitterly that prices for their olives have always been low and, also, we heard allegations that, "The old man who sits at the company, we caught him cheating ..., tipping the scales. The company is filled with thieves. But there [is] nothing anybody [can] do."

## Livestock Raising

Still, the northwest coast has its specificity, a central component of which is livestock—especially, sheep and goats. Although a state agricultural engineer from the Nile Valley told us that Bedouin livestock raising was simply a part of nature and, for that reason, had never been targeted by development programs in the northwest coast, we recognize that livestock—domesticated, of course, and thus a part of culture—are core features in the region's culture, society, and economy. Indeed, according to Awlad 'Ali and other northwest coast Bedouin, sheep and goats are capital *(ras mal)*, and they are likely to bring a higher return than is the case for money invested in banks. Moreover, profit earned from money invested in livestock is *halal*, 'righteous,' according to Islam, unlike the case for interest earned on money in a bank, which is *haram*, 'taboo.'

Thus, a Bedouin veterinarian in Marsa Matruh works diligently as a well-paid development expert to support new crop production in the steppe, and to improve the status of Bedouin women there through social programs, the production and sale of kilims, and the introduction of chickens into household economies. However, to improve her own status and economic position, she regularly invests savings directly in sheep, which she puts out to graze on the range under the hired care of a sheepherder kinsman.

Awlad 'Ali and other northwest coast Bedouin often mention the importance of sheep for *dabiha*, '[ritual] slaughter,' that is required often as an offering for social events or ceremonial occasions related to birth, male circumcision, marriage, death, return from the holy pilgrimage, settlement of a conflict, and so on. They speak of flocks in ways that suggest their significance as an element of identity, or of cultural heritage. Also, an elderly father's livestock, upon his death, is the property least likely to be divided among his heirs; and the animals are held as *jumla*, 'trust;' 'collectivity,' sometimes for years—until the heirs themselves are quite old. Meanwhile, the elderly owner of al-Qasr's largest farm insists that the farm continue to raise sheep and to keep some goats, "because our father and grandfathers had them." A son who manages the farm, however, says he would like to bring closure to the farm's livestock operation on the grounds that this activity has become too costly and is beset with too many difficulties and uncertainties.

Sheep and goats in the northwest coast have cultural and social value; and, if pressed, Awlad 'Ali and others will say that the person who herds the animals in the desert is a *baduwi*, 'Bedouin,' a role and identity imbued with cultural, social, and sometimes political meaning. However, people involved with livestock are more commonly identified by reference to a specialized, occupational role as herder or livestock raiser, fattener, trader, or exporter. Also existing within the livestock sector are the fodder merchant and people who rent out barley fields for grazing, and others who rent out access to what was formerly open range.

Sitting in a ceremonial tent with men awaiting the return of pilgrims, an Awlad 'Ali man, who is a small-scale livestock exporter, told us,

> When we export sheep, they usually go from here to Nuwayba [in Sinai] by truck. There, they cross over to 'Aqaba by ferry, and then continue on by truck to Jiddah or Kuwait. This long travel is very strenuous, and the animals suffer. Of course, before going they have to be checked for all kinds of diseases, have blood tests, all kinds of inspections. Sometimes we ship the animals by airplane, especially goats.

## Livestock Marketing and the Procurement of Fodder

In 1960, a pastoralist might have shipped his livestock by train from Marsa Matruh to Hammam or al-'Amriya for sale there, or to be taken to graze stubble and crop residues from fields in Bahayra, a Nile Valley governorate with a long history of ties to the Western Desert and the northwest coast. A pastoralist back then might also have taken animals across the border into Libya for sale, or to graze on the range there. But sending them to distant Arabia? Shipping goats by airplane to Kuwait? We doubt that he could have imagined such an innovation.

However, according to anthropologist Safia Mohsen (1975:14), northwest coast pastoralists provided Nile Valley Egypt at that time with one third or more of its mutton. Awlad 'Ali and other northwest coast livestock production thus had a strong market orientation; but commercialization of this sector has especially soared since the beginning of the 1960s, and is a change with strong parallels throughout the Arab world.[10] Two important elements of this change in the northwest coast have been the upgrading and development of cisterns for water storage in the steppe, as mentioned above, and the introduction of fodder from outside the region, which first occurred in 1963 as a form of aid from the WFP. Both of these changes have had major but unintended impacts.

Expanded water supply in the steppe has opened up large areas for more intensive use than was the case previously, when a limited water supply restricted the number of animals that could be maintained on the range. With more animals on the range, and with most of them being raised for sale, it is perhaps not surprising that informal privatization of range ownership is underway—despite Awlad 'Ali and other Bedouin claims to such land being for the *qaba'il*, and the Egyptian state's claim that this land is the private property of the state *(malkiya khassa li-l-dawla)*.

The distribution of subsidized fodder through cooperative societies has continued for about thirty years, until stopped in the early 1990s as part of Egypt's structural adjustment program agreed with the International Monetary Fund (IMF). However, fodder from the Nile Valley remains an integral part of northwest coast livestock raising and fattening operations. The availability of fodder has allowed for more sedentary herding than was the case previously, and has especially curtailed the need for migration out of the region to Bahayra or to Libya during years of drought or of little rainfall. It has also allowed for keeping more animals on the range, with the unfortunately strong potentiality for overgrazing.[11] The most spectacular aspect, perhaps, of dependence on fodder is, as one Awlad 'Ali livestock raiser said, "We now sell sheep, it seems, to buy fodder." The use of fodder also powerfully links the region to the wider Egyptian economy.

Marsa Matruh has about fifty fodder merchants, many of whom in the past sold fodder on the 'free' market to supplement the inadequate supplies provided through the cooperatives. All fodder is now provided through these merchants, many of whom are Awlad 'Ali. According to one of them, the region from Hammam to Sallum consumes about three hundred metric tons of Nile Valley fodder per day for four or five months a year, depending on the rain and also on the Egyptian state's opening and closing of the export market. These traders place orders with what are now recently privatized companies that no longer provide supplies on credit, as was the case when they were public-sector companies. As an Awlad 'Ali fodder merchant said,

> We are having a hard time. The desert consumes a lot of fodder; but we are all small merchants. The factories can always do without us. They sell to the big guys in the Nile Valley who place huge orders and make the down payment without problems. The problem with fodder is financing. When I buy, no one waits for me. I have to pay up at once. But I sell on credit. I can't refuse to give credit. Where will I sell if I don't sell on credit? This is a risky business.

Fodder consumed in the northwest coast includes the straw, and sometimes the grain of barley grown in the region. However, cotton seed cake, wheat straw, bran, and dried berseem provide the greater portion of the fodder on which the region's livestock increasingly depend. These inputs are grown mainly in the Nile Delta, and are processed in factories in Alexandria, Kafr al-Zayat, Nubariya, 'Amriya, and Mansura. The main market for this production is the Nile Valley, where it is fed mainly to that region's cattle and water buffaloes. Indeed, people in the northwest coast sometimes complain that Egypt's Nile Valley produced fodder is not particularly appropriate for their desert-bred sheep and goats.

## Local Bedouin and Complex Wider Systems

Raising, fattening, and trading in livestock are all risky businesses in the northwest coast. Awlad 'Ali and others never tire of saying that everything depends on the rain. However, Bedouin engaged in any of these activities have numerous calculations, decisions, and arrangements to make. A livestock raiser, for example, will likely consider some, or all of the following: the state of the natural range available for his use; whether to obtain fodder and how to transport, store, and finance it; whether to take or send animals to graze for fees on stubble left over in barley fields; how many animals to sell and when, and whether to deal with livestock traders operating out on the range or to take the animals for sale to a market. Livestock raisers say they expect good profits during three years out of ten—or, more optimistically, two out of five—with profits dependent on plenty of good rain, and thus no need to buy fodder.

A person involved with livestock in the northwest coast is also faced by the uncertainties of markets subject to state politics, consumer demands in distant societies, and the actions of a few large-scale exporters from the region. Libya for example, was an important export market for the region's livestock; but closure of the border in the 1970s for political reasons brought an end to that market, which was replaced by Saudi Arabia and Kuwait—countries with which Egypt, in the 1970s, reestablished friendly relations. Consumer demand in Arabia includes a strong preference for desert-raised mutton and a new niche for desert-raised goat—with its lean meat being an attraction for Arabia's increasingly cholesterol conscious public. Meanwhile, Syria and other countries compete with the northwest coast for the Arabian markets, which are themselves subject to changing local conditions. And the large-scale exporter can, and does, buy up thousands of head of livestock for fattening prior to export.

The sale of live animals in Egypt is according to supply and demand. However, a small-scale, but enthusiastic livestock trader from Awlad 'Ali explained:

> The marketing of animals is complex in Egypt. The government sets controls on the price of meat ... . [But] supply and demand sets the price for live animals. The government also controls the export of live animals. This market brings [high] prices ... [b]ut the government limits the number of animals that can be exported. [However] big dealers, who buy a lot of sheep, say a thousand head, buy cheap, put them in feed lots, and wait until they can sell at high prices for export.

Once again, as for figs and olives, the problem is marketing. A local northwest coast perception is that a few big traders, mainly from the Jumi'at, especially benefit from the export sales of the region's livestock. Others, the large majority, do not benefit so much; but when there is a good year, even the small-scale livestock raiser, as we were told, "Will be happy. He might get married. Build a house. Construct a cistern. Pay off his debts from previous years." Perhaps three good years out of ten, or two out of five, is not bad—especially if one considers that many households in the steppe, or on the range, also produce crops and have some members working for wages or in trade or transport.[12]

## Concluding Remarks

The process of change narrated above is one that we conclude to have been rather ordinary, or well within the bounds of what has taken place in similar regions in other parts of the Arab world and, indeed, elsewhere throughout the Third World. The past in the northwest coast was neither simple nor unchanging. However, transformation during the second half of the twentieth century has resulted in production primarily for use value being replaced by production for exchange value. New wage labor and trade opportunities have provided additional sources of income among the region's people, while state and international development projects have supported the successful introduction of new crops, but have failed to promote appropriate processing, marketing, and other economic institutional development for maximal benefit in the region.

The region was physically remote from Egyptian and other Arab centers; but its isolation has been ended, as even its goats now travel to other Arab countries by airplane or on modern networks of ground transportation. Meanwhile, the northwest coast—despite its desert, Bedouin, and other specificities—should be compared with other Nile Valley governorates, such as the relatively small but strategically important Governorate of Aswan.[13] It follows that it is inappropriate that the northwest coast stand as an exotic 'other' for the whole of the Egypt of the Nile Valley, as has often been the case.

## Agro-Pastoralism and Development in Egypt's Northwest Coast

Sheep, goats, and fodder are not items of glamour. Figs and olives, and other new crops are the region's prestige new agriculture, its signifiers of desert development. The state has promised, but not given landownership to those who planted tree crops. It has made arrangements for the purchase of land as private property for holiday villages. However, the state and most outsiders to the region have ignored the 'barley and pasture' part of the northwest coast. The changes we have sketched for this old dimension of the region's economy are ones that local people, Bedouin from Awlad 'Ali and other tribes, have fashioned on their own without development assistance from outside agencies. Nonetheless, these changes also constitute part of the region's development.

Figs sold in Cairo, fodder brought in from factories in the Nile Delta, sheep and goats shipped for consumption in Arabia, and olives marketed through a public sector company, all combine with summer holiday-makers, trade, and other activities as part of the region's economic scene. We are concerned about issues of sustainability, about class and other social impacts of change, and about other problems far beyond the scope of this paper. However, these concerns are not unique for the northwest coast, but have resonance for the rest of Egypt, and beyond.

We close with a comment made by the elderly *'aqila* quoted at the beginning of this paper. Suggesting a complexity that rightly embraces history, politics, and administration as basic to development (and not just the market), he said:

> We are optimistic. Development started fairly late here, only in the sixties. Before that, we had colonialism and we had military rule. We have had local government only since 1959.

## Notes

1. Some local people from the northwest coast are beneficiaries of this new land reclamation. However, this development especially accommodates people from the Nile Valley, including small-scale farmers, university and other graduates, absentee investors, and others.
2. For a detailed description and sophisticated analysis of development in an area not far from al-Qasr, where we mainly worked, see Müller-Mahn 1989.
3. Sheep seem to have predominated among Awlad 'Ali in the mid-century. A few goats were usually kept as lead animals and for their milk, but some pastoralists had relatively more goats and fewer sheep. Camels were mainly bred and herded in the southern parts of the area. Some Awlad 'Ali specialized in camels and owned large herds. However, camel herding in the region is strongly associated with the Samalus, a *murabit*, 'tied,' tribe, some of whom served as herders to Awlad 'Ali, while others

maintained their own operations.

4  Figs and olives began to be introduced into the more eastern parts of the region early in the twentieth century (see Kassas 1972). They began to be grown on a small scale in al-Qasr in the 1930s.

5  For a relevant comparative perspective, see Bradburd's (1990) excellent study of sheepherders in a pastoralist community in Iran.

6  A gender-based division of labor existed and continues. As examples, men plowed the land and sowed barley seeds. Men and women both cut the barley. After being threshed, ideally by a camel, women winnowed the barley. Men sheared the sheep; women sorted and washed the wool. Women and men both herded animals in the near vicinity of a tent, but men took them to distant pastures. At present, both men and women work for wages to harvest olives and figs; however, most 'modern' occupations are men's work among the 'rural,' or steppe, Bedouin.

7  Another important impact of monetarization and related wage labor migration that some Awlad 'Ali mention is the weakening of family relations, especially as sons with independent sources of income were able to free themselves from the demands of family and of senior kin. Awlad 'Ali who mentioned this change to us saw it as a strongly negative consequence of development during the 1960s.

8  This man reckoned in 1994, that he was spending LE800 per month for food and other expenses for a household of fifteen members. Another estimate for a household of fifteen was between LE500 and LE700 a month.

9  At the time of our field work, the Egyptian Vineyards Company was all but closed, a victim of privatization as prescribed by the IMF through its structural adjustment program for Egypt. What would replace the Egyptian Vineyards Company was not clear to us. We further note that most of the region's wool has been marketed through the central cooperative to the public sector, and thus had a future that, at least to us, was unclear.

10  We have written a comparative analysis of change on the range in the northwest coast, Saudi Arabia, Syria, and Libya (Cole and Altorki, 1998). Commercialized, range-based livestock raising (or what we call 'Bedouin ranching') is a major transformation of Arab pastoralism that has gathered momentum since the 1960s. See Lewis (1987) and Behnke (1980) for descriptive analyses of this change in Syria and in Libya, respectively.

11  Based on an estimate by Ayyad (1992:29), we guess that the northwest coast may have about 1,300,000 sheep and 400,000 goats. In around 1960, the area is said to have had fewer than 300,000 sheep and 100,000 goats.

12  This strategy of multiple occupations, plus livestock and crop production has strong survival value at the level of the household, but the mixture of different activities does not usually result in an integrated farm that combines livestock and crop production into a unified operation.

13  For an insightful comparison of Marsa Matruh and Aswan town as examples of new Egyptian cities of the 1960s or so, see Abou-Zeid 1979.

# References

Abou-Zeid, Ahmed. 1979. "New Towns and Rural Development in Egypt." *Africa* 49(3):283–90.

Ayyad, Mohamed A. 1992. "Present Conditions; Future Perspectives and Research Priorities in Dry Rangelands: Case Study of the Western Mediterranean Region (Egypt)." Cairo: International Center for Agricultural Research in the Dry Areas. Draft Report.

Behnke, Jr., Roy H. 1980. *The Herders of Cyrenaica: Ecology, Economy, and Kinship among the Bedouin of Eastern Libya*. Urbana: University of Illinois Press.

Bradburd, Daniel. 1990. *Ambiguous Relations: Kin, Class, and Conflict among Komachi Pastoralists*. Washington: Smithsonian Institution Press.

Bujra, Abdalla Said. 1967. "A Preliminary Analysis of the Bedouin Community in Marsa Matruh Town." Cairo: American University in Cairo, Social Research Center. Report.

Cole, Donald P., and Soraya Altorki. 1998. *Bedouin, Settlers, and Holiday-Makers: Egypt's Changing Northwest Coast*. Cairo: American University in Cairo Press.

Hobbs, Joseph J. 1989. "The Geography of Egypt." in Stephen M. Goodman and Peter L. Meininger, eds. *The Birds of Egypt*. Oxford: Oxford University Press. pp. 22–62.

Kassas, M. 1972. "A Brief History of Land-use in Mareotis Region, Egypt." *Minerva Biologica* 1(4):167–74.

Lewis, Norman N. 1987 *Nomads and Settlers in Syria and Jordan, 1800–1980*. Cambridge: Cambridge University Press.

Mohsen, Safia Kassem. 1975. *Conflict and Law among Awlad 'Ali of the Western Desert*. Cairo: National Center for Social and Criminological Research.

Müller-Mahn, Hans-Detlef. 1989. *Die Aulad 'Ali zwischen Stamm und Staat. Entwicklung und sozialer Wandel bei den Beduinen im nordwestlichen Ägypten*. Berlin: Dietrich Reimer Verlag.

Murray, G. W. 1935. *Sons of Ishmael: A Study of the Egyptian Bedouin*. London: George Routledge & Sons, Ltd.

Obermeyer, Gerald J. 1968. "Structure and Authority in a Bedouin Tribe: The 'Aishaibat of the Western Desert of Egypt." Ph.D. dissertation. Bloomington: Indiana University.

# 17

## Economic Changes in the Newly Reclaimed Lands: From State Farms to Small Holdings and Private Agricultural Enterprises

GÜNTER MEYER

Since the end of the 1970s, the most proclaimed goal of Egyptian agricultural policy has been the massive expansion of agricultural areas under cultivation. In 1978, in reaction to the fast increase in food imports, President Anwar al-Sadat proclaimed the so-called 'Green Revolution' with the aim of developing 1.2 million hectares of new agricultural land before the end of the century. This corresponds to an area approximately half the size of the old irrigated area of the Nile Valley and the Delta.

It was expected that economic liberalization measures would lead to another increase in agricultural production in the newly reclaimed lands. These measures include, particularly, privatization of farms belonging to the state and promotion of privately developed new land with modern agricultural technology. In the meantime, a large variety of different types of farms has been established in the new lands. The size of these farms ranges from less than two hectares to several thousand hectares, and the operational structure varies from small family-run farms to large-scale agricultural enterprises set up by urban investors and operated by permanent and seasonal labor. How successful are the different types of farms both in terms of agricultural production and in providing jobs to the rural population?

To answer these questions, the author has carried out comprehensive surveys in the newly developed irrigation areas at the western and eastern edges of the Delta. Below, a brief retrospective review of the development of land reclamation and an overview of the results of the survey are given.

## Development of the New Lands in Egypt

A few months after the 1952 Revolution, the new Egyptian government announced that it intended to reclaim several million hectares of irrigated land and to distribute them to the landless rural population—a task which developed very slowly in the 1950s (see Fig. 1). This changed in 1960, as, in anticipation of additional water through the

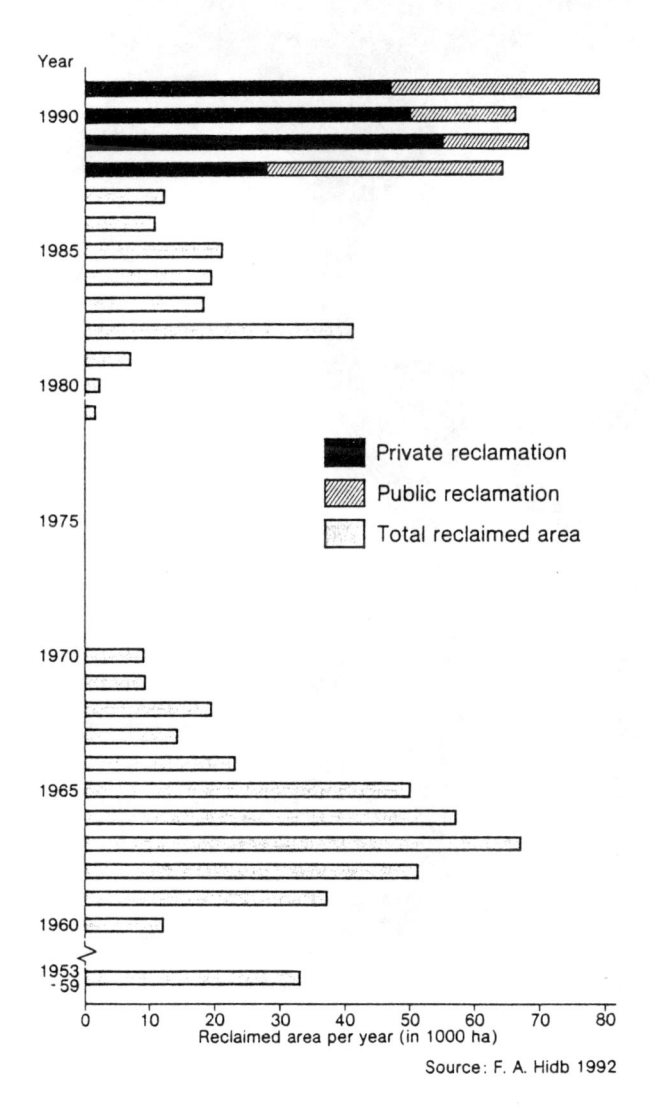

Figure 1 *Land Reclamation in Egypt, 1953–1991*

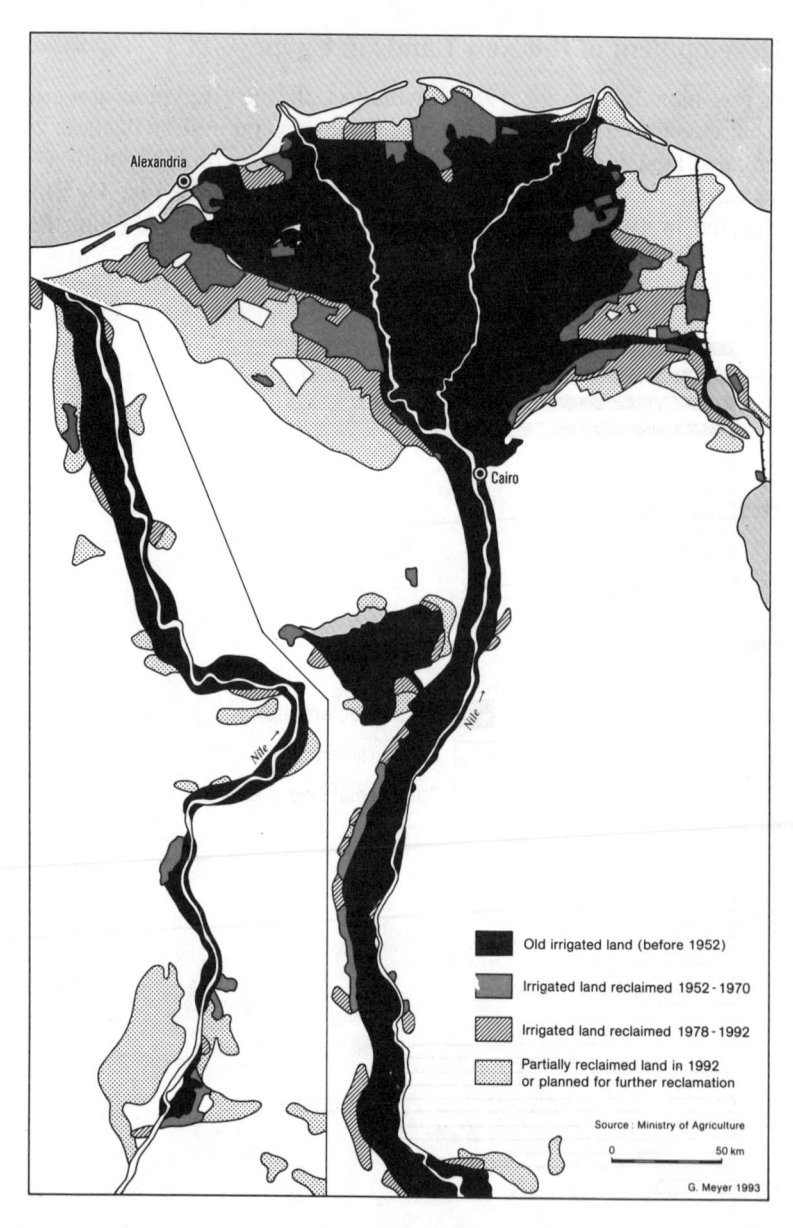

Figure 2 *Distribution of Newly Reclaimed Land in Egypt*

High Dam at Aswan, enormous efforts were undertaken to reclaim new agricultural areas. But the 1967 war with Israel, with its economic consequences, and the perception of the lack of profitability of many new irrigation projects meant a temporary end to the ambitious plans to develop the desert into irrigated land.

About 380,000 hectares had been reclaimed by 1970. These areas were mainly distributed over the fringe zones of the Nile Valley and Delta (Figure 2). Most of the land reclamation projects covered only a few hundred hectares and were cultivated by small settlers, the so-called '*muntafi'in*'. The largest projects in the area adjoining the western Delta, however, were dominated by huge state farms. When the author studied agricultural development in that area during the 1970s, the annual income from the sale of agricultural production of the state farms covered only 89 percent of the recurring costs for wages and agricultural input (Meyer 1978).

Following the *infitah* policy of 1974, a new level of interest in the reclaimed lands was generated on the part of the private sector. The government became partners in private companies or took on purely administrative roles to foster the continuation of farming and development of these lands.

Additionally, the government began the development of new desert areas (Figures 1 and 2). Some of these new-new lands were intended for sale to private owners, while some lands were developed with a complete farming and management package in mind. An example of the latter was the Salhiya project in the eastern Delta area near Isma'iliya, which was developed by Osman Ahmed Osman's Arab Contractors Company in 1981/82.

## The Salhiya Agricultural Project

This giant state farm is by far the largest agricultural enterprise in Egypt, cultivating an area of about 23,000 hectares, mainly by applying center-pivot irrigation (Figure 3). Once regarded as a bright symbol of the national battle to achieve food self-sufficiency, this prestigious project suffered from enormous financial losses and technical failures. In 1988, five animal and dairy production farms had to be closed, and fourteen greenhouses were left inoperable as a result of a lack of spare parts and chronic electrical failures. This was soon followed by the shut down of the twenty-three chicken breeding farms, the fodder factory, and the fish farm.

In an attempt to rescue the project from financial pressure, Salhiya was placed on the auction block for sale to the private sector in 1991. The offers, however, remained far short of the original asking price,

Figure 3 *Land Use of the Salhiya Public Sector Company during Winter 1991/92*

mainly because of the project's excess labor force, whose size of about 2,500 employees was apparently frightening to potential investors.

Therefore, two options were suggested to reduce the labor force. The first option was to compensate laid-off workers with cash, while the second suggested giving workers part of the land. But neither of the options was deemed feasible, since the first turned out to be too costly, while the second plan was rejected outright by the employees who feared that this large-scale project with its highly sophisticated technology would not be manageable if it were split into tiny private farms.

Finally in 1992, under a staggering debt of more than LE250 million, the project was no longer placed under the supervision of the Ministry of Agriculture but restructured into a joint-venture agricultural company owned by its four main creditors: three public banks and the Arab Contractors Company. It remains to be seen whether the new Salhiya Investment and Development Company will be more successful than the Ministry of Agriculture in solving the problems of this project (see El-Din 1993).

## Privatization of State Farms West of the Delta

In other new lands, the privatization of state farms has progressed enormously since 1991. When the author studied the impact of the latest reforms on agricultural development in the new lands along the western Delta (Figure 4) in autumn 1992, it turned out that only a relatively small proportion of the old-new lands was still controlled by public agricultural companies. Figure 5 indicates the farming activities which were, at that time, still performed on the state farms operated by the public Mariut Agricultural Company. Here, and in the areas of al-Nahda, Shimal al-Tahrir, and al-Mazra'a al-Aliya, many state farms had already been privatized, and most of the old-new lands, which still remained under government control, were offered for sale to the private sector.

About 4,800 laborers and employees who had worked at least ten years on the divested state farms received a settlement of up to ten feddans (4.2 hectares) each of old-new land in 1991/92. The size of the land differed according to the qualifications and the period of employment in the public sector, so that, uneducated workers received 0.25 feddans per year of employment with a maximum of five feddans; employees with a medium level of education (diploma) got 0.5 feddans per year, but no more than 7.5 feddans per person; and university graduates were offered ten feddans each.

According to these criteria, a total of 27,800 feddans (11,700

# 340 Günter Meyer

Economic Changes in the Newly Reclaimed Lands 341

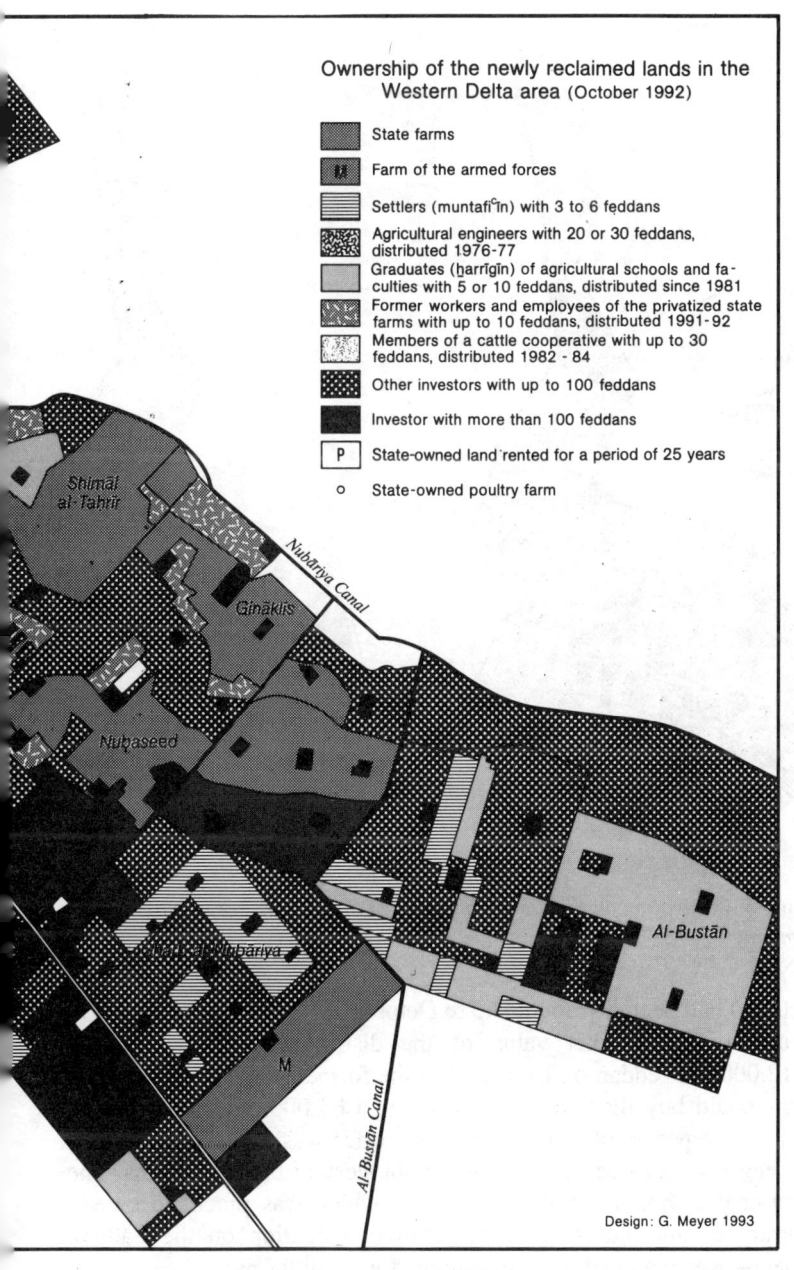

Figure 4 *Ownership of the Newly Reclaimed Lands in the Western Delta Area (October 1992)*

Figure 5 *Cultivation on the Remaining Area of the Mariut Agriculture Company*

hectares) had been distributed up to October 1992 in the area shown in Figure 4. The market value of the distributed land was about LE12,000 per feddan on average, but the former workers on the state farms could buy their plots at a price of LE1,000 per feddan, to be paid over a period of thirty years. This offer was so generous that it was eagerly accepted by all former employees of the state farms. The traditional technique of flood irrigation which was practiced here—contrary to the sophisticated center-pivot irrigation on the Salhiya project—was regarded as quite suitable for small farms.

During interviews with many of these new landowners in the autumn of 1992, it turned out that, in general, they were satisfied with the yields of their first harvest. But they complained bitterly about the collapse of farm gate prices. The new farmers claimed that they could sell their main summer crops, maize and peanuts in particular, only at prices below production costs.

The majority of the other old-new lands owned by the state farms were mainly sold by auction in small plots of three to thirty feddans. In most cases, these plots were bought by farmers from nearby villages in the Delta. Many of them had sold half a feddan or less of highly expensive old agricultural land in order to spend this money on the acquisition of a plot of newly reclaimed land which could be up to ten times as large, and would hopefully be sufficient to guarantee a family income for themselves or their sons.

The public agricultural companies responsible for the sale of the state farms had also tried to sell larger plots of old-new lands to big private investors, but such investors were only seldom to be found. One of the reasons for this was high costs to be expected from the upgrading of the traditional flood irrigation system, and the appalling state of the drainage network, the maintenance of which had been seriously neglected in some areas since its construction in the 1960s.

Other potential investors refrained from any engagement in the old-new lands due to the failure of some earlier attempts to privatize large state farms as a whole. A good example in this case is the former six thousand feddan state farm, east of Nubaseed (see Figure 4), which was acquired in 1978 by the Nile Agricultural Development Company (NADCO), a private investment company with 70 percent Saudi and 30 percent Egyptian capital. This was once a project with 1,500 dairy cows, as well as a thousand bulls and five thousand sheep for fattening, in addition to the cultivation of 1,500 feddans of fruit trees and two thousand feddans of vegetable production. The project employed five hundred permanent workers, and up to three thousand daily laborers. This farm is now completely run down and has closed operations, with the exception of 2,500 feddans which were leased in 1992 to sharecroppers for the cultivation of water melons. Bad management and insufficient investment to upgrade the technical equipment and solve the problems of inefficient irrigation and drainage were the main reasons for this failure.

A similar fate seemed to threaten the Dallah farm, southwest of Nubaseed. A Saudi Arabian investment company, owned by members of the royal family, had rented this former state farm of 6,200 feddans in 1984 in order to establish the most advanced and largest dairy project in Africa with twelve thousand cows. A Swedish company was the main contractor for setting up this highly capital-intensive enterprise, which started its operation with four thousand Friesian cows imported from Denmark.

In spite of its modern technology, the project did not make any profit, but accumulated losses of between LE22 million to LE30 million per year. This is not at all surprising if one analyses the management structure: the managing director, who changed almost every six months, was based at the company's headquarters in Cairo and visited the farm no more than once a week. The other leading staff members lived with their families in Alexandria. They did not arrive at the farm before ten o'clock in the morning and used to leave around one in the afternoon. With hardly any control by the staff, the motivation of the farm workers was extremely low.

The situation changed completely when, finally in April 1992, the company found a well-trained agricultural expert who was prepared to take over the position of managing director. He set up his office on the farm, where he also lived permanently. He immediately dismissed all fifteen leading staff members; three of whom were accused of fraud, embezzlement, and theft and sentenced to imprisonment. New employees were selected for the vacant positions on the condition of agreement to move with their families to the farm. Bachelors also had to stay on the farm the whole week, and were only allowed to leave for the weekend. Every day at 7 a.m., the staff members had to report to the managing director. An efficient system of work control was established, combined with high financial incentives for good labor performance and wage deductions for bad work. Five months after the new director took charge of the farm, the project recorded its first profit. This example is quite typical and underlines that the quality of management is one of the deciding factors in determining whether, in the majority of cases, an agricultural project in the new lands fails or succeeds.

## Distribution of Land Newly Reclaimed by State Companies

Al-Bustan, Gharb al-Nubariya, and the area irrigated with water from the Nasr Canal, west of the desert Cairo–Alexandria road (Figure 4), have been reclaimed by public companies since the 1980s. As a consequence of the liberalization policy, most of this new-new land was immediately distributed to the private sector, with the exception of the Sixth of October Farm. Located in the south of Gharb al-Nubariya, this ten thousand feddan project is operated by the armed forces. About five hundred soldiers are engaged in taking care of a thousand Friesian dairy cows, which are mainly fed with the production of 3,300 feddans of fodder crops, irrigated by twenty-two center-pivots. In addition, cereals and beans are grown on 2,700 feddans irrigated by sprinklers, fruit trees and grapes are cultivated on 1,800 feddans equipped with drip irrigation, and different kinds of vegetables are produced in 176 greenhouses. Most of the agricultural production of the farm is used by the armed forces.

The other newly reclaimed lands were distributed to three main groups: graduates from high schools and universities (*kharrigin*); small settlers, mainly former agricultural workers with their families (*muntafi'in*); and private investors *(mustasmirin)*.

## Graduates as Farmers in the New Lands

The distribution of newly reclaimed land to young graduates is part of a nationwide program which was launched by the government in 1981. At first, this program was only intended for graduates from agricultural branches of high schools and agricultural faculties. But since 1986, it has served as a general employment program for all kinds of graduates from high schools and universities.

The first five hundred graduates—most of them agricultural engineers—who benefited from this program, received, in 1981, between ten and fourteen feddans which had been cultivated before by state farms in the area of Mariyut and Shimal al-Tahrir. Four new settlements, each with 125 'villas,' were constructed for the graduates and their families. When the author visited these villages in 1992, it turned out that no more than 15 percent of the houses were permanently occupied by the graduates and their families. The other 'villas' were either empty or served as seasonal accommodation. Only about 40 percent of the graduates were still actively involved in farming operations. The others had either leased or sold their land, mainly to farmers from the Delta.

Similar conditions were found in the areas of al-Bustan and Bangar al-Sukkar, where nearly 45,000 feddans of new-new lands had been distributed in plots of five feddans to about eleven thousand graduates between 1986 and 1992. A total of thirty-one new villages were constructed here, each with small two-room core houses for two hundred to seven hundred families. One of these villages was created exclusively for young women who had to be single, in the hope that this would encourage young men wishing to start a family life to settle in the desert. The vast majority of the graduates had no agricultural background. Many of them had received arts, law, or accounting degrees. Attracted by the highly subsidized terms under which this land was offered, they had eagerly applied for such a small farm, often for purely speculative reasons. Due to their lack of experience in agriculture, it is not surprising that most of them stayed in Cairo and

Alexandria, where they looked for other jobs while either leasing, or even illegally selling their newly reclaimed land. Only a small proportion of the graduates, in particular those trained in agriculture, took up farming operations by employing wage laborers or by entering into sharecropping or partnership arrangements with agricultural workers. Other farms are managed by brothers or fathers of the graduates.

Under such conditions, one has to be rather skeptical about the economic sense of the target stated in the current five-year plan to provide graduates with 250,000 feddans of newly reclaimed land between 1992 and 1997. Such a plan is only understandable in terms of social considerations to cope with the growing problem of unemployment among high school-leavers and university graduates. But as long as there are no directives aimed at selecting only agricultural graduates—with preference for sons and daughters of farmers—it is unlikely that the productivity of this newly reclaimed land will be maximized.

## Distribution of New Lands to Small Settlers (*Muntafi'in*)

The program of distributing land to *muntafi'in*, that is, the beneficiaries of the agrarian reform, was created immediately after the revolution in 1952, when expropriated land was handed over to small settlers. These beneficiaries were selected according to socioeconomic criteria, such as experience in agriculture as landless workers or tenants, and family size, and they were expected to cultivate their land within the framework of an agricultural cooperative. Since the 1960s, the same concept has been applied for the distribution of newly reclaimed lands. Early examples of this kind are situated in the area of Mariyut and al-Nahda, where former agricultural workers employed in land reclamation received five to six feddans in 1967. The author studied the farms of these *muntafi'in* in 1977 (Meyer 1978) and in 1992. Contrary to the negative experience with settlements built for graduates, here all houses were still occupied by the families of the *muntafi'in*. Nearly all of them were running their small farms in such an efficient way that they had improved the soil fertility and agricultural productivity of the new land to a level almost comparable with the situation in the old lands of the Delta.

Basically, the same tendency was found in the new-new lands distributed between 1986 and 1989 to *muntafi'in* in the area of al-Bustan and Bangar al-Sukkar. The sons of farmers or former agricultural laborers had received a core house and five feddans at a price far below the market value. They were expected to repay this sum with an interest rate of 10 percent in fifteen annual installments, after a grace period of at least six years. It was quite obvious that the production levels achieved by these small settlers with long experience in agriculture were in most cases higher than on the farms of graduates in neighboring areas.

## Sale of New Lands to Private Investors

The majority of the investors in the area of Gharb al-Nubariya and al-Bustan had bought around twenty feddans of new-new land between 1982 and 1986. Thirty percent of the price had to be paid immediately; the rest was due after a grace period of two to four years, in up to ten annual installments, with an interest rate of 15 percent. Most of these small investors had well-paid jobs in Cairo and Alexandria, or worked as labor migrants in other Arab countries. Roughly one quarter of them were speculators who sold their new farms within ten years. The other small investors employed, in most cases, one of their relatives or an agricultural engineer, who managed the farm with at least one permanent worker and a number of seasonal laborers. A typical farm of this kind devoted about 60 percent of its land, on average, to growing fruit trees and grapes. The remaining area was mainly used to grow berseem, and rented for grazing land to sheep-rearing semi-nomads. Some wheat and vegetables were also grown.

Larger farms with more than a hundred feddans were in most cases set up by family enterprises based in Cairo and Alexandria, which were also engaged in other sectors of the economy, like trade, construction, or industry. Many of them are supported financially by Saudi investors, who have a significant share in the business, and by wealthy migrants, who had worked in the Gulf region. Most of these farms are highly profit-oriented enterprises, equipped with the latest American or West European technology, and often assisted by Israeli experts. Their agricultural produce is of first-class quality and is mainly sold to customers abroad.

The range of agricultural export production includes: the cultivation of strawberries which are sent by air freight to Scandinavia; the growing of early potatoes for customers in the Gulf states and Germany; the cultivation of early vegetables under plastic tunnels and in greenhouses for export to Saudi Arabia; and the large-scale production of fruits and grapes. Even bananas are cultivated here in huge greenhouses. Thanks to Israeli know-how, the quality of these fruits is so good that they can compete on European markets.

Typical of many similar enterprises is the 2,200 feddan farm in Figure 6, with center-pivot irrigation to cultivate wheat and fodder

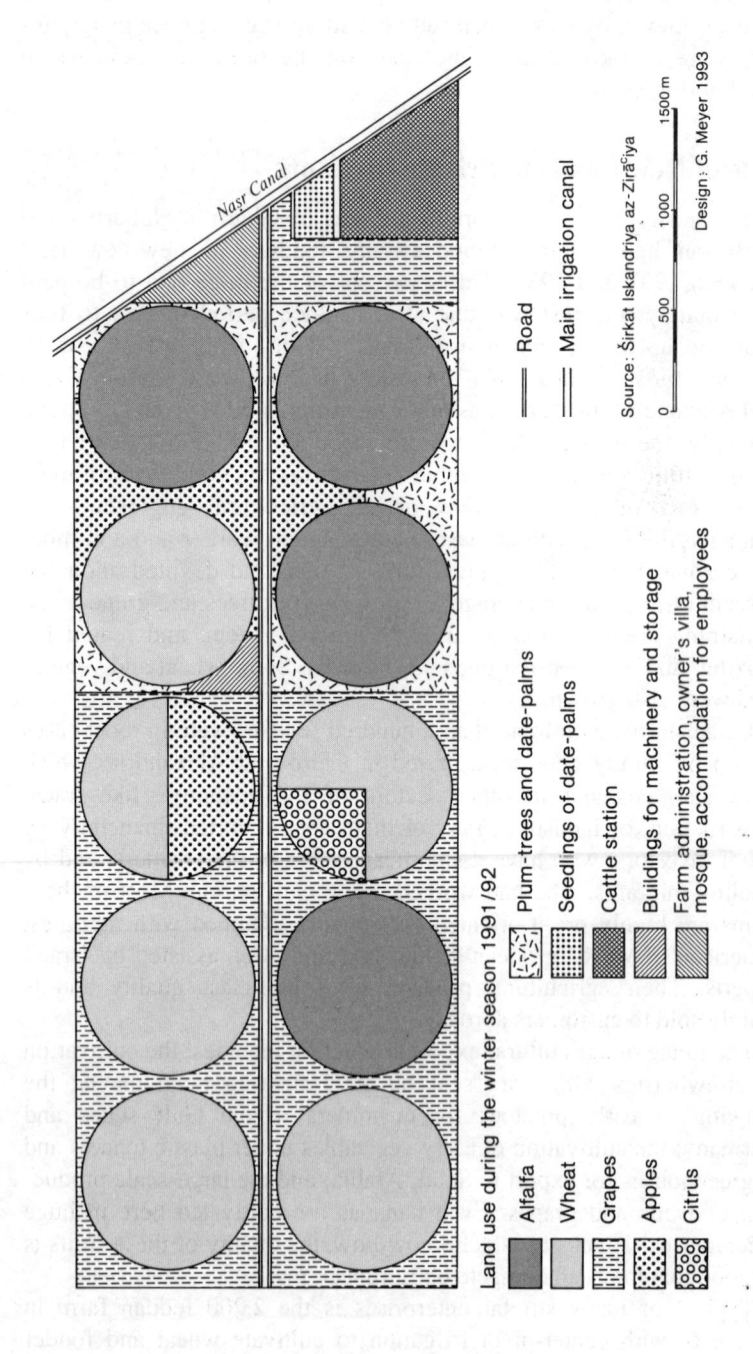

Figure 6 *Land Use on a Private 2,200 Feddan Farm in the Area of Gharb al-Nubariya*

crops for about two thousand dairy cows. In between the circular fields fruit trees are grown by drip-irrigation. The majority of these enterprises are quite successful. But there have also been some failures, like that of the 6,200 feddan farm west of the Nasr Canal, which was set up by one of the biggest Islamic shareholder companies. After this enterprise went bankrupt, due to illegal financial manipulations, the farm was deserted, with the exception of 270 greenhouses rented for vegetable production by some of the company's former employees. But even this activity collapsed when a storm destroyed all greenhouses in February 1992.

## Evaluation of the Different Types of Farms in the New Lands

Summing up the latest developments in the new lands, Table 1 provides an overview about the socioeconomic efficiency of specific types of farms in the new lands, which are the outcome of different agricultural policies before and after the introduction of the latest reforms. What kind of farms are most suited to providing new jobs for the growing population and which of them are most profitable? As a result of the author's interviews with the owners or managers of 470 farms, Table 1 shows the major types of farms that exist in the new lands along the western Delta, differentiated according to the average number of permanent and seasonal jobs per hundred feddans (forty-two hectares), and the average net profit.

State farms are obviously the worst choice for the cultivation of new lands. The number of permanent jobs is far below average, and the profitability is extremely low.

The program to distribute newly reclaimed land to graduates—so much favored by the government—is rather successful only in terms of creating employment, but in terms of agricultural profitability it is bound to be a failure, due to the lack of agricultural experience of the graduates, and because most of them are not interested in working on their own land.

Quite the opposite applies to the *muntafi'in*, former agricultural laborers or sons of farmers from the old lands in the Nile Valley and Delta, who live with their families on their small holdings. Here, by far the highest number of people are provided with a source of income, and agricultural profitability is also relatively high.

Last but not least, the economically most successful farms belong to private investors cultivating three hundred to a thousand feddans (that is, 126–420 hectares). They employ relatively few permanent workers, but the number of seasonal laborers is extremely high. These are

Table 1 *Evaluation of Farm Types in the Newly Reclaimed Lands*

| Farm type | Jobs per 100 feddan permanent | seasonal * | Profit per 100 feddan ** |
|---|---|---|---|
| 1. State farms | 3.5 | 3.9 | – – – |
| 2. Graduates (*kharrigin*) | 19.3 | 6.7 | – – ( – ) |
| 3. Settlers (*muntafi'in*) | 69.3 | 1.3 | + |
| 4. Investors who bought old-new land from state farms | 29.2 | 3.9 | – ( + ) |
| 5. Investors who bought new-new land reclaimed by the public sector | | | |
| -2–15 fed | 41.3 | 2.0 | + ( + + ) |
| -16–30 fed | 18.4 | 4.2 | – ( + ) |
| -31–100 fed | 14.4 | 5.6 | – ( + ) |
| -101–300 fed | 9.4 | 10.8 | + ( + + ) |
| -301–1000 fed | 7.9 | 13.9 | + + ( + + + ) |
| -1001–6200 fed | 5.7 | 8.1 | – ( + ) |
| 6. Former workers of privatized state farms | 35.5 | 3.0 | – ( + ) |

\* The period of employment of the seasonal labor force was summed up for one year and transformed into the equivalent of permanent jobs.

\*\* The scale for the average profit in 1992 ranges from + + + (extremely high) to – – – (extremely low). The symbols in brackets indicate the profit which is to be expected by recently established farms when the quality of the soil and the newly planted fruit trees will reach the average level of productivity.

mainly girls and young women who are brought every day by labor contractors from nearby villages in the Delta.

## Prospects for Future Development and Expansion of the New Lands

Summing up the latest economic changes in the new lands, it is obvious that agricultural development in these regions has improved significantly due to the policy of privatization and liberalization. Small farmers and experienced private investors with medium-sized estates, in particular, have proved to be much more efficient than state farms in the utilization of the newly reclaimed lands.

This does not mean, however, that turning the desert into agricultural land is necessarily the best solution for Egypt's problems of insufficient increase in agricultural output and rising unemployment. Concerning the economic viability of land reclamation and the sustainability of farming in the new lands, one has to keep in mind the enormous public subsidies for the construction and maintenance of the infrastructure in the desert and for the provision of irrigation water—which is a very scarce resource. Most experts agree that investment in the improvement of the irrigation system in the old lands of the Nile Valley and the Delta would raise agricultural production to a much higher level than the same amount of capital spent on reclaiming desert land with extremely poor soils.

Even more serious is the question about sufficient water supply. Egypt uses already more water than the annual 55.5 billion cubic meters share of Nile water to which the country is entitled according to the 1959 Nile Waters Agreement with Sudan (Chesworth 1990). In spite of the utilization of this extra water, many farmers in the Delta suffer from serious shortages of irrigation water, mainly due to the recent massive expansion of rice cultivation. This situation will deteriorate further after the opening of the al-Salam Canal in October 1997, which is planned to divert five billion cubic meters of water per year from the Nile to the area west of the Suez Canal and to North Sinai (see Figure 7) to be used for the irrigation of some 620,000 feddans of newly reclaimed land (Halawi 1997).

At least the same quantity of water is needed for the expansion of agricultural land in the Western Desert in connection with the New Delta project in southern Egypt. Here, the construction of the 590 kilometer-long Shaykh Zayid Canal started in January 1997. This canal is intended to carry water from Lake Nasser into the New Valley Governorate to irrigate as much as one million feddans of newly reclaimed land.

Various studies have revealed that the 3.5 billion cubic meters of water needed can be made available annually through the rationing of irrigation and drainage water. Another water saving measure would entail a 50 percent reduction in the area allocated for rice cultivation, down to 500,000 feddans from the current level of 1.4 million feddans. Such a move would save around 3.5 billion cubic meters of water per year. Similarly, another 1.5 billion cubic meters of water can be saved by improving irrigation technique (Qassem 1997). When added together, this still means a shortage of at least 1.5 billion cubic meters of water, not to mention a potentially high cost incurred in the form of reducing rice production.

Under these circumstances, and taking into account the unreliability of the Nile water supply—during the period 1972–1989, the average naturalized annual flows at Aswan were seven billion cubic meters

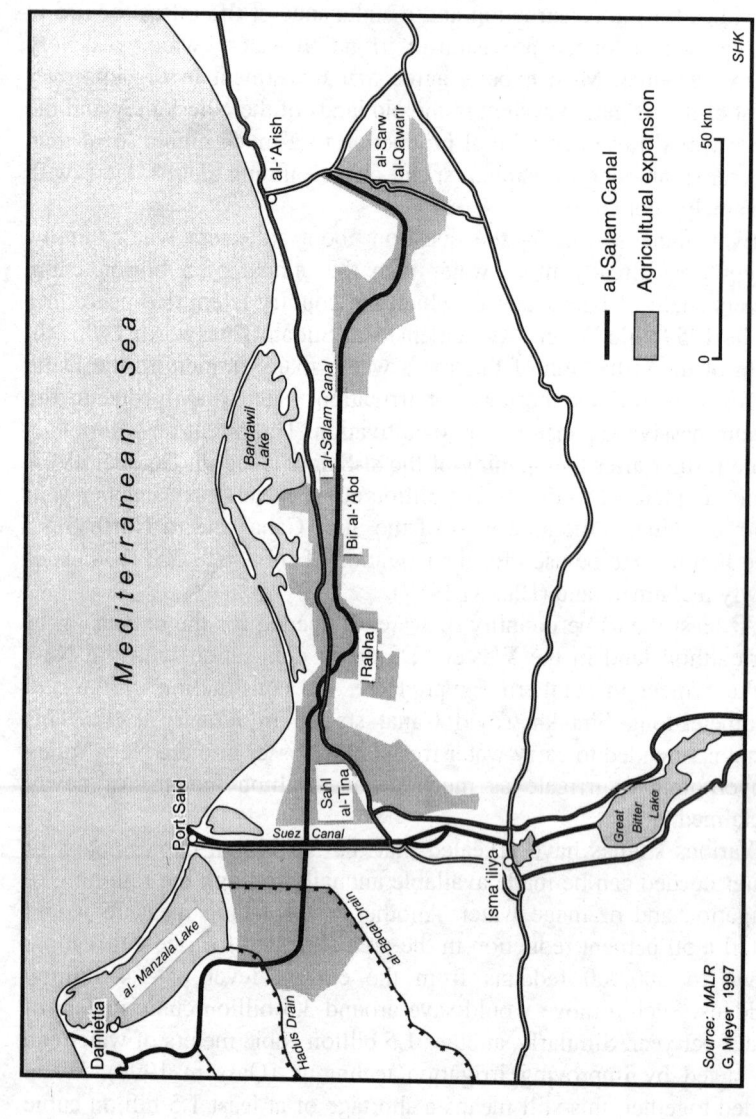

Figure 7 Agricultural Expansion in North Sinai

below the expected average flow on which the Nile Water Agreement was based (Evans 1990)—one has to be very skeptical about the sustainability of the new land reclamation projects.

## References

Abu Hidb, Fu'ad. 1992. "Reclamation of New Lands and Their Utilization." Conference on *Strategies of Egyptian Agriculture in the 1990s* (in Arabic). Cairo.

Chesworth, Peter M. 1990. "The History of Water Use in Sudan and Egypt" in P. P. Howell and J. A. Allan, eds. *The Nile. Resource Evaluation, Resource Management, Hydropolitics and Legal Issues*. London: School of Oriental and African Studies. pp. 41–57.

El-Din, Gamal Essam. 1993. "The Quagmire of El-Salhiya." *Al-Ahram Weekly* no. 142:6, November 11, 1993.

Evans, T. E. "History of the Nile Flows." in P. P. Howell and J. A. Allan, eds. *The Nile. Resource Evaluation, Resource Management, Hydropolitics and Legal Issues*. London: School of Oriental and African Studies. pp. 5–40.

Halawi, Jailan. 1997. "Debating the Development Agenda." *Al-Ahram Weekly* no. 153:2, January 27, 1994.

Meyer, Günter. 1978. "Erschliessung und Entwicklung der Aegyptischen Neulandgebiete." *Erdkunde* 32:212–27.

Qassem, Mona. 1997. "Toshki in the Balance." *Al-Ahram Weekly* no. 158:8, March 3, 1994.

# VII
## DISPUTE SETTLEMENT: SOCIETY AND POLITICS

# 18

# Men of Authority – Documents of Authority: Notes on Customary Law in Upper Egypt

HANS-CHRISTIAN KORSHOLM NIELSEN

## Introduction

Descriptions of traditional courts and customary law (*'urf*) in the Middle East are most commonly found under headings such as 'Bedouin justice' or 'Bedouin law,'[1] and describe conditions among the Bedouins of the desert; while studies concerned with the subject among sedentary people[2] and, in particular, among the rural population of the Nile Valley, are very rare.[3]

This paper is a preliminary excursion into this field, based on a collection of documents obtained during ethnographic field research carried out in the district of Idfu, Aswan governorate, Upper Egypt in the 1990s. I focus on how the authority of such documents is established, and how this authority is related to the men who issue the documents. I also focus on how the power of persuasion is established, and what means are implemented to make people comply with the content of these documents.[4]

## The District of Idfu

The district of Idfu is the northernmost in the Governorate of Aswan. The main city and district capital is Idfu. The population of Idfu district is about 300,000, of which more than 70,000 live in the city of Idfu.

As in other areas of Upper Egypt, the dominant occupation is farming and the main cash crop is sugarcane; although recent developments have encouraged a change toward other crops. Farming is intensive and dependent on irrigation, and the plots are small. Today 'work as a civil servant' is also widespread, and even in the more remote villages, a large share of the population obtains at least a part of their income from government positions. A few larger industries are also found in the district: most notable are the ferrosilicon complex, which employs more than 2,000 people; a phosphate plant; and the Idfu sugar factory which, during the season, also employs more than 2,000 workers. The city of Idfu is a popular stop for Nile cruise ships because of its famous Horus temple, and quite a few people obtain their income from the tourist industry, selling souvenirs or transporting the visitors from the river landing to the temple. As district capital, the city also contains a number of public institutions, such as a district court, a general hospital, the headquarters of the district police, the telephone exchange, and the premises of the local and district councils.

The majority of the people in the district claim descent from the tribes of the Arabian Peninsula, and although the term 'tribe' *(qabila)* is used in numerous, and often contradictory ways, covering everything from a group of people living together in one area, to lineage-based organizations, the idiom of tribalism is still a significant marker of local identity.[5]

Most famous of the numerically dominant tribes are the Ga'afra and the 'Ababda, but the number of smaller 'tribes' is very large. The Ga'afra claim descent from the House of the Prophet, and thereby hold a special status as *ashraf*; while the 'Ababda, one of the tribes formerly inhabiting the Eastern Desert, claim a more modest line of descent. Over the last hundred years, the majority of the people from the 'Ababda have settled in the Nile Valley.

A number of villages or hamlets in the district are solely inhabited by a section of one of the tribes, but the majority comprise a mixture of people. There is a broad variation in the social composition of the different villages, and the characteristics or identities ascribed to the inhabitants of one village by their neighbors are numerous.

## Dispute Settlement

When disputes or hostilities arise between villagers or townspeople in Upper Egypt, on such a scale that the disputing parties decide—or are persuaded—that the intervention of an outsider is necessary in order to reach a solution to the dispute, two different, although in many ways complementary, institutions are commonly utilized.

On the one hand, a case may be brought before the official courts in order to engage the official legal system in finding a solution to the dispute. In the district of Idfu, a case would be taken to the district courts, situated in the city. This is often done, and the seat of the district court is a busy and bustling place, that demonstrates how some of the people of the district have what, to a European, seems like an 'American' approach to the legal system—starting legal proceedings whenever an opportunity arises.

On the other hand, a solution may also be sought through the system of traditional 'reconciliation councils,' which in Upper Egypt are known by a number of different names, but most commonly as *majlis al-sulh, majlis 'urfi,* or *majlis al-'arab*. When a case has been settled by one of these councils it is common to prepare a document which states a number of details from the meeting. The documents mention who the parties were, who presided at the meeting, the central facts of the case, the adjudication of the council, and often a number of sanctions which may be imposed if the involved parties do not comply with the council's 'ruling.' These documents are issued under a range of titles such as *mahdar sulh* and *mahdar tahkim* ('statement of reconciliation' and 'statement of arbitration'), but may also be issued without titles.

The following discussion is based upon a study of fifty documents drafted within the last twenty-five years in the district of Idfu. The documents are usually handwritten and issued in triplicate; one for each of the parties and one for the council. The content of the documents is brief and concise, and includes numerous detailed references to the local geography, local agricultural practices, and other features of the area. In brief, they are condensed records of who, what, and when.

Although keeping the documents as evidence of the solution reached by the councils is most important, they are not treated with any great respect. They are simply stored at home in a cupboard or a chest along with other written material such as old school books, scraps of paper, or old bills.

The writing of documents in connection with settlements is often described as being a recent innovation[6] brought about by the pace of modern life. People move around a great deal, and where there once was daily personal contact between those witnessing the proclamation of the 'ruling' and those involved in the case, this is now not always the case. These documents are, in many ways, notes of what is fundamentally an oral practice. This is in line with the commonly described predominance of the oral over the written in legal matters under Islamic jurisprudence. However, there are also other reasons for the recent dissemination of this practice, such as the increasing rate of literacy[7] and, perhaps more significantly, a tendency toward emulating official administrative procedures, most Egyptians being well versed in the importance which official bureaucracy ascribes to 'documents' and signatures. Nevertheless, a widespread notion among older people is that the writing of these documents is a result of the rapid decline in traditional virtues such as closeness, respect, and honesty, and that this makes it necessary to keep a written record of what has been decided.

The documents are in principle 'public,' because the information they contain has already been announced by a council, and often to a large crowd of men. Although these documents are secondary in the reconciliation process, I still found that, as has been noted by Brinkley Messick, "Documents are the meeting point for the law and its social uses" (Messick 1990: 61), or in this case, the meeting point between the tradition and its social uses. At the same time, the contents offer a detailed insight into numerous aspects of the day-to-day reality of Upper Egypt.

It should be noted that the term *sulh*, often translated as 'amicable truce' (see Schacht 1964), pertaining to both the reconciliation councils and the documents, is applied in numerous situations where a reconciliation is reached between members of a community, and may cover a number of different situations; from cases where men from a local community interfere in order to stop quarrels between spouses, to cases where an official *majlis* is appointed and thousands of men gather to witness the proclamation of its adjudication. An almost classic example of the latter is in cases where a truce is reached between families or tribal sections which have been engaged in a blood feud. In a way these two examples—the quarreling spouses and the blood feud—depict the range of situations where the community experiencing the problems acts in order to create a truce between disputing parties in order to restore stability to the society.

In minor cases involving few people, no actual council is appointed and no documents are written. Usually those who interfere in such cases are an ad hoc group of villagers, who take the initiative and offer to look into the matter. The holding of large meetings and the drafting of documents only occur in cases large enough to merit the appointment of a council.

The documents from which this presentation takes its point of departure are all from cases which, both in intensity and in the number of people they involve, fall somewhere in between the two extremes mentioned above. They all deal with subjects which are related to the civic legal code, and cover a range which includes disputes over inheritance, over land, and where one party is accused of insulting the other.

As mentioned, the councils are known by a number of names: first of all, '*majlis al-sulh*,' which indicates that the function of the council is to reach an 'amicable truce' between the two parties, which is of course different from the objectives of the official courts, whose purpose is to reach a verdict without taking into consideration whether any settlement or truce between the disputing parties has been reached, or whether the parties agree to the verdict. The second name, '*majlis al-'arab*,' contains a reference to the general idea that the settlement of disputes between people by a council consisting of men of an established reputation, is similar to, or a reenactment of, what is believed to be standard classical practice among the tribes of the Arabian Peninsula. This name also refers to a notion mentioned earlier that the majority of the population are descended from the Arab tribes which settled in Egypt in the seventh century. The third name, '*majlis 'urfi*,' meaning council of traditional lore/tradition (*'urf*), indicates that the settlements reached by the councils are based on 'tradition' rather than the civic legal code or *shari'a*. However, on the other hand, it should be noted that quite often people express the view that *'urf* is *shari'a*, or at least should be understood as an extension of the religiously based legal code, in the sense that *'urf* specifies, for instance, the nature of a particular compensation being sanctioned by *shari'a*.

The legal base is, in other words, the tradition in a non-specified form. No written codes are found, but knowledge about what is right and wrong, tradition, and education in the skills of mediating and negotiating are transmitted from individual to individual, through participation in the councils as mediators or as spectators. The number of standardized solutions, cases where a right or a wrong, or a particular compensation may be applied automatically, are limited. Inquiries about what *'urf* is are most commonly met with a reference to the whole concept of the reconciliation councils and the decisions they reach, and only rarely do people mention the known rules about such issues as compensation in cases of injury, theft, or adultery.[8]

In ideal terms, *'urf* is to be understood as a practical discourse articulated through the rulings pronounced by the councils—a description, or an indication, of the content of this discourse would demand a large number of different cases dealing with various different subjects in order to disclose a consensus in the verdicts. But as Bourdieu noted; "customary law always seems to pass from particular case to particular case, from the specific misdeed to the specific sanction, never expressly formulating the fundamental principles which 'rational' law spells out explicitly (that is, all men are equal in honor)" (Bourdieu 1977:16). The accumulation of knowledge that takes place is, simultaneously, closely related to the individuals participating in the councils, and especially to the limited group of men who are mentioned below; it is 'homeostatic' in the sense used by Goody and Watt (1963), and not reified in a body of legal text. *'Urf* mainly depends on precedents, and a general idea of what is seen as being proper. The provocation and crisis caused by the dispute makes the particular issue at hand explicit, and the central function of the *majlis* is that it should ideally formulate a solution based on common—but not articulated—knowledge. In the terminology of Bourdieu, the members of the council should "awaken," so to speak, "the schemes of perception and appreciation deposited in their incorporated state in every member of the group, i.e. the dispositions of the habitus" (Bourdieu 1977:17).

## The Authorization

Before going into a more detailed description of the documents it should be noted that the writing of these constitutes the last part of the process of reconciliation. However, early in the process a document known as the *mahdar tafwid* (statement of authorization) is signed. The purpose of this is to get the agreement of the parties that they will accept whatever conclusion is reached by the *majlis*.[9] This is one of the central measures in supporting the authority of the council, investing it with a power which may force the acceptance of the verdict. And through this, the disputing parties are forced to concede a degree of their social person to the council. When the statement of authorization is signed, it is done before the *majlis*, whose members also sign as witnesses. The authorization usually contains a clause stating an amount of money which the parties are obliged to pay if they violate the ruling of the *majlis* or—in other words—the statement of authorization they have signed. This amount may be anything from a hundred pounds to cases where 'blank checks' are signed by the parties, and where it is up to the *majlis* to decide the proper amount and the use of the money.

It should be noted that it is very rare that this money is actually paid; the rules of the game always leave room for a receiving part to drop the claim. Often this is linked to the aspect of honor implicit in such a gesture.

## The Councils

The selection of the members of the council is based on numerous considerations, an important one of which is that they should be acceptable to both of the disputing parties. Certain rules for the selection are followed, where each party has the opportunity to turn down persons suggested for the council, on the grounds that they will not be favorable to his case, or at least not impartial. Curiously enough, one of the documents mentions the possibility of appeal, that is, the final clause states that if any of the parties disagrees with the ruling reached, the council is ready to be 'tried' by a new council. This may seem contradictory to the whole idea of the parties handing over all rights to the council, but it is an indication that the skills, power, and impartiality of the appointed council are also on trial.

The idea of the disinterestedness of the council is always a major concern. I am of course not talking about the interest which individual members may have in sitting on the council in order to enhance their personal status—an aspect which is in itself very important. While other anthropologists describe cases where the mediators are deeply involved, and where the outcome of the case is of great importance to them (for example, Sally Falk Moore 1977), the arrangements surrounding the formation of the *majlis al-sulh* are focused, to a large degree, on removing doubts about the impartiality of the council.

First of all, the mediators are chosen from a group of outsiders, that is, in a dispute between two sections of the same tribe, the mediators are chosen from outside the tribe; where the two disputing parties are from two different tribes, mediators are called in from a third tribe; if the dispute is internal—between members of an extended family—the mediators are chosen from outside the family. In addition, men from a group of more or less 'professional truce-makers' from the district are also usually engaged.

This group of men consists of twenty to thirty highly respected, mainly elderly men, who take part in most councils held in the district. Negotiations may be initiated without their participation, but during the later stages, they are consulted and actively involved in almost every case. When participating, they often take a leading role in the negotiations and in formulating the rulings. Very often the documents finalizing the process are kept with them. Their reputation as 'truce-makers,' and their knowledge about the tradition is commonly recognized among people in the district. Some of the men in this group are well-educated, while others have received only limited formal education. Most are farmers of a certain economic standing, and they are all known to have a large network of friends and relatives, and their homes—their *diwans* or *khaymas*—are natural meeting points where gossip and information is exchanged. Their knowledge about who is who, and who is related to whom is often encyclopedic. The men of this group are well aware of their own status and position in the system, as well as that of others in the group. To some extent they constitute a fraternity based on common influence, knowledge, and experience.

Although their involvement in this field is based on their individual reputation, their status is often enhanced by their family background.

A large part of them are from the families of the former *'umda* (village leader). In those few places where the position of *'umda* is still officially recognized as a part of the administrative system, they might occupy that post, otherwise they often hold other positions which are related to the old administrative system of rural Egypt (such as, *shaykh al-balad*). Beside the general respect surrounding the *'umda* families, their presence is also related to the formerly ascribed function of the *'umda* as the local representative of justice. In the earlier days, the *'umda* was "given statuary authority to 'adjudicate' minor offenses, to levy small fines, and to imprison for short periods," although "the authority [was] specifically withheld over disputes involving land" (Hill 1979:39).

Today, many of these men take up positions in the modern political and administrative system, being elected leaders or members of the different local or district councils. It is also common for other members of families which have produced men famous for their participation on the councils to be involved in politics at the governorate and national level.

## The Documents

Besides stating the date and the place, the documents start by enumerating the men sitting on the council. The number of men and their position is indicative of the severity of the dispute. In extreme cases, the governor and the chief of police may preside over the *majlis*. Usually, however, the list contains men from all walks of life who command respect in the local community, and at least a few representatives from the group mentioned above. In addition, the councils often include a number of experts, such as land inspectors, who are invited due to their professional capacities. On the other hand, in cases where professional lawyers appear on the council, they do so on account of their personal standing and not their professional experience.

The second clause of the documents mentions the disputing parties, who are seen as the legal 'parties' *(taraf/atraf)*. A party may either be an individual, a group of men (most often relatives), or it may be a whole section of a village, often described as the tribe of so-and-so. During the meeting, the 'tribe' is represented by a limited number of persons, who are then responsible to the *majlis*. Minors and women are most often represented by guardians. However, in a number of cases concerned with inheritance claims, females appear before the *majlis* in person.

The third clause of the documents usually states the 'facts' of the case which are reached through interviewing the parties and the witnesses, and, most often, from the inspection of the 'scene of the crime' by a group of men from the *majlis*. The negotiations are of the utmost importance; through these, the facts are sorted into those of importance and those of non-importance, and they are arranged in a new narrative—the one recorded in a condensed form in the documents. This narrative is the one to which the opposing parties should be ready to agree and contrasts with the narratives created by the disputing parties and their supporters. And although it is not the 'truth' about the case, it is a version acceptable to both parties and to the community, or at least one to which a temporary consensus may be reached.[10]

This new narrative is created through a bargaining process where the two parties have a certain influence—they may try to have certain facts included which they find important, and they may try to leave some out. Certain facts may be rejected outright. The successful mediator is always making sure that room is left for a retreat, in order to avoid the whole process going into deadlock. That this negotiation process involves the integrity of the individual concerned is reflected in what is referred to as the '*mulaka*,' where members of the council take one of the parties aside in order to persuade them to accept the truce proposed by the council.[11] It is easier to accept the rearrangement of the story, or a reorganization of the facts, when this is done in privacy, shielded from the gaze of the spectators or the community. The new narrative is, ideally, invested with a certain power, or may have a soothing quality which may impel the parties to accept it; the narrative has rearranged the facts while leaving room for the parties to accept it without suffering humiliation.

Following the clause or clauses containing the 'facts' comes the actual verdict. Here, the council announces what should be done; for example, a piece of land should be divided or exchanged for another, a wall should be removed or rebuilt, windows should be closed in order to avoid people from looking into private quarters, or an irrigation canal should be cleaned in order to ensure that all farmers in an area receive their share of the water.

Then follows a clause which, in most cases, states that the adjudication should be valid both according to tradition and according to the court, meaning that this should be the final statement concerning the case, and that none of the parties have the right to try to raise the issue in the official courts. In some cases, the documents state that if any of the parties do not comply with the ruling of the *majlis*, the other party has the right to bring the case before a judge. In other words, the legal system which the *majlis al-sulh* is to some degree seen as challenging, is invoked to sanction the verdict of the council. It is worth noting that it is generally accepted that if a case which has been settled through the traditional system of reconciliation councils is later taken to the court, the judge will favor the party which is supported by the ruling of the *majlis*. In some instances, the court has proved to be reluctant to take up cases on the basis that they have already been settled through the *majlis al-sulh*.

The final clause of the documents always contains a religious quote invoking the Supreme Witness. After this come the signatures (or thumb prints) of the disputing parties and the men of the council. Often a stamp—it may be that of the local popular council—is added to the document, giving it additional authority.

As indicated above, each step in the reconciliation process and each clause of the documents described above contain elements which are intended to persuade the disputing parties to follow the adjudication of the *majlis*. Most important is the idea of handing over all responsibility to the council through the *mahdar tafwid*, where the parties agree to abide by whatever conclusion the council may reach, and, of course, by the possible financial or legal penalties. But numerous other elements partake in the creation of the authority of the council and the ensuing documents.

First of all, there are the members of the *majlis*, who invest their personal authority and their persuasive powers in the process, based on their standing or the standing of their families. Secondly, there is the public announcement of the agreement; it is common for cases of a certain magnitude to be concluded in front of a large gathering. Here, the agreement is announced, and the public or the community is involved in order to guarantee that the disputing parties comply with the terms of the truce. The publication of the adjudication has several consequences in larger cases; members of the public of course witness what has been agreed upon, and thereby act as guarantors, but also the whole arrangement, involving the gathering of a large number of people who are looked after and fed at the expense of either one of the members of the reconciliation council or by another prominent figure in the community who is hosting the event, has an effect in itself. There would be little point in going through the whole process and incurring the expenses if the parties were not to comply with what had been agreed upon. Of further importance is the whole process of negotiating the facts brought to light by the condensed clauses of the documents which state what has been agreed upon through interviews with the separate parties, the witnesses, and the different experts and prominent men who visit the site (to inspect the borders of disputed land, for example). The persuasive power of this narrative lies in its expression of an agreement reached through prolonged negotiations and 'shuttle diplomacy' carried out by the members of the *majlis*. And finally, the adjudication of the *majlis*, along with the religious quote which invokes the Supreme Witness, 'awakens' the tradition shared by the men of the community, and thereby reinforces the fundaments of the community.

On the other hand, due to the formalized procedures surrounding the negotiations, and the powers given to the small group of men mentioned, room is also left for cunning. One of the most famous 'truce-makers' in Idfu district, Hajj Ahmad, known from "Qina to Kum Umbu" for his ability to make people negotiate and create the background for a reconciliation, was himself dragged into a dispute concerning a piece of land connected to a house occupied by his son. A neighbor insisted that he had a prior right to the piece of land, a claim which the truce-maker did not accept. The quarrel continued for more than two years, and in the end a group of men from the neighboring village attempted to find a solution to the problem. This included visiting the two parties, listening to their arguments, and trying to get them to accept a solution. It seemed that a solution was emerging, so a council was appointed and a meeting was arranged in the *khayma* of one of the men who had initiated the negotiations.

Being 'a friend of the family,' I was invited to attend. On the scheduled Friday, around sunset, I turned up and expected the family members to be ready to leave. They were not: The old man had left, along with one of his sons in order to attend to some business, while the other son was busy repairing the roof of one of the family's other houses. The meeting had been canceled—and no real explanation for the cancellation was given, other than that "some problems had come up." Later, another friend of the family explained, laughing, that the *hajj* had been informed by some of the members of the council that their ruling would be that the piece of land should be divided between the two parties; a solution which the family was not at all interested in. They wanted the whole piece or nothing. But, more importantly, it transpired that the old man had, for a long time, been trying to get hold of the disputed piece of land through the district court in Idfu, and he had now been informed that the court would rule in his favor. What he had expected was that the council would create a reconciliation between the two families based on the verdict of the court. He had been aware of the possibility of the council coming up with a different solution, and had, therefore, until the day where he had been aware of the outcome of their deliberation, postponed the signing of the *mahdar tafwid*; in a sense, entering into mock negotiations knowing the rules of the game. When he was informed about the outcome of the negotiations of the council, he could insist that he had never agreed to accept a verdict and had never signed any document stating that he was ready to do so. Hence, the *majlis* had been canceled on that Friday evening.

One would think that this would reduce the standing of the old man as a trustworthy mediator, but those whom I consulted on the issue were of the opinion that he was the expert, and had acted correctly, while those arranging the reconciliation and the *majlis* were less knowing and not properly trained in the tactics and art of negotiation. The actions of the *hajj* are—at least when seen from the outside—much more similar to those of a cunning lawyer than those of a respected elder and expert of traditional lore, and would seem—if interpreted correctly—to support what I mentioned earlier about a tendency toward an increasingly professional negotiation process, and an increased distinction between those who know and those who do not.

## Conclusion

The persuasive power, and thereby the authority which is embedded in the institution of the traditional reconciliation councils of Upper Egypt is dependent on a wide range of instances and procedures, starting with the agreement of the disputing parties to engage in a reconciliation, the process of the negotiations, and the signing of the statement of authorization, which introduces explicit sanctions, such as the threats of financial or juridical penalties. To the range of much more subtle forms of persuasion involving the person through the articulation of the tradition, is added the negotiations and the adjudication of the council. At the same time, the ritual frame, together with the proclamation of the ruling before a group of men who as witnesses guarantee that the ruling is in line with tradition and ensure that it is known by the community, engage the council in forcing the parties to comply with the rulings.

Within the last twenty to thirty years, new practices have been established. First, the rulings of the councils are now written down in documents. Second, the development of the means of communication have made it possible to engage men from different parts of the district, and thereby create the foundation for the development of a group of more or less professional truce-makers, whose advice and participation is today seen as necessary in order to ensure that a reconciliation is reached and that the proper procedures are followed.

The combination of the introduction of written documents and the establishment of a specialized group of truce-makers could easily be interpreted as being related developments, supported by the manipulation of the formalized procedures related to the signing of documents.

However, the character of the documents, their schematic form, and their close connection to unique cases do not support an actual parallel development. Although the documents are kept by a small group of men as evidence of the rulings, they are not assembled into coherent collections, and no one (beside a researcher) would think of treating them as a coherent body of text. Each document is seen as reflecting a single case, the settlement of a specific dispute. Although there is a tendency toward concentrating the insight into the tradition into fewer hands, the knowledge is still carried by the individual men. The documents are mnemonic devices—an answer to current developments—and do not constitute a body of legal texts.

## Notes

1 For example, see Kennett 1968 (1925); and Stewart 1987 for a review of the literature.
2 An exception is the material from Yemen published in recent years. See Dresch 1989 and Messick 1990.
3 According to Stewart 1987, only one publication has been fully dedicated to the subject: *al-Tha'r*, by Abu Zayd 1965. Information is also found in Hopkins (1987:165–69) and Ammar, H. (1966:57–60).
4 I take this opportunity to thank Hajj 'Abd al-Hakim Muhammad Abu Nasr for his help in acquiring the documents, and later with the translations.
5 Besides the 'tribespeople,' the population includes Orthodox Coptic Christians and Nubians. The number of Nubians living in Idfu district is limited; the majority of those relocated after the erection of the High Dam in the 1960s are living south of Idfu, in Kum Umbu district.
6 This is also supported by the fact that all of the documents, except one, have been issued within the last twenty-five years.
7 On the other hand, in several of the documents, the part dedicated to the signatures contains the fingerprints of the involved parties. According to official statistics, in 1986, the percentage of illiterates was 60 percent in the rural areas of Idfu, and 40 percent in the urban areas.
8 Examples would be the number, age, and sex of camels which should be paid in compensation in case of a killing. In Khalifah 1940, a short list is given of compensation to be paid in case of animals being injured or stolen, and adultery and other offenses being committed among the (then) non-sedentary 'Ababda of the northern Sudan in the 1930s.
9 In some cases, the *mahdar tafwid* is actually incorporated in the final document.
10 See Rosen 1989 and Geertz 1983 for a discussion of the negotiability of 'facts.'
11 Ammar, who uses the term 'Arab Council,' writes that in order to persuade a person, the "usual form of pressure is to appeal to the person to 'consider the Arabs, or the people, or his kinsfolk'" (Ammar 1966:59). In other words there is a personification of *'urf*.

# References

Abu Zayd, Ahmad. 1965. *Al-Tha'r*. Cairo: Dar al-Ma'arif.
Ammar, Hamed. 1954. *Growing Up in an Egyptian Village: Silwa, Province of Aswan*. London: Routledge and Kegan Paul.
Dresch, Paul. 1989. *Tribes, Government, and History in Yemen*. Oxford: Clarendon Press.
Geertz, Clifford. 1983. "Local Knowledge: Facts and Law in Comparative Perspective" in *Local Knowledge: Further Essays in Interpretive Anthropology*. New York: Basic Books. pp. 167–234.
Goody, Jack, and Ian Watt. 1963. "The Consequences of Literacy." in *Comparative Studies in Society and History* 1962/63: 304–45.
Hill, Enid. 1979. *Mahkama! Studies in the Egyptian Legal System*. London: Ithaca Press.
Hopkins, Nicholas S. 1988. *Agrarian Transformation in Egypt*. Cairo: American University in Cairo Press.
Kennett, Austin. 1968 [1925]. *Bedouin Justice: Law and Custom among the Egyptian Bedouins*. London: Frank Cass.
Khalifah, Hasan Ahmad. 1940. *Fi-l-sahara al-sharqiya wa sharq al-Sudan: al-'Ababdah wa qaba'il akhra*. Berber, Sudan.
Messick, Brinkley. 1990. "Literacy and the Law: Documents and Document Specialists in Yemen" in D. H. Dwyer, ed. *Law and Islam in the Middle East*. South Hadley MA: Bergen and Garvey. pp. 61–67.
Moore, Sally Falk. 1977. "Individual Interests and Organizational Structures: Dispute Settlement as 'Events of Articulation'" in I. Hamnett, ed. *Social Anthropology and Law*. London, ASA Monograph 14.
Moore, Sally Falk. 1995. "Imperfect Communications" in P. Caplan, ed. *Understanding Disputes*. Oxford; Providence, R.I.: Berg. pp. 11–38.
Rosen, Lawrence. 1989. *The Anthropology of Justice: Law as Culture in Islamic Society*. Cambridge: Cambridge University Press.
Schacht, Joseph. 1964. *An Introduction to Islamic Law*. Oxford: Clarendon Press.
Stewart, F. H. 1987. "Tribal Law in the Arab World: A Review of the Literature." *International Journal of Middle East Studies* 19:473–90.

# 19

## Culture and the Mediation of Power in an Egyptian Village

AHMED ZAYED

### Introduction

Studies on the politics of Egyptian peasants can be classified into three categories. The first category of studies was clearly influenced by modernization theory and concentrated on the 'passing' of traditional peasant society into a modern one and, therefore, the replacement of the old traditional leadership with a modern educated one (Ghayth 1959; Awda 1971). A more developed version of this category focused on the wider formative context of peasant society and politics, with special reference to the process of political mobilization of peasants (Harik 1974), and the rise of a new middle class (Halpern 1963), or a second stratum (Binder 1978). The second category took a Marxist stand, focusing on the development of a capitalist mode of production in rural Egypt that was accompanied by the rise of a landed class which ruled the political arena at both the regional and central levels ('Abd al-Mu'ati 1975; 'Abd al-Nabi 1978). A developed version of this category merged Marxist analysis with the theory of clientelism, arguing that power in rural Egypt is constituted around patriarchal relations in which members of large families act as patrons (Hopkins 1988). The third category, influenced by world systems theory, concentrated on the transformation of peasant society in the precolonial and postcolonial eras. Therefore, the studies focused on issues such as the relationship between state and peasants (Awda 1979), the relation between elite formation and class domination (Zayed 1981), and the development of a non-capitalist mode of production, along with the continuation of traditional modes of reproduction, domination, and relations with the state (Stauth 1983; Glavanis and Glavanis 1983).

This paper has been written in light of my argument on the formation of rural elites published in the early 1980s (Zayed 1981). In this study, elites were examined in close relationship with the class structure, and an attempt was made to differentiate between old elites drawn from the dominant landed class, and new elites drawn from the new middle class. However, in the writing of this paper, for which I revisited one of the two villages I studied in the late 1970s ("Village A"), I have revised my theory. I am now reluctant to use the term elite. Instead I use the concept of mediators of power. This concept might enable us to transform the analysis from the institutional–structural level to everyday practices and strategies through which power practices are 'structurated' (Giddens 1984) and symbolic capital is accumulated (Bourdieu 1977). Mediation is not only understood here as a conflict resolution strategy, but also as a strategy in which cultural capital (time, verbal discourse, symbols, and so forth) is used to achieve political domination and to reinforce traditionalization and self-regulation. Strategies of mediation are diffused on both local (village) and district (town/city) levels. The modes of domination that result on the local level are connected with the modes of domination on the district level. On the district level, state strategies enter into play and they combine with local strategies to reinforce the traditionalization of society and politics.

This paper is based on field work in an Upper Egyptian village. The field work was accomplished in two phases, separated by a relatively long interim. Phase one took place in the 1970s, and phase two after the mid-1990s. Moreover, I frequented the village from time to time to remain acquainted with all the details related to the social and political life over this relatively long period. I observed the details through participant observation and open interviews. I have also tried to examine power relations in the village through an approach that extends the concept of power so as to include social and economic life in the village, thereby focusing on understanding power relations through the everyday practices of individuals. The issues raised by these practices, and the ways people deal with them, have to be examined as well. This, I hope, will help clarify the nature of fusion between culture and politics, and the nature of the limits separating the modern and the traditional in these political practices.

## Village A

Village A (population of 6,916 in 1986) is located on the east bank of the Bahr Yusif Canal, about eighteen kilometers from the nearest town. There is a hamlet about two kilometers to the north. The buildings of the village have extended north, while those of the hamlet have extended south, so at present they almost form one unit. The hamlet is not an *'izba* in the traditional sense of the word; that is, it is not owned by some definite person from the village or elsewhere. Rather, it is simply a small village. No large landowners are found in the village or the hamlet, since the acreage of the village is relatively small—only 794 feddans. As a result of this, the inhabitants have rented and farmed plots of land located within the boundaries of other nearby villages. Over the last ten years, many kin groups have purchased the land which they were farming.

The village, as a whole, did not benefit from the agrarian reforms because there were no large estates subject to redistribution. However, four households did benefit from these reforms by receiving land in an adjacent village. The peasants in Village A cultivated traditional, commercial, and subsistence crops, such as corn, wheat, cotton, beans, and garlic. The means of production were undeveloped. Until the 1970s, the whole village had only one agricultural tractor, owned by the Agricultural coop. No machinery was used in irrigation. The peasants used water scoops, or the Archimedes screw *(tanbur)*, for irrigation, both of which required an exhausting physical effort. Moreover, the expansion of the built-up area was relatively slow. The standard of living was low, and the construction of a new house was quite costly.

However, since the late 1960s, more attention has been paid in the village to modern commercial crops, like coriander, sunflower, and soya beans. This change in the village crop structure was linked to individual initiatives on the part of a limited number of farmers. Other changes, however, were related to different circumstances. There were two significant factors that led to major changes in the village. The first was emigration, which started in the 1970s, first to Libya, then, to Jordan, Iraq, and Saudi Arabia (most emigrants were laborers, petty farmers, or graduates of technical high schools, in addition to a limited number of university graduates). The second factor was the shortage of irrigation water during the 1980s. The first factor led to a drastic shortage of labor and a flow of remittances to the households of emigrants. The second factor—relatively connected to the first—led to a search for alternatives to the primitive irrigation tools. This trend was enhanced by the increasing supply of agricultural technology as a result of the Open Door Economic Policy and the economic liberalization of the Egyptian market.

Thus, the village's face entirely changed within two decades. Part of the remittances and crop revenues were directed to purchasing tractors (mostly by families whose members had emigrated and who owned land). There are more than fifteen tractors in the village at present, in the late 1990s. Some of the average-sized landowners have purchased pump sets to use in irrigating their lands, and also rent this technology to their neighbors. There are more than a hundred pump sets currently in the village. This, in turn, has resulted in a major development in the cultivation and irrigation systems. The farmers do not rely any more on the traditional tools to lift water, plow the land, and thresh the crop. Now donkey carts or tractors are used to haul soil, local fertilizers, and crops. This is a new development in the village.

Meanwhile, the flow of emigration money resulted in an unprecedented construction boom and expansion in the village. The constructed area has doubled in size and now almost extends to the hamlet which had previously been two kilometers away. Construction in Village A, as well as in the adjacent villages, served to increase the number of builders in the village (their number amounted to three hundred, mostly former agricultural laborers). This change has also allowed a large number of households to devote part of their household labor supply (husband, wife, and children) to the manufacture of adobe or red brick, thus earning extra income. A smaller number of the village youth turned to brick manufacturing as a permanent, albeit minor, commercial activity.

Among the activities that have remarkably increased during the last decade is commerce, especially petty grocery stores. This kind of activity is mostly linked to educated persons who are also civil servants in the village or in one of the neighboring villages, or to those who had formerly worked in an Arab country.

The evidence cited above indicates an important change in the contemporary Egyptian village, that is, the differentiation of the 'peasantry.'

## The Political Arena: Substance of Politics

It is hard to determine the political arena in Village A or in any other village. This is due to two reasons. First, the arena does not take on an official, institutional character that might help provide a better knowledge of the nature of issues circulating within it. In fact, there are certain official institutions and organizations that overlap with the political arena in the village, such as the elected local council (a body that includes this village as well as some other villages), the police station (located in a nearby village), and various government agencies in the city. Nevertheless, these institutions do not interfere in the village's affairs in a way that would establish an official frame for all the issues being raised in the village. It is true that some relationship exists between these institutions and certain issues being raised on the political arena in the village, but this relationship does not cover all the politics in the village.

The second reason is that this political arena has no specific political agenda. Rather, the agenda is determined in the light of daily practices. Moreover, it may vary according to the context in which it takes place (household, neighborhood, the village as a whole, inter-village relationships, or the relationship with the state).

Based on this, the village's political arena is undetermined and is structured in accordance with its inputs (that is, the issues that are continuously raised) and outputs (the way those issues are treated and their relevant decisions, which are obligatory not by virtue of law, but by virtue of conventions). Therefore, adequate knowledge of the political arena in the village can be obtained only by becoming acquainted with the issues raised, and the practices that evolve around them. It not our intention here to study issues, but to use them as a means to discover modes of practices of power. Let us look at different levels of issues.

1. There are issues forced on the village from above. These issues are often linked to certain regulations or decisions which the peasants have to abide by, such as restricting construction on agricultural land, skimming the topsoil, or building kilns to fire clay into red bricks. Although these regulations are obligatory, they are overtly violated by the villagers in spite of possible penalties. These violations turn these issues into inputs that evoke political practices. And despite the fact that this kind of issue has a purely official character, the village, through those who control political practice, often confronts these issues with a traditional norm, for there exists an agreement inside the village that anyone who reports a violation should be conventionally punished. Practice of power at this level contradicts with the interests of the state and overlaps with regional politics. Powerful people in the village, as well as some educated people who hold governmental positions, emphasize in their daily discourse that they stand as a wall to protect the village against any evil that comes from outside. They also criticize anybody who stands against their rules if they are not able to punish them. One educated man who holds a position in the Ministry of Agriculture, and who was adamant in enforcing the law, was criticized as being 'rude' and 'ungrateful' to his village.

2. Some issues forced on the village from above require a response from the village, such as when the education authority took a decision to build a preparatory school in the village, when the youth and sports authority decided to establish a clubhouse, or when the local council decided to found a workshop to train young women in sewing and needlework. In this kind of issue, the village is supposed to have a definite reaction, such as donating a piece of land, a certain amount of money, or organizing the activity in question. Such issues are often discussed within a small group of individuals who are influential

within their kin groups, or who are members of the local council. These individuals bring such issues to the village through their contacts with higher levels in the local organization. It was found that an issue often remains unsettled for a long period of time because it is hard to create a consensus before presenting it to the village, or because of a conflict between the influential groups.

These sorts of issues are supposed to bring benefits to the village. Those who are involved in them tell people about their roles and the efforts they have made in cooperation with the authorities to have their demands implemented. However these issues may evoke conflicts within the village. Thus, the clubhouse issue, which was raised in the 1960s, turned into a non-issue as a result of a conflict between a number of village youth and the mayor, and the clubhouse has been shut ever since. There is also the school issue, which was raised in the late 1970s, and almost failed because of the resistance shown by the owner of the old school, who had rented the building to the Ministry of Education, and because of the village's inability to donate a feddan of land plus LE3,000. The project was carried out only when a local contractor (who belonged to the village and was a member of the governorate council) showed enthusiasm for it. He suggested building a school on land owned by the state, and pursued the issue in higher circles until he obtained a formal approval. He also had the idea of building the school with funds from the Ministry of Education. The third issue, that of the workshop for young women, is still being discussed by virtue of a suggestion by the local council. Here, too, appeared the problem of space and the village inability to allocate or rent a place for this purpose. The problem is being solved at present through individual cooperation between the local council and a villager. The latter has been commissioned by the council to collect the fines imposed on those farmers who store piles of fertilizers on the village roads. It has been decided that the workshop will be built with this money.

3. A third type of issues is raised from within the village, and concerns the village as a whole. It is a relatively new type of issue that requires formal recognition, and is basically concerned with the activity of civil society. In the 1970s (specifically following the October War in 1973), as a result of a shortage of food, a number of youth sought to establish a consumer cooperative. The cooperative was created and run for a while by a board. Nevertheless, it failed as a consequence of an attempt by some individuals to take possession of its money and to run it to their own advantage. In the late 1980s, a number of educated youth (mostly from social categories with less influence in the life of the village) sought to found a society to care for

orphan children. The idea was greatly resisted by the village's mayor and sheikhs who feared that the appeal to found such a society might be linked with certain religious attitudes. The project came into reality only when it was entrusted to an influential person in the village who was known to be honest and trustful. This influential person was able to stand by the group of youth and to bring the proposed society into reality.

The latest issue being raised at this level appeared in 1996, when a young village man sought to organize a developed form of *mawa'id al-rahman* (providing food to the poor in the fasting month of Ramadan) by distributing foodstuffs purchased with money donated by the financially well-off. Although the project met with some opposition in the beginning, it was in fact realized. As a result of its success in the first year, a large number of village notables became enthusiastic to contribute to it in the following year, even forming a board for the project. In fact, no other issue has ever found a similar level of consensus.

Power mediators in such issues are convinced that they are working for the interests of the village, not their own. This is why they consider their actions to be the source of all gifts and good for the village. Although conflict might emerge on this level of power practice, the historical trend manifests a tendency toward consensus and traditional choices.

4. Large-scale problems and disputes are linked to the life of the village as a whole, such as a dispute between two or more kin groups, between the village and another village, or a conflict between two prestigious figures in the village that may attract people's attention. Such a dispute may start as a trivial question, that then becomes so serious that it may not be confined only to two individuals. It may also be a dispute between two parties of such economic and political power that many people become involved. Sometimes, the villagers may even take sides in a way that reveals the loyalty of the poor to the powerful. Inter-village conflicts usually break out at marketplaces, where large numbers of people from different villages gather. They may also occur after a villager attacks someone from another village. When such a dispute arises in the village, the village consensus falls apart and power practices turn into family-based actions.

5. The fifth pattern is confined to disputes over land, water, and inheritance; the latter may involve land, houses, or property. The source of dispute here is often an attempt made by some individuals to encroach upon others' rights to inheritance. The source of land disputes, however, is an encroachment on boundaries. This type of dispute over the boundaries of agricultural land has remarkably

increased over the last ten years. These disputes reach their peak during the period of land preparation for cultivation. Disputes over water, however, have greatly decreased during the same period of time. This is due to the fact that most of these disputes occurred in the context of the surface irrigation system. Now that mechanical irrigation has spread, disputes of this type have almost disappeared. In this domain, a wider number of mediators enter the political arena. Conflicts here are between individuals, and kinship groups are no longer relevant units.

6. The sixth pattern consists of what we may call 'limited problems.' These include disputes that may break out between a number of individuals within the same neighborhood. The parties here may, or may not, belong to one kinship group, and the problems here may be of a limited nature (so long as they do not involve other parties, which may lead to the involvement of the whole village). There are two major causes of this type of problem. One is quarrels among children or women; the other is conflicts over space. For example, some may try to prevent their neighbors from placing certain objects in front of their house, from tethering animals next to their place, from building a wall or opening a window or a door onto their land, or they may ask the neighbors to pay for the costs of a wall separating their houses, if the neighbors' houses were more recently built. Sometimes, several residents of a certain area may have a dispute with a landowner who seeks to sell his land for road building. Disputes may also result from encroachment upon the land of an already existing road. These disputes, especially those concerning construction, have obviously increased lately, given the increase in construction activity in the village.

7. Simple disputes may break out within the same household between two brothers, a man and his wife, a father and his son (or sons), or a woman and a member of her family-in-law. It was observed that disputes within a family increase immediately after one of its members gets married. It seems that a new wife goes through a difficult adaptation process after marriage. Disputes usually break out between her and the members of the new family, especially the mother-in-law. This is not true in all cases, of course. It depends on several variables, such as the degree of kinship between the two families, and the similarity (or dissimilarity) of the economic level of the two families. These disputes gradually diminish with the wife's conformity to the nature of the new household, and her ability to play her role in it. The simple disputes that arise between two brothers are due to the quantity of labor done by each of them, or because of a dispute between their wives or children. A dispute between a father

and his sons may arise over disagreements between his wife and daughter-in-law, or possibly over the division of properties.

## Who Governs: Local Mediators

The village has a form of kinship organization based on tribal segmentation. In most kin groups in the village, kinship is not based on blood alone. Rather, kinship has a political nature; each kin group includes a core kin group, which involves most of the kin group members. This group is often based on blood ties. But the family also includes other groups or members who are not linked by blood ties with the core group. Marginal kin groups in the village (Copts or strangers from distant regions) affiliate to established kin groups. This indicates that the kin group is basically a political one. The social organization of the community is based on a balance of power between kin groups. This is facilitated by the fact that no group in the village is economically powerful enough to overpower the rest. The kin group from which the village's mayor is elected is a small group that is politically affiliated to a larger one. That is why the mayor's family is always considered an extraneous kin group. There is a consensus among all parties that the office should continue to be inherited within that group. In the 1960s, a certain person from one of the biggest kin groups in the village nominated himself against the mayor of the time, and, as expected, failed to win the office. Following the new law concerning the abolition of elections for mayors and sheikhs, no one from the village came forward to compete with the present mayor, even though his legal term in office had ended months earlier.

The mayor makes efforts to reconcile the divided kin groups, and to keep the balance between them. Among the mechanisms employed by the mayor's family to keep this balance, especially since the 1952 Revolution, with the number of educated people increasing, and ambitions to gain power flourishing, is to rely on the influential individuals within each group (the elders or those who are financially or educationally distinguished) to solve the problems that may arise between or within kin groups. The mayor always tends to form a 'committee' of the notables of various families, including family elders and some of the village's influential persons, to whom he assigns the task of solving the problems and disagreements that may arise. He has even tried to introduce a formal character to the work of this 'committee.' The members call themselves a 'committee,' and write down the proceedings of their discussions in a 'report' whenever asked. Committees may also vary depending on the circumstances. Thus, the committee assigned to deal with agricultural land boundaries differs from that handling a particular dispute. However, a certain degree of interrelationship exists between them all. Any individual who is influential within his kin group may find himself a member of this type of committee. But the extent of diffusion of power sharing does not mean that any person who seeks power can gain it, as will be seen later. When we talk about this mechanism, we show the extent to which a degree of equilibrium can be achieved within this segmented kin structure.

This group, consisting of the village mayor, sheikhs, educated notables, and the financially distinguished (by land, property, or capital), controls the political arena of everyday life, as well as that of higher practices (in the village's relations with other villages, with the city, and with the state). The practices of this group contribute to reproducing their social status and power. The issues raised in the village, by the state or local organizations, are often handled within a limited circle of village members. An issue may even be settled without any of the village population knowing anything about it, unless it has a concrete effect on them. Under these circumstances, the individuals who are influential within their kin groups may seem like mediators between the village and the state; and they are indeed, even with regard to the relationship between peasants and the city. They take their ill kin to physicians in the city, and buy them what they need for weddings and construction (such as, furniture, jewelry, material, and wood).

Mediation is an open field for practicing, or training to practice, power. Mediation is based on the principle of intervention. Whenever a dispute occurs between two parties, one or more individuals act as a go-between to solve the problem and to reconcile the two parties. Intervention may be undertaken automatically by those who are interested in the issue of the dispute. It may also occur when one or both parties complain to one of those who are expected to assume the role of a go-between. Sometimes, one party may complain about the other to one of the latter's kin who is considered prestigious within his kin group. Then kin group elders contact each other and seek to solve the dispute. The duration, success, or failure of this process depends on how large the dispute is. Small-scale or marriage disputes may be solved in a brief gathering of two or three persons with the two disputing parties. The larger the scale of the dispute, the wider the gathering. Large-scale disputes may involve two families or two villages. In this case, the reconciliation gathering is usually called a 'customary assembly' *(majlis 'urfi)* or 'appointment' *(maw'id)*. The following is a description of this type of gathering.

## Al-Majlis al-'Urfi or al-Mi'ad

Holding a customary assembly becomes a necessity in two cases: when the dispute involves a large number of parties or two prestigious ones, or when mediation fails to solve a particular problem. In this latter case, the parties of the dispute may reject any solution being proposed unless they 'sit' or 'assemble' *(yuq'ud)* to settle all their problems. The word 'sit' or 'assemble' here refers to a customary 'assembly,' which is also called *mi'ad* (appointment). From this latter term, the verb *yuma'id* is sometimes used instead of the verb *yuq'ud* (sit), meaning to sit in an appointment. One of the parties tells the mediator, "I must sit with him," in reference to the other party.

Preparation for a customary assembly starts with one or more individuals mediating between the parties of the dispute in question. After both parties agree to hold a customary assembly, disagreement arises over two aspects. The first is the location of the proposed assembly. In this respect, public culture has imposed certain rules which are well-known to the experienced figures in such an assembly, as well as to the villagers. A customary assembly must be held at the place of the defendant, or the party expected to have the 'right' on their side, or at the place of one of the defendant's relatives. The logic behind this lies in the fact that the defendant, or the party of 'right,' would certainly feel some sort of endorsement by seeing everyone coming to his/her place. In case both parties are equally to blame, or each party refuses to go to the other party's place, the assembly may be held at some neutral place; often at the house of some prestigious figure in the village, whether or not this figure is a relative of one of the parties, or at the mayor's house. In extreme cases, where the problem is very intense, the assembly may be held at the police headquarters in the district town.

The second aspect concerns the individuals who attend the assembly to undertake arbitration and dispute resolution. Each party seeks not to let these arbitrators be selected by the other party. Here again, there exist certain regulations imposed by culture on the process of selecting the arbitrators. The selection process depends on the nature as well as the size of the problem. In a small-scale problem, which could be solved in a customary assembly, the mediators, upon consulting the two disputing parties, may select certain figures from those attending the assembly, who are often prestigious kinsfolk of both parties. One of the parties may insist that the assembly be attended by certain figures whom they expect to be on their side. In this case, they have the right to invite whomever they wish to attend the gathering. In case of more complex problems, or those which cannot be solved by mediators in the village, each party has the right to invite whomever he wants to the assembly. Each party or both parties together may name one or more individuals from neighboring villages, who are known for being experienced in these matters (most often, though not necessarily, those with an official capacity, such as those who hold official positions in the elected assemblies, including the People's Assembly). These experienced figures are called 'men of assemblies.' The assembly may also include some of the Bedouin who live nearby in the Western Desert, and who are often known as experts in arbitration.

However, customary assemblies are not confined to the those who are invited. Any of the two parties' supporters may attend. I observed that many people would attend these gatherings without being invited. They would come just to show support. Most of them are youth, who usually show a degree of enthusiasm and partisanship. They stand watching the assembly through windows, or squat on their heels in front of the door, ready to defend their parties, or just to show their support. Among the ways employed by the elders to control and mollify these zealous young men is to hit them, which the young men accept out of respect for their elder kinfolk.

The customary assembly proceeds in a way that makes it seem more like a negotiation. The task assigned to those present at the assembly is to try to bridge the gap between the viewpoints of the two parties, each one of whom claims to have the right on their side. In the assemblies held to solve minor problems, the attendants may ask each of the two parties not to tell their side of the 'story,' and, instead, to recite the opening sura of the Quran as a sign of 'consent and compliance.' However, the discussions gradually reveal all the details of the dispute. Where the gap between the two parties is very wide, the assembly elders start by asking the attendants to recite the opening sura of the Quran, and then ask each party to tell their side of the story, that is, the details of the dispute. Each party naturally highlights their viewpoint and tries to make it seem as right as possible. When each party of the dispute involves several individuals, the story may sometimes be told by more than one person. It may also be heard from a neutral party.

After hearing the story, which is usually interrupted by both parties or by their supporters, or even by the assembly elders themselves, the latter would try to reconcile all viewpoints. They would attempt to convince the party taking a more rigorous stand to accept reconciliation. However, the other party may then take a harsher stand, forcing the elders to convince them to accept reconciliation, and so on. The means of convincing reveal how oral discourse is used as symbolic capital. The people who are taking responsibility for reconciling the disputing parties not only use the time they spend as cultural capital, but also gain power and respect through the way they talk, their management and control of the oral discourse, and their body discipline (the way they dress, sit, and speak). The following mechanisms reveal how this kind of cultural capital is used:

1. The elders may use verbal persuasion in the form of 'exemplification' *(tamthil)*, that is, quoting proverbs and parables, and assimilating the incident in a symbolic way that is linked to agriculture, animals, and food;
2. They may justify their decisions by narrating similar stories in which the two parties acted in a way different from that of the two parties of the dispute in question. These stories might have happened to the narrator or to one of his kinfolk, or even in a different dispute which he helped resolve;
3. They may exert personal influence over the parties by emphasizing that the elders came to the meeting even though they do not have time, and that the two parties should take this into consideration;
4. They may exercise direct influence by talking louder than the parties, or rebuking them, in order to show the tougher party that they are not achieving anything and that they should yield to 'the men;' and
5. They may impose silence on the assembly because of frequent interventions and/or infringements on assembly rules.

These mechanisms are often used sequentially or alternately, depending on the circumstances. As things get tougher and tension rises inside the assembly, one of the participants asks the rest to recite the opening sura of the Quran, and the gathering surely calms down as a result.

Equivocation is often used in the assembly by the disputing parties so that the words may have a double meaning. This dissimulation is sometimes accepted by the party being addressed. Where a party is angered by such use of words, the speaker, or someone else, may repeat the statement in different words. The receiver may even be accused of ignorance for not properly understanding. In any case, reconciliation eventually takes place between the two parties.

In some cases, the assembly elders might acknowledge that one of the two parties has right on his side. This is usually done by comparing faults and, ultimately, finding out who is right and who is wrong. In such a case, there are two alternative solutions:

1. The aggressive party may confess to being wrong; or
2. Compensation may be estimated at a certain amount of money.

Financial compensation is estimated in the course of the assembly. Sometimes, however, a separate sub-committee is formed to make a decision on the amount of compensation. The sentenced party pays the compensation as it is decided. The other party takes the compensation in their hand, but immediately returns it, saying: "I've obtained my rights already." In a few cases, however, money is not returned, which is often judged by others as being mean and inconsiderate.

Sometimes, those in charge of the assembly not only find a solution for the dispute, but may even go as far as to determine certain mechanisms for controlling the dispute in the future. Three such mechanisms, which may be combined, are listed here:

1. The two parties recite the opening sura of the Quran once or more, which is to be taken as a commitment that they will not return to the dispute;
2. The two parties take an oath on the Quran to show that they have reconciled and that no dispute will arise between them in the future (the one who turns his back on such an oath is damned); and
3. A penal code, which establishes the penalty, usually a cash fine, for violating the terms of the reconciliation, is agreed to and signed by the two parties.

## Engineering of Consent

Political practices, whether in relation to the state or to the continuity of the social and political life of the village, are 'structurated' in rules acceptable to all individuals of the community. These rules are inherited without any fundamental change. One might even safely claim that they obviously enhance the traditional structure of political practices in the village.

Political practices play a major role in the reproduction of these rules. They also contribute to the constant production of new rules to assert particular stands or to impose controlling precepts on those who may join or leave the circle of political practices. Therefore, political practices determine what should and what should not be done under certain circumstances. The production and reproduction of rules take place on various levels, which the case studies and observations reveal, as follows:

1. There are rules related to the respectability of senior citizens and prominent individuals within each kin group. This rule of respectability is reproduced first by constant verbal emphasis or by reference to certain examples of kin group notables in the past, in whose presence no one dared talk loudly, or to kin group examples, past and present, of obedient and loyal individuals who would not

raise their eyes to kin group elders, who might even slap their faces in hard times (in fights among families for instance). Second, the rules are reproduced by emphasizing certain practices, for example, younger people should not smoke or feel free to lay back in the presence of their respectable elders, who assert seniority in food, tea, talk, or sitting. Third, the one who might violate the rule of respectability risks punishment. It once happened that someone who was influential within his kin group, as well as the village as a whole, was walking on the street and saw an educated (preparatory level) young member of his kin group fighting with his neighbor. He tried to stop him, but the young man would not yield. The older person slapped his face, but the young man slapped him back. The old person left him and went home, and the following day, he related the incident in public. Three men from his kin group took the young man and his father to the elder's place, where they beat the young man severely in front of him. But this was not enough for the elder; so he beat the youth with his shoe, as he had sworn to do. Thus, the rule of respectability is emphasized by punishing whoever rebels against it.

2. There are rules related to intervention for solving disputes and how dispute-solving is conducted. First, there are rules related to the necessity of consulting the elders in case any dispute should arise. When someone is offended or encroached upon, he says to the aggressor: "You've got an elder to be complained to." One's right may be lost should he refrain from reporting the aggressor's encroachment to the latter's elder. Once the elder intervenes to solve the problem, the injured party makes sure not to address the aggressor, but the elder instead. Then, the elders of both parties solve the dispute together. That is why village people say in their proverbs: "He who has no elder should create one," or "The village has men of its own."

Second, there are rules related to the words used during the process of intervention. These are rules for speech in general, which should be observed in the public sphere of the village (roads, coffee shops, and house gatherings). They are also observed at problem-solving gatherings, as a public sphere. Rules of this type determine who should talk first, how to talk, who controls the course of the talk, who should listen, and who should be silent. The rules fixed for answering these questions are the ones that determine how the pattern of everyday cultural practices are transformed into a pattern of power, and how cultural symbols overlap with power practices and the pattern of domination.

Third, there are rules with regard to refraining from the rejection of the elders' judgments or mediation efforts. These rules are reproduced by negative references to those who happen to have rejected the elders' judgments or mediation efforts, and by local mediators continuously declaring that they only seek goodness, that their efforts cost them much, and that they have no self-interest whatsoever. Here again, words lead to the reproduction of rules.

3. The third type of rule relates to the exclusion of the poor from political mobility. So the poor have the least chance in political conflict. Two cases of poor individuals trying to enter the circle of political and social influence in the village were examined by the author. The two cases resulted in mechanisms to ensure the continuity of domination and to attempt to freeze political mobility.

The first case was of a man whose family came from another village and settled in Village A as part of a kin group. The man was literate, and therefore disdained to work in farming. Instead, he helped the peasants get identity cards, food ration cards, and similar services. Then he began to develop political ambitions. He tried to nominate himself to the Arab Socialist Union, in the late 1960s and the early 1970s, but he failed. Thereupon, he started reporting various infractions. It happened once that some village men who happened to have close links with the government authorities found some telegrams with this man's signature on them at the post office. The man's family elders were summoned from his old village, and he was forced to pay all the fines which had been paid by those whom he had denounced, or else he would have to leave the village for good. He chose to pay. On the same day, the village elders articulated an agreement that the same principle should be followed by anyone who might report infractions in the village, that is, that this individual should pay for the damage resulting from his/her actions.

The second case is of a young man from a small kin group living on the margins of a core kin group in the village. His father was a poor petty vendor, with physical disabilties, who eventually turned into a charlatan, going from one village to another on the back of his donkey, selling magic spells to peasants. The son finished his intermediate education and went to work in Iraq for more than five years. When he came back, his father had died. Then he worked as a teacher at the village school, and managed to build a new house. His house was the only one in the village with the owner's name written on it (his father's name to be precise). Then the young man, who was stout, started wearing dark glasses, carrying a staff and a rosary in his hand, and wearing a shawl on his shoulders. In this new look, he would frequent the village's public places (marketplaces, wedding parties, mourning ceremonies, coffee shops, outdoor stone benches, and roads). This behavior was mocked by villagers, but he was indifferent. He even announced that he would nominate himself as a candidate in the elections to the People's Assembly. For this, he got no response but mockery and disapprobation, which led him to change his mind. Surprisingly, he did nominate himself in the most recent elections in 1995. He campaigned, disseminating his fliers in villages. Nonetheless, he encountered great contempt inside and outside the village. Only a very limited number of his village people supported him. Not surprisingly, he did not win in the elections. However, he still possesses his great political ambitions.

Thus, political resistance from below always encounters resistance from above. This results in minimizing the conflict on the level of the village as a whole, between those who dominate the political arena and those who are weaker. In this context, the conflict turns into a negative, verbal form of resistance in private spheres. Moreover, the forms of individual conflict within each separate kin group increase, and this functions to foster the continuity of political domination.

## Conclusion

It is now more than two hundred years since Egypt entered into contact with European culture. When social science established the conditions for studying non-Western societies after World War II, faith was very strong in the theory of modernization, that emphasized the imperatives of social and cultural transformation in non-Western societies.

However, evidence presented here opens the way to question the modernization thesis and to rethink the role of traditional practices in reproducing social life in peasant societies, and in creating social, in addition to economic and political modes of distinction. It also opens the way to reflection upon the pattern of modernity that is developing in the peripheries of the capitalist world system, where it seems that globalization of modernity goes side by side with traditionalization and mythification of social and cultural life in the peripheries of the capitalist world system.

## References

'Abd al-Mu'ati, A. 1975. *al-Sir'a al-tabaqi fi qarya misriya*. Cairo: Dar al-Thaqafa al-Jadida. (In Arabic.)

'Abd al-Nabi, M. 1978. "Bina' al-qawa fi qarya misriya." M.A. Dissertation, 'Ayn Shams University, Cairo. In Arabic.

Awda, M. 1971. *Asalib al-itisal wa-l-taqhayyur al-ijtima'i*. Cairo: Dar al-Ma'rif. In Arabic.

Awda, M. 1979. *al-Falahun wa-l-dawla: dirasat fi asalib al-intaj wa-l-takwin al-ijtima'i li-l-qarya al-misriya.* Cairo: Dar al-Thaqafa li-l Tiba'a w-al-Nashr. In Arabic.

Binder, L. 1978. *In a Moment of Enthusiasm: Political Power and the Second Stratum in Egypt.* Chicago: University of Chicago Press.

Bourdieu, P. 1977. *An Outline of a Theory of Practice.* (translated by R. Nice). New York: Cambridge University Press.

Ghayth, A. 1959. *al-Qarya al-mutaghayyir: al-Qatun, al-Daqahliya.* Cairo: Dar al-Ma'rif. In Arabic.

Giddens, A. 1984. *The Constitution of Society: An Outline of Theory of Structuration.* Cambridge: Polity Press.

Glavanis, K. R. B. and P. M. 1983. "The Sociology of Agrarian Relations in the Middle East: The Persistence of Household Production." *Current Sociology* 31(2):1–74.

Halpern, M. 1963. *The Politics of Social Change in the Middle East and North Africa.* Princeton: Princeton University Press.

Harik, I. 1974. *The Political Mobilization of Peasants.* Bloomington, Indiana: Indiana University Press.

Hopkins, N. S. 1988. *Agrarian Transformation in Egypt.* Cairo: The American University in Cairo Press.

Stauth, G. 1983. "Capitalist Farming and Small Peasant Households in Egypt." *Review* 7(2):285–313.

Zayed, A. A. 1981. "al-Tafa'ul al-ijtima'i baina jama'at al-safwa al-qadima wa-l-safwa al-jadida fi-l-rif al-misri." Ph.D. Dissertation, Cairo University, Cairo. In Arabic.

# Contributors

Mohamed Hassan Abdel Aal is Research Professor in the Social Research Center, American University in Cairo, and Professor of Agricultural Extension, Department of Rural Sociology and Agricultural Extension, Faculty of Agriculture, Cairo University, Egypt.

Lila Abu-Lughod is Associate Professor of Anthropology at New York University, USA.

Soraya Altorki is Professor of Anthropology at the American University in Cairo, Egypt.

Kamran Asdar Ali is Assistant Professor of Anthropology at the University of Rochester, USA.

Kirsten Haugaard Bach, an anthropologist, is Research Associate at the Centre for Development Research, Copenhagen, Denmark.

Ray Bush is Head of the Department of Politics and Director of the African Studies Unit, University of Leeds, UK.

Donald P. Cole is Professor of Anthropology at the American University in Cairo, Egypt.

Nicholas S. Hopkins is Professor of Anthropology and affiliated to the Social Research Center at the American University in Cairo, Egypt.

François Ireton, an anthropologist, is research associate at the Centre d'Etudes et de Documentation Economiques, Juridiques et Sociales (CEDEJ) in Cairo, Egypt.

Sohair Mehanna is Research Associate at the Social Research Center, American University in Cairo, Egypt

Günter Meyer is Professor of Geography at the University of Mainz, Germany.

Timothy Mitchell is Associate Professor of Political Science, New York University, USA.

Mohamed M. Mohieddin is Associate Professor of Sociology in the Faculty of Arts, Minufiya University, Shabin al-Kum, Egypt.

## Contributors

Detlef Müller-Mahn, a geographer, is on the faculty of the Oriental Institute of the University of Leipzig, Germany.

Hans-Christian Korsholm Nielsen is Ph.D. candidate in the Department of Ethnography and Social Anthropology, University of Aarhus, Moesgaard, Denmark.

Malak S. Rouchdy is Adjunct Assistant Professor of Sociology at the American University in Cairo, Egypt.

Reem Saad, an anthropologist, is Research Associate in the Social Research Center, American University in Cairo, Egypt.

Hania Sholkamy, an anthropologist, is Junior Research Fellow, St. Anne's College, Oxford, UK, and works with the Consulting Association, Population Council Regional Office, Cairo, Egypt.

James Toth is Associate Professor of Anthropology at the American University in Cairo, Egypt.

Kirsten Westergaard, a political scientist, is Research Director at the Centre for Development Research, Copenhagen, Denmark.

Peter Winch, MD, MPH, is Assistant Professor, Department of International Health, School of Hygiene and Public Health, Johns Hopkins University, USA.

Ahmed Zayed is Professor of Sociology at Cairo University, Egypt, and Cultural Attaché in the Egyptian Embassy in Riyadh, Saudi Arabia.

# Index

Abbas Hilmi II, Khedive, 135
Abdel Aal, Muhammed Hassan, 9, 12, 102
Abd al-Nasir, Gamal, 68, 70, 94, 137, 169, 252, 257
Abnub, 204
Abu-Lughod, Lila, 8, 12, 132, 177
actors, agents, 1, 124
advertisements, 156, 195
agrarian reform [see land reform]
agrarian reform beneficiaries, 168, 186, 346
agriculture, 3, 5
Alexandria, 83, 124, 131, 134, 141-49, 244, 320, 329, 344
Altorki, Soraya, and Donald Cole, 9, 11, 85n2
antiquities, 149, 162
Arab socialism, 68
Arab Socialist Union, 77, 137, 139, 386
Armant, 26, 140
armed forces, 74, 344
Asdar Ali, Kamran, 12
Aswan, 49, 51, 53, 54, 55, 59, 61, 62, 69, 74, 114, 120, 282, 330, 357
Asyut, 49, 54, 62, 204
authority, patriarchal, 148, 166, 173; of documents, 357
Awlad Ali, 131ff, 318ff
Azharite schools, 116, 121, 128n4, 157 [see Islam]

Bach, Kirsten, 8, 12, 275n16
badiyah, 131, 320
Bahayra, 49, 51, 53, 58, 59, 61, 167, 184
baking, 22, 30, 190
bananas, 246, 347
barley, 138, 320

Bedouin, 11, 131ff, 220, 226, 260, 263, 318ff, 357
beet sugar, 27
Beni Hilal, 119-20, 126 [see tribes]
Beni Sulaym, 133, 136 [see tribes]
Beni Swayf, 49, 54, 61, 62
berseem, 25, 347
Blackman, Winifred, 306, 311-12
Bourdieu, Pierre, 8, 185, 197, 361-62, 372
bread, 22, 29, 32-33, 67, 156, 190, 321-22
brickmaking, 271, 374
Brown, Nathan, 76, 88, 95
buffalo, 30, 162
bureaucracy, 90, 161, 174
bureaucrats, 114, 197, 187ff, 357 [see employment]
Bush, Ray, 6, 10, 274n1

cadastral maps, 238, 266, 268
Cairo, 57, 61, 83-84, 85n4, 117, 133, 156-57, 168, 186, 195, 256, 312
camels, 25
capital, 326, 351
    cultural, 197, 383
    economic, 198
    symbolic, 382
    social, 8
capitalism, 19, 33-34, 268, 371
    precapitalist, 20
    noncapitalist, 34-35
Caribbean, 27
census (1996), 2
    agricultural, 42-63
charitable organizations, 78
children, 161, 173, 179, 203ff
    child survival, 219
    child labor, 194; on TV, 159
    child and infant mortality, 212

## 392    Index

girls healthier than boys, 211
cholesterol, 329
cities, 80-84, 130, 158, 169, 252 [see urbanization]
citrus, 246
civil society, 90
class, 78, 79, 88, 96, 98-100, 157, 167, 181
    elites, 371
    rural bourgeoisie, 96, 251
    rural middle, 79, 125, 371
    underclass, 77-79
Cleland, Wendell, 66
clinics (health units), 137, 153, 168, 207, 220ff
clothing, 156-58
Cole, Donald, and Soraya Altorki, 12, 85n12
colonialism, 135
commodity, 237, 273, 322
    commoditization, 93, 205, 237
    commodification, 273
common property, 106
community, 21, 113, 124, 127, 365
Community Development Association, 117, 119, 123, 124
Company, 90, 328
    Arab Contractors Co., 337, 339
    Beheira Land Co., 241
    Egyptian Sugar and Refining Co., 27
    Egyptian Vineyards Co., 325
    Gianaclis Co., 325
    Mariut Agricultural Co., 339
    al-Nil Co., 250;
    Nile Agricultural Development Co., 343
    Salhiya Investment and Development Co., 339
conflict, 375-79 [see disputes]
consumption, 7, 145, 156, 172, 184-91, 197, 205, 304, 307
    of red meat, 212
cooperatives, 29, 68, 70, 118, 137, 257, 279ff, 283, 322, 346
    boards: 282ff
    consumer, 376

history, 280-81
    land reform, 28, 168-69, 186, 283
Copts (Christians), 119-21, 126, 270, 379
corporatism, 72
corruption, 82, 92, 123, 149
    fraud and embezzlement, 344, 349
cosmopolitans, 155-58
cotton, 22, 23, 33, 68, 71, 168, 242
council, reconciliation [see reconciliation council]
council, village (Local Popular Council), 114, 119, 139, 315, 366, 374-75
courts, 358, 366-67
cows, 24
credit, 328
criminals, 150
cropping intensity, 56, 57, 64n13
crop mix, 57, 223
culture, 97, 206
    consumer, 156
    cultural construction, 1, 204
currency devaluation, 68
customary law [see *'urf*]

DANIDA, 114, 123, 124
Daqahliya, 49, 54, 61, 72, 102
    Mansura, 238
Delta (Lower Egypt), 44-49, 51, 101, 166
Denmark, 343
deregulation, 23, 43
Description de l'Egypte, 306
Desert Governorates, 44-48, 85, 132, 153, 220
development
    agencies, 114, 137, 322
    projects, 29, 178, 330
differentiation, 7, 118, 274, 374
discourse, 159, 361, 375, 382 [see silence]
    critical vs authoritative, 205
diseases, 219ff [see dysentery, schistosomiasis]
dispute settlement, 358, 377
    among women, 360, 378

division of labor, 66, 89, 184
divorce, 193
drainage, 103, 343 [see sewage; self-help]
Dumyat, 49, 53, 61, 102
dysentery, 207, 210, 232

ecological conditions, 4, 238, 252, 324
economic growth, 185
  rate: 89
economy, market, 1, 5, 19ff, 62, 98, 99, 154, 279, 296, 319
  planned: 1, 279
education, 1, 8, 149ff, 154, 78, 80, 184, 188, 297, 376
educated people (*muta'allimin*), 184ff
elections, 9, 76, 82, 97-98, 115, 119, 123, 140, 243, 316, 364, 379
  CDA, 119
  Cooperative, 140, 286-87
  Union, 73
employment, 41, 75, 122, 166, 169, 313, 345 [see occupation]
entropy, 14
environment, 96, 100, 103, 216, 220, 324 [see ecological conditions]
  environmental assets, 95
  pollution, 273
environmental sustainability, 101, 331, 353
ethnic groups, 119, 260
  ethnicity, 263
European Union, 27
evil eye, 196, 208-09, 211
exports, 68, 70, 89, 93, 327 [see imports]

*fallah*, 3, 100, 133, 174, 184, 220, 260 [see farmer, peasant]
family, 115, 171, 176, 204, 208-17, 268, 282, 346, 364, 378
  family emotions, 177
  marriage, 174
  family roots, 197
  family size, 346
  family history, 237, 268
  big families, 282, 363

family planning, 152
fantasies, 158
farmer, 3, 285, 373 [see *fallah*, peasant]
farms, 48-49, 334
favor, 119
Fayum, 49, 51, 54, 55, 56, 57, 59, 61
fertility rate, 4, 53, 204, 219 [see population]
fertilizer, 90, 92, 170, 194, 288, 292, 295, 376
feuds (*al-tha'r*), 9, 83, 148, 369n3
figs, 325
fines, 362, 384
flood, 245, 247
flour, 27, 29
fodder, 327-28, 337
Food and Agricultural Organization, 322
food security, 249
  food sufficiency: 337
funerals, 116, 121, 160

gender roles, 166ff, 173, 332n6 [see women]
  autonomy, 166-78
  emancipation of women, 167
genealogy, 115, 122, 133
GUAMW [Union], 71-74
generations, 187, 376
  elders, 385
  youth, 376
Gharbiya, 49, 51, 54, 62, 64n10
Gibson-Graham, J.K., 20, 34
Giddens, Anthony, 257, 372
Gini coefficient, 59-62, 64n15-16
Giza, 51, 54, 55, 59, 61, 102
globalization, 387
Government of Egypt, 28, 70, 88, 153, 323, 337
Government of the US, 28, 32, 71
government employees [see bureaucrats]
graduates, 78, 345, 349
Gramsci, Antonio, 97
grazing, 221 [see livestock]
Green Revolution, 334

## Index

Gross Domestic Product, 31, 100
Gross National Product, 73
guest house, 115, 121, 363
Gulf (Arabian), 80, 169
Gurna resettlement, 162, 164n16

habits, 172, 180 (body)
handicaps, physical, 206, 386
Hawwara, 160
healer, 208, 226
health, 203ff, 380
health units [see clinics]
High Dam, 58, 64n13, 68-69, 247, 260, 273, 337
history, 235, 305
  oral, 133, 136, 240, 266
Hiwan, 119-20, 126
hiyaza, 63n3, 257, 270 [see land tenure]
honor, 176, 217
household, 22, 23, 28, 96, 104, 115, 320
  household food budget, 32-33, 104, 215
  extended and nuclear, 185
houses, 138, 156, 168, 171, 189-91, 266, 345, 346
  bathrooms, 157, 150, 171-72, 195
  construction, 374

identity card, 151
Idfu, 37n16, 123, 357ff
images, 158
imports, 70 [see exports]
income, 313, 330
  off-farm income, 102, 170, 187, 330
individualism, 184
industry, 32, 358
inequality, 59, 89, 166
inflation, 73
informal sector, 74, 76, 271
information flow, 314, 324, 362
inheritance, 53, 64n14, 245, 326, 360, 364, 377
integration (into a wider system), 13, 90, 94, 124, 132, 191, 328, 331

intellectuals, 161
interest, 290, 326, 346
  banks, 339
International Financial Institutions (IFIs), 88ff
International Labor Organization (ILO), 322
International Monetary Fund (IMF), 21, 23, 28, 32, 71, 75, 76, 84, 328, 332n9
investment, 199, 326, 334, 343
  investors, 345, 349
Iraq, 80, 137, 171
Ireton, François, 10, 181n4
irrigation, 6, 57, 58, 64n13, 258-60, 337, 342, 349, 373
Islam, 8, 125, 157, 180,, 326 [see Azharite schools]
  festivals, 116, 313, 326, 377
  militant organizations, 8, 67, 77, 148-49, 179, 315, 377
  saint cult, 8, 81, 266, 313, 315
  scripturalist, 9, 78, 81, 125, 180
  sufis, 8, 81
Islamic investment companies, 78, 349
Isma'il, Khedive, 240
Isma'iliya, 49, 51, 58, 61, 62, 220ff
Italy, 79, 158
'izba, 168, 220, 242, 258, 372

Jahin, Salah, 302
Japan, 64n16, 99

Kafr al-Shaykh, 49, 51, 53, 62
knowledge, 361

labor, 84, 346
  labor force, 339 [see workers, employment, occupation]
land dispute, 250, 367, 377
land distribution, 270, 339
land holders, 89
  large (landlords), 70, 92, 100, 187, 242ff
  small, 22, 90, 257, 271, 285, 296, 337 (small settlers), 373
land market, 170, 186-87

## Index 395

land reclamation, 47, 68, 186, 238, 244, 334
 new lands, 350, 335
land reform, 5, 32, 37n23, 43, 68, 70, 168, 186, 197, 241, 242, 246, 263, 280, 346
 land counterreform, 32, 88 [see Law 96 of 1992]
 land reform land, 168, 186, 270
 land reform law, 89, 257 [see Law 96 of 1992]
land tax, 32, 170
land tenure, 42, 57
 consolidation, 42, 61, 170
 fragmentation, 42, 61, 187
 holdings, 114, 169, 186, 257, 292, 296, 324 (titles)
 new owners, 342
 rented, 53, 169-70, 186 [see tenants]
 state land, 328
land use, 260, 264
landlessness, 89, 92, 187, 249, 258, 335, 346
Larson, Barbara, 305
Law [see *'urf*, *sharia*, courts]
Law 96 of 1992, 6, 33, 99, 102, 170, 189, 254n19, 270 [see land reform law]
lentils, 215
Lewis, W. A., 66, 84
liberalization, 88, 90, 334, 373
Libya, 80, 134, 137, 322, 329
Lipton, Michael (urban bias), 118
Literacy, 152, 195, 223-24, 284, 359 [see education]
 Literacy classes, 151, 153
livestock, 221, 292, 304, 312, 326-29
 sheep and goats, 326-29
loans, 290, 339
logic, 20, 24, 26, 28, 35, 216, 381
Lower Egypt [see Delta]
Luxor, 22, 30, 147, 150, 157, 162

maize, 25
*majlis*, gatherings, assemblies, 131, 139 [see reconciliation councils]

malnutrition, 32
management, 344
marginality, 47ff, 70, 89, 136, 117, 126, 148, 159, 379, 387
Marketing, 5, 19, 31, 98-99, 168, 196, 213, 246-51, 319, 324-26
 cartels, 29, 242
 periodic (weekly) market, 168, 196, 302-16
 trade as way of life, 325
marriage, 174
 marriage contract, 152
 wedding songs, 160
Matruh, 131ff, 318ff
mayor [see *'umda*]
mechanization, 25, 57 [see pumps, tractors]
mediation, 380
medicine, 203, 210, 225
Mehanna, Sohair, and Peter Winch, 12
memory (mnemonic), 369
Merchant/trader, 27-29, 103, 139, 242, 246, 248-49, 289, 298, 309, 313
 fodder merchants, 328
 Greek traders, 320
messages, 158, 215
Meyer, Günter, 12
midwife, 208
migration, 1, 7, 47, 55, 74, 85n4, 89, 102, 169, 171, 174, 187-88, 220, 263, 347, 373
 return migration, 172
milk, 30, 212, 214
Minister of Tourism, 162
Ministry of Agriculture, 21, 22, 28, 32, 106, 281, 339, 375
Ministry of Education, 376
Ministry of Social Affairs, 119, 281
Ministry of Supply, 21, 28, 29, 37n17
Minufiya, 49, 51, 54, 55, 61, 62, 304ff
Minya, 49, 51, 54, 59, 62, 257ff, 304ff
mistrust, 286
Mitchell, Timothy, 6, 10, 99, 274n1
mobility, social, 80, 237, 252
 political, 386
model, 31
modernization theory, 105, 371, 387

modes of production, 25, 371
Mohieddin, Mohammed, 12
morality, 160
Morocco, 167, 306, 312
Morsy, Soheir, 167
Mubarak, Ali, 240
Prophet Muhammed, 80, 125, 179, 358
Muhammed Ali Pasha, 95, 134, 167, 240
Müller-Mahn, Detlef, 12
*mulukhia*, 25, 29
mutual aid, 191 [see reciprocity]
myth of origin, 122

National Democratic Party (NDP), 119, 243
New Valley, 48
newspaper, 158
Nielsen, Hans-Christian, 8, 13
non-governmental organizations (NGOs), 114, 206

Obermeyer, Gerald, 132, 320
occupation, 221, 271, 295 [see employment, labor, workers]
olives, 325
Open Door policy, 75, 252, 337, 373
oral testimony, 359 [see history]
owners and tenants law [see Law 96 of 1992]

Parliament, 68, 72, 123, 139, 387
participation, 116
  political participation, 79, 122, 140
pastoralism, 319
paternalism, 80
patron-client relations, 80, 119, 371, 377
peasant, 3, 42, 88, 132, 241 [see *fallah*, farmer]
  worker-peasant, 94
peasantry, 88ff
People's Assembly [see Parliament]
pest control, 69
  boll weevil, 68
  pesticides, 288, 292
physician, 225

piety, 80
Polanyi, Karl, 304
police, 139, 315, 358, 364, 374, 381
politics, rural, 89, 103, 122, 139, 243, 250, 371
  political arena, 90, 374-80
  of street-naming, 124
  opposition, 100, 140
  protest, 100
population, 2, 43, 51, 66, 91, 142 [see census]
  population growth (rate), 43, 95 [see fertility rate]
  of villages, 114, 185, 204, 21, 238, 264, 372
postcolonial, 158
potatoes, 244
potters, 119-20
poverty, 70, 169, 210, 256
  poverty rate, 4
power, 192, 262, 363, 372, 375
  power structure, 279-98, 375
pricing, 91
prices, 28, 29, 31, 67, 288, 313, 314, 343
price controls, 31, 33, 68, 170
Principal Bank for Development and Agricultural Credit (PBDAC), 6, 90, 92, 281, 289, 296

privacy, 172, 194, 365
privatization, 88, 334, 339
profit(s), 26, 326
public sector, 289, 296, 325, 339
  public sector jobs, 271
public health, 215, 231
pumps, 240, 245, 373 [see mechanization]

Qalyubiya, 49, 54, 57, 61, 64n10, 102, 103
Qina, 22, 51, 53, 54, 55, 59, 61, 62, 148, 282
quota, 29, 33
Quran, 302, 382-84

rain, 318

reciprocity, 116, 321 [see mutual aid]
reconciliation councils (majlis al-sulh), 359, 362-64, 379-84
relations of production, 90
religion [see Islam]
representation, 7, 147
resistance, 141, 387 (political)
revolts, 168
Revolution of 1952, 132, 168, 346, 379
rice, 22, 24, 68
rights, human and civil, 98, 205
riots, 21, 76, 78, 85
risk, 208, 210, 307, 328-29
Rouchdy, Malak, 8, 9, 12, 275n16
rules, 362, 375, 384
    for speech, 385

Saad, Reem, 9, 11, 164n20, 275n16
sabotage, 250
Sa'id (Upper Egypt), 44-48, 51, etc., 78, 203, 372ff
Salhiya, 337-38
Sallum, 163, 328
Sanusiya, 134
Saudi Arabia, 130, 307, 329, 343, 347
Saunders, Lucie, and Sohair Mehanna, 95
savings account, 154
schistosomiasis (bilharzia), 220, 223, 232
schools, 155 [see education]
sedentarization, 133, 138, 263
seeds, 288, 297
self, 133, 136, 161, 175, 197
self-help, 116-17, 195
self-provisioning [see subsistence]
sesame, 23
settlements, 260, 263
settlers, small, 345, 349
sewage, 195, 251 [see drainage; self-help]
sharecropping, 187, 241, 321, 343, 346
*sharia*, 361 [see law, courts, *'urf*]
Sharqiya, 49, 51, 54, 57, 59, 61, 167, 184
*shaykh al-balad*, 246 [see *'umda*]
Sholkamy, Hania, 8, 12

Shura Council, 100, 117, 125
signs, 156
silence, 153, 383, 385
Sinai, 160, 327, 351
Siwa, 320
smuggling, 138, 318
snakes, 120
social distance, 270
social justice, 95, 216
space, spatial analysis, 257, 264, 273, 306, 309-10, 378
State, 215, 315, 375
    allocates land titles, 331
    owns property, 328
    rent-seeking, 91
    solves problems: 285
    state culture, 150
    state decisions, 375
    state resources, 91
    strategies, 372
    supervisory role, 282
state farms, 337, 339
status, 176, 184, 192
    family, 363
    work, 176
status quo, in rural areas, 94
strategies, 24, 96, 237-52, 241, 243, 263, 274, 297, 332n12, 367-68, 386
    of mediation, 372
strawberries, 347
structural adjustment, 5, 19, 62, 42, 88ff, 105, 173, 176, 258, 281ff, 328
subsidies, 28, 29, 32, 33, 43, 77, 170, 351
    fodder, 328
    inputs, 287
    land, 345
subsistence agriculture, 23, 25, 30, 34, 57, 214, 242
sugarcane, 22, 23, 25, 26, 114, 260, 279, 295, 357 [see beet sugar]
sugar refinery, 25, 279, 358
Suhag, 51, 53, 54, 55, 61, 62
surplus, 94
surveys, 205, 227, 325, 334
symbols, 125

Ta'amir al-Sahari (desert development organization), 137, 322-23
Tahrir, 69, 74, 339-45
technology, 194
television, 1, 117, 131, 147-63, 194-95, 232
tenants, tenancy, 246-47, 256, 346 [see land holders]
texts, legal, 369 [see law]
time, 286, 306
Toth, James, 6, 9, 10, 95, 175, 182n6
tourism, 24, 161, 318, 358
tractors, 24, 26, 57, 373 [see mechanization]
trade/commerce, 374 [see markting, merchants]
tradition, traditional practices, 20, 357ff, 387
transportation, 29, 226, 260
Tribes/tribal, 83, 115, 116, 122, 132ff, 263, 282, 319, 325, 331n3 (tied tribes), 358, 363, 379 [see Awlad Ali, Beni Hilal, Beni Sulaym, Hawwara]
Tushka/New Delta, 351

unemployment, 31, 66, 153, 192, 346
UNICEF, 219
United States, 27
USAID, 23, 32, 91, 93, 153
Universities, 78, 345
urbanization, 9, 51, 48, 67, 76, 231 [see cities]
'umda, 246, 268, 270, 315, 364, 377, 379-80
Upper Egypt [see Sa'id]
'urf (customary law), 131, 137, 140, 357ff, 381-84

values or norms, 20, 97, 151, 160, 163, 360
  market, 342
  mathematical, 59

vegetables, 23, 347
veiling (*hijab*), 83, 157, 179-80
village leadership, 117, 118, 122, 140, 379-80
violence, 9, 100, 121, 139, 148 [see feud, sabotage]
  interpersonal, 382, 385
visits, visiting, 116, 177, 196

wages, 31, 69, 70, 74, 153, 175
War, 74, 134
  Gulf (1990-91), 24, 372;
  October (1973), 76, 376;
  Six Day (1967), 73, 75, 337;
  World War One (1914-18), 135, 244;
  World War II (1939-45), 135
water, 351
  piped water, 195
  water harvesting, 323
Wolf, Eric, 3
women, 4, 22, 24, 30, 89, 104, 153, 176, 271, 311, 345, 375
  farm work, 175
  household tasks, 30, 154, 153, 191-96, 311, 314, 321
  as hired labor, 350
  single women, 345
wheat, 21ff, 27ff, 71, 347
workers, 26, 41ff, 66ff, 263, 268, 283, 321 [see laborers]
World Bank, 91, 93, 104, 282, 322
World Food Program (WFP), 137, 322, 327
World Health Organization (WHO), 219
world systems theory, 13, 371

yields, 4, 31, 57

zakat, 79, 81, 82-83
zar [see healer]
Zayed, Ahmed, 8, 9, 13, 275n16